COMMON CORE CURRICULUM MAPS

IN ENGLISH LANGUAGE ARTS

Grades K–5

COMMON
CORE

JOSSEY-BASS
A Wiley Imprint
www.josseybass.com

OTHER BOOKS IN THE COMMON CORE SERIES:

Common Core Curriculum Maps in English Language Arts, Grades 6–8

Common Core Curriculum Maps in English Language Arts, Grades 9–12

Published by Jossey-Bass
A Wiley Imprint
989 Market Street, San Francisco, CA 94103–1741—www.josseybass.com

Readers should be aware that Internet websites offered as citations and/or sources for further information may have changed or disappeared between the time this was written and when it is read.

Limit of Liability/Disclaimer of Warranty: While the publisher and author have used their best efforts in preparing this book, they make no representations or warranties with respect to the accuracy or completeness of the contents of this book and specifically disclaim any implied warranties of merchantability or fitness for a particular purpose. No warranty may be created or extended by sales representatives or written sales materials. The advice and strategies contained herein may not be suitable for your situation. You should consult with a professional where appropriate. Neither the publisher nor author shall be liable for any loss of profit or any other commercial damages, including but not limited to special, incidental, consequential, or other damages.

Jossey-Bass books and products are available through most bookstores. To contact Jossey-Bass directly call our Customer Care Department within the U.S. at 800-956-7739, outside the U.S. at 317-572-3986, or fax 317-572-4002.

Jossey-Bass also publishes its books in a variety of electronic formats. Some content that appears in print may not be available in electronic books.

Library of Congress Cataloging-in-Publication Data
Common Core curriculum maps in English language arts, grades K–5.—1st ed.
    p. cm. — (The Common Core series)
  Includes index.
  ISBN 978-1-118-10822-2 (pbk.)
  ISBN 978-1-1-181-3710-9 (ebk.)
  ISBN 978-1-1-181-3711-6 (ebk.)
  ISBN 978-1-1-181-3712-3 (ebk.)
  1. Language arts (Elementary)—Curricula—United States—States. 2. Language arts (Elementary)—Standards—United States—States. I. Common Core, Inc.
  LB1576.C5785 2012
  372.6'044—dc23

                                                                2011029324

Printed in the United States of America
FIRST EDITION
PB Printing   10 9 8 7 6 5 4

CONTENTS

FOREWORD

Good Schools: The Salt of Society

Carol Jago

Three hundred years ago Cotton Mather preached, "A Good School deserves to be call'd the very Salt of the Town that hath it." Without a school "wherein the Youth may by able Masters be Taught the Things that are necessary to qualify them for future Serviceableness," a community will founder.[1] Mather's advice to townspeople in Puritan New England reflects one of the philosophical underpinnings of the Common Core Curriculum Maps in English Language Arts: Schools matter. Curriculum matters. Teachers matter.

In order to determine which things should be taught, we must of course first define what it means to be serviceable in a twenty-first-century democratic society. To ensure a capable workforce and build a strong economy, high levels of literacy and numeracy are obviously essential. But what about the need for students to develop empathy and thoughtfulness? It is short-sighted to equate the value of education with economic growth. Like salt, good schools with rich curricula enhance the community by adding depth—and piquancy. Like salt, they are a preservative, ensuring that a society's values endure.

Many of the benefits we've come to demand as our rights in a modern society depend upon high levels of employment, but if we shift the discussion of the purpose of school from job training to preparing America's children to lead a worthwhile life, the calculus changes. Is simply working nine-to-five for forty years what you most aspire to for your children? Or do you want them to have an education that invites exploration of essential questions, inspires challenges to the status quo, and somehow prepares them for what we cannot yet know? Most parents want both.

The conundrum for curriculum developers is to avoid becoming so caught up in preparing students to make a living—which starts with paying attention in kindergarten; earning good grades through elementary school, middle school, and high school; achieving competitive SAT and ACT scores; and winning a place in college or in the workplace—that we lose sight of educating students to enrich their lives.

In *Not for Profit: Why Democracy Needs the Humanities,* philosopher Martha Nussbaum warns that, "With the rush to profitability in the global market, values precious for the future of democracy, especially in an era of religious and economic anxiety, are in danger of getting lost."[2] I share her concern. The movement to reform education primarily in order to make the United States more globally competitive seems wrong-headed and even counterproductive. Maybe I lack a competitive spirit, but I have always

---

1. Cotton Mather, "The Education of Children," http://www.spurgeon.org/~phil/mather/edkids.htm.
2. Martha Nussbaum, *Not for Profit: Why Democracy Needs the Humanities* (Princeton: Princeton University Press, 2010), 6.

wanted more for my students than just coming in first. I want them to learn about and to think about the world—today's world and yesterday's. Nussbaum explains, "World history and economic understanding must be humanistic and critical if they are to be at all useful in forming intelligent global citizens, and they must be taught alongside the study of religion and of philosophical theories of justice. Only then will they supply a useful foundation for the public debates that we must have if we are to cooperate in solving major human problems."[3] One means of learning about the problems that have beset and continue to bedevil humanity is through the study of the humanities—literature and art, history and philosophy. This is the kind of education the Common Core Curriculum Maps offer. I believe it is the education that every generation of citizens needs.

Unit Three of the Grade One curriculum map, Life Lessons, offers young children opportunities to explore the kind of education Martha Nussbaum recommends. As they work through the unit, "Students read and listen to fables with morals. They learn about rules for life in a book of manners. Reading the life story of George Washington Carver, students learn about a man who had to overcome obstacles in life to make important contributions to science and agriculture. Students learn about Thomas Edison's work with electricity and the rules for its safe use. Descriptive words are the focus of a lesson centered on the artwork of Georgia O'Keeffe. Finally, the children write narratives focused on life lessons and create informative posters focused on electrical safety." This interdisciplinary approach integrates the study of science and builds students' background knowledge. In so doing, it strengthens their reading comprehension and develops their facility with reading informational texts—a key expectation of the Common Core State Standards. It also invites children to investigate Georgia O'Keeffe's paintings and build their cultural literacy.

Some readers of the Common Core Curriculum Maps may argue that their students won't read nineteenth-century novels, that twenty-first-century students raised on Twitter need a faster pace and different kinds of text. I say language arts classrooms may be the last place where young people can unplug themselves from the solipsism of Facebook postings and enter a milieu different from their own. "But my students won't do the homework reading I assign," teachers wail. It isn't as though students don't have the time. A 2010 study by the Kaiser Family Foundation reports that children aged eight to eighteen spend an average of seven and a half hours daily "consuming entertainment media."[4] And this does not include the hour and a half a day they spend texting friends. Today's students have the time to read; many of them simply choose not to.

To those who look at the suggested works for the high school Common Core Curriculum Maps and think, "Our students could never read those books," I urge perusal of the primary grade curriculum maps. If children were immersed in rich literature and nonfiction from the first days of kindergarten and engaged in classroom conversations that encouraged them to think deeply about what they read, then negotiating Ralph Ellison's *Invisible Man* in eleventh grade and Jane Austen's *Sense and Sensibility* in twelfth is certainly possible. Though such books pose textual challenges for young readers, as part of a continuum and under the tutelage of an "able Master," the work is achievable. In our effort to provide students with readings that they can relate to, we sometimes end up teaching works that students can read on their own at the expense of teaching more worthwhile texts that they most certainly need assistance negotiating.

We need to remind ourselves that curriculum should be aimed at what Lev Vygotsky calls students' zone of proximal development. Writing in 1962, Vygotsky said, "the only good kind of instruction is that which marches ahead of development and leads it."[5] Classroom texts should pose intellectual challenges for readers and invite them to stretch and grow. Students also need books that feed their personal interests and allow them to explore "the road not taken." Reading a broad range of books makes students stronger readers and, over time, stronger people. Rigor versus relevance doesn't need to be an

---

3. Ibid., 94.
4. Ulla G. Foehr, Victoria J. Rideout, and Donald F. Roberts, "Generation M^2: Media in the Lives of 8- to 18-Year-Olds," (Menlo Park, CA: Kaiser Family Foundation, January 2010), http://www.kff.org/entmedia/8010.cfm.
5. Lev Vygotsky, *Thought and Language*, trans. Eugenia Hanfmann and Gertrude Vakar (Cambridge, MA: MIT Press, 1962), 104.

either-or proposition. With artful instruction by able masters, students can acquire the literacy skills they need — not only to meet the Common Core State Standards, but also to meet the challenges this brave new world is sure to deal them.

Reading literature also helps students explore hypothetical scenarios and consider the ramifications of what might prima facie seem to be a good or profitable idea. Consider the Common Core Curriculum Maps' final Grade Seven unit, Literature Reflects Life: Making Sense of Our World. Addressing Common Core Reading Standard RL.7.6, "Analyze how an author develops and contrasts the points of view of different characters or narrators in a text," the map recommends students read Robert Louis Stevenson's *The Strange Case of Dr. Jekyll and Mr. Hyde*. This nineteenth-century novella invites young readers to reflect upon their own conflicting natures and offers a cautionary tale regarding experimentation. When we consider how best to prepare tomorrow's doctors, scientists, programmers, and engineers for the twenty-first century, it seems to me that reading stories about investigations that go very wrong is quite a good idea.

Later in his sermon, Cotton Mather states that "the Devil cannot give a greater Blow to the Reformation among us, than by causing Schools to Languish under Discouragements." The Common Core Curriculum Maps offer hope to discouraged teachers. They offer a plan for developing young minds, a plan that is both rigorous and has never been more relevant. It may seem odd to be taking guidance from a seventeenth-century Puritan, but I know I couldn't say it better. "Where schools are not vigorously and Honourably Encouraged, whole Colonies will sink apace into a Degenerate and Contemptible Condition, and at last become horribly Barbarous. If you would not betray your Posterity into the very Circumstances of Savages, let Schools have more Encouragement." Amen.

WRITTEN BY TEACHERS, FOR TEACHERS

To My Fellow Teachers:

Participating in the development of these Maps has been an eye-opening and incredibly rewarding professional development experience for me. I was especially drawn to the project because I knew that the Maps would be offered *for free* to teachers around the country. Since my first years as a classroom teacher, I've witnessed the powerful results that come from a marriage between rich content and literacy instruction; I wanted the Maps to exhibit this component. As an administrator, I approached this project from the perspective of creating resources that provide enough support for you without taking away your creative freedom. As a mother, I've thought about what an impact these Maps could and will—I hope—have on the education my children receive.

The new Common Core State Standards Initiative presented my colleagues and me—now close friends—with an ideal opportunity for twenty-first-century collaboration: we live in three different states, yet developed these Maps together. After much trial and error regarding our approach, we decided to pair the best literary and informational texts we know into meaningful thematic units, allowing students to develop literacy in a humanities-rich environment. We hope that the closely related components of these Maps will give you confidence to use them in various permutations in your classroom. We also hope you will collaborate with your colleagues to refine and create new activities that will not only ensure the standards are taught and learned, but will also yield deeper levels of student work and satisfaction.

In the middle school Maps of this volume, we have worked to provide the perfect juxtaposition of substantive and challenging content with engaging and interesting instructional approaches for middle school students. We have made every effort to engage students in a variety of age-appropriate and social ways, encouraging them to take complex ideas and apply them to their daily experiences inside *and outside* of class.

Our own collaboration on these Maps has been intellectually gratifying and joyful, and we hope they provide you with a similarly rewarding experience. These Maps are our gift to you, and we sincerely hope you enjoy the journey of making them your own.

Cyndi Wells
Lead coach and fine arts facilitator, Charlottesville, Virginia
Lead writer, fourth through eighth grade,
Common Core Curriculum Maps in ELA

To My Fellow Teachers:

For years we have been deluged with reform initiatives from on high that claimed they would improve student achievement. Few have actually brought progress. I joined the Common Core team of teachers out of conviction that the Common Core State Standards (CCSS) would make a difference and have a positive impact on our work in the classroom. The standards provide a framework for composing a rich, well-planned curriculum that guides our instruction.

Classroom teachers know that imaginative planning is at the heart of any successful lesson. The seventy-six Sample Lesson Plans (SLP), one for each of the units, are instructional road maps. The purpose of each SLP is to demonstrate how to create the necessary link between the literary and informational texts and the CCSS. The SLPs vary in focus and content—from a novel or selection of poems to a play or informational text. Each has a clear topic, a set of objectives, and suggested activities, as well as helpful guides for differentiated instruction. Consider these plans as a place to start. Use them directly or as a model for developing your own lessons.

Writing the maps and the SLPs has been both intellectually rewarding and joyful to us as classroom teachers. I hope you find that working with these volumes becomes equally joyful and useful in your own classrooms.

Dr. Ruthie Stern
High school teacher, New York City
Lead writer, Sample Lesson Plans, Common Core Curriculum Maps in ELA

To My Fellow Teachers:

Creating these curriculum maps has been, by far, the most exciting project I have been part of in my twenty-two-year teaching career. As a classroom teacher, I (like many of you) have hung on to the pendulum as it has swung back and forth from prescriptive, mandatory educational initiatives to long periods with no guidance at all—always trying to find a way to provide students with a rich and rigorous education. The Common Core Curriculum Mapping Project presented us with a perfect opportunity to strike a new balance.

We have brought excellent literary and informational texts alive in new ways by pairing them with the skills and expectations in the Common Core State Standards (CCSS). These maps offer terrific new choices to teachers who wish to use the CCSS to create classes that are rich not just with great literature and literary nonfiction, but also with art, history, mythology, and science.

If you peeked into my fifth-grade classroom, you would see me enjoying the difference these maps make. I see poetry brought into a new light with the guidance of our sample lesson plans. I am amazed by students who are working hard to read a book like *Walk Two Moons* because they have been lured by the study of a complex plot and the enticing "coming of age" genre. Teaching has become fun again!

We have worked as a team. Cyndi Wells wrote the fourth and fifth grades, providing a seamless entry into the middle grades' curricula. Ruthie Stern masterfully wrote the sample lesson plans, giving the maps articulated lessons aligned vertically as the standards progress from kindergarten toward college and career readiness.

And so we . . . along with all those who wrote, critiqued, wrote again, revised, rewrote, and edited . . . give this gift to you! And we can't wait to see it interpreted in classrooms by creative teachers, with new twists and turns, evolving into an even richer and more rigorous curriculum that suits your students, your school, and your community.

Lorraine Griffith
Fifth-grade teacher, Asheville, North Carolina
Lead writer, kindergarten through third Grade
Common Core Curriculum Maps in ELA

INTRODUCTION

Few educators or policymakers would have guessed, even a year or so ago, that nearly all states would jettison their standards and embrace new, largely uniform standards for the teaching of ELA and math. Fewer still would have expected all of this to happen as quickly as it has.

The rapid rise of the Common Core State Standards (CCSS) is an unprecedented event at the national level—and more importantly, at the school level, where its implications are profound. For educators in most states, the CCSS raise the bar for what students should know and be able to do.[1] If you are reading this, you are probably responsible for implementing the CCSS in your school, district, or state. You will find that the CCSS contain explicit guidance about the reading, writing, speaking, listening, and language skills students are expected to master. Almost any single standard in the CCSS illustrates this. Here's one of the reading standards from seventh grade:

> Determine two or more central ideas in a text and analyze their development over the course of the text; provide an objective summary of the text. (RI.7.2)

The CCSS call for the new standards to be taught within the context of a "content-rich curriculum." But the CCSS do not specify what content students need to master, as this fell outside the scope of the standards-setting project. Here is how this is explained in the introduction to the CCSS:

> [W]hile the Standards make references to some particular forms of content, including mythology, foundational U.S. documents, and Shakespeare, they do not—indeed, cannot—enumerate all or even most of the content that students should learn. The Standards must therefore be complemented by a well-developed, content-rich curriculum consistent with the expectations laid out in this document.[2]

Responsibility for developing such a curriculum falls to schools, districts, and states. Common Core's Curriculum Maps in ELA are designed to meet the needs of the teacher, principal, curriculum director, superintendent, or state official who is striving to develop, or to help teachers to develop, new ELA curricula aligned with the CCSS. The Maps can also serve as a resource for those endeavoring to conduct professional development related to the standards.

---

1. Sheila Byrd Carmichael, Gabrielle Martino, Kathleen Porter-Magee, and W. Stephen Wilson, "The State of State Standards—and the Common Core—in 2010" (Washington, DC: Thomas B. Fordham Institute, July 2010), 13.
2. *Common Core State Standards for English Language Arts & Literacy in History/Social Studies, Science, and Technical Subjects* (Washington, DC: Common Core State Standards Initiative), 6.

The Maps provide a coherent sequence of thematic curriculum units, roughly six per grade level, K–12. The units connect the skills outlined in the CCSS in ELA with suggested works of literature and informational texts and provide activities teachers could use in their classrooms. You will also find suggested student objectives in each unit, along with lists of relevant terminology and links to high quality additional resources. *Every standard in the CCSS is covered in the Maps*, most more than once. Standards citations are included after each sample activity/assessment to indicate alignment. Each grade includes a "standards checklist" showing which standards are covered in which unit. And most of the works the CCSS lists as "exemplar texts" are included in the Maps.

Moreover, each unit in this print edition of the Maps features a Sample Lesson Plan, a road map showing how to use one or more of the suggested texts in that unit to meet specific standards. Each Sample Lesson Plan includes step-by-step guidance for classroom activities tied to the lesson, questions that engage students in a deeper analysis and appreciation of the texts, and even suggestions for differentiated instruction. Many of the Sample Lesson Plans, particularly in the earlier grades, also include detailed guidance for connecting ELA lessons to other subjects, including math, science, history, geography, music, and art.

An important feature of Common Core's curriculum Maps is their attention to building students' background knowledge of a diverse array of events, people, places, and ideas. Cognitive science has demonstrated that students read better if they know something about the subject they are studying.[3] With this in mind, Common Core incorporated into its Maps themes, texts, and activities that teach students about "The Great Big World," as one of the kindergarten Maps is called. The content cloud shown in Figure I.1 includes much of the key content knowledge in the Maps. The larger an event, name, or idea appears in the cloud, the more emphasis it receives in the Maps. As you examine this cloud, do keep in mind that the Maps contain much that is not included here.

Figure I.1

Common Core's Maps were written by teachers for teachers. More than three dozen public school teachers had a hand in drafting, writing, reviewing, or revising the Maps. Collectively, these teachers brought dozens of years of experience to the mapping project. Each of the lead writers is deeply knowledgeable about the CCSS; some even served as feedback providers to the standards' writers. These

---

3. Daniel T. Willingham, *Why Don't Students Like School? A Cognitive Scientist Answers Questions About How the Mind Works and What It Means for the Classroom* (San Francisco: Jossey-Bass, 2009).

teachers looked to model curricula, including the International Baccalaureate, and at excellent, content-specific standards, such as the Massachusetts English Language Arts Curriculum Frameworks, for suggestions of what topics and titles to include at each grade. Most importantly, the teachers drew on their own considerable experience of what students enjoy learning about, and infused the Maps with that knowledge.

The Maps also reflect the contributions and perspective of the many teachers who reviewed them. Twice, the American Federation of Teachers convened the same panel of teachers that reviewed the CCSS to review Common Core's Maps. The Milken Family Foundation connected us with a dozen winners of the Milken Educator Award. These teachers, nationally recognized for excellence in the classroom, provided invaluable input and insight. And the National Alliance of Black School Educators identified superintendents, teachers, and content area specialists from across the country who reviewed the Maps in draft form. A public review of our draft Maps, conducted in the fall of 2010, elicited numerous helpful comments.

And the Maps will continue to evolve and improve. The second online edition of the Maps is open to public comment twenty-four hours a day, seven days a week. Anyone is able to critique any aspect of the Maps—any essential question, any student objective, any text suggestion. Viewers can rate each unit Map as a whole, and many other Map elements, such as suggested works and sample activities. Comments on the Maps are open for public view. Also, teachers can submit sample lesson plans that will be reviewed by a committee of teachers who will decide which ones to add to the official Maps website. In these ways and more, Common Core's Curriculum Maps in ELA are living documents, expanding and improving over time as they absorb and reflect the experience and perspective of educators across the nation.

We are thrilled that, as of this writing, the website featuring the maps (www.commoncore.org) has attracted more than three million visitors and that six state departments of education have recommended the Maps for use by districts statewide. The publication of the Maps is a momentous step for the mapping project. If you find this volume of interest we hope you will follow our project as we develop more inspiring and instrumental Maps-related resources for America's educators.

September 2011

Lynne Munson
President and Executive Director, Common Core

HOW TO USE THE COMMON CORE CURRICULUM MAPS

Common Core's Curriculum Maps in ELA are brand-new curriculum materials, built around the Common Core State Standards (CCSS) in English Language Arts. The CCSS dictated both the goals and contours of our Maps. The "exemplar texts" listed in the CCSS figure significantly in our unit Maps, which break down each grade, K–12, into a series of themed units. Each unit pairs standards with suggested student objectives, texts, activities, and more.

The Maps are intended to serve as "road maps" for the school year, as aids for jump-starting the lesson planning process. As common planning tools, these Maps can facilitate school and district-wide collaboration. They also can become the backbone of rich, content-based professional development as teachers work together to create and then refine curricula for their particular schools and classrooms.

The units are designed to be taught in sequence (particularly in elementary school), but teachers could certainly modify the units if they need to be taught in a different order. We do not expect teachers to use every text, nor to do every sample activity or assessment. The suggested texts simply offer a range of rich and relevant materials from which teachers may choose. The suggested activities or assessments are neither prescriptive nor exhaustive. Teachers can select from among them, modify them to meet their students' needs, and/or use them as inspiration for creating their own activities.

Each unit Map contains the following elements:

Overview. This is a brief description of the unit. It explains the unit's theme and provides a summary of what students will learn. It explains the structure, progression, and various components of the unit. It may offer some guidance regarding the selection of texts. The unit descriptions illuminate the connections between the skills identified in the standards and the content of the suggested works.

Essential question. The "essential question" highlights the usefulness, the relevance, and the greater benefit of a unit. It is often the "so what?" question about material covered. It should be answerable, at least to some degree, by the end of the unit, but it should also have more than one possible answer. It should prompt intellectual exploration by generating other questions. Here's an example from eighth grade: "How does learning history through literature differ from learning through informational text?"

Focus standards. These standards are taken directly from the CCSS and have been identified as especially important for the unit. Other standards are covered in each unit as well, but the focus standards are the ones that the unit has been designed to address specifically.

Suggested student objectives. These are the specific student outcomes for the unit. They describe the transferable ELA content and skills that students should possess when the unit is completed. The objectives are often components of more broadly worded standards and sometimes address content and skills necessarily related to the standards. The lists are not exhaustive, and the objectives should not supplant the standards themselves. Rather, they are designed to help teachers "drill down" from the standards and augment as necessary, providing added focus and clarity for lesson planning purposes.

Suggested works. These are substantial lists of suggested literary and informational texts. In most cases (particularly in the middle and high school grades), this list contains more texts than a unit could cover; it is meant to offer a range of options to teachers. Several permutations of the list could meet the goals of the unit. The suggested texts draw heavily from the "exemplar texts" listed in the CCSS. Exemplars are works the CCSS identified as meeting the levels of complexity and rigor described in the standards. These texts are identified with an (E) after the title of an exemplar text. An (EA) indicates a work by an author who has another work cited as an exemplar text.

Art, music, and media. These sections list works of visual art, music, film, and other media that reflect the theme of the unit and that a teacher can use to extend students' knowledge in these areas. Each unit includes at least one sample activity involving the works listed under this heading. ELA teachers who choose to use this material may do so on their own, by team teaching with an art or music teacher, or perhaps by sharing the material with the art or music teacher, who could reinforce what students are learning during the ELA block in their classroom. The inclusion of these works in our ELA Maps is *not* intended to substitute for or infringe in any way upon instruction that students should receive in separate art and music classes.

Sample activities and assessments. These items have been written particularly for the unit, with specific standards and often with specific texts in mind. Each activity addresses at least one standard in the CCSS; the applicable standard(s) are cited in parentheses following the description of each activity. The suggested activities or assessments are not intended to be prescriptive, exhaustive, or sequential; they simply demonstrate how specific content can be used to help students learn the skills described in the standards. They are designed to generate evidence of student understanding and give teachers ideas for developing their own activities and assessments. Teachers should use, refine, and/or augment these activities as desired, in order to ensure that they will have addressed all the standards intended for the unit and, in the aggregate, for the year.

Reading foundations. Our kindergarten through second-grade Maps include a section titled Reading Foundations that provides a pacing guide of instructional goals for the teaching of the CCSS reading Foundational Skills. This guide complements our Maps and was prepared by reading expert Louisa Moats, who also helped develop the reading standards for the CCSS.

Additional resources. These are links to lesson plans, activities, related background information, author interviews, and other instructional materials for teachers from a variety of resources, including the National Endowment for the Humanities and ReadWriteThink. The standards that could be addressed by each additional resource are cited at the end of each description.

Terminology. These are concepts and terms that students will encounter—often for the first time—over the course of the unit. The list is not comprehensive; it is meant to highlight terms that either are particular to the unit, are introduced there, or that play a large role in the work or content of the unit. These terms and concepts are usually implied by the standards, but not always made explicit in them.

Making interdisciplinary connections. This is a section included only in our Maps for the elementary grades. Here we very broadly list the content areas the unit covers and then suggest opportunities for making interdisciplinary connections from the Common Core ELA Maps to other subjects, including history, civics, geography, and the arts. We hope this section will be particularly helpful for K–5 teachers, who typically teach all subjects.

Sample lesson plans. Each unit includes a supplementary document that outlines a possible sequence of lessons, using one or more suggested unit texts to meet focus standards. Many of the texts used in the sample lesson plans are also CCSS exemplar texts. These sample lessons include guidance for differentiated instruction.

Standards checklist. Each grade includes a standards checklist that indicates which standards are covered in which unit—providing teachers an overview of standards coverage for the entire school year.

Addressing all of the CCSS. The curriculum writers worked carefully to ensure that the content and skills in each unit would build on one another so that in the aggregate, all standards would be addressed in a coherent, logical way. They grouped standards that they could envision fitting together in one unit. For example, if a unit were focused on asking and answering questions in informational text, then standards for shared research and expository writing were included in that unit as well. *All standards are addressed at least once,* if not a number of times, in the activities and assessments sections.

Interpreting CCSS citations. Our citations for the standards follow the format established by the CCSS (found in the upper right-hand corners of the pages in the CCSS ELA document):

strand.grade.number

For example, the first Reading Literature (RL) standard in grade four would be cited as RL.4.1. You will find our citations in the front of each focus standard and at the end of each sample activity/assessment. Where standards clearly corresponded to lessons listed under Additional Resources, standards also have been cited.

Understanding unit themes. The unit themes grew organically out of the process of selecting which standards would be the focus of each unit and consulting the list of exemplar texts. The teachers who wrote the Maps intentionally chose themes that would resonate with students, as well as lend coherence to the skills and content addressed. Some of the themes introduced in the early elementary grades, such as courage, re-emerge in later years. We have done so in a deliberate attempt to invite students to wrestle with some of the "great ideas," a hallmark of a liberal education. We hope that as students progress through school, they will consider the themes at greater levels of depth.

Teaching reading. Under the Reading Foundations sections for the kindergarten through second-grade Maps (and embedded into the third- through fifth-grade Maps) is a pacing guide for reading instruction. This guide is aligned with the CCSS reading Foundational Skills. The guide paces instruction in reading foundations logically across the grades. Concepts of print, phonological awareness, phonics, and text reading fluency are all addressed and woven into a developmental progression that leads to word recognition and text reading. Accomplishment of these milestones can be achieved with daily practice and brief activities that would require thirty to forty minutes of instructional time per day. A sample of those activities is also provided. Explicit, sequential, and cumulative teaching of these skills in no way should detract from, substitute for, or prevent the teaching of the oral language, comprehension, and literature-focused instruction, also described in the units.

The curriculum Maps are not tailored for any specific reading instruction method or management technique. *It is up to local school districts and teachers to determine how reading will be taught.* The sample activities and assessments reflect a mix of teacher- and student-centered instruction, but emphasize eliciting evidence of student understanding through authentic assessments.

Selecting materials. Many of the texts listed as exemplars in the CCSS Appendix B are included in our Maps. These texts take priority in our units and indeed shape unit themes. Like the exemplar texts themselves, the additional texts suggested in our Maps include literary works and informational texts that have stood the test of time, as well as excellent contemporary titles. The suggested texts include novels, short stories, poetry, essays, speeches, memoirs, biographies, autobiographies, fables, folktales, and mythology. Teachers will find texts written by authors of wide-ranging diversity: young and old, living and dead, male and female, American and foreign.

In the early grades, the Maps prioritize students' exposure to traditional stories and poetry, Mother Goose rhymes, and award-winning fiction and nonfiction chosen for quality of writing and relevance to themes. They also emphasize concepts of print, phonological awareness, phonics, and text reading fluency. In upper elementary and middle school grades, students read a variety of fiction and nonfiction on science and history topics, as well as diverse selections of classic and contemporary literature. High school begins by establishing in ninth grade a common understanding of literary and informational genres, subgenres, and their characteristics. Grades ten through twelve each focus on a different literary tradition, both American and international. Along the way, the Maps highlight numerous points of connection with history, science, and the arts.

Much consideration has been given to readability. Whenever possible, we have used Lexile level ranges, as described in the CCSS Appendix A, as a guide. We realize that there still will be a range of texts within each grade span. We also recognize that simple texts may be read at upper grades with more nuanced analysis. For this reason, some texts appear in more than one grade. Texts that fall outside the CCSS-recommended grade span are noted.

At the elementary and middle school levels, the text availability and readability levels also were cross-checked with the Scholastic Reading Wizard Reading Levels section, Amazon.com, and the Lexile levels (as available) on the Barnes & Noble website.

Evaluating student work. Aside from the inclusion of a scoring rubric for high school seminars, the Maps do not provide sample student work or scoring rubrics. We do hope that the interactivity feature of the online edition of the Maps may allow teachers to submit these kinds of materials, if they so desire. We expect to develop such additional tools as teachers and curriculum developers use and customize the Maps, and as we conduct ongoing professional development.

Differentiating instruction. The sample lesson plans provide specific guidance for differentiated instruction for advanced and struggling students. As with student work and scoring rubrics, we expect to develop further guidance on differentiation as the Maps are implemented and customized.

Incorporating art, music, and media. While literature is of course a vital component of the standards, some standards in the CCSS address the arts as well. Because Common Core promotes the importance of all students studying the arts, we have highlighted places where ELA instruction could be enhanced by connecting a work of literature or an objective of the unit to art, music, or film. For example, students might compare a novel, story, or play to its film or musical rendition. Where a particular period of literature or the literature of a particular region or country is addressed, works of art from that period or country may also be examined. We suggest, for example, that students study self-portraiture when they are encountering memoirs. In each case, connections are made to the standards themselves.

Promoting student understanding through recitation and memorization. Recitation requires close reading and therefore nurtures deeper levels of students' understanding. Students also benefit from the satisfaction of making a poem or piece of prose one's own for life. In addition, many teachers observe that memorization and recitation help develop a student's experience and confidence in public speaking, which could help students marshal evidence and make effective arguments in other contexts. Keep in mind that our suggestions for memorization activities are not meant to be mandatory in every unit.

KINDERGARTEN

Children enter kindergarten with a wide range of knowledge. Some have already learned to read simple books, while others have not yet learned the alphabet. Over the course of this year, all students begin to read, write, and advance their existing skills. The kindergarten curriculum map consists of a rich array of "read-aloud" stories, nonfiction, and poems, combined with phonics and writing, as well as listening and speaking activities. The units include a section devoted to the CCSS reading foundations. While not a comprehensive reading program, this pacing guide provides guidance for instruction in print concepts, phonological awareness, phonics, word recognition, fluency, and some of the writing and language skills. Students listen to a wide variety of excellent literary and nonfiction texts: poems and informational texts about counting; poems and songs with strong rhythm and rhyme; stories about exploring; books about American symbols and celebrations; and books about plants, insects, and frogs. They learn to retell and discuss what they have learned, putting events in order and explaining why they occurred. By the end of the year, students have learned to decode and encode one-syllable regular words and recognize high-frequency sight words. They have been exposed to historical and biographical nonfiction, as well as fiction, poetry, and fables. In the following year, they will continue to learn to read while building knowledge of an array of topics.

Standards Checklist for Kindergarten

Standard	Unit 1	Unit 2	Unit 3	Unit 4	Unit 5	Unit 6	Standard	Unit 1	Unit 2	Unit 3	Unit 4	Unit 5	Unit 6
Reading—Literature							2a		FA	A			
1		A					2b			A			
2		FA			A		2c			A			
3		A	FA	A		A	2d			F	A	FA	A
4	A		FA				3						
5	FA	A	A				4				A		F
6		A					4a				A		
7		A		A			4b				A		FA
8 n/a							5	F	A				
9		FA	FA		FA		5a	FA	A				
10				A	A	FA	5b	A	A		A	A	A
Reading—Informational Text							5c	A	A	A	A		
1		FA	A	FA			5d			A	A	A	
2			FA	A			6				A	A	
3				A			Reading Foundations (addressed in units)						
4	FA			A			1	A	A				
5	A		A				1a	A	A				
6	A	A					1b	A	A				
7			A	A			1c	A	A				
8				A		FA	1d	A	A				
9			A		FA	FA	2	F					
10					A	A	2a	FA	A				
Writing							2b						
1	FA	A	A		A		2c						
2	A	A	FA	A	A	A	2d						
3		FA	A			A	2e						
4 n/a							3						
5		A		A	A	A	3a			A			
6					FA	FA	3b	A					
7				FA	A	A	3c						
8		A		A	FA		3d					A	
9 n/a							4						FA
10 n/a							Reading Foundations (addressed in *Reading Foundations: A Pacing Guide*)						
Speaking and Listening							1	A	A	A			
1	FA	FA	A	A	A	A	1a	A	A	A			
1a	FA	A	A	A	A	A	1b	A	A	A			
1b	A	FA	A	A	A	A	1c	A	A	A			
2			A	A	A		1d	A	A	A	A	A	A
3			A	A	A		2						
4			A	FA	A	A	2a	A	A	A			
5	A		A	A			2b			A	A		
6			A		A	A	2c			A	A	A	A
Language							2d			A	A	A	A
1			F				2e					A	
1a	A	A	A	A			3					A	A
1b		A		A			3a	A	A	A	A	A	A
1c		A		A			3b	A	A	A	A	A	A
1d			FA				3c				A	A	A
1e		A					3d					A	A
1f				FA			4				A	A	A
2		F	F	F	F								

F = Focus Standard; A = Activity/Assessment

A Colorful Time with Rhythm and Rhyme

In this first six-week unit of kindergarten, students are introduced to colorful picture books, traditional poetry, and nursery rhymes filled with rhythm and rhyme.

ESSENTIAL QUESTION

? How does rhyme affect the way that we hear and read poetry?

OVERVIEW

Focusing on phonological awareness, students are challenged to listen for rhythm and rhyming words within the literature. Concepts of print are taught as students read poems on wall charts and in informational books. Descriptions of gathered objects and artworks highlight the secondary focus on color, encouraging rich description, discussion in spoken language, and vocabulary development. In this early stage of writing, students use a combination of drawing, dictation, and writing to give opinions about favorite colors.

FOCUS STANDARDS

These Focus Standards have been selected for the unit from the Common Core State Standards.

RI.K.4: With prompting and support, ask and answer questions about unknown words in a text.

RL.K.5: Recognize common types of texts (e.g., storybooks, poems).

RF.K.2: Demonstrate understanding of spoken words, syllables, and phonemes.

RF.K.2(a): Recognize and produce rhyming words.

W.K.1: Use a combination of drawing, dictating, and writing to compose opinion pieces in which they tell a reader the topic or the name of the book they are writing about and state an opinion or preference about the topic or book (e.g., "My favorite book is . . . ").

SL.K.1: Participate in collaborative conversations with diverse partners about kindergarten topics and texts with peers and adults in small and larger groups.

SL.K.1(a): Follow agreed-upon rules for discussions (e.g., listening to others and taking turns talking about the topics and texts under discussion).

L.K.5: With guidance and support from adults, explore word relationships and nuances in word meanings.

L.K.5(a): Sort common objects into categories (e.g., shapes, foods) to gain a sense of the concepts the categories represent.

SUGGESTED STUDENT OBJECTIVES

- Recognize the difference between a storybook and a poem.
- Understand that poems (poetry) are written by poets and that they often rhyme.
- Distinguish between a verse (stanza) and a line in a poem.
- Identify the author and illustrator of a storybook and of an informational book.
- Ask questions about unknown words in a text.
- Understand the organization and basic features of print.
- Identify the front cover, back cover, and title page of a book; follow the words from left to right, top to bottom, and page by page.
- Understand that words are separated by spaces in print.
- Use a combination of drawing, dictating, or writing to share an opinion.
- Listen to others and take turns speaking while discussing favorite rhymes.
- Expand vocabulary by sorting objects (e.g., by color, noticing colorful places in school and describing objects with "color" adjectives).

SUGGESTED WORKS

(E) indicates a CCSS exemplar text; (EA) indicates a text from a writer with other works identified as exemplars.

LITERARY TEXTS

Picture Books (Read Aloud)

- *Red, Green, Blue: A First Book of Colors* (Alison Jay)
- *Colors! Colores!* (Jorge Lujan and Piet Grobler)
- *Brown Bear, Brown Bear* (Bill Martin Jr. and Eric Carle)
- *If Kisses Were Colors* (Janet Lawler and Alison Jay)
- *My Many Colored Days* (Dr. Seuss) (EA)
- *Mary Wore Her Red Dress* (Merle Peek)
- *The Red Book* (Barbara Lehman)
- *Chicka Chicka Boom Boom* (Bill Martin Jr., John Archambault, and Lois Ehlert)
- *Rap a Tap Tap, Here's Bojangles: Think of That!* (Leo and Diane Dillon)
- *And the Dish Ran Away with the Spoon* (Janet Stevens and Susan Stevens Crummel)
- *The Real Mother Goose* (Blanche Fisher Wright)
- *Red Is for Dragon: A Book of Colors* (Roseanne Thong and Grace Lin)
- *Clang! Clang! Beep! Beep! Listen to the City* (Robert Burleigh and Beppe Giacobbe)

- *Itsy Bitsy Spider* (Iza Trapani)
- *Grandmother's Nursery Rhymes: Las Nanas de Abuelita* (Nelly Palacio Jaramillo)

Poems (Read Aloud)
- "Halfway Down" (A. A. Milne) (E)
- "Singing Time" (Rose Fyleman) (E)
- "Mary Had a Little Lamb" (Sarah Josepha Hale)
- "Time to Rise" (Robert Louis Stevenson)
- "Twinkle, Twinkle, Little Star" (Ann and Jane Taylor)

Nursery Rhymes (Read Along)
- "Diddle, Diddle, Dumpling"
- "Early to Bed"
- "Georgie Porgie"
- "Hey Diddle Diddle"
- "Humpty Dumpty"
- "Jack and Jill"
- "Jack Be Nimble"
- "Little Bo Peep"
- "Little Boy Blue"
- "Little Jack Horner"
- "Little Miss Muffet"
- "Old Mother Hubbard"
- "Pat-a-Cake"
- "Ring Around the Rosey"
- "Rock-a-bye, Baby"
- "Roses Are Red"
- "Simple Simon"
- "Star Light, Star Bright"

INFORMATIONAL TEXTS
Informational Books
- *My Five Senses* (Aliki) (E)

Informational Books (Read Aloud)
- *All the Colors of the Rainbow* (Rookie Read-About Science Series) (Allan Fowler)
- *The Magic School Bus Makes a Rainbow: A Book About Color* (Joanna Cole, Carolyn Braken, and Bruce Degan)
- *Colors and Shapes: Los colores y las figuras* (Gladys Rosa-Mendoza, Carolina Cifuentes, and Michele Noiset)
- *I Spy Colors in Art* (Lucy Micklethwait)
- *Colors* (Learning with Animals) (Melanie Watt)
- *Matisse: The King of Color* (Laurence Anholt)
- *A World of Colors: Seeing Colors in a New Way* (Marie Houblon)

ART, MUSIC, AND MEDIA

- Henri Matisse, *The Dessert: Harmony in Red* (1908)
- James Abbott McNeill Whistler, *Arrangement in Black and Gray: The Artist's Mother* (1871)
- Diego Rivera, *Flower Day* (1925)
- Pieter Bruegel, *The Hunters in the Snow* (1565)
- Helen Frankenthaler, *Mountains and Sea* (1952)
- Paul Gauguin, *The Midday Nap* (1894)
- Pablo Picasso, *Le Gourmet* (1901)

SAMPLE ACTIVITIES AND ASSESSMENTS

1. POETRY/PRINT CONCEPTS

As students read a rhyme, ask them to focus on listening for rhyming words and hearing the rhythm of the lines. By teaching the children to follow along with you on wall charts or an interactive whiteboard, they are able to enjoy rich vocabulary in context and become familiar with sight words and word families. Adding the simple melodies to the nursery rhymes will enhance the students' perception of rhythm. By using musical recordings of the nursery rhymes, students can move to the rhythm of the rhymes in song and recite the words with ease. (RF.K.1, RF.K.3c)

2. POETRY/PHONOLOGICAL AWARENESS

While reading (reciting) "Humpty Dumpty," snap your fingers on the word at the end of a line (e.g., "wall"). The children will snap when they hear the word that rhymes with it (e.g., "fall"). Continue with various rhymes and poems. Afterwards, put up a second nursery rhyme, but leave out the end word of every other line (i.e., "Humpty Dumpty sat on a wall, Humpty Dumpty had a great _____"). Some students can pick from a list of words the appropriate one to fill in the blank. Once they've mastered that, repeat the exercise without providing the list of words. (RF.K.2a)

3. POETRY/PRINT CONCEPTS

As students read a nursery rhyme (or poem) from a chart or interactive whiteboard in the front of the class, choose a student to come up and follow the words from left to right with a pointer. Instruct the students that if there is a word they do not understand in this rhyme, they should raise a hand to ask about it. (RF.K.1a, RL.K.4, RL.K.5)

4. INFORMATIONAL TEXT/LITERARY TEXT

As the class reads an informational or literary book, introduce the idea of author and illustrator. Describe their roles in the creation of a text. Do a "text walk" by carefully showing the front cover, back cover, and title page of the book. As you read an informational text such as *All the Colors of the Rainbow,* pause to ask the children questions. Encourage them to ask questions about the text and unfamiliar words. (RI.K.4, RI.K.5, RI.K.6, RL.K.4)

5. CLASS DISCUSSION/POETRY

Arrange small groups of students and place an object (e.g., a block) in the middle of each circle. Instruct the students to discuss which poem in this unit is their favorite. Students pick up the block when ready to share. Ask them to put the block back in the middle when finished. When working with a group, ask the student who has the floor to think of/share a word that rhymes with the last word of a sentence in the chosen poem. (SL.K.1, SL.K.1a)

6. ART/WRITING

Show students the Whistler and the Rivera. Ask them to discuss how Whistler used a mostly black and white palette, while Rivera used a wide range of colors. Then ask them to choose to draw their favorite of the two works, either in black and white or using a wide range of colors. (W.K.2, SL.K.5)

7. LANGUAGE/VOCABULARY

Prepare a basket of colored objects. Invite students to come to the basket and choose something to tell the class about. This is the rule: Each student must describe the object using at least two "describing words" (i.e., adjectives). Example: a bright red apple, a small green block. Extend this activity by introducing opposites of one of the adjectives. "You showed me a small block. Now find a large block." You could have another vocabulary activity with the same collection by sorting the same objects into color categories such as "red" and "green" or by asking the students to think of rhyming words that describe. (L.K.5a)

8. ART/CLASS DISCUSSION/VOCABULARY CONNECTION

Display the works by Matisse and Picasso. Ask the students what color dominates each work. Ask the students why they think Picasso chose blue and Matisse chose red. Ask how the paintings are the same (e.g., both figures are preparing food and neither is looking at us) and how they are different (e.g., we can see outside in the Matisse, whereas Picasso's is a close-up), preparing the way for literature conversations in comparing and contrasting texts. (SL.K.1, SL.K.5)

READING FOUNDATIONS: A PACING GUIDE FOR READING INSTRUCTION

See Kindergarten, Level One, in the Reading Foundations section for a complete pacing guide for this unit.

ADDITIONAL RESOURCES

Generating Rhymes: Developing Phonemic Awareness (ReadWriteThink) (RF.K.2a)
Growing Readers and Writers with Help from Mother Goose (ReadWriteThink) (RF.K.1b, RF.K.2a)
Hats Off to Color (ArtsEdge, The Kennedy Center) (L.K.5a)
Interview with Eric Carle (RL.K.6)
"Twinkle, Twinkle, Little Star" video
"Rap A Tap Tap" video (Shirley Temple and Bill Robinson)
Spicy Hot Colors video
"Halfway Down" video
Chicka Chicka Boom Boom video

TERMINOLOGY

Artist	Illustrator	Poem	Rhythm
Author	Informational book	Poet	Stanza
Description	Line	Poetry	Story book
Illustration	Opinion	Rhyme	Verse

MAKING INTERDISCIPLINARY CONNECTIONS

This unit teaches:

Art: Color in painting (e.g., Matisse, Whistler, Rivera, Bruegel, Frankenthaler, Gauguin, Picasso)

Science: Color in nature (e.g., rainbows), the five senses (e.g., seeing color—eyes, hearing rhythm and rhyme—ears)

This unit could be extended to teach:

Art: Color (e.g., the color wheel, warm and cool colors, and primary and secondary colors)

Science: the five senses (e.g., touch—skin, smell—nose, taste—tongue)

Math: Patterns (e.g., rhyming patterns in Mother Goose rhymes)

Kindergarten, Unit One Sample Lesson Plan

"Halfway Down" by A. A. Milne

In this series of four lessons, students read "Halfway Down" by A. A. Milne, and they:

- Identify the form of the poem (RL.K.5)
- Note the connection between form and content (RL.K.1, RL.K.5)
- Examine the theme of the poem (RL.K.1)
- Explore a different reading interpretation of the poem (RL.K.1, SL.K.2)
- Reflect on the power of a poem to provoke thoughts and feelings (SL.K.1a, SL.K.1b)

Summary

Lesson I: Meet A. A. Milne and "Halfway Down"	Lesson II: Kermit the Frog Meets Milne
Note the form of Milne's "Halfway Down" (RL.K.5)	Examine Kermit the Frog's performance of Milne's poem "Halfway Down" (SL.K.2)
Meet A. A. Milne (RL.K.6)	Note the differences between the reading and the singing of the poem (RL.K.1, SL.K.2)
Identify repeating sounds in the poem (rhyming) (RF.K.2a)	Evaluate Kermit's interpretation of the poem (SL.K.2)
Identify the setting of the poem (RL.K.3)	(Through memorization) develop ownership of Milne's words
Probe the shift from the first to the second stanza	
Explore what the poem is about (RL.K.1)	
Examine the theme of the poem (RL.K.1)	
(Through illustrations) individualize response to the theme (W.K.1, W.K.3, SL.K.5)	

Lesson III: We Write Along with Milne

Revisit Milne's "Halfway Down" (RL.K.2)

Revisit Kermit's interpretation of the poem (SL.K.2)

(While citing the poem) revisit its rhymes (RF.K.2a)

Explore the purpose of the rhymes (RF.K.2a)

Compose a new stanza (W.K.2)

Lesson IV: Halfway Down and Halfway Up

Assimilate the varying components of the unit: Milne's poem; Kermit's song; the students' new stanza and the students' illustrated poems (RL.K.2)

Reflect on the power of a poem to provoke thoughts and feelings (SL.K.1a, SL.K.1b)

Lesson I: Meet A. A. Milne and "Halfway Down"

Objectives

Note the form of Milne's "Halfway Down" (RL.K.5)

Meet A. A. Milne (RL.K.6)

Identify repeating sounds in the poem (rhyming) (RF.K.2a)

Identify the setting of the poem (RL.K.3)

Probe the shift from the first to the second stanza

Explore what the poem is about (RL.K.1)

Examine the theme of the poem (RL.K.1)

(Through illustrations) individualize response to the theme (W.K.1, W.K.3, SL.K.5)

Required Materials

- ☐ Enlarged copy of A. A. Milne's "Halfway Down"
- ☐ Copies of the poem (free of illustrations) to distribute to the students
- ☐ Markers and colored pencils

Procedures

1. Lead-In:
   a. The purpose of this part of the lesson (even before reading the poem) is to help the students note the form of the poem.
      Point to the enlarged copy of A. A. Milne's "Halfway Down."
      Ask the students what they notice.
      They will note that it is not very long (i.e., they can count the number of words).
      Ask if anyone knows what we call this "grouping of words."

If there is no response from the students, introduce the term *poem*.

You may want to hold up a chapter book to help the students visualize the difference between prose and verse.

b. Continue to probe with students (i.e., "What else do you notice about the poem?")

c. Introduce the word *stanza*.

2. Step by Step:

a. The teacher will read the poem aloud (at least twice).

Halfway Down

(A. A. MILNE)

Halfway down the stairs
Is a stair where I sit.
There isn't any other stair
Quite like it.
I'm not at the bottom,
I'm not at the top;
So this is the stair
Where I always stop.
Halfway up the stairs
Isn't up and isn't down.
It isn't in the nursery,
It isn't in the town.
And all kinds of funny thoughts
Go running round my head:
"It isn't really anywhere!
It's somewhere else instead!"

b. Introduce A. A. Milne (this part can be moved up and become activity a.)

For example, produce a poster with Milne's picture and perhaps a picture of Winnie the Pooh. This is a good opportunity to connect with some of the students' prior knowledge.

c. Back to the poem.

Read the poem to the students again; at this point, some of the students may join as the teacher points to the words that she reads. The purpose of this step is to emphasize rhyme.

Introduce the term *rhyme* through probing and repeating pairs of words (e.g., sit/it, top/stop).

d. Before reading the poem again (with the help of the students), ask the students to notice the difference between the first and the second stanzas. The students will notice the shift from "halfway down" to "halfway up." Through a series of questions, demonstrate the difference between the two stanzas, for example:

What does the speaker say in the first stanza?

—The focus is on the speaker; "I" is repeated four times; (point to the "I's"); he sits there because it is "halfway down."

What does he say in the second stanza?

—There are no "I's." Instead, the speaker pays more attention to the stairs, especially in the first four lines.

What happens in the last four lines?

—The speaker refers to himself again, but he makes a confusing statement: "It isn't really anywhere! It's somewhere else instead!"

e. This is a good time to introduce the students to the idea that sometimes you need to think carefully to figure out what a poet is saying. Provide them with time to discuss their ideas.

3. Closure:

A good way to conclude the lesson is to let the students absorb the information and spend some quiet time, on their own, reflecting. Distribute the individual copies of the poem and ask the students to draw upon their reflections to illustrate the poem.

Differentiation

Advanced

- Expand the students' exposure to and enjoyment of more Milne poetry, using poems such as "Solitude," "Waiting at the Window," or "Us Two." Discuss the themes of these poems and ask students to illustrate them. A multi-stanza poem could be cut into stanzas and glued into a book illustrated by the students.

Struggling

- If there is a staircase in your school, physically take students to the staircase. Have various students experience going halfway up and halfway down the stairs. If a staircase is not available, draw it on the board and have a student finger-walk up the stairs and down the stairs, stopping at the halfway point.
- Spend some time exploring rhyming sounds by doing rhyming word pairs like: red/bed, blue/shoe, yellow/fellow, black/sack, brown/clown, white/kite.

Homework/Assessment
N/A

Tell a Story, 1-2-3

In this second six-week unit of kindergarten, students focus on sequence as they enjoy Counting Books, both fictional and informational, and stories based on three.

ESSENTIAL QUESTION

? How are the beginning, the middle, and the end of a story different from each other?

OVERVIEW

Building on the wide exposure to text types in the first unit, students now focus on the sequence of a text: the beginning, middle, and end of a story. They learn to retell rich stories and, by listening to versions of traditional stories, recognize familiar storylines embedded in different settings with different characters. Counting rhymes and reading a number of counting books will continue the first unit's focus on phonological awareness and listening for more rhythm and rhyme, as well as on sequencing. Students study three paintings, which are used for a creative storytelling activity and are related to the idea of multiple versions of a familiar story.

FOCUS STANDARDS

These Focus Standards have been selected for the unit from the Common Core State Standards.

RL.K.2: With prompting and support, retell familiar stories, including key details.

RL.K.9: With prompting and support, compare and contrast the adventures and experiences of characters in familiar stories.

RI.K.1: With prompting and support, ask and answer questions about key details in a text.

SL.K.1: Participate in collaborative conversations with diverse partners about kindergarten topics and texts with peers and adults in small and larger groups.

SL.K.1(b): Continue a conversation through multiple exchanges.

W.K.3: Use a combination of drawing, dictating, and writing to narrate a single event or several loosely linked events, tell about the events in the order in which they occurred, and provide a reaction to what happened.

L.K.2: Demonstrate command of the conventions of Standard English capitalization, punctuation, and spelling when writing.

L.K.2(a): Capitalize the first word in a sentence and the pronoun *I*.

SUGGESTED OBJECTIVES

Name the author and illustrator of both the fictional and informational texts in this unit.

Orally retell familiar stories, including details and events at the beginning, middle, and end.

Recite and produce rhyming words from nursery rhymes and rhyming texts.

Use a combination of writing, drawing, and dictating to retell stories with a beginning, middle, and end.

Distinguish shades of meaning among simple adjectives.

Recognize the importance of sequence in storytelling, informational and fictional counting books, and nursery rhymes.

Appreciate the difference between an original story and other versions of the same story.

SUGGESTED WORKS

(E) indicates a CCSS exemplar text; (EA) indicates a text from a writer with other works identified as exemplars.

LITERARY TEXTS

Counting Books (Read Aloud)

- *Ten, Nine, Eight* (Molly Bang) (EA)
- *Chicka Chicka 1, 2, 3* (Bill Martin Jr., Michael Sampson, and Lois Ehlert)
- *Ten Apples Up on Top!* (Dr. Seuss and Roy McKie) (EA)
- *One is a Snail, Ten is a Crab: A Counting by Feet Book* (April Pulley Sayre, Jeff Sayre, and Randy Cecil)
- *Anno's Counting Book* (Mitsumasa Anno)
- *Grandfather Counts* (Andrea Cheng)

Traditional Stories and Variations (Read Aloud)

- *Goldilocks and the Three Bears* (Jan Brett)
- *Horrible Harry Bugs the Three Bears* (Suzy Kline and Frank Remkiewicz)
- *The Three Billy Goats Gruff* (Paul Galdone)
- *The Three Cabritos* (Eric A. Kimmel and Stephen Gilpin)
- *Three Cool Kids* (Rebecca Emberley)
- *The Three Little Pigs* (James Marshall)
- *The Three Pigs* (David Wiesner)
- *The True Story of the Three Little Pigs* (Jon Scieszka and Lane Smith)
- *The Three Little Wolves and the Big Bad Pig* (Eugene Trivizas and Helen Oxenbury)
- *The Three Little Javelinas: Los Tres Pequenos Jabalies* (bilingual) (Susan Lowell)

Stories (Read Along)

- *Pancakes for Breakfast* (Tomie dePaola) (E)
- *Ten Black Dots* (Donald Crews) (EA)
- *The Very Hungry Caterpillar* (Eric Carle)

Poems (Read Aloud)

- "Three Little Kittens" in *The Oxford Illustrated Book of American Children's Poems* (Eliza Lee Follen)
- "Zin! Zin! Zin! A Violin" (Lloyd Moss and Marjorie Priceman) (E)
- "Mix a Pancake" in *The Complete Poems* (Christina Rossetti) (E)

Nursery Rhymes (Read Along)

- "Three Blind Mice"
- "One, Two, Buckle My Shoe"
- "A Diller, A Dollar"
- "Hot Cross Buns"
- "Hickory, Dickory, Dock"
- "Old King Cole"
- "Baa, Baa, Black Sheep"
- "This Little Pig Went to Market"

INFORMATIONAL TEXTS

- *Can You Count Ten Toes? Count to 10 in 10 Different Languages* (Lezlie Evans and Denis Roche)
- *One Is a Drummer: A Book of Numbers* (Roseanne Thong and Grace Lin)
- *Arlene Alda's 1-2-3: What Do You See?* (Arlene Alda)
- *Moja Means One: Swahili Counting Book* (Muriel and Tom Feelings)
- *The Year at Maple Hill Farm* (Alice and Martin Provensen) (E)
- *Our Animal Friends at Maple Hill Farm* (Alice and Martin Provensen) (EA)
- *Farm Animals* (Young Nature Series) (Felicity Everett)
- *Pigs* (Gail Gibbons) (EA)
- *Beatrice's Goat* (Page McBrier and Lori Lohstoeter)
- *Pigs* (Animals That Live on the Farm) (JoAnn Early Macken)
- *Goats* (Animals That Live on the Farm) (JoAnn Early Macken)

ART, MUSIC, AND MEDIA

Art

- Jean-Francois Millet, *First Steps* (1858–1859)
- Vincent van Gogh, *First Steps, after Millet* (1890)
- Pablo Picasso, *Mother and Child (First Steps)* (1943)

SAMPLE ACTIVITIES AND ASSESSMENTS

Note: Continue work on rhythm and rhyme from Unit One as more of the students show readiness to hear and see rhyming words. (RF.K.2a)

1. CLASS DISCUSSION/LITERATURE

Arrange small groups of students and place an object (e.g., a block) in the middle of the circle. As a class, tell the story of *Goldilocks and the Three Bears*, having students take turns telling the events in the story. Students pick up the block when ready to fill in part of the story and put the block back in the middle when finished. Encourage the students to identify all the characters and setting, as well as the major events of the story, when retelling. Encourage the students to note the importance of describing words (adjectives) in the telling of the story. For example, note the different ways the characters are described. Storytelling is shared with all the members of the group. (RL.K.2, RL.K.3, SL.K.1a,b, L.K.5b)

2. LITERATURE/WRITING

Ask students to retell the story of *Goldilocks and the Three Bears*. Tell them to use illustrations, dictating, and/or writing. Tell them to be sure to focus on the beginning, middle, and end of the story by using transitional words (e.g., ordinal numbers: *first, second, . . .*"). You may use paper folded into three sections to help some students organize their ideas for the beginning, middle, and end. Encourage students to include all the characters in the story and to add as many details as they can remember. You may extend this writing activity for advanced students by asking them to write a new version of *Goldilocks and the Three Bears*. Be sure to have them change the characters and the setting and to illustrate the new story to create a class book. (RL.K.1, RL.K.2, L.K.1a,b,c; L.K.2a, L.K.5b, W.K.3, W.K.5)

3. LITERATURE

Using the book of illustrations *Pancakes for Breakfast* (Tomie DePaola), have students look at the illustrations and note how the pictures tell a story. Point out the importance of looking very closely at the details in the illustrations to tell what happens next. Encourage active thinking by asking what might happen when the page is turned to the next illustration. Because this is a wordless book, point out how the illustrator is telling a story without words. Even picture books with words tell a story through the illustrations. Write the students' dictated stories on sentence strips and place them in a pocket chart. Focus on modeling the capital letter required at the beginning of a sentence and the word *I*. (Extend this activity by reversing this process: read aloud the text of a simple book without showing the illustrations. Ask students to illustrate the story, creating their own wordless book. The students' illustrations can then be compared to the book.) (RL.K.5, RL.K.6, RL.K.7, L.K.2a)

4. ART/LITERATURE CONNECTION

To introduce "versions" of a story to your class, use Millet's *First Steps* as the original "story." Allow the class to study the painting, giving plenty of time to notice details and create a possible story about the painting. Then show them van Gogh's *First Steps, after Millet* and have the class note how the "original characters are still in the story," but also that it all looks different (e.g., the Millet is in pencil while the van Gogh is an oil painting; in the Millet the people are prominent, whereas in the van Gogh, other elements—such as the gate, the wheelbarrow, and the tree—are also emphasized). Finally, show them Picasso's *First Steps* to see how another artist expressed the same idea in a completely different way. (RL.K.9)

5. ART/NARRATIVE WRITING

After looking closely at three paintings with the same title, *First Steps*, choose one of the paintings and imagine it shows the beginning of a story. Pair students to create the middle and end of the story to share with the class. *Prompt:* Choose one of the paintings and write (or dictate) a sentence telling why you chose that painting as your favorite. Be sure to begin your sentence with a capital letter and put a period at the end. (W.K.1, W.K.3)

6. ART/WRITING CONNECTION

Ask students to choose the painting they like best and to write (or dictate) a sentence saying why they chose that painting as their favorite. Remind them to begin their sentences with capital letters and to put periods at the end. (W.K.1, W.K.3)

7. LITERATURE

Read the traditional version of a story first. Then read a different version of the story. For example, read the Galdone version of "The Three Billy Goats Gruff" and discuss the beginning, middle, and end of the story. Then read one of the other versions discussing how the beginning, middle, and end are similar, but also how the setting and characters make it a different story. Note how important the varied shades of meaning for action words (verbs) are crucial to each story. (RL.K.9, L.K.5b)

8. READING FOUNDATIONS AND INFORMATIVE/EXPLANATORY WRITING

Create a counting book using the letters covered so far this year. Each student will choose a favorite letter and then brainstorm words that begin with that letter. Using the numbers one through five and five different things that begin with the chosen letter, create a book (e.g., *A Counting Book for T: 1 Tadpole, 2 Turkeys, 3 Toads, 4 Tigers, 5 Trout*). Title each student's book *A Counting Book for* _____. Be sure to write the name of the author and illustrator (student) on the cover of the book. Place the finished books in a basket for other students to enjoy. (RF.K.1a,b,c,d; RF.K.3a)

9. INFORMATIONAL TEXT

Today you will have to think, ask questions, and answer questions while we read an informational counting book titled *One Is a Drummer: A Book of Numbers* (Roseanne Thong and Grace Lin). (RI.K.1, RI.K.6)

10. INFORMATIONAL TEXT

Because pigs and goats are talking characters who have personalities in these stories, students will enjoy reading about real pigs and goats. Beginning with books and digital resources on pigs or goats, keep a chart of animal needs that are met on the farm. Extend this work by writing a class book about real pigs or real goats. Be sure to talk about their needs and how those needs are met on farms. In an effort to pave the way for focused research, you may want to demonstrate the use of key word searches on a web browser with an interactive whiteboard or other projection device. (RI.K.1, RI.K.6, W.K.2, W.K.7, W.K.8)

11. POETRY/ILLUSTRATION

"Mix a Pancake" is a poem written by Christina Rossetti. Have students draw illustrations that match the words to show the steps in making pancakes. When finished, they can share the illustrations with a friend and read (recite) the poem together. (RL.K.5, RL.K.7, W.K.2)

READING FOUNDATIONS: A PACING GUIDE FOR READING INSTRUCTION

See Kindergarten, Level Two, in the Reading Foundations section for a complete pacing guide for this unit.

ADDITIONAL RESOURCES

Comparing Tales through Performance: The Three Little Pigs (ArtsEdge, The Kennedy Center) (RL.K.9)
Poetry Portfolios: Using Poetry to Teach Reading (ReadWriteThink) (RL.K.5)
Story Kit (a free application available from iTunes) (K.W.1., K.W.2, and/or K.W.3)
Interview with Tomie DePaola (RL.K.6)

TERMINOLOGY

Author	Illustration	Ordinal number	Retelling
Beginning	Illustrator	words (*first, second,*	Sequence
Characters	Middle	*third*)	Storybook
End	Number words	Poem	Versions

MAKING INTERDISCIPLINARYS CONNECTIONS

This unit teaches:

Art: Millet, van Gogh, Picasso
Science: Farm animals (e.g., pigs and goats; what farm animals need to live)

This unit could be extended to teach:

Science: Animals and their needs (e.g., farm, pet, and wild animals; what animals need to live) or farming (e.g., crops from field to table)

Kindergarten, Unit Two Sample Lesson Plan

Pancakes for Breakfast by Tomie dePaola

In this series of two lessons, students examine *Pancakes for Breakfast* by Tomie dePaola, and they:

Explore the story behind the illustrations of *Pancakes for Breakfast* (RL.K.7, SL.K.3)

Note the strength of a story that has few words (RL.K.7, SL.K.3)

Summary

Lesson I: *Pancakes for Breakfast* – An Introduction

Identify the author/illustrator of *Pancakes for Breakfast* (RL.K.6)

Note the absence of narration in *Pancakes for Breakfast* (RL.K.5, RL.K.7)

Explore the setting of *Pancakes for Breakfast* (RL.K.3, RL.K.7, SL.K.1, SL.K.4)

Tell the story of *Pancakes for Breakfast* (RL.K.1, RL.K.7, SL.K.1)

Lesson II: *Pancakes for Breakfast* – The Plot

Examine the characteristics of the protagonist of *Pancakes for Breakfast* (RL.K.3)

Identify additional characters in the story (RL.K.3)

Explore the plot of *Pancakes for Breakfast* (RL.K.1, SL.K.1, SL.K.3)

Probe the moral of the story (SL.K.3)

Note the strength of the story despite the presence of only a few words (RL.K.7, SL.K.3)

Lesson II: *Pancakes for Breakfast*—The Plot

Objectives

Examine the characteristics of the protagonist of *Pancakes for Breakfast* (RL.K.3)

Identify additional characters in the story (RL.K.3)

Explore the plot of *Pancakes for Breakfast* (RL.K.1, SL.K.1, SL.K.3)

Probe the moral of the story (SL.K.3)

Note the strength of the story despite the presence of only a few words (RL.K.7, SL.K.3)

Required Materials

☐ *Pancakes for Breakfast*, by Tomie dePaola

Procedures

1. Lead-In:

Students retell the story of *Pancakes for Breakfast*.

2. Step by Step:

a. Students reexamine the story's illustrations and describe the protagonist; they notice her looks, her expressions, and her actions.

b. Students note the role of the cat and the dog in the story.

c. In a class discussion, with the help of the teacher's probes, students identify the story's introduction, the development of its plot, and its conclusion.

d. Students discuss the moral of the story: "If at first you don't succeed try, try, again."

3. Closure:

Students evaluate the illustrator's ability to tell a story without words.

Differentiation

Advanced

- A small group of students could create a story to accompany the illustrations. After creating a sound to match to page turns, students could record their story on a digital recording device.

Struggling

- Before introducing this book to the class, make pancakes from scratch in the classroom. As you are making the pancakes with the students, discuss the verbs related to cooking, such as "mixing," "stirring," "blending," and "cracking." Be sure that the students understand the process of making a pancake, from mixing the batter to pouring the syrup onto the pancake. Incorporate the phrase, "Try, try again" if there is any difficulty with cracking an egg or flipping the pancake.

Homework/Assessment

N/A

Kindergarten ▶ *Unit 3*

Exploring with Friends in the Neighborhood

In this third six-week unit of kindergarten, students explore fictional characters in literary texts and neighborhoods in informational texts.

ESSENTIAL QUESTION

? How is reading like exploring?

OVERVIEW

Building on basic retelling of a familiar story, this unit focuses on introducing the differences between literary and informational texts (though not by name necessarily). Students explore characters, settings, and events in both literary and informational texts by asking questions about unknown words, characters, settings, and events. Students compare the first adventure of *Little Bear* with other stories in the book. As they read stories of other characters, as in *Frog and Toad Together,* students extend their skills of comparing and contrasting. *Winnie the Pooh* provides the context for students to learn to ask questions when they lose their way in following the story or in understanding Pooh's special language, such as the made-up word "expotition." The informational texts offer a comparable opportunity for students to ask questions about real people in their communities, such as firefighters and police officers.

FOCUS STANDARDS

These Focus Standards have been selected for the unit from the Common Core State Standards.

RL.K.3: With prompting and support, identify characters, settings, and major events in a story.

RL.K.4: Ask and answer questions about unknown words in a text.

RL.K.9: With prompting and support, compare and contrast the adventures and experiences of characters in familiar stories.

RI.K.2: With prompting and support, identify the main topic and retell key details of a text.

W.K.2: Use a combination of drawing, dictating, and writing to compose informative/explanatory texts in which they name what they are writing about and supply some information about the topic.

L.K.1: Demonstrate command of the conventions of Standard English grammar and usage when writing or speaking.

L.K.1(d): Understand and use question words (interrogatives) (e.g., *who, what, where, when, why, how*).

SUGGESTED STUDENT OBJECTIVES

- Use the words *who, what, where, when,* and *why* to explore informational texts.
- Ask questions about unknown words in both fictional and informational texts.
- Locate basic information in a nonfiction text.
- Identify characters, settings, and key events in a story.
- Compare and contrast the adventures of one character in a collection of stories.
- Compare and contrast the adventures of different characters in different books through the use of a graphic organizer.
- Understand the difference between real (nonfiction) and imagined (fiction) explorations.
- Use a combination of drawing, dictating, or writing to compose an informative text.
- Name and identify periods, question marks, and exclamation points.
- Understand and correctly use the prepositions *to/from, on/off,* and *in/out.*

SUGGESTED WORKS

(E) indicates a CCSS exemplar text; (EA) indicates a text from a writer with other works identified as exemplars.

LITERARY TEXTS

Chapter Book (Read Aloud)

- *The Complete Tales of Winnie-the-Pooh* (A. A. Milne) (EA)

Picture Books (Read Aloud)

- *Frog and Toad Together* (Arnold Lobel) (E)
- *Little Bear* (series) (Else Holmelund Minarik and Maurice Sendak) (E)
- *The Story About Ping* (Marjorie Flack and Kurt Wiese)
- *Blueberries for Sal* (Robert McCloskey)
- *Make Way for Ducklings* (Robert McCloskey)
- *Curious George* (series) (H. A. Rey and Margret Rey)
- *Officer Buckle and Gloria* (Peggy Rathmann)
- *Where the Wild Things Are* (Maurice Sendak)
- *Knuffle Bunny: A Cautionary Tale* (Mo Willems)
- *Owl Moon* (Jane Yolen and John Schoenherr)
- *Little Fur Family* (Margaret Wise Brown and Garth Williams)
- *Harold and the Purple Crayon* (Crockett Johnson)
- *The Snowy Day* (Ezra Jack Keats)

- *The Jolly Postman* (Allan Ahlberg and Janet Ahlberg)
- *Margaret and Margarita: Margarita y Margaret* (Lynn Reiser)

Stories (Read Along, Wordless Books)

- *A Dog, a Boy, and a Frog* (Mercer Mayer) (E)
- *Trainstop* (Barbara Lehman)

Poems (Read Aloud)

- "Us Two" in *The Complete Tales and Poems of Winnie-the-Pooh* (A. A. Milne) (EA)
- "The Swing" in *A Child's Garden of Verses* (Robert Louis Stevenson)

INFORMATIONAL TEXTS

- *Fire! Fire!* (Gail Gibbons) (E)
- *The Post Office Book: Mail and How it Moves* (Gail Gibbons) (EA)
- *Check It Out!: The Book about Libraries* (Gail Gibbons) (EA)
- *Community Helpers from A to Z* (Bobbie Kalman and Niki Walker)
- *Whose Hat is This?* (Katz Cooper, Sharon Muehlenhardt, and Amy Bailey)
- *Whose Tools Are These?* (Katz Cooper, Sharon Muehlenhardt, and Amy Bailey)
- *Jobs Around My Neighborhood: Oficios en mi vecindario* (Gladys Rosa-Mendoza and Ann Iosa)
- *A Day in the Life of a Police Officer* (First Facts: Community Helpers at Work) (Heather Adamson)
- *A Day in the Life of a Doctor* (First Facts: Community Helpers at Work) (Heather Adamson)
- *A Day in the Life of a Teacher* (First Facts: Community Helpers at Work) (Heather Adamson)
- *A Day in the Life of a Firefighter* (First Facts: Community Helpers at Work) (Heather Adamson)

ART, MUSIC, AND MEDIA

Art

- Romare Bearden, *The Block* (1972)
- Pieter Bruegel, *Netherlandish Proverbs* (1559)

Music and Songs (Read Along)

- Henry Mancini, *Baby Elephant Walk* (1961)
- Camille Saint-Saëns, *Carnival of the Animals, Fifth Movement*, "The Elephant" (1886)
- "Do You Know the Muffin Man?"
- "The People in Your Neighborhood" (Jeff Moss)
- "What Shall We Do When We All Go Out?"

SAMPLE ACTIVITIES AND ASSESSMENTS

1. CLASS DISCUSSION/INFORMATIONAL TEXT

While reading informational books about community helpers, create a chart with the following headings: *Who, What, Where, When,* and *Why.* Encourage children to listen for answers to those questions as you read the book aloud. Remind the students to pay close attention to the illustrations for details. To ensure each child's participation, give them sticky notes or whiteboards on which to write or draw their ideas. Begin by talking about the author, illustrator, and front, back, and title page of the book. Fill in the chart each time you read a new book about community helpers. Use this chart as inspiration to change the lyrics for "Do You Know the Muffin Man?" for community helpers in your neighborhood (e.g., "Do you know the fireman … That works on 12th and Main!"). (RI.K.1, RI.K.2, RI.K.5, RI.K.7, L.K.1d, SL.K.1, SL.K.3, SL.K.4)

2. CLASS DISCUSSION/INFORMATIONAL TEXT

Using two books that describe different jobs but are in the same series of informational books (such as the *Community Helpers at Work* series), create a graphic organizer to compare and contrast the days of various community helpers. Discuss the ways the jobs are similar and different. Require each student to dictate, draw, write, or act out something one of the community helpers does (e.g., a postal worker weighs packages). Ask if the other community helper does something similar (e.g., a nurse weighs patients). (RI.K.2, RI.K.9)

3. MUSIC CONNECTION/LITERATURE

As a musical illustration of comparing and contrasting, use the work of Henry Mancini ("Baby Elephant Walk") and Saint-Saëns (*Carnival of the Animals*, "The Elephant") to compare and contrast two musical compositions that are inspired by elephants. Introduce the activity by telling the students that they are going to hear two different musical pieces that are based on elephants. As they listen to "Baby Elephant Walk" and "The Elephant," ask them to decide which piece reminds them more of an elephant. Extend this activity by having the students move to the music as they listen, deciding whether the music makes them want to dance or lumber like elephants. (L.K.5d, RL.K.9)

4. LITERATURE

After reading the first story in the *Little Bear* collection of stories, use a chart to organize ideas about each of the three stories. Remind students of the *who, what,* and *where* questions to be answered. Create headings for *Character, Setting,* and *Events*. Assign students one of the three categories to think about each time you read, encouraging them to write or draw ideas on sticky notes. Fill in the chart each time you read a new *Little Bear* story. (*Extension:* Create a similar chart to compare other fictional explorations and adventures by characters such as Frog and Toad, Curious George, and more.) (RL.K.3, RL.K.9)

5. LITERATURE

Read *Winnie-the-Pooh* aloud to check for student understanding. To be sure that students are following the story and understanding the words, encourage students to monitor their own comprehension. Tell the children that if they lose their way or a word is confusing them, they should put a hand on their own shoulder. If you see a student do so, stop reading at a good stopping place, reread the confusing section, and allow other students to participate in clearing up the confusion. (RL.K.4)

6. WRITING/LANGUAGE

"Write about a community helper in your neighborhood. Be sure to name the community helper and to tell what she/he does to help the community." (For example, "A trash collector picks up stinky garbage all over our city and takes it to the dump.") (W.K.2, L.K.1a, L.K.2a,b,c; L.K.5c)

7. LANGUAGE

Tell the students that they are going to practice giving and following directions. Create directions that focus on using prepositions such as *to/from, on/off,* and *in/out.* Pull a child's name out of a basket and then give them a command. For example, "Tian, walk *from* your desk *to* the teacher's desk." "Jaxton, put your hand *in* the basket and then take it *out.*" Extend this activity by placing the prepositions on cards and having the students make up directions using the words. You could also play the game of Simon Says as you give the commands. As students develop confidence, increase the commands by two or three additional steps. (L.K.1e)

8. LITERATURE/POETRY

Read a poem such as "The Swing." Assign the students the task of drawing an illustration for each stanza of the poem. Do the same activity with other poems, such as "Us Two." Using key words such as *who, what, where, why, when,* and *how,* compare and contrast the two poems. Encourage the children to work on the recitation of their favorite poem. (RL.K.9, L.K.1d)

9. ART/CLASS DISCUSSION

View Bearden's collage. Note that the work is four feet high and eighteen feet long. Compare that to the size of a wall in the classroom. Try to get the students to look at the collage for as long as possible. The following questions will help guide a fifteen-minute discussion: What do you notice first in this collage and why? Where do you think this might be? What do you see that makes it look like this place? How did Bearden make the buildings look different (e.g., color and texture)? Do you notice any people? (SL.K.1, SL.K.2, SL.K.4, SL.K.5, SL.K.6)

10. ART/INFORMATIVE/EXPLANATORY WRITING

Assign students a section from *Netherlandish Proverbs* to work with. Ask them to study it closely. Partner the students to compose one sentence describing what the people seem to be doing or who they might be. Have students share their sentences with the whole group. (W.K.1, W.K.3)

11. ART/CLASS DISCUSSION

Display the Bearden and Bruegel pieces side by side. Note that these works were created more than four hundred years apart. Ask the students to find similarities and differences between the two works. Which place seems like a real place, and which one seems more like a dream or fantasy? Document the answers on a chart for future discussion. (SL.K.1, SL.K.2, SL.K.4, SL.K.5, SL.K.6)

READING FOUNDATIONS: A PACING GUIDE FOR READING INSTRUCTION

See Kindergarten, Level Three, in the Reading Foundations section for a complete pacing guide for this unit.

ADDITIONAL RESOURCES

- *Imagination or Observation: Frog and Toad are Friends* (Indiana Department of Education) (RL.K.5)
- *Exploring Neighborhoods Through Art: Harold and the Purple Crayon* (ArtsEdge, The Kennedy Center) (RL.K.7)

- *Reading Illustrations* (ArtsEdge, The Kennedy Center) (RL.K.7)
- *Make Way for Ducklings* statue (Nancy Schon's website)

TERMINOLOGY

Character	Fiction	Question mark	When
Compare	How	Questioning	Where
Contrast	Imaginary	Real	Who
Exclamation mark	Key events	Setting	Why
Fantasy	Nonfiction	What	

MAKING INTERDISCIPLINARY CONNECTIONS

This unit teaches:

Music: *Carnival of the Animals, Fifth Movement* "The Elephant" (Camille Saint-Saëns); elements of music (e.g., moving responsively to music)

Social Studies: Community helpers (e.g., wide range of careers)

Geography: Community (i.e., town, city, or community)

This unit could be extended to teach:

Music: *Carnival of the Animals*, Movements I–XIV (Camille Saint-Saens) (e.g., recognizing the instruments within the performance); elements of music (e.g., fast/slow, high/low, and loud/quiet)

Science: The human body (e.g., focus on the medical field through health of your body: exercise, cleanliness, healthy foods, rest, and dental care)

Geography: Locate continent, country, and state where the community is located.

Kindergarten, Unit Three Sample Lesson Plan

Frog and Toad Together by Arnold Lobel

In this series of six lessons, students read *Frog and Toad Together* by Arnold Lobel, and they:

Explore the adventures of the two characters, Frog and Toad (RL.K.1, RL.K.2, RL.K.3, SL.K.2)

Identify the differences between the two characters (RL.K.1, RL.K.2, RL.K.3)

Examine the relationship between Frog and Toad (RL.K.1, RL.K.3)

Note the author's use of humor (RL.K.1)

Imagine and share new adventures of Frog and Toad (W.K.1, W.K.2, W.K.3, SL.K.5, SL.K.6)

Summary

Lesson I: "A List"

Examine the book cover and identify the two leading characters in the book (RL.K.2)

(Together) spell out their names (RF.K.3, RF.K.3)

Note their activity (RL.K.2, RL.K.7, SL.K.2)

Become aware of the author/illustrator's name (RL.K.5, RL.K.6)

Note the purpose of "Contents" and list the five stories in the book (RL.K.5)

(After listening to the teacher reading the story, "A List") list all the facts that have been learned about Frog and Toad (RL.K.1, RL.K.2, SL.K.2)

Ponder the ways that Frog and Toad demonstrate their friendship (RL.K.3)

Lesson II: "The Garden"

Recall details about Frog and Toad from "A List" (RL.K.2, SL.K.2)

(After listening to "The Garden") recall the story's events (RL.K.1, RL.K.2, RL.K.3)

Examine Lobel's illustrations (RL.K.7)

Explore Toad's dedication to his garden (RL.K.1, RL.K.2, RL.K.3)

Note Frog's support of Toad's efforts (RL.K.1, RL.K.2, RL.K.3)

Lesson III: "Cookies"

Explore the details of Frog and Toad's friendship so far (RL.K.1, RL.K.2, RL.K.3)

(After listening to "Cookies") revisit the term *willpower* and examine its use in the story (RL.K.1, RL.K.2, RL.K.3)

Determine if Frog and Toad are successful in their attempts to exercise willpower (RL.K.1, RL.K.2, RL.K.3, SL.K.1)

Revisit the ending of the story and discuss Toad's statement: "I am going home now to bake a cake." (RL.K.1, RL.K.2, RL.K.3)

Lesson IV: "Dragons and Giants"

Note the way that the story begins when Toad says: "The people in this story are brave." (RL.K.1)

(After listening to the story) consider whether Frog and Toad are brave (RL.K.1, RL.K.2, RL.K.3)

Determine if their friendship helps them when they try to be brave (RL.K.3)

Discuss the humor in the story (RL.K.1)

Recall other humorous moments in the previous stories (RL.K.1)

Lesson V: "The Dream"

Consider how this story is different from the others (RL.K.1, RL.K.2, RL.K.3)

Explore Lobel's use of the dream (RL.K.1, RL.K.2, RL.K.3)

Note the purpose of Lobel's use of capital letters

Examine the different expressions on Toad's face (RL.K.7)

Explore what one learns about Frog when he tells Toad: "I always do." (RL.K.1, RL.K.2, RL.K.3)

Lesson VI: Our Own Stories

Revisit Frog and Toad and list the lessons that that they have learned (RL.K.1, RL.K.2, RL.K.3)

Explore the details that show they are friends (RL.K.1, RL.K.2, RL.K.3, RF.K.3)

Imagine new adventures for the two characters (SL.K.6)

Translate the new adventure into illustrations (W.K.1, W.K.2, W.K.3)

Share Frog and Toad's new adventures (SL.K.5, SL.K.6)

Lesson VI: Our Own Stories

Objectives

Revisit Frog and Toad and list the lessons that they have learned (RL.K.1, RL.K.2, RL.K.3)

Explore the details that show they are friends (RL.K.1, RL.K.2, RL.K.3)

Imagine new adventures for the two characters (SL.K.6)

Translate the new adventures into illustrations (W.K.1, W.K.2, W.K.3)

Share Frog and Toad's new adventures (SL.K.5, SL.K.6)

Required Materials

☐ *Frog and Toad Together*, by Arnold Lobel
☐ Markers
☐ Drawing paper

Procedures

1. Lead-In:

   Students take turns discussing:
   - The plot of each of the five stories
   - The characteristics of Frog and Toad
   - The nature of their friendship

2. Step by Step:

   a. Imagining new adventures. Students (either individually, in groups, or with the entire class) invent new adventures for Frog and Toad. Students consider what they already know about the two characters.

   b. Students draw pictures of the new adventures of Frog and Toad, labeling the characters' names.

   c. While the students work, they explain their choices, drawing upon their familiarity with the two characters.

   d. Students may share their ideas with their neighbors while they work.

   e. Display the students' work.

   f. Students share the details of their stories and answer questions from their peers.

3. Closure:

   At the conclusion of the lesson, offer specific details regarding the students' work. Point to the students' ability to:
   - Understand what a plot is
   - Differentiate between the two characters
   - Apply their understanding as they imagine new adventures
   - Describe the stories that they drew

Differentiation

Advanced

- Students will create a graphic organizer (such as a Venn diagram or digital organizer that compares and contrasts the two characters, Frog and Toad).

Struggling

- Students will first act out one of the stories previously read in the unit, showing the difference between the two characters, Frog and Toad, and demonstrating the understanding of the beginning, middle, and end of the story. Students will then receive a new situation for Frog and Toad. In a small group, students will discuss a story plot and act out the story.

Homework/Assessment
N/A

America: Symbols and Celebrations

In this fourth six-week unit of kindergarten, students explore America's symbols and celebrations through literary and informational texts; they begin to write informative/explanatory pieces.

OVERVIEW

Building on asking questions about neighborhoods, students begin this unit by asking questions about a local symbol. They progress to asking questions for more detailed information in nonfiction texts. Students learn to write informative pieces with richer content. Through shared writing, students also learn to expand complete sentences by using more details about American symbols. To be sure the content resonates with the children, celebrations from the student's own ethnicity or religion will be encouraged as part of the information gathering.

ESSENTIAL QUESTION

? Why are symbols important?

FOCUS STANDARDS

These Focus Standards have been selected for the unit from the Common Core State Standards.

RI.K.1: With prompting and support, ask and answer questions about key details in a text.

W.K.7: Participate in shared research and writing projects (e.g., explore a number of books by a favorite author and express opinions about them).

L.K.1: Demonstrate command of the conventions of Standard English grammar and usage when writing or speaking.

L.K.1(f): Produce and expand complete sentences in shared language activities.

L.K.2: Demonstrate command of the conventions of Standard English capitalization, punctuation, and spelling when writing.

L.K.2(d): Spell simple words phonetically, drawing on knowledge of sound-letter relationships.

SL.K.4: Describe familiar people, places, things, and events and, with prompting and support, provide additional detail.

SUGGESTED STUDENT OBJECTIVES

- Describe the connection between two events or ideas in a text.
- Recognize cause and effect relationships (e.g., the contributions of Martin Luther King Jr. and the holiday celebrating his life).
- Review characters, setting, and key events in fictional stories when retelling them.
- Answer questions about unknown words, details, and events in both fiction and informational texts.
- Gather information from text sources and experiences to answer questions about a given topic (e.g., about holidays).
- Use a combination of drawing, dictating, and writing to compose an informative text on a given topic (e.g., about holidays).
- Ask questions to get information, to seek help, or to clarify something that is not understood.
- Produce and expand complete sentences in shared writing about a given topic (e.g., symbols in America).
- Identify new meanings for familiar words and apply them accurately (e.g., march—verb, March—month, march—musical piece).
- Use newly learned words in conversation (e.g., new words related to celebrations and symbols).

SUGGESTED WORKS

(E) indicates a CCSS exemplar text; (EA) indicates a text from a writer with other works identified as exemplars.

LITERARY TEXTS

Picture Books (Read Aloud)

- *Duck for President* (Doreen Cronin and Betsy Lewin)
- *Clifford Goes to Washington* (Norman Bridwell)
- *This Land Is Your Land* (Woody Guthrie and Kathy Jakobsen)
- *My Country, 'Tis of Thee* (Samuel Francis Smith)
- *America the Beautiful* (Katharine Bates and Wendell Minor)
- *Pledge of Allegiance* (Scholastic, Inc.)
- *I Pledge Allegiance* (Bill Martin Jr., Michael Sampson, and Chris Raschka)

  (Tailor to represent the cultures in your classroom.)

- *Apple Pie and the Fourth of July* (Janet S. Wong and Margaret Chodos-Irvine)
- *Family Pictures: Cuadros de familia* (Carmen Lomez Garza) (E)

Poems (Read Aloud)

- "Celebration" in *Song and Dance* (Alonzo Lopez) (E)
- Selections from *I Am America* (Charles R. Smith)
- "Thanksgiving Day" in *Flowers for Children*, Vol. 2 (Lydia Maria Child)

INFORMATIONAL TEXTS

Informational Books

- *In Our Country* (Emergent Reader) (Susan Canizares and S. Berger)
- *The American Flag* (Welcome Books) (Lloyd G. Douglas)
- *The White House* (Welcome Books) (Lloyd G. Douglas)
- *The Statue of Liberty* (Welcome Books) (Lloyd G. Douglas)
- *The Bald Eagle* (Welcome Books) (Lloyd G. Douglas)
- *The Liberty Bell* (Welcome Books) (Lloyd G. Douglas)
- *Giving Thanks: The 1621 Harvest Feast* (Kate Waters and Russ Kendall)
- *Independence Day* (Rookie Read-About Holiday Series) (Trudi Strain Trueit)
- *Martin Luther King Jr. Day* (Rookie Read-About Holiday Series) (Trudi Strain Trueit)
- *Veterans Day* (Rookie Read-About Holiday Series) (Jacqueline S. Cotton)
- *John Philip Sousa: Getting to Know the World's Greatest Composers* (Mike Venezia)
- *El Dia de los Muertos: The Day of the Dead* (Rookie Read-About Holiday Series) (Mary Dodson Wade)
- *Cinco de Mayo* (Rookie Read-About Holiday Series) (Mary Dodson Wade and Nanci R. Vargus)
- *Chinese New Year* (Rookie Read-About Holiday Series) (David F. Marx)
- *Kwanzaa* (Rookie Read-About Holiday Series) (Trudi Strain Trueit)
- *Christmas* (Rookie Read-About Holiday Series) (Trudi Strain Trueit)
- *Diwali* (Rookie Read-About Holiday Series) (Trudi Strain Trueit)
- *Chanukah* (Rookie Read-About Holiday Series) (David F. Marx)
- *Ramadan* (Rookie Read-About Holiday Series) (David F. Marx)

ART, MUSIC, AND MEDIA

Music and Songs (Read Along)

- John Philip Sousa, *Stars and Stripes Forever* (1896)
- John Philip Sousa, *The Liberty Bell* (1893)
- John Philip Sousa, *The Washington Post* (1889)
- "America the Beautiful" (Katharine Lee Bates and Samuel A. Ward)
- "America (My Country, 'Tis of Thee)" (Samuel Francis Smith)
- "Yankee Doodle" (Traditional)
- "You're a Grand Old Flag" (George M. Cohan)

SAMPLE ACTIVITIES AND ASSESSMENTS

1. INTRODUCTORY DISCUSSION/VOCABULARY

To introduce the concept of a symbol, choose a symbol well known to the students in your class (e.g., professional sports team logo or school mascot). Discuss why a symbol is important for unifying fans behind a team or school. Go on to discuss the meaning behind the symbol as a source of inspiration. Learning (reciting) the lyrics to the songs featured in this unit will reinforce the inspiration drawn from common songs as symbols. (RI.K.4, SL.K.2, SL.K.3, SL.K.4, L.K.4, L.K.6)

2. INFORMATIVE/EXPLANATORY WRITING

Use a theme-related short sentence to begin your unit, such as "The flag waves." Challenge the class to think of details to add to the sentence to make it more interesting (e.g., "The red, white, and blue flag waves"; "The red, white, and blue American flag waves in the strong winds of March"). (W.K.5, L.K.1, L.K.5b)

3. READING (INFORMATIONAL TEXT)/GATHERING INFORMATION

Create a KWL chart for American symbols and holidays to set the stage for asking questions, answering questions, and gathering information under main topics. Teachers may need to model the questioning until the students begin to generate research questions on their own. As the class reads an informational book (e.g., *The Liberty Bell*, by Lloyd G. Douglas), gather information about the main topic, noting elements of informational text, such as photographs or text boxes. Remind the students of the importance of also studying illustrations for information. Add the information to the KWL chart. Look for connections between ideas as you add information to the charts. Use sticky notes or whiteboards for students to fully participate in adding information to the charts. (RI.K.1, RI.K.2, RI.K.3, RI.K.7, RI.K.8)

4. INFORMATIVE/EXPLANATORY WRITING

Use the following prompt to direct students to communicate research findings: "Write an informative/ explanatory piece about a symbol or holiday from our class research (KWL chart in Activity 3). Write about the symbol or holiday and what it means. Be sure to use the information on your chart as you write. Illustrate your ideas before you write or after you are finished." (W.K.2, W.K.8, SL.K.5, L.K.1a, L.K.2d)

5. CLASS DISCUSSION/READING/LITERATURE

Introduce a book showing a diverse viewpoint of an American holiday such as *Apple Pie and the Fourth of July* (Janet Wong). As you read the book, ask the students to look for ways that the main character sees one of the traditional American holidays. Encourage the students to look closely at the illustrations and to listen closely to the story. When you are finished reading, ask students to discuss how people see holidays and celebrations differently, depending on their family and ethnic experience. Before turning to whole-group discussion, have students draw a picture or "turn and talk" in preparation for sharing ideas. Pay particular attention to whether the students confirm understanding of what they have read. Encourage listeners to ask relevant questions and speakers to answer them carefully. (RL.K.3, RL.K.7, RL.K.10, SL.K.1, SL.K.2, SL.K.3)

6. WRITING ACTIVITY/HOME CONNECTION

Send a note to parents asking them to find a photograph of the child taken during a family celebration. Ask parents to name the celebration and to tell what makes it special as their family celebrates it. Use this information to create a display of your class's celebrations and to prepare for the shared research project on community celebrations. Scanning the holiday photographs digitally or receiving them in a digital format would enable a slide show presentation (such as PowerPoint) to accompany the sharing time. (SL.K.4, W.K.8)

7. CLASS DISCUSSION/SHARED RESEARCH/WRITING ACTIVITY

Choose a holiday celebrated in your community. Gather information about the holiday by reading books and asking people in your community to tell you why it is celebrated, when it is celebrated, who celebrates it, and how it is celebrated. Create a large cube for the holiday and assign small groups of students to prepare an illustration for each face of the cube. Use the guiding research questions above to assign the faces of the cube. Repeat this activity with several holidays celebrated by the members of your classroom. Extend this work with the following writing activity to communicate findings: "After researching a community holiday and creating an information cube, write a class book about the holiday and illustrate each page." (SL.K.4, L.K.5c, W.K.2, W.K.7, W.K.8)

8. LANGUAGE/VOCABULARY

Tell the students that there are words that are spelled the same and sound the same, but have very different meanings. Listen to John Philip Sousa's music and "march" around the room. Explain that in this case, "march" is an action word. The name of this type of song is a "march," because you want to march to it. And you could even do this "march" in the month of "March." The lesson: Some words are used differently to mean different things. This activity can be repeated with the word *flag,* using the word as a verb and as a noun. (L.K.1b, L.K.4a, L.K.5d)

9. LANGUAGE/VOCABULARY

Create a word bank to collect new words from this unit. These words can be used in discussion and in journal writing to reinforce their proper use. Use the word bank to practice making nouns plural (e.g., statue, statues). (L.K.1b,c, L.K.6)

READING FOUNDATIONS: A PACING GUIDE FOR READING INSTRUCTION

See Kindergarten, Level Four, in the Reading Foundations section for a complete pacing guide for this unit.

ADDITIONAL RESOURCES

- *Martin Luther King Jr. and Me: Identifying with a Hero* (ReadWriteThink) (W.K.7, W.K.8)

TERMINOLOGY

Cause	Effect	KWL chart	Symbol
Composer	Informational text	Questioning	

MAKING INTERDISCIPLINARY CONNECTIONS

This unit teaches:

Music: Patriotic songs (e.g., "America the Beautiful," "America [My Country, 'Tis of Thee,"] "Yankee Doodle," "You're a Grand Old Flag"); band music (e.g., marches of John Philip Sousa)
Geography: United States
History: Celebrations of diversity (e.g., Chinese New Year, Cinco de Mayo, Kwanzaa, Chanukah, and Christmas)

This unit could be extended to teach:

Art: Sculpture
History: Native Americans (e.g., a tribe or nation located near your students compared/contrasted to a tribe or nation farther away); voyage of Christopher Columbus; presidents, past and present

Kindergarten, Unit Four Sample Lesson Plan

Family Pictures by Carmen Lomas Garza

In this series of three lessons, students read *Family Pictures* by Carmen Lomas Garza, and they:

> Explore the stories of Carmen Lomas Garza (RL.K.1, RL.K2, RL.K.3)
>
> Generate their own families' stories (W.K.3, W.K.5, W.K.8, SL.K.4, SL.K.5)
>
> Interpret the stories through illustrations (RL.K.7, SL.K.3)
>
> Share their stories (SL.K.6)

Summary

Lesson I: Family Pictures

Examine the family pictures of Carmen Lomas Garza (RL.K.7)

Identify the themes of Garza's pictures (RL.K.7, SL.K.3)

Notice Garza's use of details (RL.K.2)

Explore the power of pictures to depict family events (SL.K.3)

Lesson III: Telling our Families' Stories

Introduce personal stories (SL. K.4, SL.K.6)

Explore classmates' stories (SL.K.1, SL.K.3)

Evaluate the experience (SL.K.1)

Lesson II: Our Family Pictures

Revisit Garza's family stories (RL.K.1, RL.K.2, RL.K.3, RL.K.7, SL.K.3)

Generate ideas for their own families' stories (W.K.3, W.K.8)

Explore the details of the stories (W.K.5, SL.K.4)

Interpret the stories through illustrations (W.K.3, SL.K.4, SL.K.5)

Lesson II: Our Family Pictures

Objectives

Revisit Garza's family stories (RL.K.1, RL.K.2, RL.K.3, RL.K.7, SL.K.3)

Generate ideas for their own families' stories (W.K.3, W.K.8)

Explore the details of the stories (W.K.5, SL.K.4)

Interpret the stories through illustrations (W.K.3, SL.K.4, SL.K.5)

Required Materials

☐ Class set of *Family Pictures* by Carmen Lomas Garza

☐ Drawing paper

☐ Pencils and markers

Procedures

1. Lead-In:

Revisit Garza's pictures.

2. Step by Step:

a. In small groups, the students begin to share family stories.

b. The students select a specific story to tell and begin to think of the details of the event. Some may choose to look at one of Garza's pictures for help. For example, the picture titled "Oranges" includes the tree, a boy in the tree, and the oranges and the leaves. Such an exploration will help the students grasp the meaning of the type of details that they may choose to include in their pictures.

c. The students draw their families' pictures.

3. Closure:

With teacher assistance, students will prepare an exhibition of their pictures.

Differentiation

Advanced

- Students will write a narrative including all of the details in their illustration.
- Students will choose one of the Garza illustrations to compare and contrast with their illustration.

Struggling

- Using key question prompts such as *who, what, where, why,* and *when,* work with the students to elicit their understanding of key details in the story.
- To enhance vocabulary, make a copy of the student's illustration and label all of the details, enabling a stronger re-telling of the story during the sharing time. Work with students on learning each detail in the illustration.

Homework/Assessment

N/A

The Great Big World

In this fifth six-week unit of kindergarten, students focus on the difference a setting can make in the creation of a story.

ESSENTIAL QUESTION

? Why is it important for writers to describe settings carefully?

OVERVIEW

Building on the diversity of family celebrations, students read about the greater world beyond America. By reading *Mr. Popper's Penguins*, students are lured into dreaming of far-away places. Focusing on the pairing of fiction and informational text, students see how fictional settings can reflect real places. By using an atlas, nonfiction books, video, and interactive online media, students also see how different types of texts give us similar and different information. During these activities, students write words using what they know about vowel sounds, beginning and ending sounds, and word families. Viewing landscapes by master painters reinforces the concept of comparing and contrasting settings.

FOCUS STANDARDS

These Focus Standards have been selected for the unit from the Common Core State Standards.

RL.K.3: With prompting and support, identify characters, settings, and major events in a story.

RL.K.9: With prompting and support, compare and contrast the adventures and experiences of characters in familiar stories.

RI.K.9: With prompting and support, identify basic similarities in and differences between two texts on the same topic (e.g., in illustrations, descriptions, or procedures).

W.K.6: With guidance and support, explore a variety of digital tools to produce and publish writing, including in collaboration with peers.

W.K.8: With guidance and support, recall information from experiences or gather information from provided sources to answer a question.

L.K.2: Demonstrate command of the conventions of Standard English capitalization, punctuation, and spelling when writing.

L.K.2(d): Spell simple words phonetically, drawing on knowledge of sound-letter relationships.

SUGGESTED STUDENT OBJECTIVES

- Describe the connection between the settings of fictional works and informational books about the same place.
- Learn about the similarities and differences between fictional and informational texts on the same topic.
- Compare and contrast characters' adventures that are set in different continents.
- Use a combination of drawing, dictating, and writing to offer an opinion (e.g., about a continent to visit); include details that explain/support the opinion.
- Demonstrate understanding of common verbs and adjectives by relating them to their opposites (e.g., in the context of describing places).

SUGGESTED WORKS

(E) indicates a CCSS exemplar text; (EA) indicates a text from a writer with other works identified as exemplars.

LITERARY TEXTS

Chapter Book (Read Aloud)

- *Mr. Popper's Penguins* (Richard Atwater and Florence Atwater) (E)

Picture Books (Read Aloud)

North America

- *Arrow to the Sun* (Gerald McDermott)
- *Song of the Swallows* (Leo Politi)
- *The Story of Jumping Mouse* (John Steptoe)

South America

- *Morpha: A Rain Forest Story* (Michael Tennyson and Jennifer H. Yoswa)
- *Rain Player* (David Wisniewski)

Europe

- *Little Red Riding Hood* (Trina Schart Hyman)
- *One Fine Day* (Nonny Hogrogian)
- *The Story of Ferdinand* (Munro Leaf and Robert Lawson)

Asia

- *The Paper Crane* (Molly Bang) (E)
- *Lon Po Po: A Red-Riding Hood Story from China* (Ed Young) (E)
- *Once a Mouse . . .* (Marcia Brown)
- *The Fool of the World and the Flying Ship* (Arthur Ransome and Uri Shulevitz)

Africa

- *A Story, A Story* (Gail E. Haley) (E)
- *Why Mosquitoes Buzz in People's Ears* (Verna Aardema, Leo Dillon, and Diane Dillon)
- *Shadow* (Blaise Cendrars, translated by Marcia Brown)

Australia

- *Lizzie Nonsense* (Jan Ormerod)
- *Possum Magic* (Mem Fox and Julie Vivas)
- *Koala Lou* (Mem Fox and Pamela Lofts)

Antarctica

- *Something to Tell the Grandcows* (Eileen Spinelli and Bill Slavin)
- *Eve of the Emperor Penguin* (Mary Pope Osborne and Sal Murdocca)

INFORMATIONAL TEXTS

Informational Books (Read Aloud)

- *Continents and Maps* (Big Book, Pearson Learning)
- *Me on the Map* (Joan Sweeney and Annette Cable)
- *As the Crow Flies: A First Book of Maps* (Gail Hartman and Harvey Stevenson)
- *Beginner's World Atlas* (National Geographic)

Informational Books (Read Aloud/Independent)

- *The Seven Continents* (Rookie Read-About Geography) (Wil Mara)
- *North America* (Rookie Read-About Geography) (Allan Fowler)
- *South America* (Rookie Read-About Geography) (Allan Fowler)
- *Europe* (Rookie Read-About Geography) (Allan Fowler)
- *Asia* (Rookie Read-About Geography) (Allan Fowler)
- *Africa* (Rookie Read-About Geography) (Allan Fowler)
- *Australia* (Rookie Read-About Geography) (Allan Fowler)
- *Antarctica* (Rookie Read-About Geography) (Allan Fowler)
- *Count Your Way Through China* (series) (Jim Haskins)

ART, MUSIC, AND MEDIA

Art

North America

- Albert Bierstadt, *Valley of the Yosemite* (1864)
- Piet Mondrian, *Broadway Boogie Woogie* (1942–1943)

Europe

- John Constable, *The Hay Wain* (1821)
- Paul Cézanne, *Straße vor dem Gebirge Sainte-Victoire* (1898–1902)

Asia

- Guo Xi, *Early Spring* (1072)
- Ando Hiroshige, panel from *Famous views of 53 stations of the Tōkaidō Road* (1855)

Africa

- J. H. Pierneef, *Trees* (date unknown)
- *The Linton Panel* (18th or 19th century)

Australia

- Emily Kam Kngwarreye, *Earth's Creation* (1994)
- Emily Kam Kngwarreye, *The Alhalkere Suite* (1993)

Music and Songs (Read Along)

- Mary F. Higuchi (compiled by), "Geography Songs on the Continents" (2000)
- "It's a Small World" (Walt Disney)
- "London Bridge Is Falling Down" (Tinkerbell Records)

Film

- Luc Jacquet, dir., *March of the Penguins* (2005)
- Jon Stone, dir., *Big Bird in China* (1983)

SAMPLE ACTIVITIES AND ASSESSMENTS

1. MAKING CONNECTIONS: LITERATURE/INFORMATIONAL TEXT

Throughout this unit, read fictional stories set in a continent and then read informational text (both from books and digital sources) that describe the continent. Students will develop an appreciation for the setting of the story—the connection between a fictional setting and a real place. Require students to record what they have learned on either sticky notes or a whiteboard to prepare for sharing with the whole group. Following each reading, they record new information, using these details to compare one continent to another. Note the opposites, such as *cold* and *hot,* or *rainy* and *dry*. If possible, arrange a conversation via the Internet with a classroom or individual on another continent. Prepare for the conversation by asking specific, child-generated questions about the continent. (RI.K.9, L.K.1b, L.K.5b)

2. INFORMATIVE/EXPLANATORY WRITING

Explain that Mr. Popper loved the idea of "dreaming big." Remind them that he daydreamed about faraway places and that he wished he could have visited Antarctica to explore all that was there. Ask the students, "If you could choose to visit any of the continents we studied, which one would you choose? Be sure to support your choice with one or two strong reasons." Allow students to choose one of the continents studied during this unit that they might like to visit someday. To help the children plan their work, use a program such as Kidspiration to create a graphic organizer on each of the continents chosen by the students. Students can draw pictures of animals, people, and objects one might find on that continent. Write two sentences about the continent using a combination of drawing, dictation, and writing. Share the work with the class. (SL.K.6, W.K.1, W.K.5, W.K.6, W.K.8, L.K.2d, RF.K.3d)

3. STORY RETELLING/WRITING

The literature in this unit is conducive to storytelling. Pair students so that they can practice retelling a favorite story from this unit. Ask them, "Using illustrations and writing, retell _____. Be sure to focus on the beginning, middle, and end of the story." Introduce the concept of major events, and ask them to focus on major events and the most important details. To make the activity more challenging, after retelling the story, ask if they can retell a similar story with a completely different setting and character. For example, they may retell *Story of Ferdinand*. How would the story be different if it took place in South America? Which animal would be the main character? Extend this activity by doing a class write: "Write a new version of *The Story of Ferdinand*. Be sure to change the characters and the setting. Illustrate the new story to create a class book." As students volunteer words for creating this story, encourage them to provide letters for sounds as you write. (RL.K.2, W.K.3, W.K.7 L.K.2d)

4. COMPARING TEXTS/INFORMATIONAL TEXT

Choose two of the books (or maps) of the seven continents. Read the books aloud to the students. Students will then tell how these two books are the same and how they are different. Students will work with a partner or in a small group to discuss similarities and differences between the books or maps. Teachers will record students' contributions on a compare-and-contrast graphic organizer. (RI.K.9)

5. COMPARING TEXTS/LITERATURE

After reading two books, *Little Red Riding Hood* and *Lon Po Po*, discuss how the two stories are the same and how they are different. Generate ideas from among the children through writing, drawing, or acting out parts of each story. (RL.K.9, RL.K.10)

6. WORD ACTIVITY/LANGUAGE

Mr. Popper's Penguins is filled with alliteration based on the letter *p*. Encourage the children to listen for *p* words that they hear as you read. The vocabulary words will be challenging and fun to use in classroom discussions. (L.K.6)

7. WORD ACTIVITY/LANGUAGE

Create a word bank of all of the words with *r*-controlled vowels (ar, er, ir, ur, or) as you find them in this unit. Create active listeners by encouraging the students to listen for the words and act as "sound detectives." Sort the words by their respective spellings, noting how the letter combinations create similar sounds (e.g., "A W**or**ld of W**or**ds"). (L.K.6)

8. ART/VOCABULARY

View the Bierstadt and Guo Xi paintings. Note that they were painted eight hundred years apart and on opposite sides of the world. Ask the students to describe what they see. Note similarities (e.g., the monumentality of both works) and differences (e.g., different color palettes). This is an opportunity to extend the idea of comparing and contrasting the settings in stories to comparing and contrasting the settings in paintings. (SL.K.2)

9. ART/CLASS DISCUSSION

View the Mondrian. Share the title and ask what clues it provides about the painting's subject. Ask the students what they notice first in this work and what place they think this might be. ("What do you see that makes it look like this place?") Ask whether the place looks busy or slow and how the artist made it appear that way. Compare this work to another painting (e.g., the Kngwarreye), noticing similarities and differences and focusing on the idea of both place and painting style. Document responses on a chart. (SL.K.1, SL.K.3, SL.K.4)

10. ART/NARRATIVE WRITING

Select two or three works to study that include people or man-made structures (e.g., Cézanne, Constable, Hiroshige, Linton Panel). Ask the students to find the people or structures and discuss how they compare, in scale, to the natural elements in the works. Ask the students to write a new title for the work that interests them the most. Share titles in small groups and possibly post them next to a reproduction of the work of art for future sharing. (W.K.1, W.K.2)

READING FOUNDATIONS: A PACING GUIDE FOR READING INSTRUCTION

See pages Kindergarten, Level Five, in the Reading Foundations section for a complete pacing guide for this unit.

ADDITIONAL RESOURCES

- *Lon Po Po: A Chinese Fairytale Lesson Plan* (Elizabeth Mazzurco, Scholastic, Inc.) (RL.K.9)
- *Lon Po Po: A Red Riding Hood Story from China Lesson Plan* (Chinese Childbook) (RL.K.9)
- "All About World Geography: World Map with a Continent Matching Puzzle" (Sheppard Software)

TERMINOLOGY

Antonyms	Details (most important)	Main idea	Similar
Compare		Opposites	
Contrast	Different	Settings	

MAKING INTERDISCIPLINARY CONNECTIONS

This unit teaches:

Art: Landscapes from around the world
Geography: Working with maps and globes (e.g., locating and naming the seven continents)

This unit could be extended to teach:

Art: Portraits from around the world
Science: Animal habitat preservation (e.g., Jane Goodall's work with chimpanzees in East Africa or attempts to preserve Giant Pandas in China)
Geography: Working with maps and globes (e.g., locating oceans, poles, rivers, lakes, and mountains on globes and maps)

Kindergarten, Unit Five Sample Lesson Plan

Lon Po Po: A Red-Riding Hood Story from China by Ed Young

In this series of three lessons, students read *Lon Po Po: A Red-Riding Hood Story from China* by Ed Young, and they:

Follow the plot of the story *Lon Po Po* (RL.K.1, RL.K.2, RL.K.3)

Explore Shang's wise scheme (RL.K.10, SL.K.2)

Revisit the tale of "Little Red Riding Hood" (RL.K.1)

Juxtapose the stories of "Little Red Riding Hood" and "Lon Po Po" (RL.K.9)

Summary

Lesson I: *Lon Po Po*

Meet Shang, Tao, and Paotze (RL.K.3)

Explore the plot of *Lon Po Po: A Red-Riding Hood Story from China* (RL.K.1, RL.K.2, RL.K. 3)

Examine Shang's plan (RL.K.10, SL.K.2)

Identify the reasons for the sisters' success (SL.K.2)

Lesson III: *Lon Po Po* and "Little Red Riding Hood"

Recall details of *Lon Po Po* and "Little Red Riding Hood" (RL.K.1)

Chart the recalled details of the two stories (RL.K.9)

Revisit Shang's scheme (RL.K.10, SL.K.2)

Explore the climax of each of the two stories (RL.K.9, SL.K.2)

Juxtapose the two stories (RL.K.9)

Lesson II: "Little Red Riding Hood"

Retell the story of "Little Red Riding Hood" (RL.K.9)

Explore the plot of the story (RL.K.3)

Examine the story's resolution (SL.K.2)

Lesson III: *Lon Po Po* and "Little Red Riding Hood"

Objectives

Recall details of *Lon Po Po* and "Little Red Riding Hood" (RL.K.1)

Chart the recalled details of the two stories (RL.K.9)

Revisit Shang's scheme (RL.K.10, SL.K.2)

Explore the climax of each of the two stories (RL.K.9, SL.K.2)

Juxtapose the two stories (RL.K.9)

Required Materials

☐ Class set of *Lon Po Po: A Red-Riding Hood Story from China*, by Ed Young

☐ Class set of "Little Red Riding Hood"

Procedures

1. 1. Lead-In:
   Students recall the details of the two stories.

2. Step by Step:
   a. With assistance, students create charts that will help them note the differences between the two stories.

	Lon Po Po	"Little Red Riding Hood"
List of Characters		
Characters' Actions		
Climax		
Conclusion		
Theme of the story		

   b. Help the students investigate the dissimilarities between the plots.
   c. Students will revisit the wisdom and the strength of Shang, since she is the force that drives the plot.
   d. Provide prompts that will help point to the thematic differences in the two stories.

3. Closure:
   Re-read, aloud, *Lon Po Po: A Red-Riding Hood Story from China*, by Ed Young.

Differentiation

Advanced

- Students will use a Venn diagram or other compare/contrast graphic organizer.
- Students will use a digital version of a graphic organizer to transfer the information from the chart in this lesson into a different format.
- Students will compare and contrast the artwork of Ed Young in *Lon Po Po* to the artwork in a version of "Little Red Riding Hood," such as the one illustrated by Trina Schart Hyman.

Struggling

- Divide this lesson into two lessons, dealing with only one story at a time.
- Use a video version of "Little Red Riding Hood" and then allow the students to act out the story before comparing it to *Lon Po Po*.

Homework/Assessment
N/A

Wonders of Nature: Plants, Bugs, and Frogs

In this sixth six-week unit of kindergarten, students enjoy reading emergent-reader informational texts and listening as picture books by Eric Carle and Robert McCloskey are read aloud.

ESSENTIAL QUESTION

? How does nature inspire us as readers, writers, and artists?

OVERVIEW

Students build on the phonological and phonemic work done all year in kindergarten by reading with the support of teachers and peers. Focusing on the relationships among ideas in texts, students recognize that growth and change occur in both fiction and informational texts. Learning about "cause and effect," students recognize interactions in nature and note the role that people can play in preserving nature. Students read about Monet, a painter who was inspired by light and the wonder of nature, as an introduction to revision in the creative process.

FOCUS STANDARDS

These Focus Standards have been selected for the unit from the Common Core State Standards.

RL.K.10: Actively engage in group reading activities with purpose and understanding.

RI.K.8: With prompting and support, identify the reasons an author gives to support points in a text.

RI.K.9: With prompting and support, identify basic similarities in and differences between two texts on the same topic (e.g., in illustrations, descriptions, or procedures).

RF.K.4: Read emergent-reader texts with purpose and understanding.

W.K.6: With guidance and support, explore a variety of digital tools to produce and publish writing, including in collaboration with peers.

L.K.4: Determine or clarify the meaning of unknown and multiple-meaning words and phrases based on kindergarten reading and content.

L.K.4(b): Use the most frequently occurring inflections and affixes (e.g., *-ed, -s, re-, un-, pre-, -ful, -less*) as a clue to the meaning of an unknown word.

SUGGESTED STUDENT OBJECTIVES

- Articulate cause-and-effect relationships (e.g., as they occur in the natural world).
- Recognize the basic similarities and differences between two texts on the same topic (e.g., when both are informational or when one is fiction and one nonfiction).
- Read emergent-reader texts with purpose and understanding.
- Write, draw, or dictate a narrative (e.g., describing something that happened in nature and a subsequent reaction).
- Relate the idea of writing revision to a visual artist's creative process (i.e., continuously improving the work).
- Use common affixes as clues to the meaning of an unknown word.

SUGGESTED WORKS

(E) indicates a CCSS exemplar text; (EA) indicates a text from a writer with other works identified as exemplars.

LITERARY TEXTS

Picture Books (Read Aloud)

- *Days with Frog and Toad* (Arnold Lobel) (EA)
- *The Carrot Seed* (Ruth Krauss and Crockett Johnson)
- *The Tiny Seed* (The World of Eric Carle) (Eric Carle)
- *A Tree Is Nice* (Janice May Udry and Marc Simont)
- *Time of Wonder* (Robert McCloskey)
- *One Morning in Maine* (Robert McCloskey)
- *Jack and the Beanstalk* (Steven Kellogg)
- *Kate and the Beanstalk* (Mary Pope Osborne and Giselle Potter)
- *There Was an Old Lady Who Swallowed a Fly* (Simms Taback)
- *Fireflies* (Julie Brinckloe)
- *The Very Lonely Firefly* (Eric Carle)
- *The Grouchy Ladybug* (Eric Carle)
- *The Very Quiet Cricket* (Eric Carle)
- *The Very Clumsy Click Beetle* (Eric Carle)
- *It's Earth Day!* (Mercer Mayer)
- *The Magical Garden of Claude Monet* (Laurence Anholt)

Picture Book (Read Aloud/Independent)

- *Hi! Fly Guy* (Tedd Arnold) (E)

Poems (Read Aloud)

- "Two Tree Toads" in *Orangutan Tongs: Poems to Tangle Your Tongue* (Jon Agee) (E)
- Selections from *Insectlopedia* (Douglas Florian)
- "Little Black Bug" (Margaret Wise Brown)
- "The Caterpillar" in *Rossetti: Poems* (Christina Rossetti) (EA)
- "Trees" (Sarah Coleridge)
- *Over in the Meadow* (John Langstaff and Feodor Rojankovsky) (E)

Poem (Read Along)

- "Wouldn't You?" in *You Read to Me, I'll Read to You* (John Ciardi) (E)

Nursery Rhymes (Read Along)

- "Mary, Mary Quite Contrary"
- "Ladybug, Ladybug"

INFORMATIONAL TEXTS

INFORMATIONAL BOOKS (READ ALOUD)

- *Follow the Water from Brook to Ocean* (Arthur Dorros) (E)
- *Water, Water Everywhere* (Mark Rauzon and Cynthia Overbeck Bix) (E)
- "Our Good Earth" in *National Geographic Young Explorer!* (April 2009) (EA)
- "Garden Helpers" in *National Geographic Young Explorer!* (September 2009) (E)
- *The Reasons for Seasons* (Gail Gibbons) (EA)
- *The Seasons of Arnold's Apple Tree* (Gail Gibbons) (EA)
- *Red-Eyed Tree Frog* (Joy Cowley and Nic Bishop)
- *A Blue Butterfly* (Bijou Le Tord)

Informational Books (Read Aloud/Independent)

- *Living Sunlight: How Plants Bring the Earth to Life* (Molly Bang and Penny Chisholm) (EA)
- *A Tree Is a Plant* (Let's-Read-and-Find-Out Science) (Clyde Robert Bulla and Stacey Schuett) (E)
- *From Seed to Pumpkin* (Let's-Read-and-Find-Out Science) (Wendy Pfeffer and James Graham Hale) (E)
- *From Tadpole to Frog* (Let's-Read-and-Find-Out Science) (Wendy Pfeffer and Holly Keller) (E Series)
- *From Caterpillar to Butterfly* (Let's-Read-and-Find-Out Science) (Deborah Heiligman and Bari Weissman) (E Series)
- *How a Seed Grows* (Let's-Read-and-Find-Out Science) (Helene J. Jordan and Loretta Krupinski) (E Series)
- *Frogs and Toads and Tadpoles, Too!* (Rookie Read-About Science) (Allan Fowler)
- *From Seed to Plant* (Rookie Read-About Science) (Allan Fowler)
- *Taking Root* (Rookie Read-About Science) (Allan Fowler)
- *Inside an Ant Colony* (Rookie Read-About Science) (Allan Fowler)
- *Maple Trees* (Rookie Read-About Science) (Allan Fowler)

- *Pine Trees* (Rookie Read-About Science) (Allan Fowler)
- *Cactuses* (Rookie Read-About Science) (Allan Fowler)
- *It Could Still Be a Flower* (Rookie Read-About Science) (Allan Fowler)
- *Plants That Eat Animals* (Rookie Read-About Science) (Allan Fowler)
- *It's a Good Thing There are Insects* (Rookie Read-About Science) (Allan Fowler)
- *Spiders Are Not Insects* (Rookie Read-About Science) (Allan Fowler)
- *Earth Day* (Rookie Read-About Holidays) (Trudi Strain Trueit)
- *From Seed to Pumpkin* (Wendy Pfeffer)

ART, MUSIC, AND MEDIA

Art

- Claude Monet, *Water Lilies (The Clouds)* (1903)
- Claude Monet, *Water Lilies* (1906)
- Claude Monet, *Water Lilies* (1916–1923)

Music and Songs (Sing Along)

- "The Ants Go Marching One by One"
- "Itsy Bitsy Spider"

Media

- *Linnea in Monet's Garden* (1999)

SAMPLE ACTIVITIES AND ASSESSMENTS

1. CLASS DISCUSSION/READING/INFORMATIONAL TEXT/WRITING

Create a cause-and-effect table (as shown next) to record your class work. Read a book such as *Earth Day* (Trudi Strain Trueit). As you read, encourage the students to think about whether we need Earth Day and how celebrating this special day helps the earth. Build in personal accountability by asking students to draw, write, dictate, or act out their ideas before adding them to the chart. Add a writing dimension to this work by giving students the following whole-class writing prompt: "Write a class book titled *Earth Day: Making a Difference*. Use the cause-and-effect chart to plan each page of the book. Work in teams to illustrate." (RI.K.8, RI.K.10, SL.K.6, W.K.2, W.K.7, L.K.1f)

Cause (why we have a problem): People are careless and throw trash on the ground.

"Earth Day Activities" (event): Pick up trash around a stream.

Effect (how we help the earth): Fish have a healthier place to live. Water is cleaner.

2. NARRATIVE WRITING

Give students this prompt: "Write (or draw or dictate) a story about something amazing you have seen in nature. Be sure to include the name of what you saw (e.g., a firefly), the setting (e.g., a dark night in June, in my yard), and two events that happened (e.g., I chased it and caught it). Tell about how you reacted to the events (e.g., I screamed because I had a bug in my hand and didn't know what to do with it!)" (W.K.3, SL.K.4, L.K.2a)

3. ART/WRITING/REVISION

Claude Monet painted water lilies over and over again. Tell the students to look at his paintings to see how they changed. Explain that one of the reasons for this change was the shifting light in his garden, but also that painters sometimes paint the same subject many times as a way to innovate. Display the three paintings in chronological order, spending time on each individually. What changes did Monet make when he painted the same subject again and again? Relate this idea to the revision process when writing stories. Return the students' nature stories (see Narrative Writing, in Activity 2) and ask the students to try writing them again, but to make them a little different this time, perhaps by adding new details. Publish the writing in a digital format by scanning the student work and inserting it into a PowerPoint presentation. Students will present the work to parents as a culminating writing activity for the year. (SL.K.1, W.K.5, W.K.6)

4. INFORMATIVE/EXPLANATORY WRITING

After reading a chapter from *Days with Frog and Toad* (Arnold Lobel) and *From Tadpole to Frog* (Let's-Read-and-Find-Out-Science) (Wendy Pfeffer and Holly Keller), lead the following activity with the students: Work together to make a list of the ways the frog in the fictional book (Lobel) was similar to the frog in the nonfiction book (Pfeffer and Keller). Make a list of how the two frogs are different. Students may be ready to create this list themselves on their own personal graphic organizer. (RL.K.3, RL.K.10, RI.K.10, SL.K.6)

5. CLASS DISCUSSION/READING/INFORMATIONAL TEXT

Read a book such as *From Tadpole to Frog* (Let's-Read-and-Find-Out-Science) (Wendy Pfeffer and Holly Keller) and then read *Red-Eyed Tree Frog* (Joy Cowley and Nic Bishop). (These are both nonfiction books, and they both talk about toads.) Ask what the students noticed about how these books were the same and how they were different. (RI.K.9, RI.K.10, SL.K.6)

6. INFORMATIVE/EXPLANATORY WRITING

After reading an informational text detailing a process, such as the life cycle of a butterfly or frog, give the students the following writing prompt: "Write a four-page booklet explaining the life cycle of a frog or butterfly using illustrations and sentences." (W.K.2, L.K.2a)

7. VOCABULARY/DRAMA

Create a word bank for "Ways Animals Move" (e.g., dart, fly, hop, and swim). Use these verbs to teach the -*ed*, -*s*, and -*ing* suffixes. Act out the words, adding adverbs to make the actions opposite in speed like "hopping slowly" or "hopping fast." Have some fun with the word bank by creating a "wordle" with the verbs describing animal movements. (L.K.1b, L.K.4b, L.K.5b)

8. READING/FLUENCY/INFORMATIONAL TEXT/POETRY

Since students are reading, introduce them to the easy science texts in this unit. Spend time having the students read the books aloud with partners or alone. When reading (reciting) poetry, encourage the dramatic expression of poems such as "Wouldn't You." (RF.K.4)

READING FOUNDATIONS: A PACING GUIDE FOR READING INSTRUCTION

See Kindergarten, Level Six, in the Reading Foundations section for a complete pacing guide for this unit.

ADDITIONAL RESOURCE

- *Animal Study: from Fiction to Facts* (ReadWriteThink) (RI.K.10)

TERMINOLOGY

Cause	Different	Explanatory writing	Revision
Creative process	Effect	Oral presentation	Similar

MAKING INTERDISCIPLINARY CONNECTIONS

This unit teaches:

Art: Monet (e.g., painting, "Water Lilies" series)

Science: Plants (e.g., what plants need to grow; seeds, flowers, and the parts of a plant); Earth Day (e.g., pollution, recycling, conservation); seasons; bugs and frogs (e.g., habitats and life cycles)

This unit could be extended to teach:

Art: More famous artworks inspired by nature

Science: Weather (e.g., local weather patterns and daily weather changes)

Kindergarten, Unit Six Sample Lesson Plan

From Seed to Pumpkin by Wendy Pfeffer

In this series of two lessons, students read *From Seed to Pumpkin* by Wendy Pfeffer, and they:

Trace the growth of a plant from a seed to a pumpkin (RI.K.1, RI.K.2, RI.K.4, SL.K.1, SL.K.2, SL.K.5)

Appreciate the growth process by charting the growth of the plant and the passage of time (SL.K.6, RF.K.4)

Summary

Lesson I: *From Seed to Pumpkin*	Lesson II: *From Seed to Pumpkin*—Charting the Process
Trace the development of the seeds (RI.K.1, RI.K.2, RI.K.4, SL.K.1, SL.K.2, SL.K.5)	Identify the steps that begin with the seed and end with a pumpkin (RI.K.1, RI.K.2, RI.K.3, SL.K.2)
Closely observe the illustrations depicting the growth from a seed, to a plant, to a pumpkin (RI.K.6, RI.K.7)	Chart the steps identified (RI.K.10, W.K.2, RF.K.4)
Note the passage of time (RI.K.1, RI.K.2, SL.K.1, SL.K.2)	Illustrate the chart (W.K.2)
	Revisit the process (SL.K.6)

Lesson II: *From Seed to Pumpkin*—Charting the Process

Objectives

Identify the steps that begin with the seed and end with a pumpkin (RI.K.1, RI.K.2, RI.K.3, SL.K.2)

Chart the steps identified (RI.K.10, W.K.2, RF.K.4)

Illustrate the chart (W.K.2)

Revisit the process (SL.K.6)

Required Materials

☐ Markers
☐ Paper

Procedures

1. Lead-In:
   Discuss the book *From Seed to Pumpkin* with students. Students revisit the transition of the pumpkin from a seed to a plant.

2. Step by Step:
   a. Introduce the class project.
      - Students chart the growth of the pumpkin plant.
      - Students write about (with teacher assistance) and illustrate the process.
   b. Collaboratively, returning to the book for details when necessary, students work on the chart.

3. Closure:
   Students reflect about what they have learned from the book *From Seed to Pumpkin*.

Differentiation

Advanced

- Create an electronic slide for each step of the growth of the pumpkin seed. Create a narration to go with the slides and record it. Share the presentation with another class.
- Using a familiar tune like "The Farmer in the Dell," write verses for a song that show the steps of growth for a pumpkin.

Struggling

- Before this lesson set begins, create a KWL chart about pumpkins. If possible, show students what a real pumpkin looks like and what a pumpkin seed looks like.
- Spend some time talking about sequence, reviewing how plants in the classroom have grown from seeds.

Homework/Assessment
N/A

GRADE 1

In first grade, students build on the reading, writing, listening, and speaking that they practiced in kindergarten. As in kindergarten, these units include a section devoted to the CCSS reading foundations. While not a comprehensive reading program, this pacing guide provides guidance for instruction in print concepts, phonological awareness, phonics, word recognition, fluency, and some of the writing and language skills. Students should enter first grade with basic decoding skills and familiarity with a range of fiction, nonfiction, and poetry. As their reading and writing skills become more advanced, they begin to apply their knowledge to new topics and situations. Students are exposed to a rich variety of "read-aloud" stories, nonfiction, and poems, including stories about animals, fables, and other life lessons, stories and nonfiction accounts about contributors to America, versions of the "Cinderella" tale from many nations, and more. They have opportunities to draw interesting connections between literature and other subjects: for example, in the unit "Winds of Change," they consider changes in nature as well as changes in characters' feelings. They explore the arts throughout the year: in one unit they look at paintings by Matisse, and in another they compare masks from around the world. They start to produce writing—journal entries, brief descriptions, opinion pieces, and stories—and to collaborate on simple research projects (such as finding out about an animal). They learn to create short books with a table of contents and numbered pages. By the end of first grade, they are able to sound out and recognize many one-syllable and multisyllabic words, and they have a strong repertoire of sight words.

Standards Checklist for Grade One

Standard	Unit 1	Unit 2	Unit 3	Unit 4	Unit 5	Unit 6
Reading—Literature						
1	FA					A
2		FA	FA		A	A
3			FA	A		
4				FA		
5	A	FA			A	A
6		A	A			A
7			A		A	
8 n/a						
9			A			FA
10				A		
Reading—Informational Text						
1	FA					
2		FA				A
3					FA	A
4				A		
5		A				A
6			FA			
7	A					
8				FA		
9						FA
10		A		FA	A	
Writing						
1			A		FA	FA
2	A	FA	A			
3			FA	A		
4 n/a						
5	A	A	A	FA	A	
6						F
7	FA	A	A			A
8	A		A			A
9 n/a						
10 n/a						
Speaking and Listening						
1	FA			A	A	
1a	A			A	A	
1b	A	A		A	A	
1c	A			A	A	
2	A	FA				
3		A		A	FA	
4		A		FA	A	A
5	A		A	A		FA
6	A		A	A	A	A
Language						
1	FA					
1a	A					
1b	A	A				
1c	A		A			
1d	A			A		
1e	A		A	A		
1f	A		A			
1g	A			A		
1h	A					
1i	A			A		
1j	FA	A	A			
2			F			A
2a					A	A
2b	A		FA		A	A

Standard	Unit 1	Unit 2	Unit 3	Unit 4	Unit 5	Unit 6
2c				A		
2d	A					A
2e	A					A
3 n/a						
4						
4a	A					
4b				A		
4c				A		
5		FA		F		F
5a		A				
5b		FA				
5c					A	
5d				A	FA	FA
6					A	
Reading Foundations (addressed in units)						
1						
1a	A					
2						
2a						
2b						
2c						
2d						
3						
3a						
3b						
3c						
3d						
3e						
3f						
3g						
4	A	A	F		F	A
4a	A	A			A	A
4b	A	A	FA		A	A
4c	A	A			FA	A
Reading Foundations (addressed in *Reading Foundations: A Pacing Guide*)						
1				A		
1a	A	A		A		
1b				A		
1c				A		
1d				A		
2						
2a	A					
2b		A	A			
2c				A	A	
2d			A	A	A	A
2e						
3						
3a	A	A	A	A	A	
3b	A	A	A	A	A	
3c	A	A	A	A	A	
3d						
3e				A		
3f					A	A
3g	A	A	A	A	A	A
4		A	A	A	A	A
4a		A	A	A	A	A
4b		A	A	A	A	A
4c	A	A	A	A	A	A

F = Focus Standard; A = Activity/Assessment

Alphabet Books and Children Who Read Them

In this first six-week unit of first grade, students are welcomed to school as readers and begin reviewing the alphabet and concepts of print through books about the library, friendship, and the ABCs.

ESSENTIAL QUESTION

Why is it important to ask questions while you are reading?

OVERVIEW

By conducting shared research, students learn that investigating is foundational to learning. By using books that require conversation, such as *The Graphic Alphabet*, students understand that ideas are processed through inquiry, thought, and conversation. After the students perform shared research based on a class question, they write a class ABC book about their topic. During this writing, they review the formation of a sentence with proper punctuation. Students respond to a question (prompt) to write what they know about healthy habits (e.g., exercise, healthy eating), focusing on their topic and supporting it with facts. Finally, they apply their knowledge of questioning to poetry and perform the poetry as a choral reading.

FOCUS STANDARDS

These Focus Standards have been selected for the unit from the Common Core State Standards.

RL.1.1: Ask and answer questions about key details and events in a text.

RI.1.1: Ask and answer questions about key details in a text.

W.1.7: Participate in shared research and writing projects.

SL.1.1: Participate in collaborative conversations with diverse partners about Grade One topics and texts with peers and adults in small and larger groups.

L.1.1: Demonstrate command of the conventions of Standard English grammar and usage when writing or speaking.

L.1.1j: Produce and expand complete simple and compound declarative, interrogative, imperative, and exclamatory sentences in response to prompts.

SUGGESTED STUDENT OBJECTIVES

- Use pictures, illustrations, and details in a text to discern and describe key ideas.
- Help shape research questions.
- Gather information on a given topic.
- Listen to one another in conversations and speak one at a time.
- Capitalize names, places, and dates.
- Punctuate sentences correctly with a period and question mark.
- Perform poetry as a choral reading.

SUGGESTED WORKS

(E) indicates a CCSS exemplar text; (EA) indicates a text from a writer with other works identified as exemplars.

LITERARY TEXTS

Stories

- *Little Bear's Visit* (Else Holmelund Minarik and Maurice Sendak) (EA)
- *A Kiss for Little Bear* (Else Holmelund Minarik and Maurice Sendak) (EA)
- *Morris Goes to School* (Bernard Wiseman)

Stories (Read Aloud)

- *Tomas and the Library Lady* (Pat Mora and Raul Colon) (E)
- *¡Marimba! Animales from A to Z* (Pat Mora and Doug Cushman) (EA)
- *Dr. Seuss's ABC: An Amazing Alphabet Book!* (Dr. Seuss) (EA)
- *Chicka Chicka Boom Boom* (Bill Martin Jr., John Archambault, and Lois Ehlert)
- *Our Library* (Eve Bunting and Maggie Smith)
- *The Library* (Sarah Stewart and David Small)
- *Alphabet Mystery* (Audrey Wood and Bruce Wood)
- *I Can Read with My Eyes Shut!* (Dr. Seuss) (EA)

Poems

- "Good Books, Good Times!" (Lee Bennett Hopkins)
- "You Read to Me, I'll Read to You" (Mary Ann Hoberman and Michael Emberley)

Poems (Read Aloud)

- "Read to Me" (Jane Yolen)
- "How to Eat a Poem" (Eve Merriam) (EA)
- "Books to the Ceiling" (Arnold Lobel) (EA)
- "Books Fall Open" (David McCord)

INFORMATIONAL TEXTS
Informational Books

- *I Read Signs* (Tana Hoban) (E)
- *26 Letters and 99 Cents* (Tana Hoban) (EA)
- *Look Book* (Tana Hoban) (EA)
- *Exactly the Opposite* (Tana Hoban) (EA)
- *School Bus* (Donald Crews) (EA)
- *Alphabet City* (Stephen T. Johnson)
- *Exercise* (Rookie Read-About Health) (Sharon Gordon)
- *Germs! Germs! Germs!* (Hello Reader Science Level 3) (Bobbi Katz and Steve Bjorkman)

Informational Books (Read Aloud)

- *A Good Night's Sleep* (Rookie Read-About Health) (Sharon Gordon)
- *Museum ABC* (New York Metropolitan Museum of Art)
- *An A to Z Walk in the Park* (R.M. Smith)
- *I Spy: An Alphabet in Art* (Lucy Micklethwait)
- *The Graphic Alphabet* (David Pelletier)
- *Eating the Alphabet: Fruits & Vegetables from A to Z* (Harcourt Brace Big Book) (Lois Ehlert)
- *The Turn-Around, Upside-Down Alphabet Book* (Lisa Campbell Ernst)
- *The Hidden Alphabet* (Laura Vaccaro Seeger)

ART, MUSIC, AND MEDIA
Art

- Pieter Bruegel, *Children's Games* (1560)

SAMPLE ACTIVITIES AND ASSESSMENTS

1. ART/CLASS DISCUSSION

Look at *Children's Games* by Pieter Bruegel. Ask the students to study it closely for a few minutes and write down any questions they have about what they see. When the time is up, have them ask their questions. As the students begin to ask questions aloud, write all of the questions on a chart (e.g., "What are they doing? Is that like a hula hoop? Was this painted a long time ago? . . ."). Talk about the value of asking questions and how we begin to open our minds to think deeply about something. (The painting was done in the sixteenth century, and the artist was perhaps trying to show all of the games he knew. You may want to note the few toys children had—sticks, hoops, etc.) (SL.1.2)

2. CLASS DISCUSSION/READING/INFORMATIONAL TEXT

Tell the students that just because books are called "ABC books" does not mean they are always easy to understand. Therefore, to understand them, we have to be willing to ask questions and to think deeply and look for key details. Tell the students that they are going to look at *The Graphic Alphabet*. Using a document camera for viewing this book would be helpful. On each page, there is a letter, but there is something more going on than just that letter. Look at *A*. Have the students ask questions about the page and try to answer them (e.g., "Why is the letter *A* crumbling? Could the letter be a mountain? Is that an *avalanche*?"). As you go through the book and throughout the unit, introduce the new vocabulary. (RI.1.1, RI.1.7, L.1.1j, SL.1.2)

3. LANGUAGE/WRITING

Introduce the writing of declarative and interrogative sentences by focusing on an informational ABC book, such as *Eating the Alphabet: Fruits & Vegetables from A to Z* (Lois Ehlert). On a chart, write a question such as "What is your favorite fruit?" Teach the students to answer the question with a complete declarative response, such as "My favorite fruit is a strawberry." Discuss the end punctuation. Continue this activity to teach the expansion of sentences to include details, such as "Strawberries are my favorite fruit because they are juicy, sweet, and delicious." (L.1.1j, L.1.2b, W.1.5, SL.1.6)

4. CLASS DISCUSSION/POETRY/FLUENCY

The theme of the poetry in this unit is the love of books and language. By visually displaying the poems (i.e., an interactive whiteboard, document camera, overhead projector, or chart paper), students will review sight words and see the way the poem is written (i.e., with lines and stanzas). Using a poem such as "Good Books, Good Times!" (Lee Bennett Hopkins) or "How to Eat a Poem" (Eve Merriam), encourage the students to read with you repeatedly and to ask questions until they understand the poem. Poetry is easily transformed into choral reading (reciting) by highlighting lines from one punctuation mark to the next, and then assigning groups to read those highlighted sections. (SL.1.2, RF.1.4)

5. INFORMATIVE/EXPLANATORY WRITING

Give students this prompt: "Children should eat healthy foods, exercise, and take care of their bodies. Name one way to stay healthy. Supply some facts about the topic you chose and provide closure at the end of your writing." As students write, watch closely that they focus on just one way to stay healthy and that they compose an essay supported by facts. Encourage students to write complete sentences and to use the correct end punctuation. (W.1.2, L.1.1j, L.1.2b)

6. WRITING/SHARED RESEARCH

Using the ABC books as a model, generate some ideas for writing a class ABC book. Work together as a class to come up with potential research questions. Begin by asking questions such as, "Is it possible to create an ABC book with *Games to Play* as our title?" Allow the class to give some ideas (e.g., names, authors, books, plants, insects). After ideas have been shaped into a research question, allow the children to vote on a theme for the class ABC book. Once the theme is chosen, gather information from a variety of texts and digital resources for each letter of the alphabet. Decide on a design for the book. Assign each student a letter in the book. Each page should include an upper and lower case letter, the key word, an illustration, and a sentence using the key word. Be sure to have them follow rules for spelling and punctuating correctly. (SL.1.1, W.1.2, W.1.7, W.1.8, L.1.1a.j, L.1.2, RF.1.1a)

7. PREDICTION/LITERARY TEXT

As you read the book *Tomas and the Library Lady*, pause periodically and encourage students to ask questions. By using "I wonder" as the beginning of the question, have students predict what is coming next in the story and clarify understanding. Use sticky notes or whiteboards to keep each child engaged in the questioning. (RL.1.1)

8. CLASS DISCUSSION/READING

Throughout this unit, students read from a variety of texts: stories, poems, and informational texts. When you have a ten-minute block, play "I Spy" with the children (e.g., "I spy an informational book,"

"I spy a nonfiction book"). The students then have to guess which book you are looking at in the display of unit books. (RL.1.5, L.1.1)

READING FOUNDATIONS: A PACING GUIDE FOR READING INSTRUCTION

See Grade One, Level One, in the Reading Foundations section for a complete pacing guide for this unit.

ADDITIONAL RESOURCES

- *Book Sorting: Using Observation and Comprehension to Categorize Books* (ReadWriteThink) (RL.1.5)
- *Adventures in Nonfiction: A Guided Inquiry Journey* (ReadWriteThink) (W.1.7, W.1.8)

TERMINOLOGY

Alphabet books	Informational	Question marks	Sort
Author	Key details	Questions	Stories
Capitalization	Periods	Research question	Topic
Illustrator	Poems	Shared research	

MAKING INTERDISCIPLINARY CONNECTIONS

This unit teaches:

Art: Pieter Bruegel (*Children's Games*)
Science: Healthy living (e.g., eating fruits and vegetables, exercise, sleep, avoiding germs)

This unit could be extended to teach:

Science: Healthy living (e.g., body systems, Jenner, Pasteur)

Grade One, Unit One Sample Lesson Plan

A Kiss for Little Bear by Else Holmelund Minarik

In this series of two lessons, students read *A Kiss for Little Bear* by Else Holmelund Minarik, and they:

Follow the plot of the story as they trace the path of the kiss (RL.1.1, RL.1.2, RL.1.3)

Explore the use of illustrations (RL.1.7, SL.1.2)

Summary

Lesson I: A Picture for Grandmother	Lesson II: A Kiss for Little Bear
Meet Little Bear, the painter (RL.1.3)	(Continue to) follow Little Bear's kiss (RL.1.1, RL.1.2, RL.1.3, RL.1.7)
Note the use of illustrations (RL.1.7, SL.1.2)	(Continue to) examine the use of illustrations (RL.1.7)
Examine Little Bear's painting (RL.1.1, RL.1.3, RL.1.7, SL.1.2)	Chart the path of the kiss (RL.1.2)
Explore Grandmother's response (RL.1.1, RL.1.2, RL.1.3, SL.1.2)	Explore the ending of the story (RL.1.1, RL.1.2, SL.1.2)
(Begin to) follow Little Bear's kiss (RL.1.1)	Reread *A Kiss for Little Bear*

Lesson II: A Kiss for Little Bear

Objectives

(Continue to) follow Little Bear's kiss (RL.1.1, RL.1.2, RL.1.3, RL.1.7)

(Continue to) examine the use of illustrations (RL.1.7)

Chart the path of the kiss (RL.1.2)

Explore the ending of the story (RL.1.1, RL.1.2, SL.1.2)

Reread *A Kiss for Little Bear*

Required Materials

☐ Class sets of *A Kiss for Little Bear*, by Else Holmelund Minarik

Procedures

1. Lead-In:

The students conclude the reading of *A Kiss for Little Bear*. Depending on the students' reading levels, you may choose to read the story to the students or have them read it.

2. Step by Step:

a. In several small groups, students chart the path of Little Bear's kiss.

  Little Bear draws the picture→

  Little Bear decides to send his picture to Grandmother→

  Little Bear asks Hen to take the picture to Grandmother→

  Grandmother sends a kiss back with Hen→

  Hen passes it to Frog→

  And Frog asks Cat to deliver the kiss→

  Cat asks Skunk to bring Little Bear the kiss→

  But Little Skunk meets another Little Skunk and gives her the kiss→

  And she kisses him back→

  Hen sees all that kissing→

  And takes the kiss to Little Bear.

b. Reconvene the students to discuss the story's ending.

c. Ask students to introduce and explain their group's chart/s.

3. Closure:

The class rereads *A Kiss for Little Bear*.

Differentiation

Advanced

- Allow students to read silently or with a partner.
- Ask the students to work together to find text evidence for each step in the path of Little Bear's kiss.

Struggling

- Before you read the story aloud, assign the students to be characters with name cards in front of their seats: Little Bear, Grandmother, Hen, Frog, Cat, Skunk, and Little Skunk.
- When the "kiss" is introduced, physically hand the "kiss" from one character to the next person. (You could use a candy kiss or just "blow a kiss" to the next person.)

Homework/Assessment

N/A

Grade 1 ▶ *Unit 2*

The Amazing Animal World

In this second six-week unit of first grade, students read informational texts about animals and learn how to strengthen their own informative/explanatory writing.

ESSENTIAL QUESTION

? How can reading teach us about writing?

OVERVIEW

Building on the informative/explanatory writing in the first unit, students focus on constructing stronger informative/explanatory writing pieces. Then, students revise their work with an adult. They also learn about the creative process through studying the artwork of Henry Matisse, and create a piece of art to go with their informative writing. The class explores informative/explanatory writing by explaining the technique used to create their own artistic works. As they read fictional texts, they continue to retell a story using details and focusing on a central message.

FOCUS STANDARDS

These Focus Standards have been selected for the unit from the Common Core State Standards.

RL.1.2: Retell stories, including key details, and demonstrate understanding of the central message or lesson.

RL.1.5: Explain major differences between books that tell stories and books that give information, drawing on a wide reading of a range of text types.

RI.1.2: Identify the main topic and retell key details of a text.

L.1.5: With guidance and support, demonstrate understanding of word relationships and nuances in word meanings.

L.1.5(b): Define words by category and by one or more key attributes (e.g., a *duck* is a bird that swims; a *tiger* is a large cat with stripes).

W.1.2: Write informative/explanatory texts in which they name a topic, supply some facts about the topic, and provide some sense of closure.

SL.1.2: Ask and answer questions about key details in a text read-aloud or information presented orally or through other media.

SUGGESTED STUDENT OBJECTIVES

- Describe how a text can group information into general categories.
- Write an informative/explanatory text about a given topic (e.g., about an animal), supplying factual information and providing a sense of closure.
- In a revision process, and under the guidance and support of an adult, add details to an informative text.
- Confirming understanding of information, present the information orally by restating key elements and answering questions about key details.
- Write an informative/explanatory text explaining how to do something (e.g., how Matisse created the large-scale cut-out, *The Snail).*
- Use sentence context clues to help determine word meanings.
- Use common, proper, and possessive nouns in speech and writing.

SUGGESTED WORKS

(E) indicates a CCSS exemplar text; (EA) indicates a text from a writer with other works identified as exemplars.

LITERARY TEXTS

Stories
- *Are You My Mother?* (Philip D. Eastman) (E)
- *Mouse Tales* (Arnold Lobel) (EA)
- *Uncle Elephant* (Arnold Lobel) (EA)
- *Mouse Soup* (Arnold Lobel) (EA)

Story (Read Aloud)
- *Finn Family Moomintroll* (Tove Jansson) (E)

Poem
- "Fish" (Mary Ann Hoberman)

Poems (Read Aloud)
- "The Fox's Foray" in *The Oxford Nursery Rhyme Book* (anonymous) (E)
- "The Owl and the Pussycat" in *The Complete Nonsense of Edward Lear* (Edward Lear) (E)
- "I Know All the Sounds that the Animals Make" in *Something Big Has Been Here* (Jack Prelutsky)
- "The Pasture" in *The Poetry of Robert Frost* (Robert Frost)
- "The Purple Cow" in *The Burgess Nonsense Book: Being a Complete Collection of the Humorous Masterpieces of Gelett Burgess* (Gelett Burgess)

INFORMATIONAL TEXTS

Informational Books

- *Starfish* (Let's-Read-and-Find … Science) (Edith Thacher Hurd and Robin Brickman) (E)
- *What Lives in a Shell?* (Let's-Read-and-Find … Science) (Kathleen Weidner Zoehfeld and Helen K. Davie) (E series)
- *Big Tracks, Little Tracks: Following Animal Prints* (Let's-Read-and-Find … Science) (Millicent E. Selsam and Marlene Hill Donnelly) (E series)
- *Where Are the Night Animals?* (Let's-Read-and-Find … Science) (Mary Ann Fraser) (E series)

Informational Books (Read Aloud)

- *Earthworms* (Claire Llewellyn and Barrie Watts) (E)
- *What Do You Do With a Tail Like This?* (Steve Jenkins and Robin Page) (E)
- *Biggest, Strongest, Fastest* (Steve Jenkins) (EA)
- *What Do You Do When Something Wants To Eat You?* (Steve Jenkins) (EA)
- *Never Smile at a Monkey: And 17 Other Important Things to Remember* (Steve Jenkins) (EA)
- *Amazing Whales!* (Sarah L. Thomson) (E)
- *How Animals Work* (DK Publishing)
- *Creature ABC* (Andrew Zuckerman)
- *A Nest Full of Eggs* (Let's-Read-and-Find … Science) (Priscilla Belz Jenkins and Lizzy Rockwell) (E series)
- *What's It Like to Be a Fish?* (Let's-Read-and-Find … Science) (Wendy Pfeffer and Holly Keller) (E series)
- *Where Do Chicks Come From?* (Let's-Read-and-Find … Science) (Amy E. Sklansky and Pam Paparone) (E series)

ART, MUSIC, AND MEDIA

Art

- Albrecht Dürer, *A Young Hare* (1502)
- Marc Chagall, *I and the Village* (1945)
- Paul Klee, *Cat and Bird* (1928)
- Henri Rousseau, *The Flamingoes* (1907)
- Susan Rothenberg, *Untitled (Horse)* (1976)
- Henri Matisse, *The Snail* (1953)
- Louisa Matthíasdóttir, *Five Sheep* (no date)

SAMPLE ACTIVITIES AND ASSESSMENTS

1. MAIN TOPIC AND KEY DETAILS/INFORMATIONAL TEXT

While reading a book such as *What Do You Do With a Tail Like This?* (Steve Jenkins), make a chart to record the name of each animal (main topic) mentioned. Record key details, such as where the animal lives (i.e., its habitat), what the animal eats (i.e., whether it is an herbivore, carnivore, or omnivore), and an interesting fact (e.g., its method of adaptation) on the chart. Ask students to supply at least one piece of information on a sticky note when you are finished reading. Create and add to similar charts about animal facts as you read to the children and as they read independently. Use these charts to create oral and written sentences about the animals. (RI.1.2, L.1.1j, L.1.5b)

2. CLASS DISCUSSION/READING/INFORMATIONAL TEXT

Before beginning this lesson, ask students what they are experts at doing (e.g., bike riding, roller skating, or back flips). Allow some time to share. Remind the students that an author is a real person who has worked hard to know the information to fill a book such as *What Do You Do With a Tail Like This?* (Steve Jenkins). Ask the students to think about how authors become experts on a topic, such as the tails of animals. If possible, invite a speaker who has expertise in something. Talk about how they became an expert. Talk about why this makes informational texts better and how having good information can help improve one's writing. (RI.1.2, SL.1.3)

3. ART/INFORMATIVE/EXPLANATORY WRITING

Using a projector and computer, display the Tate's website for Matisse's *The Snail*. Encourage students to comment about the colors and what they see in the artwork. As you read the background information and move through the site, students will see the process Matisse used to create his work. Students will then create a work of their favorite animal from this unit using torn pieces of painted paper. Later, do a shared writing in which the students explain the steps taken to create an art piece in the style of Matisse. This activity could be a model for a piece of informative/explanatory writing later. (W.1.7, SL.1.2)

4. INFORMATIVE/EXPLANATORY WRITING (REVISION)

Since the students have now completed an artistic masterpiece of their favorite animal, extend the work into a writing assignment. Give the students this prompt: "Write about your favorite animal. Be sure to include interesting facts about your animal and include a catchy beginning, some facts, and a strong ending." Allow your students to begin by working in teams to gather information. Using nonfiction texts, remind them to use the index or table of contents to locate more information about the animal. When they have some basic information, have them write the first draft. Ensure that adults are available to help with revision of the writing. Display the published writing with the Matisse-style artwork (see Art/Informative/Explanatory Writing). (W.1.2, W.1.5, RI.1.5, RI.1.10, RF.1.4)

5. RETELLING/VOCABULARY

Read a fictional animal story, such as *Are You My Mother?* (Philip D. Eastman). Discuss the vocabulary in the story and work on understanding unknown words. Ask the students (if, for example, discussing *Are You My Mother?*), "What word was funny in the story because of the way it was used?" (Possible answer: "Snort.") Then ask, "How did you know what it meant?" Divide the students into groups of three and have them tell the story to each other, taking turns as each tells a part. Let them know that if they are stuck on a part of the story, you will allow them to use the book to solve the problem. Encourage the students to try to remember as many details as they can for retelling the story because details are what make the story interesting. When they are finished retelling the story, talk about what lesson might be learned from the story and what new words they learned. (L.1.4a, RL.1.2)

6. LITERARY/LANGUAGE

Follow up on a book read previously in class, such as *Are You My Mother?* (Philip D. Eastman). Go back and reread the story. As you read it this time, read for the purpose of finding all of the animals and things that baby bird thought might be his mother. As students find the words, write them on index cards (e.g., kitten, hen, dog, cow, boat, plane). Sort the words into categories (e.g., animals, modes of transportation). Think of more words for each of the categories. This activity could also be done with a poem such as "The Pasture" or "I Know All the Sounds that the Animals Make." After reading and rereading (reciting) the poem, gather the nouns in the poem and sort them according to categories (e.g., places, animals, sounds). (L.1.1b, L.1.5a)

7. LITERARY

As students read independently, remind them that different characters often tell the story at different times in a book. Using a book such as *Mouse Tales* (Arnold Lobel), allow the students to reread parts of the text where the weasel speaks, where the mouse speaks, and where the narrator tells the story. Provide elbow macaroni at each table. Ask students to place the macaroni on the quotation marks in the book, reminding them that it means someone is speaking. Assigning the parts to three readers will show others how dialogue works in literature. (RL.1.6)

8. LITERARY/READ ALOUD

Choose a fantasy read-aloud, such as *Finn Family Moomintroll* (Tove Jansson). Continuing to focus on the retelling of fiction, give the children the opportunity to retell the previous chapters by allowing them to choose an object to prompt the retelling. For example, provide a number of props (e.g., a black hat made of construction paper), and ask students to find the appropriate object when it appears in the story and put it into a "retelling basket." Before each reading time, have the students retell the story using the gathered objects as prompts for remembering characters and events. By the time the book ends, you will have an object for each chapter or key event in the book—and the students will be efficient storytellers. (RL.1.2)

9. ART/CLASS DISCUSSION

Select three or four works to view (e.g., the Klee, Chagall, and Dürer). Ask the students the following questions: What animal do you see in this work? Does anyone see a different animal? What color is the animal? Is this the real color of this animal? Why do you think the artist chose the color he or she did? Begin to introduce the concept of abstraction (versus realism) by comparing the Dürer image with either the Klee or the Chagall. Ask questions like: Is this exactly what a rabbit looks like? What about a cat? A picture of a cow? How can we tell the difference? What was the artist trying to do? (SL.1.1.b, SL.1.3, SL.1.4)

10. ART/INFORMATIVE/EXPLANATORY WRITING

Ask the students to draw an animal of their choice. They will then color it using the animal's real colors, or they could choose to use other colors. Students may also choose to do either a realistic or abstract version of their animal. Ask the students to write an informative/explanatory text based on their drawing, using their choice of realistic or creative coloring. (W.1.2)

READING FOUNDATIONS: A PACING GUIDE FOR READING INSTRUCTION

See Grade One, Level Two, in the Reading Foundations section for a complete pacing guide for this unit.

ADDITIONAL RESOURCES

- *Animal Study: From Fiction to Facts* (National Endowment for the Humanities) (RL.1.5)
- *Investigating Animals: Using Nonfiction for Inquiry-based Research* (ReadWriteThink) (W.1.7)
- Edward Lear home page
- Robert Frost reads "The Pasture"

TERMINOLOGY

Categories	Lesson	Retell
Context clues	Main topic	Revision
Informative/explanatory	Message	

MAKING INTERDISCIPLINARY CONNECTIONS

This unit teaches:

Art: Henri Matisse, Albrecht Dürer
Science: Animals (e.g., habitats, unique adaptations, and the food chain)

This unit could be extended to teach:

Geography: Oceans
Science: Animals (e.g., undersea life, habitat destruction, Rachel Carson)

Grade One, Unit Two Sample Lesson Plan

Are You My Mother? by P. D. Eastman

In this series of three lessons, students read *Are You My Mother?* by P. D. Eastman, and they:

- Explore the adventures of a baby bird in search of his mother (RL.1.1, RL.1.2, RL.1.3)
- Consider the importance of the illustrations in the story (RL.1.7, SL.1.1, SL.1.2)
- Appreciate the importance of rereading stories (RL.1.2)

Summary

Lesson I: Baby Bird Begins a Search

- Explore the reason for the mother bird's decision to leave the nest (RL.1.1, RL.1.3, SL.1.1, SL.1.2)
- Note the changing facial expressions of the baby bird leading up to his decision to search for his mother (RL.1.3, RL.1.7)
- Examine the baby bird's exchanges with the animals that he meets (RL.1.1, RL.1.2)

Lesson II: Continue Baby Bird' Search

- Note the shift in the narrative when the baby bird begins to run (RL.1.1, RL.1.2)
- Examine the bird's encounter with the Snort (RL.1.1, RL.1.2, RL.1.3, SL.1.1, SL.1.2)
- Explore the meeting between the mother and the baby bird (RL.1.1, RL.1.2, RL.1.3, SL.1.1, SL.1.3)
- Consider the impact of the illustrations on the reader understanding of the baby bird's emotions (RL.1.7, SL.1.1, SL.1.2)

Lesson III: Revisit Baby Bird's Adventure

Recall the baby bird's adventures with the help of passages from the text (RL.1.1, RL.1.2, RL.1.3, SL.1.1, SL.1.2)

Chart the baby bird's adventures (RL.1.1, SL.1.5)

Illustrate the baby bird's adventures (SL.1.5)

Consider what *Are You My Mother?* teaches (SL.1.1, SL.1.2)

Lesson III: Revisit Baby Bird's Adventure

Objectives

Recall the baby bird's adventures with the help of passages from the text (RL.1.1, RL.1.2, RL.1.3, SL.1.1, SL.1.2)

Chart the baby bird's adventures (RL.1.1, SL.1.5)

Illustrate the baby bird's adventures (SL.1.5)

Consider what *Are You My Mother?* teaches (SL.1.1, SL.1.2)

Required Materials

☐ *Are You My Mother?* by P. D. Eastman

☐ Large, blank poster boards

☐ Markers

☐ Colored pencils

Procedures

1. Lead-In:
   The class rereads *Are You My Mother?* aloud. (Depending on the students' reading levels, you may choose to read the story or have students read it.)

2. Step by Step:
   a. In a class discussion, the students recall the details of the baby bird's journey.

b. In small groups, students create a chart (see following sample) where they trace the baby bird's steps. They consult the book whenever they are not sure of the next step. (Since the journey begins and ends at home a circular chart makes the most sense.)

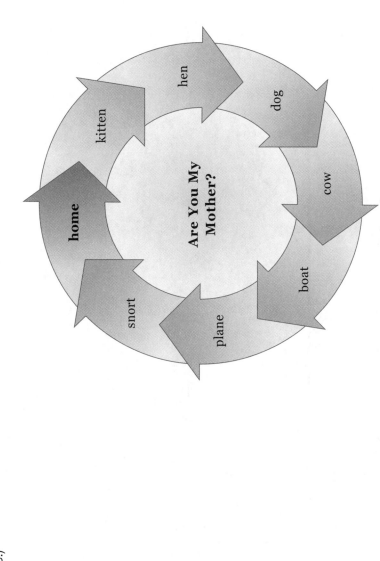

c. Students illustrate the charts. The illustrations will enable students to add individual perspective. In Lessons I and II, the students note the contribution of the illustrations to the presentation of the baby bird, his character, his mood, and his emotions. This is their opportunity to do the same.

3. Closure:
Students will introduce and discuss their groups' charts.

Differentiation

Advanced

- When students finish this activity, put them into small performance teams to read the book with expression.
- Arrange for the students to go and read the book to a kindergartener or to a kindergarten class.

Struggling

- Create a 3-by-3 table with nouns from the story printed in the table. As you review each noun, have students make a picture of the noun. For example, draw a kitten in the square labeled "kitten." If students need more work with word recognition, play bingo with the words.
- Create the circular formation for the children and allow each child in the group to write two of the words on sticky notes. Have children practice looking at story clues to put the sticky notes in the right place.

Homework/Assessment

N/A

Life Lessons

In this third six-week unit of first grade, students read literature and informational texts related to life lessons.

ESSENTIAL QUESTION

? How can stories teach us life lessons?

OVERVIEW

Building on the retelling of stories with details, students delve deeper by focusing on the categorizing of story details into the following groupings: characters, key events, and settings. Students read and listen to fables with morals. They also learn about rules for life in a book of manners. Reading the life story of George Washington Carver, students learn about a man who had to overcome obstacles in life to make important contributions to science and agriculture. Students also learn about Thomas Edison's work with electricity and the rules for its safe use. Students write narratives focused on life lessons and create informative/explanatory posters about electricity. Finally, students focus on descriptive words while studying the artwork of Georgia O'Keeffe.

FOCUS STANDARDS

These Focus Standards have been selected for the unit from the Common Core State Standards.

RL.1.2: Retell stories, including key details, and demonstrate understanding of the central message or lesson.

RL.1.3: Describe characters, settings, and major events in a story, using key details.

RI.1.6: Distinguish between information provided by pictures or other illustrations and information provided by the words in a text.

W.1.3: Write narratives in which they recount two or more appropriately sequenced events, include some details regarding what happened, use temporal words to signal event order, and provide some sense of closure.

L.1.2: Demonstrate command of the conventions of Standard English capitalization, punctuation, and spelling when writing.

L.1.2(b): Use end punctuation for sentences.

RF.1.4: Read with sufficient accuracy and fluency to support comprehension.

RF.1.4(b): Read on-level text orally with accuracy, appropriate rate, and expression on successive readings.

SUGGESTED STUDENT OBJECTIVES

- Describe characters, key events, and the setting in a story.
- Identify who is speaking in a story or fable.
- Distinguish between the information provided by the pictures or illustrations in a text and the information provided by the words.
- Using time cue words, providing some details, and ending with a sense of closure, write narratives that include at least two sequenced events.
- With the help of an adult, revise narratives.
- Produce complete sentences with correct past, present, or future verb tenses.
- Use end punctuation for sentences: periods, question marks, and exclamation points.
- Relate the use of punctuation to the way a text should be read expressively.
- Compare and contrast two versions of an Indian fable.
- Create informative/explanatory posters using both text and illustrations (e.g., to teach about electrical safety).

SUGGESTED WORKS

(E) indicates a CCSS exemplar text; (EA) indicates a text from a writer with other works identified as exemplars.

LITERARY TEXTS

Stories

- *Green Eggs and Ham* (Dr. Seuss) (E)
- *Seven Blind Mice* (Ed Young) (EA)
- *The Blind Men and the Elephant* (Karen Backstein and Annie Mitra)
- *Inch by Inch* (Leo Lionni)
- *The Lion & the Mouse* (Jerry Pinkney)
- *Lousy Rotten Stinkin' Grapes* (Margie Palatini and Barry Moser)
- *Yo! Yes?* (Chris Raschka)

Stories (Read Aloud)

- *The Boy Who Cried Wolf* (B. G. Hennessy and Boris Kulikov)
- *Town Mouse, Country Mouse* (Jan Brett)
- *The Tortoise and the Hare* (Janet Stevens)
- *The Hare and The Tortoise* (Helen Ward)
- *Fables* (Arnold Lobel) (EA)
- *The Little Red Hen* (Paul Galdone)

- *The Ugly Duckling* (Hans Christian Andersen and Jerry Pinkney)
- *Swimmy* (Leo Lionni)
- *Alexander and the Wind-up Mouse* (Leo Lionni)
- *Punctuation Takes a Vacation* (Robin Pulver and Lynn Rowe Reed)

Poems

- "By Myself" in *Honey I Love and Other Poems* (Eloise Greenfield)
- "Sharing" in *Falling Up* (Shel Silverstein)
- "Ridiculous Rose" in *Where the Sidewalk Ends* (Shel Silverstein)

Poems (Read Aloud)

- *Goops and How to Be Them: A Manual of Manners for Polite Children* (Gelett Burgess)
- "I'm Making a List" in *Where the Sidewalk Ends* (Shel Silverstein)
- "My Mother Says I'm Sickening" in *The New Kid on the Block* (Jack Prelutsky)

INFORMATIONAL TEXTS

Informational Books

- *A Weed is a Flower: The Life of George Washington Carver* (Aliki) (E)
- *George Washington Carver* (Rookie Biographies) (Lynea Bowdish)
- *Thomas Alva Edison* (Rookie Biographies) (Wil Mara)
- *What is Electricity?* (Rookie Read-About Science) (Lisa Trumbauer)

Informational Books (Read Aloud)

- *Manners* (Aliki) (EA)
- *Hello! Good-bye!* (Aliki) (EA)
- *Georgia O'Keeffe* (Getting to Know the World's Greatest Artists) (Mike Venezia)
- *My Light* (Molly Bang) (EA)
- *Flick a Switch: How Electricity Gets to Your Home* (Barbara Seuling and Nancy Tobin)
- *Watch Out! At Home* (Claire Llewellyn and Mike Gordon)

ART, MUSIC, AND MEDIA

Art

- Georgia O'Keeffe, *Red Poppy* (1927)
- Georgia O'Keeffe, *Jack in the Pulpit No. IV* (1930)
- Georgia O'Keeffe, *Jimson Weed* (1936)
- Georgia O'Keeffe, *Oriental Poppies* (1928)
- Georgia O'Keeffe, *Two Calla Lilies on Pink* (1928)
- Vincent van Gogh, *Sunflowers* (1888–1889)
- Vincent van Gogh, *Irises* (1890)
- Vincent van Gogh, *Almond Blossom* (1890)
- Vincent van Gogh, *Butterflies and Poppies* (1890)

SAMPLE ACTIVITIES AND ASSESSMENTS

1. PUNCTUATION/LITERARY TEXT

To introduce the relationship between punctuation and reading expression, use the book *Yo! Yes?* Show the students the cover of the book with its very simple title: *Yo! Yes?* Ask how someone would say those words. As you read the book with the students, have the boys read one page, and the girls the opposite page. As they focus on the illustrations and the way the author ends each sentence, they will know how to read the words, and a story will be created in their minds. Follow this reading with other books so that the children learn how important it is to read with the end punctuation in mind. *Extension:* Reading (reciting) poetry with punctuated lines such as "Sharing," would be a way to extend this knowledge of punctuation and dramatic expression into other literary forms. Follow this activity with practice using different kinds of end punctuation. (RL.1.6, RL.1.7, RF.1.4b, L.1.2b)

2. COMPARING AND CONTRASTING CHARACTERS, SETTINGS AND EVENTS/LITERARY TEXT

Tell the students that fables are stories that teach us a lesson. The characters in the story are usually animals and have one main characteristic. Read the familiar fable "The Tortoise and the Hare." Ask students what they can tell you about the tortoise. (He's slow, but steady.) What can they tell about the hare? (He's fast, but undependable.) Create a chart with cells for the title, characters (with one characteristic each), setting, key events (i.e., from the beginning, middle, and end), and the lesson learned (i.e., the moral of the story). As you read each fable in this unit, continue to fill in the chart. Give students more and more responsibility for filling in the characters, setting, and key events of a fable. Assess understanding at the end of the unit by reading a fable and then have each child write or dictate the entries on his or her own chart. (RL.1.2, RL.1.3)

3. COMPARING AND CONTRASTING FABLES/LITERATURE

Tell the students that the Indian fable "The Blind Men and the Elephant" is the original telling of a fable more commonly known in the United States as "Seven Blind Mice." Read the original story first and then read "Seven Blind Mice." (Read aloud to students, or they may read on their own if they are able.) As the two fables are added to the fable story chart, ask the students to explain how these two stories are the same and how they are different. Use a digital camera to take photographs of the process of creating the artwork. Use these photographs to guide the writing of the shared explanatory paper. (RL.1.2, RL.1.9)

4. NARRATIVE WRITING

Assign this narrative prompt: "Think of a time when you learned a lesson. Be sure to include at least two sequenced events, use time cue words, provide some details, and include a sense of closure." Encourage the students to think about the lessons learned in the fables as they write their own story. Be sure the students focus on the beginning, middle, and end (where they tell about the lesson learned). Edit to be sure that nouns (singular and plural) match verbs and that verb tenses are correct and consistent. (W.1.3, W.1.5, RL.1.2, L.1.1c,j)

5. INFORMATIVE/EXPLANATORY WRITING

One of the life lessons focused on in this unit is manners. With the students, create a list of "lunchroom manners" using a book such as *Manners* (Aliki). Students should dictate the sentences while you write them on sentence strips. In this writing lesson, focus on writing complete sentences with subject-verb agreement. To practice handwriting and correct sentence construction, have the students copy some of the sentences. Sentences such as these can be illustrated and compiled in a book titled *Lunchroom Manners*. A follow-up to this lesson would be a humorous list of lunchroom manners inspired by Prelutsky and Silverstein and written in poetic form. (SL.1.6, L.1.1c,j)

6. INDEPENDENT READING/INFORMATIONAL TEXT

Introduce the book *A Weed is a Flower: The Life of George Washington Carver*. Explain that illustrations and text are both very important in a book. Guide students as they read by asking them first to think about what you can learn from the illustrations. Create a two-column chart with "illustrations" on one side and "text" on the other side. When students learn something from studying the illustration, they will write it on a sticky note and put it in the book. When students learn something from the written words of the text, they will also note it on a sticky note. When the students are finished reading the book, use sticky notes to guide the discussion focusing on learning from illustrations and learning from the text. (RI.1.6)

7. ART/CLASS DISCUSSION

Show students images of van Gogh's works in comparison to O'Keeffe's, and discuss the following as a class: Both of these artists painted flowers. What is similar and different about their paintings? Why do you think each painter chose to paint the flowers they did? Was it because of their color or shape? Do the flowers remind you of anything—like faces or groups of people? (SL.1.3)

8. ART/INFORMATIVE/EXPLANATORY WRITING

Consider showing both O'Keeffe and van Gogh works without titles. Have students write a short description of what they see. Which flower can you see actually growing and changing? Which painter chose to make his or her works more abstract? Who painted flowers realistically? (W.1.7, W.1.8)

9. INFORMATIVE/EXPLANATORY WRITING

After reading several books about electricity, create a list of rules for safety (e.g., avoiding electrical outlets with wet hands). Divide the rules evenly among the students and assign the task of creating a safety poster for each one. Each student will write a rule neatly and show additional information (i.e., the application of the rule) in his or her illustration. Create sets of posters and allow students to present their rules to another classroom or grade level. (W.1.2, RI.1.6, SL.1.5, SL.1.6)

READING FOUNDATIONS: A PACING GUIDE FOR READING INSTRUCTION

See Grade One, Level Three, in the Reading Foundations section for a complete pacing guide for this unit.

ADDITIONAL RESOURCES

- *Building a Matrix for Leo Lionni Books: An Author Study* (ReadWriteThink) (RL.1.9)
- *Aesop and Ananse: Animal Fables and Trickster Tales* (National Endowment for the Humanities) (RL.1.2)
- The Georgia O'Keeffe Museum

TERMINOLOGY

Adjectives	End punctuation	Key events	Period
Affixes	Exclamatory	Lesson	Revision
Characters	Fable	Message	Setting
Complete sentences	Imperative	Moral	Verbs
Declarative	Interrogative	Narratives	

MAKING INTERDISCIPLINARY CONNECTIONS

This unit teaches:

Art: Georgia O'Keeffe, Vincent van Gogh

Science: Scientists (e.g., George Washington Carver, Thomas Edison); Electricity (e.g., basic principles, safety rules)

This unit could be extended to teach:

Science: Sun (i.e., as a source of energy, light, and heat)

Grade One, Unit Three Sample Lesson Plan

A Weed Is a Flower: The Life of George Washington Carver by Aliki

In this series of five lessons, students read *A Weed is a Flower: The Life of George Washington Carver* by Aliki, and they:

Explore the life of George Washington Carver (RL.1.1, RL.1.2, RL.1.3, RI.1.10)

Trace Carver's successful struggle to get an education (RI.1.1, RL.1.2, RL.1.3, RI.1.10)

Examine the kind of person Carver was (RI.1.2)

Note Carver's contributions to farming (RL.1.2, RL.1.3)

Summary

Lesson I: Meet George Washington Carver

Recognize biography as a literary genre

Discuss the function of a biography

Note that Aliki is both the author and the illustrator of the book

Observe the cover and discuss its content

Listen and consider the purpose of the introduction to the book (RI.1.10)

Lesson III: George Washington Carver Is Free

Trace Carver's struggle to get an education (RI.1.1, RL.1.2, RL.1.3, RI.1.10)

List the jobs he had

(Continue to) list Carver's characteristics (RI.1.2)

Note the point in the story where Carver remembers that his neighbors used to call him "Plant Doctor" (RL.1.2, RL.1.3)

Identify a shift in the plot

Lesson II: Young George Washington Carver

Note the basic facts of Carver's early years (RL.1.2, RL.1.3, RI.1.10)

Explore Moses Carver's attitude toward the young Carver (RL.1.2, RL.1.3)

(Begin to) list the characteristics of the young boy (RL.1.2, RL.1.3)

Investigate his actions (RL.1.2, RL.1.3)

Consider how his acts reflect who he is

Lesson IV: The Plant Doctor

Examine Carver's career as the Plant Doctor (RL.1.2, RL.1.3)

Consider how Carver's habit of asking questions helped him become successful

Investigate Carver's contribution to farming in America (RL.1.2, RL.1.3)

Lesson V: A Flower for the Plant Doctor

Study the title of the book

Revisit the life of Carver (RL.1.2, RL.1.3, SL.1.1)

Imagine words that describe his life (introduce the concepts of simile and metaphor) (L.1.6)

Consider images that portray the kind of person he was (RL.1.7, RI.1.7, RF.1.3, SL.1.4, SL.1.5)

Reflect on the lessons that Carver's life teaches (SL.1.1a)

Lesson V: A Flower for the Plant Doctor

Objectives

Study the title of the book

Revisit the life of Carver (RL.1.2, RL.1.3, SL.1.1)

Imagine words that describe his life (introduce the *concepts* of simile and metaphor) (L.1.6)

Consider images that portray the kind of person he was (RL.1.7, RI.1.7, RF.1.3, SL.1.4, SL.1.5)

Reflect on the lessons that Carver's life teaches (SL.1.1a)

Required Materials

☐ *A Weed Is a Flower: The Life of George Washington Carver*, by Aliki

☐ Large, blank poster board

☐ Construction paper

☐ Scissors

☐ Markers

☐ Colored pencils

☐ Glue

Procedures

1. Lead-In:

Students discuss the life of George Washington Carver.

2. Step by Step:

   a. Following a prompt, the students select words to describe Carver. Students use their imaginations; for example, if a child says "brave," then ask for another word or an image that evokes bravery, such as a lion. The purpose of this activity is to introduce the concepts of simile and metaphor, though students do not need to master those terms at this level. List all the words generated on the board and encourage students to use what they know about phonics and word analysis skills to help with spelling the words.

b. Once a substantial list has been generated the students choose words, write them on the construction paper, and illustrate them.

c. As the students complete their work, place the drawings on a poster board. When the students are done, the final product should be a collection of words and drawings that describe George Washington Carver. (Perhaps place the children's work in the shape of a flower.)

3. Closure:

Sit with the students and reflect on the following question: Who was Carver and why was he such a special man?

Differentiation

Advanced

- After deciding upon metaphors, students will create a graphic representation describing George Washington Carver using an online tool to generate a word cloud or other visualization.

Struggling

- To pre-teach the concept of simile, students will focus on familiar animal characteristics. Supply the beginning of a phrase and ask students to fill in the name of the animal (e.g., "as hungry as a BEAR," "as fast as a CHEETAH," "as slow as a TURTLE," and "as quiet as a MOUSE").

- To pre-teach the concept of metaphor, explain that these animals can be used to represent a human characteristic, such as a lion representing bravery in the case of George Washington Carver.

Homework/Assessment

N/A

Winds of Change

In this fourth six-week unit of first grade, students look at changes in nature through nonfiction, changes in the feelings of characters through fantasy, and changes in their own writing through revision.

ESSENTIAL QUESTION

? How do you know what a character is feeling and when these feelings change?

OVERVIEW

Building on the simple characteristics of fable characters, students describe the characters' feelings. Focusing on verbs, students act out the various ways Dorothy in *The Wonderful Wizard of Oz* could "walk" on the yellow brick road. They read an article on wind power to look at how wind can provide energy efficiently. They view the nonfiction in this unit through the lens of cause and effect. Finally, students look at writing as a moldable, changing piece of work that can improve with revision.

FOCUS STANDARDS

These Focus Standards have been selected for the unit from the Common Core State Standards.

RL.1.4: Identify words and phrases in stories or poems that suggest feelings or appeal to the senses.

RI.1.8: Identify the reasons an author gives to support points in a text.

W.1.5: With guidance and support, focus on a topic, respond to questions and suggestions from peers, and add details to strengthen writing as needed.

L.1.5: With guidance and support, demonstrate understanding of word relationships and nuances in word meanings.

L.1.5(d): Distinguish shades of meanings among verbs differing in manner (e.g., look, peek, glance, stare, glare, and scowl).

SL.1.4: Describe people, places, things, and events with relevant details, expressing ideas and feelings clearly.

SUGGESTED STUDENT OBJECTIVES

- Identify words and phrases in stories or poems that suggest feelings and appeal to the senses.
- Identify cause and effect relationships in informational text.
- Add details as needed to strengthen writing through revision.
- Distinguish shades of meaning among verbs by defining, choosing, or acting out the meanings.
- Using commas to separate the words, dictate sentences with a series of nouns.
- Write a narrative text with a focus on feelings.
- Revise writing using temporal words, feeling words, and vivid verbs.
- Distinguish between the root and affixes of verb conjugations, such as *walk, walks, walked, walking*.
- Use commas in a series and identify the conjunction (e.g., "I see monkeys, tigers, and elephants at the zoo").

SUGGESTED WORKS

(E) indicates a CCSS exemplar text; (EA) indicates a text from a writer with other works identified as exemplars.

LITERARY TEXTS

Stories

- *Owl at Home* (Arnold Lobel) (E)
- *Frog and Toad All Year* (Arnold Lobel) (EA)
- *Ten Apples Up on Top!* (Dr. Seuss) (EA)
- *When Sophie Gets Angry—Really, Really Angry* … (Molly Bang) (EA)
- *Changes, Changes* (Pat Hutchins)
- *My Name is Yoon* (Helen Recorvits and Gabi Swiatkowska)
- *The Wind Blew* (Pat Hutchins)

Stories (Read Aloud)

- *The Wonderful Wizard of Oz* (L. Frank Baum) (E)
- *Twister on Tuesday* (Mary Pope Osborne and Sal Murdocca) (EA)
- *Alexander and the Horrible, No Good, Very Bad Day* (Judith Viorst and Ray Cruz)
- *Alexander, Who's Not (Do You Hear Me? I Mean It!) Going to Move* (Judith Viorst, Ray Cruz, and Robin Preiss Glasser)
- *If You Give a Mouse a Cookie* (Laura Joffe Numeroff and Felicia Bond)
- *The Bat Boy and His Violin* (Gavin Curtis and E. B. Lewis)
- *Goin' Someplace Special* (Patricia C. McKissack and Jerry Pinkney)

Poems

- "Covers" in *The Sun is So Quiet* (Nikki Giovanni) (E)
- "It Fell in the City" in *Blackberry Ink* (Eve Merriam) (E)

- "Laughing Boy" in *Haiku: This Other World* (Richard Wright) (E)
- "Drinking Fountain" in *Random House Book of Poetry for Children* (Marchette Chute) (E)

Poems (Read Aloud)

- "Who Has Seen The Wind?" in *Rossetti: Poems* (Everyman's Library Pocket Poets) (Christina Rossetti) (E)
- "The Wind" in *A Child's Garden of Verses* (Robert Louis Stevenson)
- "Windy Nights" in *A Child's Garden of Verses* (Robert Louis Stevenson)
- "Blow, Wind, Blow!" (Traditional)

INFORMATIONAL TEXTS

Informational Books

- "Wind Power" (National Geographic Young Explorer!) (November–December 2009) (E)
- *Storms* (National Geographic Readers) (Miriam Goin)

Informational Books (Read Aloud)

- *Tornadoes!* (Gail Gibbons) (EA)
- *Tornadoes* (Seymour Simon)
- *Super Storms* (Seymour Simon)
- *Flash, Crash, Rumble, and Roll* (Franklyn M. Branley and True Kelley)
- *How People Learned to Fly* (Fran Hodgkins and True Kelley) (E)
- *Feelings* (Aliki) (EA)
- *Twisters and Other Terrible Storms: A Nonfiction Companion to Twister on Tuesday* (Will and Mary Pope Osborne, and Sal Murdocca) (EA)

ART, MUSIC, AND MEDIA

Art

- Richard Diebenkorn, *Ocean Park No. 38* (1971)
- Richard Diebenkorn, *Ocean Park No. 49* (1972)
- Richard Diebenkorn, *Ocean Park No. 54* (1972)
- Richard Diebenkorn, *Ocean Park No. 115* (1979)

Music

- Pyotr Ilyich Tchaikovsky, Violin Concerto in D major, Op. 35 (1878)
- Wolfgang Amadeus Mozart, Violin Concerto No. 4 in D Major (1775)
- Johann Sebastian Bach, Concerto for 2 Violins, Strings, and Continuo in D Minor (Double Violin Concerto) (1730–1731)
- Ludwig van Beethoven, Violin Concerto in D Major, Op. 61 (1806)

Film

- Victor Fleming, dir., *The Wizard of Oz* (1939)

SAMPLE ACTIVITIES AND ASSESSMENTS

1. READING/LITERARY

Read *The Wonderful Wizard of Oz* aloud to the class. As students meet each character in the text, guide them to think about the character's feelings and how the author shows us how the character feels. Discuss how the author helps us use our senses to see, smell, feel, hear, and even taste while we are reading a book. As you read aloud, model the way you are drawn to use your senses. For example, in the second paragraph of Chapter One, the author describes Kansas so that you can "see" the countryside clearly. Then he goes on to describe Aunt Em, Uncle Henry, Toto, and Dorothy, with a focus on their feelings. (RL.1.3, RL.1.4)

2. LANGUAGE

Choose some verbs that are rather bland, such as "to walk." Ask the students to imagine that they are in the book (*The Wonderful Wizard of Oz*) with Dorothy and that they are walking on the yellow brick road. Have them imagine that they are really happy (e.g., when they see the Emerald City). How would they walk? (Possible answers: *skip, run, dance.*) Allow students to show us how that kind of motion would look. Then, have them imagine that they are feeling scared (e.g., when walking through the forest). How would they walk? (Possible answers: *tiptoe, creep.*) Make a list of all the words that could be used as a better choice than "walk." This lesson on verbs can be extended to cover tenses, roots, and affixes *-ed, -s, -ing*. To make the extending lessons more fun, create a Wordle for each verb tense (i.e., present tense verbs for "walk," past tense verbs for "walk," . . .) (SL.1.4, L1.1e, L.1.4b, L.1.4c, L.1.5d)

3. LANGUAGE

To reinforce the idea of a wide range of alternatives for a word like *see,* write the words *look, peek, glance, stare, glare,* and *scowl* on cards. Have the students arrange the cards in order from the most to least cautious (e.g., peek → glance → look → stare → glare → scowl). Use a thesaurus to add other synonyms of "to see" and add them into the range of words. (L.1.5d)

4. NARRATIVE WRITING/REVISION

Give students this prompt: "Write a story about a time you felt happy. Be sure to include at least two sequenced events, use time cue words, provide some details, and include a sense of closure." Combining the focuses of this unit (revision, appealing to the senses with details, and using well-chosen verbs), zero in on details and synonyms while the students revise their stories. Help the students to watch for the proper use of personal, possessive, and indefinite pronouns (e.g., *I, me, my; they, them, their; anyone, everything*) as they are editing. (W.1.3, W.1.5, L.1.1d)

5. INFORMATIVE/EXPLANATORY READING AND WRITING

Introduce an informative article such as "Wind Power" (*National Geographic Young Explorer!*). First, ask students to think about what wind causes and brainstorm with the children. Then, have the students read the article independently, with partners, or with the teacher to find out what the wind causes.

Cause	Effect
Wind	"Whips up fun" (study illustration for specifics)
Wind	Kites fly
Wind	Pushes sailboats
Wind	Windmills spin, turning wind energy into electricity

Continue this activity with more nonfiction articles and books, continually giving students more of the responsibility for recording their own ideas. Throughout the unit, continue reading and reciting the poems in the unit to build a love for poetry. Blend the recording of ideas from the nonfiction works into a creative writing activity by creating an illustrated free-form poem using the wind cause-and-effect chart as inspiration. As a class, generate more effects of wind that students may have witnessed. Begin and end the poem with the word *wind*. (RL.1.10, RI.1.8, W.1.7, W.1.8)

6. MUSIC CONNECTION/MOOD

Throughout the day, play some violin concerto music in the background. Ask the students how the music made them feel. For example, ask them to finish this sentence: "During the music, I felt _____." Continue to listen to the music at any opportunity. Then, read the book *The Bat Boy and His Violin*, which is the story of a boy who loved to play the violin. After the students listen to the story, go back through the text and have the children talk about how the author used words and phrases to let the reader know how the characters in the book felt. (RL.1.4, L.1.1i)

7. LANGUAGE

To teach the use of a comma in a series, list the five senses on the whiteboard. Give students a "setting" card (e.g., zoo, farm, or beach) and have them dictate a sentence using one of the senses, naming three things they sense in that setting. Explain that when we use the word *and* we are using a conjunction. For example, "At the zoo, I smell popcorn, elephants, and cotton candy." Write the dictated sentence and then challenge them to write their own sentences using *and* in the sentences. (L.1.1g, L.1.2c)

8. READING/INFORMATIONAL TEXT

As you read books about the topic of wind or tornadoes, place the word *tornado* in the center of a display board. Look for causes of tornadoes (post on the left) and the effects of tornadoes (post on the right), creating a visual graphic organizer for cause and effect. Have students use the graphic organizer to create sentences showing cause and effect (e.g., "The high winds of the tornado tore the roof from the top of the Civic Center."). Repeat this activity as you read other informational books with a cause-and-effect structure, giving students more of the responsibility for placing sticky notes on the graphic organizer and writing out the sentences. (RL.1.10, RI.1.8)

9. ART/CLASS DISCUSSION

Show students a sampling of Richard Diebenkorn's *Ocean Park* series, which the painter began in 1967 and worked on for the rest of his life. What do you see in these images—the ocean? Clouds? Sand? What techniques has Diebenkorn used to convey the look and feel of these objects? Use adjectives and action verbs to describe what you see. (SL.1.3, L.1.1, L.1.5)

10. ART/CLASS DISCUSSION

Take time to have students look at each painting closely. What changes in Diebenkorn's series of *Ocean Park* works? Where? Discuss together the use of one subject in this selection. What aspects of the paintings stay the same? (SL.1.1, SL.1.3, SL.1.4, SL.1.6)

READING FOUNDATIONS: A PACING GUIDE FOR READING INSTRUCTION

See Grade One, Level Four, in the Reading Foundations section for a complete pacing guide for this unit.

ADDITIONAL RESOURCES

- *The Day Jimmy's Boa Taught Cause and Effect* (ReadWriteThink) (RI.1.8)
- *Lesson Plan on Tornadoes* (National Geographic)

TERMINOLOGY

Cause	Revision
Effect	Verbs

MAKING INTERDISCIPLINARY CONNECTIONS

This unit teaches:

Art: Richard Diebenkorn
Music: Violin concertos (by Tchaikovsky, Mozart, Bach, and Beethoven)
Science: Weather (e.g., wind and tornadoes)

This unit could be extended to teach:

Science: Changing states of matter (e.g., solid, liquid, and gas)

Grade One, Unit Four Sample Lesson Plan

Owl at Home by Arnold Lobel

In this series of six lessons, students read *Owl at Home* by Arnold Lobel, and they:

Explore the adventures of Owl (RL.1.1, RL.1.2, RL.1.3, RL.1.4, SL.1.1, SL.1.2)

Note Lobel's use of illustrations to depict Owl's adventures (RL.1.7)

Offer individual perspectives of Owl's character and his understanding of his environment (RL.1.2, RL.1.3, W.1.1, W.1.2, W.1.3)

Summary

Lesson I: "The Guest"

Follow the plot of "The Guest" (RL.1.1, RL.1.2, RL.1.3)

Identify Owl's guest (RL.1.3, RL.1.3)

Explore Owl's actions (RL.1.2, SL.1.1, SL.1.2)

Examine Lobel's use of illustrations to depict the events in the story (RL.1.7)

Lesson III: "Tear-Water Tea"

Follow the plot of "Tear-Water Tea" (RL.1.1, RL.1.2, RL.1.3)

Identify the strange idea of the story (RL.1.3)

Note what you learn about Owl's life (RL.1.1, RL.1.2, RL.1.3)

Explore what this strange idea reveals about Owl's character (RL.1.2, SL.1.1, SL.1.2)

Lesson II: "Strange Bumps"

Follow the plot of the "Strange Bumps" (RL.1.1, RL.1.2, RL.1.3, SL.1.1)

Probe the mystery of the "Strange Bumps" along with Owl (RL.1.2, SL.1.1, SL.1.2)

Examine the use of illustrations to depict Owl's fear (RL.1.7)

Note the humor in the story

Lesson IV: "Upstairs and Downstairs"

Follow the plot of "Upstairs and Downstairs" (RL.1.1, RL.1.2, RL.1.3)

Identify Owl's problem (RL.1.2)

Probe Owl's attempt to solve his problem (RL.1.2, SL.1.1, SL.1.2)

Examine the image of Owl at the end of the story (p. 48) (RL.1.7)

Lesson V: "Owl and the Moon"

Follow the plot of "Owl and the Moon" (RL.1.1, RL.1.2, RL.1.3)

Explore Owl's view of friendship (RL.1.2, SL.1.1, SL.1.2)

Ponder the reasons for Owl's sadness (RL.1.2. SL.1.1, SL.1.2)

Identify the purpose of the final illustration of the story (p. 64) (RL.1.7)

Lesson VI: Assessing Owl's Adventures

Revisit Owl's stories (RL.1.1, RL.1.2, SL.1.1)

Select a favorite story

Identify the reason for choosing the story (RL.1.2, RL.1.3)

Articulate a position in support of that choice (W.1.1, W.1.2, W.1.3)

Lesson VI: Assessing Owl's Adventures

Objectives

Revisit Owl's stories (RL.1.1, RL.1.2, SL.1.1)

Select a favorite story

Identify the reason for choosing the story (RL.1.2, RL.1.3)

Articulate a position in support of that choice (W.1.1, W.1.2, W.1.3)

Required Materials

☐ *Owl at Home*, by Arnold Lobel

☐ Notebooks

☐ Pencils

Procedures

1. Lead-In:
A brief teacher-led discussion revisits Owl's stories.

2. Step by Step:
   a. Students select a favorite story.
   b. With teacher assistance, students write paragraphs about the story. Students' paragraphs include:
      • A sentence that identifies the story and the name of the author,
      • A sentence that offers a point of view about the story, and
      • A sentence (or more depending on the student's individual ability) that supports the student's opinion.

3. Closure:
Student volunteers, taking turns, read their paragraphs aloud.

Differentiation

Advanced

- After students complete the best paragraph they can, give them the opportunity to revise and edit with a partner.
- Students may want to type their paragraphs and illustrate their favorite stories.

Struggling

- Prepare a "fill in the blank" version of the paragraph, giving students a structure for their writing. My favorite story in *Owl at Home* by _____ was "_____." I chose this story because _____. I also enjoyed _____. If time allows, have the students copy the paragraph onto a piece of lined paper.

Homework/Assessment

Students' paragraphs enable teachers to assess:

- Students' basic comprehension of the stories in *Owl at Home*
- Students' ability to take a position
- Students' ability to support their position

Grade 1 ▶ *Unit 5*

American Contributions

In this fifth six-week unit of first grade, students meet Americans who shaped our nation's history.

ESSENTIAL QUESTION

? How does learning about remarkable people help us learn about history?

OVERVIEW

Building on the work with fiction and informational texts in previous units, students meet important Americans in informational books and then hear fictional stories about the same people. Focusing on reading independently and fluently, students read nonfiction to learn about the contributions made by important Americans. By placing events of a similar time period on a timeline, students are able to visualize the connections among events and people. Students write and revise an opinion piece. The unit also focuses on vocabulary in context as students learn to read and reread for meaning.

FOCUS STANDARDS

These Focus Standards have been selected for the unit from the Common Core State Standards.

RI.1.3: Describe the connection between two individuals, events, ideas, or pieces of information in a text.

RI.1.10: With prompting and support, read informational texts appropriately complex for Grade One.

RF1.4: Read with sufficient accuracy and fluency to support comprehension.

RF.1.4(c): Use context to confirm or self-correct word recognition and understanding, rereading as necessary.

W1.1: Write opinion pieces in which [students] introduce the topic or name the book they are writing about, state an opinion, supply a reason for the opinion, and provide some sense of closure.

SL.1.3: Ask and answer questions about what a speaker says in order to gather additional information or clarify something that is not understood.

SUGGESTED STUDENT OBJECTIVES

- Read nonfiction independently, proficiently, and fluently.
- See and describe the connection between two key events or ideas within a text and between two texts.
- Use context to confirm or self-correct word recognition.
- Reread when necessary.
- Write an opinion about an interesting person studied in this unit, supporting their choices with reasons.
- Revise opinion writing.

SUGGESTED WORKS

(E) indicates a CCSS exemplar text; (EA) indicates a text from a writer with other works identified as exemplars.

LITERARY TEXTS

Stories (Read Aloud)

- *Little House in the Big Woods* (Laura Ingalls Wilder and Garth Williams) (E)
- *The Hatmaker's Sign: A Story by Benjamin Franklin* (Candace Fleming and Robert Parker)
- *Willie Was Different: A Children's Story* (Norman Rockwell)
- *Rockwell: A Boy and His Dog* (Loren Spiotta-DiMare and Cliff Miller)
- *A True Story About Jackie Robinson (Testing the Ice)* (Sharon Robinson and Kadir Nelson)
- *George Washington and the General's Dog* (Frank Murphy and Richard Walz)
- *A. Lincoln and Me* (Louise Borden and Ted Lewin)
- *Mr. Lincoln's Whiskers* (Karen Winnick)
- *Abe Lincoln Crosses a Creek: A Tall, Thin Tale* (Deborah Hopkinson and John Hendrix)

Poems (Read Aloud)

- "Hope" in *The Collected Poetry of Langston Hughes* (Langston Hughes) (EA)
- "Washington" in *The Random House Book of Poetry for Children* (Nancy Byrd Turner)
- "You're a Grand Old Flag" (George M. Cohan and Norman Rockwell)

INFORMATIONAL TEXTS

Informational Books

- *The Man Who Walked Between the Towers* (Mordicai Gerstein)
- *George Washington* (Rookie Biographies) (Wil Mara)
- *Let's Read About … George Washington* (Scholastic First Biographies) (Kimberly Weinberger and Bob Doucet)
- *Abraham Lincoln* (Rookie Biographies) (Wil Mara)
- *Let's Read About—Abraham Lincoln* (Scholastic First Biographies) (Sonia Black and Carol Heyer)
- *Laura Ingalls Wilder* (Rookie Biographies) (Wil Mara)

- *Paul Revere* (Rookie Biographies) (Wil Mara)
- *Let's Read About … Cesar Chavez* (Jerry Tello)
- *Benjamin Franklin* (Rookie Biographies) (Wil Mara)
- *Pocahontas* (DK Readers) (Caryn Jenner)
- *Jackie Robinson* (Rookie Biographies) (Wil Mara)

Informational Books (Read Aloud)

- *Dave the Potter: Artist, Poet, Slave* (Laban Carrick Hill and Bryan Collier) (EA)
- *John, Paul, George, and Ben* (Lane Smith)
- *A Picture Book of Paul Revere* (David A. Adler, John Wallner, and Alexandra Wallner)
- *A Picture Book of Benjamin Franklin* (David A. Adler, John Wallner, and Alexandra Wallner)
- *A Picture Book of George Washington* (David A. Adler, John Wallner, and Alexandra Wallner)
- *Betsy Ross: The Story of Our Flag* (Easy Reader Biographies) (Pamela Chanko)

ART, MUSIC, AND MEDIA

Art

- John Singleton Copley, *Paul Revere* (1768)
- Gilbert Stuart, *Dolley Madison* (1804)
- *Portrait of Harriet Tubman* (artist and date unknown)
- Gilbert Stuart, *George Washington* (1796)
- George P.A. Healey, *Abraham Lincoln* (1869)
- *Dr. Martin Luther King Jr. at The Lincoln Memorial* (artist unknown, 1963)
- Ben Wittick, *Geronimo (Goyathlay), a Chiricahua Apache; full-length, kneeling with rifle* (1887)

Songs

- "Yankee Doodle Boy" (George M. Cohan)
- "You're a Grand Old Flag" (George M. Cohan)

SAMPLE ACTIVITIES AND ASSESSMENTS

1. READING/INFORMATIONAL TEXT

To help students make visual connections between events and people during early American history, create a simple timeline and record events as you read books on this topic together or as students report back on what they read independently. Students should understand that although these informational texts focus on different people or topics, it all happened at the same time in history. By extending the timeline to include historical figures, students begin to understand chronology and the connections between events in informational texts. (RI.1.3, RI.1.10)

2. READING/INFORMATIONAL TEXT/FLUENCY

Have students choose one of the biographies they enjoyed reading. Have them practice reading the book until they can read it well (i.e., with phrasing and expression). As students read their biographies independently, look for opportunities to use context to confirm or self-correct word recognition and understanding, encouraging the children to reread as necessary. Take the books to a kindergarten class and have students read the books aloud to students there. (RF.1.4a, RI.1.4, RI.1.10)

3. OPINION WRITING

Give students this prompt: "Choose one of the people from this unit that you think is the most interesting. Write about the person. Be sure to name the person and to give two or three reasons why you think he or she is the most interesting." (W1.1)

4. READING/WORD ACTIVITY

Display the lyrics to each of the songs on an overhead projector or interactive whiteboard. After singing the songs together several times, allow the students to choose words that are interesting to them and circle them. Help students look for clues in the text to determine word meanings. Check for the correct definitions in a dictionary. Collect these and other words to add to the word bank from reading throughout the unit. Continue reviewing the songs until the lyrics are well known or memorized. (RF.1.4c)

5. WRITING/LANGUAGE

Give students this prompt: "Write three sentences about an American person we've read about recently, using at least three new words from our word bank in your work. Illustrate each sentence to demonstrate the meaning of each word." Do a mini-lesson on articles (*a, the*) and demonstrative pronouns (*this, that, these, those*) as the students write their sentences. (L.1.1h, L.1.1j, L.1.2a, L.1.2b, L.1.2d, L.1.2e, L.1.5c, L.1.6)

6. READING/LITERARY/WRITING/REVISION

Read and discuss *The Hatmaker's Sign* (Candace Fleming and Robert Parker). Talk about how it relates to revision. Instruct students to take a piece of their writing (such as the "most interesting" piece) and carefully work on revising ideas. Students should edit their pieces and publish them. (W1.5, RL.1.2)

7. READING/LITERARY/INFORMATIONAL TEXT

Create pairings of books that are literary and informational (e.g., *George Washington and the General's Dog* and *The Rookie Biography of George Washington*). Discuss how reading a story about a character/historic person differs from reading a biography of the same person. Talk about how these two books connect to each other. For example, ask questions like, "How were the books the same?" and "How were they different?" In this unit are numerous potential book pairings among the biographies, fictional stories, and even a fictional story written by the historical person himself (Benjamin Franklin). Pairing the readings presents an opportunity to highlight the different characteristics of each genre. (RI.1.3, RL.1.5, RL.1.7)

8. GUEST SPEAKER/LISTENING/QUESTIONING

Invite a person from your community who has made a notable contribution to visit your classroom. After the speaker has shared his or her story, invite the students to ask questions to gather additional information or to clarify understanding. Write thank-you notes to guest speakers, telling the speaker one new thing learned during the presentation. (SL.1.3, W.1.8)

9. ART/LANGUAGE CONNECTION

Select several works to view—for instance, you might choose to compare the Copley with the Stuart. Ask the students to turn to the person next to them and discuss such questions as: Who is this subject? How did the artist choose to depict/portray this famous American? Just by looking, search the paintings or photographs for important clues to discover who this person really is. (SL.1.1, SL.1.3, SL.1.4, SL.1.6)

10. ART/CLASS DISCUSSION

Show students Stuart's portrait of Washington, the Martin Luther King Jr. photograph, and the photograph of Geronimo. Ask students to focus on the setting that surrounds each of the subjects. In the case of Washington, how did the painter place his subject in order to convey his importance? What does the painter add to the scene? How does this differ from the Martin Luther King Jr. photograph, where the photographer had to instantly capture the setting? Can you see a merging of these two qualities in the image of Geronimo? (SL.1.1, SL.1.3, SL.1.4, SL.1.6)

READING FOUNDATIONS: A PACING GUIDE FOR READING INSTRUCTION

See Grade One, Level Five, in the Reading Foundations section for a complete pacing guide for this unit.

ADDITIONAL RESOURCES

- *Collaborative Stories 2: Revising* (ReadWriteThink) (W1.5) *Note:* Although this is a revision lesson based on a narrative, the technique would work for revising an opinion piece as well.
- *Bio-Cube* (ReadWriteThink) (RI.1.3)

TERMINOLOGY

Biography	Expression	Support	Words in context
Compare	Opinion	Timeline	
Contrast	Reread	Word bank	

MAKING INTERDISCIPLINARY CONNECTIONS

This unit teaches:

Art: portraiture, Gilbert Stuart
Music: George Cohan
Geography: United States (e.g., thirteen colonies, fifty states, territories)
History: Important Americans (e.g., George Washington, Benjamin Franklin, Harriet Tubman, Geronimo)

This unit could be extended to teach:

Geography: Appalachian Mountains, Rocky Mountains, Mississippi River
History: American Revolution (e.g., Boston Tea Party, Paul Revere's Ride)

Grade One, Unit Five Sample Lesson Plan

Little House in the Big Woods by Laura Ingalls Wilder

In this series of eleven lessons, students read *Little House in the Big Woods* by Laura Ingalls Wilder, and they:

Explore the life of Laura and her family (RL.1.3)

Consider scenes to illustrate (RL.1.2)

Recall details of the scenes (RL.1.1, SL.1.2)

Write appropriate captions for the illustrations (SL.1.4, SL.1.5, L.1.1, L.1.2)

Revisit *Little House in the Big Woods* (SL.1.2)

Explore the life of Laura Ingalls Wilder (RI.1.10, RF.1.4)

Summary

Lesson I: *Little House in the Big Woods*

Locate Wisconsin on a United States map (RI.1.5, RL.1.5)

Meet the family members who live in the "little gray house" (RL.1.3)

Note the author's name

Recall details from Ch. I (RL.1.1, SL.1.2)

Explore the family's activities (RL.1.3)

Consider scenes to illustrate (RL.1.2)

identify details in assigned scene (RL.1.1, SL.1.2)

Illustrate scene (RL.1.7, SL.1.2)

Write appropriate caption for the scene (SL.1.4, SL.1.5, L.1.1, L.1.2)

Lesson II/III: Ch. I–Ch. IV

Reflect upon activities from Lesson I

Proceed to scenes in Ch. II–Ch. IV (RL.1.3)

Examine the "sub stories" in Ch. II and Ch. III (RL.1.2)

Imagine the family "making pictures" in the snow (RL.1.4)

Explore "Prince's" story (SL.1.2)

Consider scenes to illustrate (RL.1.2)

identify details in assigned scene (RL.1.1, SL.1.2)

Illustrate scene (RL.1.7, SL.1.2)

Write appropriate caption for the scene (SL.1.4, SL.1.5, L.1.1, L.1.2)

Lesson IV/V: Ch. V–Ch. VII

Explore the lesson of the story about Grandpa (Ch. V) (RL.1.2)

Probe father's wisdom (RL.1.3)

Examine Ma's courage (Ch. VI) (RL.1.3)

Visualize Grandpa making sugar (RL.1.4)

Consider the mood of the changing seasons (RL.1.4)

Consider scenes to illustrate (RL.1.2)

Identify details in assigned scene (RL.1.1)

Illustrate scene (RL.1.7, SL.1.2)

Write appropriate caption for the scene (SL.1.4, SL.1.5, L.1.1, L.1.2)

Lesson VIII/IX: Ch. XI–Ch. XIII

Investigate the harvest season (SL.1.2)

Explore the purpose of storing food (SL.1.2)

Note the customs of autumn (SL.1.2)

Probe why Pa did not kill the deer (RL.1.3)

Consider scenes to illustrate (RL.1.2)

Identify details in assigned scene (RL.1.1, SL.1.2)

Illustrate scene (RL.1.7)

Write appropriate caption for the scene (SL.1.4, SL.1.5, L.1.1, L.1.2)

Lesson XI: The Life of Laura Ingalls Wilder

[after reading *Laura Ingalls Wilder: Author of Little House Books* (Rookie Biographies)]

Identify biography as a genre

Explore the life of Laura Ingalls Wilder (RI.1.10, RF.1.4)

Probe the similarities between *Little House* and the biography (RI.1.3)

Lesson VI/VII: Ch. VIII–Ch. X

Explore the setting of the opening scene of Ch. VIII

Imagine the smells in Grandma's kitchen (RL.1.4)

Visualize the family dancing (RL.1.3, RL.1.4)

Explore the changing seasons (RL.1.4)

Consider scenes to illustrate (RL.1.2)

Identify details in assigned scene (RL.1.1, SL.1.2)

Illustrate scene (RL.1.7)

Write appropriate caption for the scene (SL.1.4, SL.1.5, L.1.1, L.1.2)

Lesson X: Little House Revisited

Display the illustrations

Revisit *Little House in the Big Woods* (SL.1.2)

Explore new impressions (SL.1.2)

Lesson I: *Little House in the Big Woods*

Objectives

Locate Wisconsin on a United States map (Rl.1.5, RL.1.5)

Meet the family members who live in the "little gray house" (RL.1.3)

Note the author's name

Recall details from Ch. I (RL.1.1, SL.1.2)

Explore the family's activities (RL.1.3)

Consider scenes to illustrate (RL.1.2)

Identify details in assigned scene (RL.1.1, SL.1.2)

Illustrate scene (RL.1.7, SL.1.2)

Write appropriate caption for the scene (SL.1.4, SL.1.5, L.1.1, L.1.2)

Required Materials

☐ Class set of *Little House in the Big Woods*, by Laura Ingalls Wilder

☐ Markers/colored pencils

☐ Pencils

☐ Drawing paper

Procedures

1. Lead-In:
   With teacher assistance, students locate Wisconsin on a United States map.

2. Step by Step:
   a. Introduce the students to the novel, *Little House in the Big Woods*, by Laura Ingalls Wilder.
   b. Students may read along as the teacher reads Chapter I, "Little House in the Big Woods."
   c. A class discussion follows the reading. The students list the characters they meet in Chapter I. They note the family's activities. They note the setting of the story.
   d. The discussion turns to specific scenes. In small groups, the students explore assigned scenes. They recall details of the scenes and identify moments to illustrate.
   e. Students draw details of the scenes.
   f. With teacher assistance, they write captions under their illustrations.

3. Closure:
   Back in a large group, reflect upon the activities of the lesson with the students.

Differentiation

Advanced

- Students reread the book independently during independent reading time or at home.
- Students take the idea of naming the characters more seriously by also looking for clues as to what each character's personality is like. Assign students a character and look for clues as you read aloud. At the end of each chapter, students report on their assigned character. These inferred character qualities will be used to predict character actions as subsequent chapters are read.

Struggling

- Students draw their first illustration together, paying close attention to vocabulary in the story that might need explanation.
- Students label each object and character drawn.
- Guide the class through drawing the setting and characters to solidify these ideas in the students' minds.

Homework/Assessment

N/A

Around the World with a Glass Slipper

In this sixth six-week unit of first grade, students compare and contrast multiple versions of Cinderella while learning about continents and cultures.

ESSENTIAL QUESTION

? What can versions of the same story teach us about different cultures?

OVERVIEW

In the previous unit, students were introduced to writing opinion pieces in the context of studying American contributions. In this unit, students look beyond America, but continue to focus on opinion writing. Students choose a favorite version of a fairy tale, such as *Cinderella*, and write about their choices, supporting their opinions with reasons. They continue to focus on similarities and differences in fiction and nonfiction texts. As the unit closes, the students examine artistic masks from various countries and cultures and use descriptive words to describe the masks.

FOCUS STANDARDS

These Focus Standards have been selected for the unit from the Common Core State Standards.

RL.1.9: Compare and contrast the adventures and experiences of characters in stories.

RI.1.9: Identify basic similarities in and differences between two texts on the same topic (e.g., in illustrations, descriptions, or procedures).

W.1.1: Write opinion pieces in which they introduce the topic or name the book they are writing about, state an opinion, supply a reason for the opinion, and provide some sense of closure.

W.1.6: With guidance and support from adults, use a variety of digital tools to produce and publish writing, including in collaboration with peers.

L.1.5: With guidance and support from adults, demonstrate understanding of word relationships and nuances in word meanings.

L.1.5(d): Distinguish shades of meanings among verbs differing in manner (e.g., *look, peek, glance, stare, glare,* [and] *scowl*) and adjectives differing in intensity (e.g., *large, gigantic*) by defining or choosing them, or by acting out the meanings.

SL.1.5: Add drawings or other visual displays to descriptions when appropriate to clarify ideas, thoughts, and feelings.

SUGGESTED STUDENT OBJECTIVES

- Compare and contrast multiple versions of a story (e.g., *Cinderella*) by different authors and from different cultures.
- Identify the similarities and differences between two texts on the same topic.
- Write opinions about a favorite version of a story.
- Read nonfiction texts independently with a sense of purpose (e.g., to know about the continents and cultures discussed in a fairy tale version).
- Illustrate an adaptation of a scene from a story and present it to the class in a slide.
- Use vivid words to describe an object.

SUGGESTED WORKS

(E) indicates a CCSS exemplar text; (EA) indicates a text from a writer with other works identified as exemplars.

LITERARY TEXTS

Stories (Read Aloud)

- *Cinderella* (Charles Perrault, Loek Koopmans, and Anthea Bell)
- *Cinderella* (Marcia Brown)
- *The Korean Cinderella* (Shirley Climo and Ruth Heller)
- *The Way Meat Loves Salt: A Cinderella Tale from the Jewish Tradition* (Nina Jaffe and Louise August)
- *Yeh-Shen: A Cinderella Story from China* (Ai-Ling Louie and Ed Young) (EA)
- *The Egyptian Cinderella* (Shirley Climo and Ruth Heller)
- *Little Gold Star: A Spanish American Cinderella Tale* (Robert D. San Souci and Sergio Martinez)
- *Fair, Brown, and Trembling: An Irish Cinderella Story* (Jude Daly)
- *The Turkey Girl: A Zuni Cinderella Story* (Penny Pollock and Ed Young) (EA)
- *Cinderella Penguin, or, the Little Glass Flipper* (Janet Perlman and John Peterson)
- *Mufaro's Beautiful Daughters* (John Steptoe)
- *Prince Cinders* (Babette Cole)
- *James Marshall's Cinderella* (Barbara Karlin and James Marshall)
- *Cinderquacker* (Mike Thaler and Dave Clegg)

Poem

- "Star Light, Star Bright" (Traditional)

INFORMATIONAL TEXTS

Informational Books

- *North America* (Pull Ahead Books Continents) (Madeline Donaldson)
- *South America* (Pull Ahead Books Continents) (Madeline Donaldson)
- *Europe* (Pull Ahead Books Continents) (Madeline Donaldson)
- *Asia* (Pull Ahead Books Continents) (Madeline Donaldson)

- *Australia* (Pull Ahead Books Continents) (Madeline Donaldson)
- *Antarctica* (Pull Ahead Books Continents) (Madeline Donaldson)
- *Africa* (Pull Ahead Books Continents) (Madeline Donaldson)

Informational Books (Read Aloud)

- *Look What Came from China* (Miles Harvey)
- *Look What Came from Australia* (Kevin Davis)
- *Look What Came from Egypt* (Miles Harvey)
- *Ancient Egypt: A First Look at People of the Nile* (Bruce Strachan)
- *Look What Came from Africa* (Miles Harvey)
- *DK First Atlas* (Anita Ganeri and Chris Oxlade)

ART, MUSIC, AND MEDIA

Art

- North America: shaman's mask (Inuit/Eskimo, Alaska, circa early twentieth century)
- South America: Devil Dance mask (Aymara, Bolivia, circa 1974)
- Europe: Captain Scaramouche (Venice, Italy, date unknown)
- Asia: puppet mask (Japan, circa early twentieth century)
- Africa: mask (Dan, Ivory Coast, circa early twentieth century)
- Australia: display mask (East Sepik, Papua New Guinea, circa 1980)

SAMPLE ACTIVITIES AND ASSESSMENTS

1. READING/LITERARY

As you begin the set of Cinderella stories, create a wall chart to organize the similarities and differences among the versions. Use categories that review the literary terms of this school year, such as: *characters, setting, beginning, events* (middle), and *ending.* (RL.1.1, RL.1.2, RL.1.9)

2. READING/OPINION WRITING

Read many different versions of *Cinderella*. Then, give students this prompt: "Choose your favorite version of the Cinderella story. Tell at least two reasons why you liked this version the most." Students should include the title of the book, at least two reasons why they thought it was their favorite, and a strong ending. Revision should focus on word choice, elaboration, or word order as they rewrite the paragraph. (W.1.1, L.1.1j, L.1.2a,b, L.1.2d, L.1.2e, RL.1.9)

3. READING/LITERARY/MULTIMEDIA PRESENTATION

Ask the students to think about how all of the Cinderella stories are different because of the time and place in which they happen. Challenge the students to draw the "trying on the slipper" scene as if it were happening right now and in the place where they live. Scan the pictures and create a slide for each image. Students present their drawings to the class, explaining their adaptation of the "slipper scene." (SL.1.5, SL.1.6, RL.1.9)

4. READING/INFORMATIONAL TEXT/LITERARY

Have students read one of the nonfiction books about a continent or country. After the students finish, have them find and review a fairy tale that is set in a similar place or culture. Discuss what students saw in both books (e.g., geography, people, clothing, food, places, and customs). Discuss how the books are different (e.g., one tells a story; the other gives factual information). (RL.1.5, RL.1.7, RI.1.9)

5. READING/INFORMATIONAL TEXT

Choose two books about the same continent such as *Australia* (Pull Ahead Books Continents, Madeleine Donaldson) and *Look What Came from Australia* (Kevin Davis). Discuss how the books are similar (because they are about the same continent). Determine how they are also different (because they are written by different authors and have different purposes). Then, read the books as a class. Make a chart with two columns, one for each book (e.g., *Australia* and *Look What Came from Australia*). Work together to make a list of what is learned in each book and then look for similar information in both books. Challenge the students to do this activity with two books, reading with a partner or reading one independently and having the teacher read the other aloud. (RF.1.4, RI.1.2, RI.1.3, RI.1.9, RI.1.10)

6. READING/INFORMATIONAL TEXT/PRESENTATION

Partner students to research the contributions/inventions of a country introduced to them in this unit. Tell them to work together to gather information from several different sources. Building knowledge of the contributions of various countries that is gleaned from informational texts (e.g., the *Look What Came from . . .* series), have students gather actual items that represent the contributions (e.g., for China, writing paper, a compass, and paper money). Ask them to communicate findings by creating a museum of contributions by having the students design information cards to go with each item. Students could stand behind their table to explain the origins of the items as visitors come through the museum. (SL.1.5, RI.1.2, RI.1.5, RI.1.9, RI.1.10, W.1.7, W.1.8, L.1.2)

7. ART/LANGUAGE

Discuss how countries and continents, as depicted in the literature in this unit, are very different. Introduce masks from different continents. As they view each mask, ask the students to think of describing words (i.e., adjectives) you would use to tell someone about the mask. Ask such questions as: What materials do you think are used? Why do you believe each culture chooses specific colors or textures in their works of art? Can you guess how each object was used? (L.1.5d, SL.1.4)

READING FOUNDATIONS: A PACING GUIDE FOR READING INSTRUCTION

See Grade One, Level Six, in the Reading Foundations section for a complete pacing guide for this unit.

ADDITIONAL RESOURCES

- *Cinderella* (Ministry of Education, New Zealand) (RL.1.9)
- *Fairy Tales Around the World* (National Endowment for the Humanities) (RL.1.2)
- *The Meaning Behind the Mask* (National Endowment for the Humanities) (RL.1.2, RL.1.6)

TERMINOLOGY

Act out	Dialogue	Scene
Compare	Fairy tales	Setting
Contrast	Fantasy	
Culture	"Once upon a time . . ."	

MAKING INTERDISCIPLINARY CONNECTIONS

This unit teaches:

Science: The earth's surface (e.g., the seven continents, the four oceans, the two poles)
Art: Masks
Geography: Working with maps and globes (e.g., the seven continents)

This unit could be extended to teach:

History: Ancient Egypt (e.g., Africa, Nile, the Pharaohs, pyramids, mummies, and hieroglyphics)
Science: Inside the earth (e.g., layers, volcanoes, and rocks)
Geography: Working with maps and globes (e.g., North American countries, the Equator, and cardinal directions)

Grade One, Unit Six Sample Lesson Plan

Yeh-Shen: A Cinderella Story from China Retold by Ai-Ling Louie

In this series of two lessons, students reread *Yeh-Shen: A Cinderella Story from China* retold by Ai-Ling Louie, and they:

- Appreciate the history of the tale of Cinderella (RI.1. 1, RI.1.2, SL.1.1.1, SL.1.1.2)
- Retell the story of Yeh-Shen (RL.1.2, RL.1.3, SL.1.1, SL.1.2)
- Discuss the reasons for choosing Yeh-Shen (SL.1.1, SL.1.2)

Summary

Lesson I: Revisiting the Story of Yeh-Shen	Lesson II: Expressing Ideas
Locate China on a world map	Revisit previous lesson's talk (RL.1.2)
Investigate the historical background of the tale (RI.1. 1, RI.1.2, SL.1.1, SL.1.2)	(Individually) reflect on the choice of Yeh-Shen (W.1.1, W.1.5, W.1.6)
Revisit the tale of Yeh-Shen (RL.1.2, RL.1.3, SL.1.1, SL.1.2)	Illustrate written passages (SL.1.5)
Explore their choice to revisit Yeh-Shen (RL.1.9, SL.1.1, SL.1.2)	Display and share written reflections (SL.1.1)

Lesson I: Revisiting the Story of Yeh-Shen

Objectives

- Locate China on a world map
- Investigate the historical background of the tale (RI.1. 1, RI.1.2, SL.1.1, SL.1.2)
- Revisit the tale of Yeh-Shen (RL.1.2, RL.1.3, SL.1.1, SL.1.2)
- Explore their choice to revisit Yeh-Shen (RL.1.9, SL.1.1, SL.1.2)

Required Materials

- ☐ Class set of atlases
- ☐ Multiple copies of *Yeh-Shen: A Cinderella Story from China*, retold by Ai-Ling Louie

Procedures

1. Lead-In:
   Teachers introduce the students to the class activity.

2. Step by Step:
   a. In a group (where all the students are revisiting Yeh-Shen), students locate China in an atlas or world map. They also point to the rest of Asia and the Pacific Ocean. They then locate the United States and note the distance between the two countries.
   b. With teacher assistance, students investigate the historical origins of the tale. (A brief introduction, containing historical information, is included in the Puffin Books edition of the book.)
   c. In their group, the students retell Yeh-Shen's story.
   d. In their group, the students discuss why, of all the tales, this one might be their favorite.

3. Closure:
   Remind the students that the following day (Lesson II), they will write about the tale of their choice.

Differentiation

Advanced

- After students have finished the discussion described in this lesson, introduce the book *Beyond the Great Mountains* by Ed Young. Ask students to explore the illustrations of both books by Ed Young. Ask students to use the poem and illustrations of both books to discuss the beauty of China, as seen through the eyes of Ed Young.

Struggling

- Mix the groups so that students model good reasons for the selection of a story. Assign one of the confident writers to write the reasons on sentence strips as they are discussed. Allow students to review these reasons during Lesson II, when they write about the tale of their choice. (Even if they choose a different tale, these reasons will serve as a model of statements of support.)

Homework/Assessment
N/A

The unit Around the World with a Glass Slipper offers students an opportunity to choose a favorite version of the famous fairy tale. This mini-map focuses on the Chinese version of the tale. The mini-map assumes that the students have already read several versions of "Cinderella."

GRADE 2

In second grade, students become independent readers and writers, able to conduct research, write reports, and compare and contrast characters from stories. Now the "read-aloud" works are combined with books that students read for themselves, as they learn about seasons, the Wild West, the African American journey to freedom, and more. In the unit Building Bridges with Unlikely Friends, students learn about bridges—both real and imagined. Later, in Hand-Me-Down Tales from Around the World, students listen to Prokofiev's *Peter and the Wolf* as they consider why tales are passed from one generation to the next. Students learn about the physical world as well; in the final unit they read about the human body and health. The variety of topics exposes students to rich literature while building their background knowledge of a range of subjects and topics. Students use graphic organizers to clarify their ideas and plan their writing. Their writing includes reports, literary responses, opinion pieces, stories, letters, and explanations. Throughout the year, students build grammatical knowledge and practice reading and speaking with fluency and expression. They engage in discussions about literature and make use of online resources. By the end of second grade, students should be able to read simple storybooks fluently and write in print and cursive. They should be familiar with a repertoire of myths, stories, poems, and nonfiction narratives.

Standards Checklist for Grade Two

Standard	Unit 1	Unit 2	Unit 3	Unit 4	Unit 5	Unit 6
Reading—Literature						
1	A					
2		FA			FA	A
3			FA	A		
4	FA			A	A	FA
5	FA				A	
6		A	F	FA	A	
7			FA		A	
8 n/a						
9		FA			A	
10					A	FA
Reading—Informational Text						
1		A				
2	FA					
3			A	FA	A	
4		A				A
5	A	A			A	
6		FA	FA		A	
7		A			FA	A
8						FA
9				FA		
10		A			A	FA
Writing						
1				FA	A	FA
2	A	FA	FA			A
3		A		FA	FA	
4 n/a						
5		A	A			
6	A		A	FA		
7	FA	A			A	
8	A	A				
9 n/a						
10 n/a						
Speaking and Listening						
1	FA	A	A			A
1a	A					A
1b	A					A
1c	A					A
2	FA	A		A	A	A
3		A		A	FA	
4		A	A		FA	
5		A	A	A	A	F
6		A	A			A
Language						
1	A					
1a						
1b		A			A	
1c						A
1d				A		

Standard	Unit 1	Unit 2	Unit 3	Unit 4	Unit 5	Unit 6
1e	A					
1f	A					
2	A	A	F			
2a	A				A	
2b	A		FA			
2c	A					
2d	A					
2e	A					A
3	A	A				
3a	A	A		A		
4		A	F			
4a		A			A	
4b		A		A		
4c		A		A		
4d		A	FA			
4e		A	A			
5						
5a						A
5b	A			A	A	
6				A		
Reading Foundations (addressed in units)						
1 n/a						
2 n/a						
3						
3a						
3b						
3c						
3d						
3e						
3f						
4	A	A				
4a						
4b						
4c						
Reading Foundations (addressed in *Reading Foundations: A Pacing Guide*)						
1 n/a						
2 n/a						
3		A	A	A	A	A
3a	A	A	A	A	A	A
3b		A	A	A	A	A
3c	A	A	A	A	A	A
3d	A	A	A	A	A	A
3e	A	A	A	A	A	A
3f	A	A	A	A	A	A
4	A	A	A	A	A	A
4a	A	A	A	A	A	A
4b	A	A	A	A	A	A
4c	A	A	A	A	A	A

F = Focus Standards; A = Activity/Assessment

A Season for Chapters

In this first six-week unit of second grade, students focus on the beauty of language—in chapter books, informational texts, and poetry—all related to the four seasons.

OVERVIEW

Focusing on the beauty of language in poetry and fiction, students learn poetry terms and the beginnings and endings of stories. In preparation for writing informational text, students complete a research project on a seasonal activity from a region of the United States unlike their own. Enjoying the beauty of the language of music through Vivaldi's *The Four Seasons*, students use their own beautiful language when writing "seasonal" poetry. Students review the roles of authors and illustrators, and read about specific authors and poets. This unit could become a weather unit or a solar system unit by adding topic-specific titles to the informational texts.

FOCUS STANDARDS

These Focus Standards have been selected for the unit from the Common Core State Standards.

RI.2.2: Identify the main focus of a multi-paragraph text as well as the focus of specific paragraphs within the text.

RL.2.4: Describe how words and phrases (e.g., regular beats, alliteration, rhymes, [and] repeated lines) supply rhythm and meaning in a story, poem, or song.

RL.2.5: Describe the overall structure of a story, including describing how the beginning introduces the story and the ending concludes the action.

SL.2.1: Participate in collaborative conversations with diverse partners about Grade Two topics and texts with peers and adults in small and larger groups.

SL.2.2: Recount or describe key ideas or details from a text read aloud or information presented orally or through other media.

W.2.7: Participate in shared research and writing projects.

ESSENTIAL QUESTION

? When is language beautiful?

SUGGESTED STUDENT OBJECTIVES

- Independently read chapter books according to ability.
- Distinguish between the roles of author and illustrator in chapter books.
- Ask the questions *who, what, where, when, why,* and *how* after reading fictional books.
- Study the beginnings and endings of chapters and stories.
- Use digital resources to research a seasonal activity.
- Use a computer-generated graphic organizer to organize class research.
- Create an informational class book from this shared research.
- Study art pieces to see the artist's techniques in creating a sense of cold or warmth.
- Create a collection of adjectives and adverbs.
- Expand sentences by adding adjectives and adverbs from the class discussion on art.
- Write a paragraph using complete sentences.
- Write poetry based on music (e.g., Vivaldi's *The Four Seasons*).
- Enjoy and analyze poetry related to the seasons, noting alliteration, rhyme, rhythm, and repetition.
- Study the organization of informational text, specifically the purpose of paragraphs.

SUGGESTED WORKS

(E) indicates a CCSS exemplar text; (EA) indicates a text from a writer with other works identified as exemplars.

LITERARY TEXTS

Stories

- *Poppleton in Winter* (Cynthia Rylant and Mark Teague) (E)
- *Poppleton in Spring* (Cynthia Rylant and Mark Teague) (EA)
- *Poppleton in Fall* (Cynthia Rylant and Mark Teague) (EA)
- *Henry and Mudge and the Snowman Plan* (Cynthia Rylant and Sucie Stevenson) (EA)
- *Red Leaf, Yellow Leaf* (Lois Ehlert)
- *Snowballs* (Lois Ehlert)
- *Leaf Man* (Lois Ehlert)
- *Snow* (Uri Shulevitz)
- *The Days of Summer* (Eve Bunting and William Low)
- *Peepers* (Eve Bunting and James Ransome)
- *Every Autumn Comes the Bear* (Jim Arnosky)
- *The Little Yellow Leaf* (Carin Berger)

Story (Read Aloud)

- *The Mitten* (Jan Brett)

Poems

- "Autumn" (Emily Dickinson) (E)
- "Something Told the Wild Geese" (Rachel Field) (E)
- "Who Has Seen The Wind?" (Christina Rossetti) (E)
- "Weather" (Eve Merriam) (E)
- "Knoxville, Tennessee" (Nikki Giovanni) (E)
- "Stopping by Woods on a Snowy Evening" (Robert Frost) (E)
- "Summer Song" (John Ciardi) in *The Seasons* (ed. John N. Serio)

Poems (Read Aloud)

- "Bed in Summer" (Robert Louis Stevenson)
- "A Vagabond Song" (Bliss Carman) in *The Seasons* (ed. John N. Serio)
- "The Snowflake" (Walter de la Mare) in *The Seasons* (ed. John N. Serio)
- "The Locust Tree in Flower" (William Carlos Williams) in *The Seasons* (ed. John N. Serio)

INFORMATIONAL TEXTS

Informational Books

- *Sunshine Makes the Seasons* (Franklyn M. Branley and Michael Rex)
- *Why Do Leaves Change Color?* (Betsy Maestro and Loretta Krupinski)
- *How Do You Know It's Winter?* (Rookie Read-About Science) (Allan Fowler)
- *Look How It Changes!* (Rookie Read-About Science) (June Young)
- *How Do You Know It's Fall?* (Rookie Read-About Science) (Allan Fowler)
- *How Do You Know It's Spring?* (Rookie Read-About Science) (Allan Fowler)
- *Energy from the Sun* (Rookie Read-About Science) (Allan Fowler)
- *How Do You Know It's Summer?* (Rookie Read-About Science) (Allan Fowler)
- *What Do Authors Do?* (Eileen Christelow)
- *What Do Illustrators Do?* (Eileen Christelow)
- *Cynthia Rylant: A Writer's Story* (Alice Cary and Susan Spellman)

INFORMATIONAL BOOKS (READ ALOUD)

- *Snowflake Bentley* (Jacqueline Briggs Martin and Mary Azarian)
- *Snowflakes in Photographs* (W. A. Bentley)
- *A River of Words: The Story of William Carlos Williams* (Jennifer Bryant and Melissa Sweet)

ART, MUSIC, AND MEDIA

Art

- Vincent van Gogh, *Sunflowers* (1889)
- Artist unknown, *Snow-Laden Plum Branches* (1098–1169)
- Louis Comfort Tiffany, *Dogwood* (1900–1915)
- Pieter Bruegel, *Hunters in the Snow* (1565)

- Gustave Caillebotte, *Paris Street, Rainy Day* (1877)
- Georges Seurat, *Une Baignade, Asnieres* (1883–1884)
- Vincent van Gogh, *Mulberry Tree* (1889)
- Maurice de Vlaminck, *Autumn Landscape* (1905)

Music

- Vivaldi, *The Four Seasons* (1723)

SAMPLE ACTIVITIES AND ASSESSMENTS

Note: Your choice of texts for this unit can be made in a few different ways, such as completing a few weeks of fiction and then shifting to poetry, and finally to nonfiction, or the unit could move along by seasons, with all of the winter materials used during two weeks of the unit before moving on to the other seasons in a logical order.

1. CLASS DISCUSSION/LITERATURE

Ask students to pick a favorite book from the easy section of the library. To introduce the characteristics of a good solid beginning and ending of a story, ask the students to read aloud to a partner just the first paragraph or two and then the last paragraph. Later, allow students to share the books in small groups to see what each child notices about these solid beginnings and solid endings. For example, they may notice things such as a clearly described setting with vivid words at the beginning, the book coming full circle, and the ending providing a sense of satisfaction. (RL.2.5)

2. STORY BEGINNINGS AND ENDINGS/LITERATURE

Introduce and read the first chapter of *Poppleton in Winter* by Cynthia Rylant. The following day, look at the chapter again. Explain to the class that Cynthia Rylant is an author who knows exactly how to write the beginning of a story and how to wrap it up with a strong ending. Direct the students to look closely at how the story begins. Reread the section where the story is set up. Students will see the setting, characters, and situation/problem in the first two sentences of the story: "Poppleton's house grew very long icicles in winter. Poppleton was proud of them." Create a bulleted list as the students discuss what they see, finishing the sentence "A strong beginning has . . ." Then turn to the end of the story and discuss the attributes of a strong ending. Read Rylant's final sentences: "Poppleton was glad his icicles were knocked down. Icicles always melted. But a new friend would stay." Continue the bulleted list, having students finish the sentence "A strong ending has . . ." As the students read each successive chapter independently, with a partner, or with the teacher, make these charts a focus of discussion. Eventually add a chart for the action in the middle of the story. (RL.2.5, RF.2.4)

3. ASKING AND ANSWERING QUESTIONS/LITERATURE

After reading the fictional read-aloud picture books for each of the seasons, have students ask and answer questions using *who, what, where, when, why,* and *how.* Challenge students to create questions from these stems that apply directly to the books you are reading. Encourage students to answer the questions on sticky notes under each question on the following chart. (RL.2.1)

Who?	What?	Where?	When?	Why?	How?

4. FEATURES OF INFORMATIONAL TEXT/RECOGNIZING AND WRITING PARAGRAPHS

This unit contains a wide variety of informational texts. To introduce the work of organizing informational text, choose a book with a variety of text features and strong paragraphs. Explain to the children that as you read for information, you will also be looking at the author's craft. Guide students to look closely at the way each informational book on the four seasons is arranged (e.g., through the use of headings, subheadings, and paragraphs). Choose one page to look for the purpose of paragraphs in organizing the information in the text. You might want to make a copy of the page for the students to examine as you demonstrate the topical chunks of information in paragraphs. Extend this lesson by listing text features in multiple books on seasons and related topics. Focus on the purposes of the text features in the books. Follow this reading lesson with having students write a paragraph as a shared write. Choose one topic related to the book read, and write a paragraph with a strong topic sentence, detailed information, and a satisfying conclusion. (RI.2.2, RF.2.4)

5. LANGUAGE ACTIVITY

Use the informational book *How Do You Know It's Fall?* to introduce apostrophes. Discuss the concept of contractions by creating sentences starting with "It is . . ." and then contracting the words to "It's." Continue generating lists of contractions for "he is," "she is," "they are," "we are," and so on. Ask the students to create detailed sentences related to the season of fall using a variety of contractions. Extend the lesson by discussing apostrophes used to show possession. Staying with the fall theme, generate a list of possessives focusing on nature's preparation for winter (e.g., a bear's thick coat, a squirrel's collection of acorns, a tree's slow growth.) (L.2.2c)

6. SHARED RESEARCH/WRITING

Focus a discussion on the characteristics of seasons in your local climate. Discuss activities that your students might associate with each season. Talk about how one of the season's activities might help the local economy more than others by generating research questions such as, "Which season is most important to our community?" Use digital resources and speakers who have visited to gather information. Conclude the research and communicate findings with a class write such as: "Research a sport or activity in your community that relates to a specific season. Create a nonfiction text about the season, the sport, and the way it affects your community." (RI.2.5, SL.2.1, SL.2.2, W.2.2, W.2.8, L.2.3)

7. SHARED RESEARCH/GRAPHIC ORGANIZER/WRITING

Follow the local community research with a new research challenge. This time, organize small groups to research and to write about a community in a contrasting climate and geographical location. Focus on the seasons there, a sport (or activity) that is important, and the way they affect their community. Help students generate the research questions that will guide their work. Ask them to gather information from a variety of online sources and possibly hold a conversation via the Internet with the Chamber of Commerce from the community. Introduce a digital tool for organizing information. Model the organization of gathered information into broad topics through webbing. Use one part of the graphic organizer (web) to demonstrate to the class how to write one well-developed paragraph. Working in small groups, students should use the webbed information to write the remaining paragraphs. When the paragraphs are completed, combine them into books. Students can add illustrations by drawing or by collecting photographs from online sources. (RI.2.2, W.2.2, W.2.6, W.2.7, L.2.2)

8. CLASS DISCUSSION/POETRY

The Seasons (ed. John N. Serio) is a book of collected poems by different poets. Introduce the poem "Summer Song." Ask the students, "What did you notice about the first four lines of the poem?" (*Possible answer:* Repetition of "By the . . .") Note the pattern of rhyme in the first four lines (i.e., ABAB) and how it changes as it progresses through the poem (i.e., AABB). Continue to look at the features of poetry as you read other seasonal poems in this unit. Each of the poems from *The Seasons* exemplifies at least one of the characteristics of the Grade Two standards: rhyme, rhythm, alliteration, and repetition. Encourage students to choose a poem to perform (recite) for the class. (RL.2.4)

9. CLASS DISCUSSION/MUSIC APPRECIATION

Listen to one of the four concertos in Vivaldi's *The Four Seasons*. Instruct the students to write down words or phrases that come to them as they are listening. After they are finished, tell them to work together as a class to compile a list of words and phrases they thought of while listening. Choose a descriptive word or phrase and then challenge them to think in simile or metaphor (e.g., falling leaves—like what? Like jewels falling from the sky). Use the collection of words and phrases to write a class poem titled "Spring," "Summer," "Autumn," or "Winter." Be sure to use rhythm, rhyme, alliteration, and/or repetition in your class poem. (RL2.4, L.2.5b)

10. ART/LANGUAGE

View the Bruegel, Caillebotte, and Seurat images. As the class studies each piece, ask the students how the artist creates a sense of warmth or cold, dryness or wetness in the painting. As the students use adjectives and adverbs in the conversation, write them down under the appropriate category on a whiteboard or chart paper. Use these words to create and expand sentences (e.g., "The artist painted snow. The talented artist painted snow with cool colors. Using an icy blue color, the artist painted a snowy scene."). Extend the activity by using the word bank to create free-form poems to go with each painting. (L.2.1e,f)

11. ART/INFORMATIVE/EXPLANATORY WRITING

Select a work to study—for instance, you might choose the Seurat for a clear depiction of a season. Ask the students to name the season that the artist has painted. Then have students write a two- or three-sentence explanation identifying elements in the work that led them to their observation. (W.2.2)

12. ART/CLASS DISCUSSION

Artists often convey a sense of season in their depictions of flowers or trees. Ask students to study the Tiffany image, van Gogh's *Mulberry Tree*, and the work titled *Snow-Laden Branches*. Note that these works were created on three different continents at around the same time period. Ask students to discuss similarities and differences in these artists' techniques for depicting the seasons. (SL.2.2)

READING FOUNDATIONS: A PACING GUIDE FOR READING INSTRUCTION

See Grade Two, Level One, in the Reading Foundations section for a complete pacing guide for this unit.

ADDITIONAL RESOURCES

- *English Spelling Rules* (Reading from Scratch) (L.2.2d)
- *All Together Now: Collaborations in Poetry Writing* (National Endowment for the Humanities) (L.2.1e,f)
- The Weather Channel

TERMINOLOGY

Alliteration	Ending	Repetition
Author	Illustrator	Research
Beginning	Introduction	Rhyme
Chapter	Main idea	Rhythm
Conclusion	Paragraph	Shared writing
Digital graphic organizer	Poet	Spelling patterns
Digital sources	Poetry	

MAKING INTERDISCIPLINARY CONNECTIONS

This unit teaches:

Art: van Gogh, Seurat, Bruegel, Caillebotte, Tiffany
Music: *The Four Seasons* (Vivaldi)
Geography: U.S. landforms (e.g., mountains, coast, plains, hills, and deserts)
Science: Seasonal cycles

This unit could be extended to teach:

Geography: U.S. geography (e.g., the Mississippi River, mountain ranges such as the Appalachian and Rocky Mountains, and the Great Lakes)
Science: Weather, the water cycle, and/or the solar system

Grade Two, Unit One Sample Lesson Plan

"Autumn" by Emily Dickinson

"Something Told the Wild Geese" by Rachel Field

"Who Has Seen the Wind?" by Christina Rossetti

"Knoxville, Tennessee" by Nikki Giovanni

"Weather" by Eve Merriam

In this series of six lessons, students read "Autumn" by Emily Dickinson, "Something Told the Wild Geese" by Rachel Field, "Who Has Seen the Wind?" by Christina Rossetti, "Knoxville, Tennessee" by Nikki Giovanni, and "Weather" by Eve Merriam, and they:

Explore the various ways that poets describe the changes in weather (RL.2.1, SL.2.1, SL.2.2, SL.2.3)

Identify several poetic devices that poets use (RL.2.4)

Offer personal reflections on the readings through illustrations and brief passages (W.2.1)

Summary

Lesson I: "Autumn" by Emily Dickinson	Lesson II: "Something Told the Wild Geese" by Rachel Field
Observe the form of the poem (RL.2.4)	Observe the form of the poem (RL.2.4)
Note the name of the poet	Note the name of the poet
Conduct first reading of the poem (RL.2.1)	Conduct first reading of the poem (RL.2.1)
Identify new vocabulary words	Identify new vocabulary words
(After a second reading) explore the dominant colors of the poem (RL.2.1, SL.2.1, SL.2.2, SL.2.3)	(After a second reading) examine the pending changes in nature (RL.2.1, SL.2.1, SL.2.2, SL.2.3)
Examine the changes in nature that the speaker depicts (RL.2.1, SL.2.1, SL.2.2, SL.2.3)	Explore what the "something" is, and what it told the wild geese (RL.2.1, SL.2.1, SL.2.2, SL.2.3)
Probe the speaker's decision to "put a trinket on" (RL.2.1, SL.2.3)	Consider why the poem is in the past tense (RL.2.1, SL.2.1, SL.2.2)

Lesson III: "Who Has Seen the Wind?" by Christina Rossetti Observe the form of the poem (RL.2.4) Note the name of the poet Conduct first reading of the poem (RL.2.1) Identify new vocabulary words (After a second reading) note the speaker's repeated question (RL.2.1, RL.2.4, SL.2.3) Explore the purpose of the repetitions (RL.2.4, SL.2.1, SL.2.2) Point to and examine the purpose of the two parts of the poem (RL.2.1, SL.2.1, SL.2.2)	**Lesson IV: "Knoxville, Tennessee" by Nikki Giovanni** Observe the form of the poem (RL.2.4) Note the name of the poet Conduct first reading of the poem (RL.2.1) Identify new vocabulary words (After a second reading) explore the absence of punctuation in the poem and consider the poet's purpose (RL.2.4, SL.2.1, SL.2.2) Examine the speaker's list (RL.2.1, SL.2.3) Explore the objective of the list (RL.2.1, SL.2.1, SL.2.2)
Lesson V: "Weather" by Eve Merriam Observe the form of the poem (RL.2.4) Note the name of the poet Conduct first reading of the poem (RL.2.1) Note the unusual words that the poet uses (RL.2.4) (During a second reading) listen to the sounds of the words the poet uses (RL.2.4) Explore the impact of what the sounds make (RL.2.1, RL.2.4, SL.2.1, SL.2.2, SL.2.3)	**Lesson VI: Revisiting the Seasons Poems** Revisit the poems of Lessons I–V (RL.2.1, RL.2.4, SL.2.1, SL.2.2, SL.2.3) Individually select a favorite poem Illustrate the poem Explain the purpose of the illustrations (W.2.1) Assess results (SL.2.1)

Lesson VI: Revisiting the Seasons Poems

Objectives

Revisit the poems of Lessons I–V (RL.2.1, RL.2.4, SL.2.1, SL.2.2, SL.2.3)

Individually select a favorite poem

Illustrate the poem

Explain the purpose of the illustrations (W.2.1)

Assess results (SL.2.1)

Required Materials

- [ ] "Autumn" by Emily Dickinson,
- [ ] "Something Told the Wild Geese" by Rachel Field
- [ ] "Who Has Seen the Wind?" by Christina Rossetti
- [ ] "Knoxville, Tennessee" by Nikki Giovanni
- [ ] "Weather" by Eve Merriam

Procedures

1. Lead-In:

Student volunteers read the five poems aloud.

2. Step by Step:

a. A class discussion reminds the students of the uniqueness of each of the five poems:
   - The colors in "Autumn"
   - The mystery in "Something Told the Wild Geese"
   - The repeated question in "Who Has Seen the Wind?"
   - The list in "Knoxville, Tennessee"
   - The new words and sounds in "Weather"

b. Students select a favorite poem.

c. Students illustrate the poems. Their illustrations must reflect the readings. For example, students who choose "Autumn" use warm colors of fall.

d. Students write two or three sentences explaining their illustrations.

e. Students, with the teachers' help, hang the illustrated poems.

3. Closure:

Students discuss their work and note the many ways that poets describe the changing seasons.

Differentiation

Advanced

- Students choose one of the poems to use as a craft model for writing their own poem. For example, a student could write a "Winter" poem modeled after "Autumn" using the idea of winter colors. A student could choose to write a mystery poem about another seasonal phenomenon.

Struggling

- Take one of the poems and cut it up. Glue each of the lines on a blank page, making a book out of the poem. Divide the pages to be illustrated among a small group of students. Students illustrate the page after discussing the meaning of their line with other students and/or an adult. Tell students to assemble the pages in order. Encourage students to enjoy reading the picture book they have illustrated.

Homework/Assessment
N/A

Grade 2 ► *Unit 2*

The Wild West

In this second six-week unit of second grade, students read literature set in the Wild West: chapter books, informational texts, songs, tall tales, and fairy tales.

ESSENTIAL QUESTION

? How does setting affect a story?

OVERVIEW

Building on the shared research in the first unit, students research an interesting person from the 1800s in the American Wild West and write an informative/explanatory essay. Students read tall tales and then discuss where the fiction is stretched beyond belief, and why the tale has been told through the years. Students also read their choice of fantasy and chapter books set in different time periods of life in the West. Finally, students will study the art of George Catlin to understand his role in creating historic images of Native Americans.

FOCUS STANDARDS

These Focus Standards have been selected for the unit from the Common Core State Standards.

RL.2.2: Recount stories, including fables and folktales from diverse cultures, and determine their central message, lesson, or moral.

RL.2.9: Compare and contrast two or more versions of the same story by different authors or from different cultures.

RI.2.6: Identify the main purpose of a text, including what the author wants to answer, explain, or describe.

W.2.2: Write informative/explanatory texts in which they introduce a topic, use facts and definitions to develop points, and provide a concluding statement or section.

SUGGESTED STUDENT OBJECTIVES

- Create a list of collective nouns related to topics studied (e.g., "herd," "flock," etc., in this unit on the West).
- Read tall tales and learn the distinct characteristics of this type of tale.

- Compare and contrast an original fairy tale with one that has been rewritten in a different setting.
- Read multiple perspectives on a given topic.
- Research the life of a real person.
- Write an informational essay based on research about a real person.
- Read informational texts to answer the questions *who, what, where, when, why,* and *how.*
- Read chapter books in the fantasy genre, paying careful attention to the varied voices of the characters.

SUGGESTED WORKS

(E) indicates a CCSS exemplar text; (EA) indicates a text from a writer with other works identified as exemplars.

LITERARY TEXTS

Stories

- *Cowgirl Kate and Cocoa* (Erica Silverman and Betsy Lewin) (E)
- *Cowgirl Kate and Cocoa: Partners* (Erica Silverman and Betsy Lewin) (EA)
- *Ghost Town at Sundown* (Mary Pope Osborne) (EA)
- *Buffalo Before Breakfast* (Mary Pope Osborne and Sal Murdocca) (EA)
- *Little Red Cowboy Hat* (Susan Lowell and Randy Cecil)
- *Little Red Riding Hood: A Newfangled Prairie Tale* (Lisa Campbell Ernst)
- *The Gingerbread Man* (Karen Lee Schmidt)
- *Justin and the Best Biscuits in the World* (Mildred Pitts Walter and Catherine Stock)
- *Dancing with the Indians* (Angela Shelf Medearis)
- *The Cowboy and the Black-Eyed Pea* (Tony Johnston)
- *The Gingerbread Cowboy* (Janet Squires and Holly Berry)
- *The Tortoise and the Jackrabbit* (Susan Lowell)
- *Gift Horse: A Lakota Story* (S. D. Nelson)
- *Crazy Horse's Vision* (Joseph Bruchac, S. D. Nelson, Curtis Zunigha, and Robert Tree Cody)
- *A Boy Called Slow* (Joseph Bruchac and Rocco Baviera)

Stories (Read Aloud)

- *Little Red Riding Hood* (Trina Schart Hyman)
- "The Princess and the Pea" in *Fairy Tales from Hans Christian Andersen* (Hans Christian Andersen)
- *The Toughest Cowboy: or How the Wild West Was Tamed* (John Frank and Zachary Pullen)

Tall Tales

- *Paul Bunyan* (Steven Kellogg)
- *John Henry* (Julius Lester and Jerry Pinkney)
- *Pecos Bill* (Steven Kellogg and Laura Robb)
- *Johnny Appleseed* (Steven Kellogg)

Poem

- "How I Spent My Summer Vacation" (Mark Teague)

Poems (Read Aloud)

- "Buffalo Dusk" (Carl Sandburg)
- "Home on the Range" (Brewster Higley)

INFORMATIONAL TEXTS

Informational Books

- *Cowboys* (Lucille Recht Penner)
- *I Want to Be a Cowboy* (Dan Liebman)
- *The Very First Americans* (Cara Ashrose)

Informational Books (Read Aloud)

- *Cowboys and Cowgirls: Yippee-Yay!* (Gail Gibbons) (EA)
- *Black Cowboy, Wild Horses: A True Story* (Julius Lester and Jerry Pinkney)
- *Bill Pickett: Rodeo-Ridin' Cowboy* (Andrea D. and Brian Pinkney)
- *Wild Tracks! A Guide to Nature's Footprints* (Jim Arnosky) (E)
- *B is for Buckaroo: A Cowboy Alphabet* (Louise Doak Whitney and Sue Guy)
- *Cactus Hotel* (Brenda Z. Guiberson)
- *Wild West* (DK Eyewitness Books) (Stuart Murray)
- *You Wouldn't Want to Live in a Wild West Town!* (Peter Hicks, David Salariya, and David Antram)
- Online biographical sources for:
  - Annie Oakley
  - Buffalo Bill
  - Wild Bill Hickock
  - Will Rogers
  - Kit Carson

ART, MUSIC, AND MEDIA

Art

- George Catlin, *The White Cloud, Head Chief of the Iowas* (1830–1870)
- George Catlin, *A Comanche Family Outside Their Teepee* (1841)
- Edward S. Curtis, *Cheyenne Maiden* (1930)
- Edward S. Curtis, *A Smoky Day at the Sugar Bowl—Hupa* (1923)
- Frederic Remington, *Fight For The Water Hole* (1903)
- Frederic Remington, *A Dash for the Timber* (1899)

Music and Song

- "Git Along, Little Dogies" (traditional cowboy ballad)

SAMPLE ACTIVITIES AND ASSESSMENTS

1. LANGUAGE/INFORMATIONAL TEXT

Create a running list of collective nouns in this unit (e.g., a herd or drove of cows; a herd or band of horses; a flock of sheep; and a band, tribe, or nation of Native Americans). Keep a growing word bank of people, vocabulary, and phrases that appear in this unit. Reading (reciting) poetry such as "Buffalo Dusk" and "Home on the Range" will give the students rich opportunities to collect vocabulary and to learn the words in context. These words can be used in later student writing. (RI.2.4, L.2.1b, L.2.4, RL.2.4, RL.2.10)

2. CLASS DISCUSSION/LITERATURE

Introduce the genre of tall tales by explaining that they are stories about a special kind of hero who is bigger than life. Even though the story is based on a real person, the person is exaggerated to be stronger or bigger than any real hero can ever be. Read about a hero from the 1800s named John Henry. As you read the story, challenge the students to think about the part of the story that is so amazing we know it is not really true. After the students have read the story, go back through the story and have the students write down one thing that might be real and one thing they think is fantasy. Ask questions such as, "Why do you think we have this tall tale? Why do you think the story has a race between a machine and a human? Why do you think the man beats the machine?" (RL.2.2, SL.2.2)

3. GRAPHIC ORGANIZER/LITERATURE

After reading the fairy tale *The Princess and the Pea,* introduce another version of the story, *The Cowboy and the Black-Eyed Pea.* Before reading the book, challenge the students to think about how the two stories are the same and how they are different. Create a Venn diagram or other graphic organizer to compare and contrast the two stories. Have the students use sticky notes to add their ideas to the Venn diagram. When they are finished, ask them to use the graphic organizer to construct sentences that describe two ways in which the stories are the same and two ways in which they are different. Continue this activity with other traditional stories and their alternative versions. (RL.2.9, SL.2.2)

4. CLASS DISCUSSION/INFORMATIONAL TEXT

Bill Pickett: Rodeo-Ridin' Cowboy (Andrea Davis Pinkney) is a true story of an African American cowboy. After you have read the story, display the same kind of chart from the Unit One segment on fiction (see the following sample). Again, remind the students that these are only question stems and must be amplified to focus on the story. Ask students to choose two questions to answer and write on their whiteboards. Share the responses from the students and add to the class chart. (RI.2.1, SL.2.2)

Who?	What?	Where?	When?	Why?	How?

5. CLASS DISCUSSION/INFORMATIONAL TEXT

Remind students that when they are doing research in the classroom, they start with a question. Similarly, authors of informational books also begin their work with a question or the desire to explain something. Have the students read an informational book such as *Cowboys and Cowgirls: Yippee-Yay!* (Gail Gibbons). After they finish the book, ask students to think about what question the author wanted to answer or what she wanted to explain in this book. When they are finished reading and writing down their questions, begin a discussion on how authors base research in asking and answering questions. (RI.2.6)

6. INFORMATIVE/EXPOSITORY WRITING

By reading the informational books in this unit, students learn about Native Americans, African Americans, and Caucasians during the 1800s in the American Wild West. Give the students this prompt: "Write about the person most interesting to you from the Wild West days. Be sure to answer the questions *who, what, where, when, why,* and *how* as you write about the person you chose." Using the question stems, students will generate their own research questions. Encourage the use of a variety of sources as they gather additional information using online sources and books. When students are finished with their research, pair them according to related choices to allow sharing of organized gathered information. Have them practice talking through the information to lay the groundwork for writing focused paragraphs. Students write drafts. After the first draft is written, have them spend time revising the work with peers or the teacher. (RI.2.1, RI.2.5, RI.2.10, W.2.2, W.2.5, W.2.7, W.2.8, SL.2.1, SL.2.2, SL.2.6, L.2.1, l.2.2, L.2.3)

7. DRAMATIZATION/FLUENCY

Introduce the story about a modern-day cowgirl, *Cowgirl Kate and Cocoa* (Erica Silverman). As they read the first chapter, ask students to think about whether this story could really happen or if it is a fantasy. Ask students to find evidence in the text to support their choices. Use a whiteboard or sticky notes to record their thinking. As they finish reading and writing, pair students to discuss their ideas. After they are finished discussing, ask them to remain partners and to experiment with reading using different voices for different characters in the book. Monitor the reading by listening for reading with expression and character voices. (RL.2.6, RF.2.4)

8. ART/CLASS DISCUSSION

Explain to the students that George Catlin was a famous artist who traveled west on horseback during the 1800s to paint pictures of Native Americans. Display his works. Ask students what they notice first in these paintings. What do they have in common with other portraits they have seen? (For example, Washington, Revere—see Unit Five in the section on first grade.) Note the titles of the works. Explain that Catlin was unique in his time because he painted Native Americans individualistically. (SL.2.2)

9. ART/OPINION WRITING

Select one Curtis and one Catlin artwork to study. Have the students compare Curtis's and Catlin's approaches to depicting Native Americans. Does Curtis's use of the environment expand our understanding of the Native Americans in his photographs? If so, how? (W.2.1, W.2.3)

10. ART/CLASS DISCUSSION

Have students close their eyes and "turn on" their imaginations. Tell them to imagine traveling back to the nineteenth century as if they were artists studying the Native Americans. Ask questions like: What do you see? What types of people are there; plants, animals, landscapes? Have students write a few sentences about their imagined picture, as well as sketch a picture. If time permits, turn the sketched image into a landscape image: add significant aspects, like characters, a setting, and any meaningful details. Use listed artworks as inspiration for students. (SL.2.3, SL.2.4, SL.2.5)

11. ART/CLASS DISCUSSION

View the two Remington paintings of cowboys. Ask students to look at the individual cowboys and see if they can find many differences in their appearances. Was Remington depicting cowboys individually (like Catlin) or more like types (like Curtis)? What can we learn about cowboy life by looking at these works? (SL.2.3, SL.2.4, SL.2.5)

READING FOUNDATIONS: A PACING GUIDE FOR READING INSTRUCTION

See Grade Two, Level Two, in the Reading Foundations section for a complete pacing guide for this unit.

ADDITIONAL RESOURCES

- *Cowboys and Fairy Tales: Interacting With Fractured Texas Tales* (ReadWriteThink) (RL.2.9, W.2.3)
- *An Interactive Biographical Dictionary Profiling Men and Women Portrayed in "The West"* (PBS) (W.2.8)
- George Catlin, various paintings of Native Americans (1796–1872)

TERMINOLOGY

Biography	Compare	Fantasy	Real
Characters	Contrast	Fluency	Tall tale
Collective nouns	Expression	Point of view	Venn diagram

MAKING INTERDISCIPLINARY CONNECTIONS

This unit teaches:

Art: George Catlin, Edward S. Curtis, Frederic Remington
Geography: the western United States
History: American westward expansion (e.g., the role of the railroad) and Native Americans (e.g., Plains Indians and the effect of the railroad on Native American communities)

This unit could be extended to teach:

History: American westward expansion (e.g., the steamboat, wagon trains, the Pony Express) and Native Americans (e.g., Sequoyah and the Trail of Tears)
Science: Simple machines used by the Native Americans and technology related to westward movement (e.g., arrows and wagon wheels)

Grade Two, Unit Two Sample Lesson Plan

Cowgirl Kate and Cocoa by Erica Silverman

In this series of two lessons, students read *Cowgirl Kate and Cocoa* by Erica Silverman, and they:

- Explore the relationship between Kate and Cocoa (RL.2.2, RL.2.3)
- Examine the lessons that Kate and Cocoa's experiences teach (RL.2.2, RL.2.3, SL.2.1, SL.2.2)
- Identify components of paragraphs (L.2.1)
- Compose paragraphs (W.2.1)

Summary

Lesson I: Meet Kate and Cocoa	Lesson II: Lessons That Kate and Cocoa Teach Us
Independently read *Cowgirl Kate and Cocoa*, by Erica Silverman (RL.2.10, RF.2.3, RF.2.4)	Revisit the lessons that we learn from Kate's and Cocoa's stories (RL.2.2, RL.2.3)
(In small groups) explore the themes of the stories of Kate and Cocoa (RL.2.2, SL.2.1, SL.2.2)	Select a story to discuss (SL.2.1, SL.2.2)
Identify a story to write about (SL.2.1)	Identify the necessary component of a paragraph (L.2.1)
	Compose paragraphs (W.2.1)
	Edit paragraphs (W.2.5, L.2.1, L.2.2, L.2.3)
	Share paragraphs (SL.2.6)

Lesson II: Lessons That Kate and Cocoa Teach Us

Objectives

Revisit the lessons that we learn from Kate's and Cocoa's stories (RL.2.2, RL.2.3)

Select a story to discuss (SL.2.1, SL.2.2)

Identify the necessary components of a paragraph (L.2.1)

Compose paragraphs (W.2.1)

Edit paragraphs (W.2.5, L.2.1, L.2.2, L.2.3)

Share paragraphs (SL.2.6)

Required Materials

☐ *Cowgirl Kate and Cocoa*, by Erica Silverman

☐ Loose-leaf paper

☐ Pencils

Procedures

1. Lead-In:

Capable student volunteers will read *Cowgirl Kate and Cocoa*, by Erica Silverman, aloud.

2. Step by Step:

a. In several small groups, students discuss the content of a story they choose to write about.

b. Introduce the students to the paragraph template below.

Sentence I: Identify the story and the author					
Topic sentence: State the lesson that the story teaches					
Supporting detail					
Supporting detail					
Supporting detail					
Concluding sentence					

c. Students compose their paragraphs with teacher's support.

d. Students edit their work based on their teacher's comments.

3. Closure:

Student volunteers read their paragraph aloud.

Differentiation

Advanced

- Students will revise and edit, with final editing done by an adult.
- Students will go through each story and create a "six-word lesson" for each one. The "six word lessons" will be written on sentence strips for the rest of the class to match to the correct story.

Struggling

- Students may need modeling of an entire paragraph before they are ready to do this work independently.
- Choose a story, for the class or small group, to do as a modeled lesson before teaching from step b on to the end with an expectation of independent work.
- Using adult volunteers to scribe, allow students to dictate paragraph components into the chart before asking them to write out the paragraph themselves. Students will then be able to focus on the content of the paper. Students will learn from copying the correct spelling and punctuation of their ideas.

Homework/Assessment

Using a template, teachers assess their students' compositions.

Grade 2 ▶ *Unit 3*

Building Bridges with Unlikely Friends

In this third six-week unit of second grade, students explore literal and figurative language through the theme of building bridges.

ESSENTIAL QUESTION

❓ Why do authors use figurative language?

OVERVIEW

Students read informational (how-to) texts on building bridges and view these amazing structures on the Internet. Through realistic fiction, they examine the possibility of friendship in conflict-filled settings. Reading fantasy texts that depict animals' experiences with "bridge-building" completes their exploration. Building on the writing of previous units, they write a letter to a character in *Charlotte's Web*. Students also gather words from poetry and explore the meanings of idioms and words with common roots.

FOCUS STANDARDS

These Focus Standards have been selected for the unit from the Common Core State Standards.

RL.2.3: Describe how characters in a story respond to major events and challenges.

RL.2.7: Use information gained from the illustrations and words in a print or digital text to demonstrate understanding of its characters, setting, or plot.

RI.2.6: Identify the main purpose of a text, including what the author wants to answer, explain, or describe.

W.2.2: Write explanatory texts in which they introduce a topic, use facts and definitions to develop points, and provide a concluding statement or section.

L2.2: Demonstrate command of the conventions of Standard English capitalization, punctuation, and spelling when writing.

L.2.2(b): Use commas in greetings and closings of letters.

L.2.4: Determine or clarify the meaning of unknown and multiple-meaning words and phrases based on Grade Two reading and content, choosing flexibly from an array of strategies.

L.2.4(d): Use knowledge of the meaning of individual words to predict the meaning of compound words.

SUGGESTED STUDENT OBJECTIVES

- Read a how-to book.
- Write an explanatory piece on how to do something.
- Discern the difference between the use of literal and figurative language.
- Discern authors' techniques for describing characters.
- Write friendly letters to one of the characters in a book.
- Use commas correctly in the greeting and closing of a friendly letter.
- Write responses to a letter from a character's point of view.
- Use knowledge of a root word, such as *bridge,* to predict the meaning of compound words and idioms.
- Describe the use of riddles and other language in Haiku poetry.

SUGGESTED WORKS

(E) indicates a CCSS exemplar text; (EA) indicates a text from a writer with other works identified as exemplars.

LITERARY TEXTS

Stories

- *Henry and Mudge: The First Book* (Cynthia Rylant and Sucie Stevenson) (E)
- *The Fire Cat* (Esther Holden Averill) (E)
- *George and Martha: The Complete Stories of Two Best Friends* (James Marshall)

Stories (Read Aloud)

- *The Cricket in Times Square* (George Selden and Garth Williams) (E)
- *Charlotte's Web* (E. B. White and Garth Williams) (E)
- *Zen Shorts* (Jon J. Muth)
- *Pop's Bridge* (Eve Bunting and C. F. Payne)
- *Mackinac Bridge: The Story of the Five-Mile Poem* (Gloria Whelan and Gijsbert van Frankenhuyzen)
- *One Green Apple* (Eve Bunting and Ted Lewin) (EA)
- *Four Feet, Two Sandals* (Karen Lynn Williams, Khadra Mohammed, and Doug Chayka)
- *Snow in Jerusalem* (Deborah da Costa, Ying-Hwa Hu, and Cornelius Van Wright)
- *The Day of Ahmed's Secret* (Florence P. Heide, Judith H. Gilliland, and Ted Lewin)
- *My Father's Shop* (Satomi Ichikawa)
- *Silent Music* (James Rumford)
- *The Little Painter of Sabana Grande* (Patricia Maloney Markun and Robert Casilla)

Poems (Read Aloud)

- "The Bridge Builder" (Will Allen Dromgoole)
- *If Not for the Cat* (Jack Prelutsky and Ted Rand)
- *I Am the Dog I Am the Cat* (Donald Hall)

INFORMATIONAL TEXTS

Informational Book

- *Bridges* (See More Readers) (Seymour Simon) (EA)

Informational Books (Read Aloud)

- *Bridges Are To Cross* (Philemon Sturges and Giles Laroche)
- *Bridges: Amazing Structures to Design, Build & Test* (Carol A. Johmann, Elizabeth Rieth, and Michael P. Kline)
- *Owen and Mzee: The True Story of a Remarkable Friendship* (Isabella Hatkoff, Craig Hatkoff, Paula Kahumbu, and Peter Greste)
- *Owen and Mzee: The Language of Friendship* (Isabella Hatkoff, Craig Hatkoff, Paula Kahumbu, and Peter Greste)
- *Tarra and Bella: The Elephant and Dog Who Became Best Friends* (Carol Buckley)

ART, MUSIC, AND MEDIA

Art

- *Album Quilt*, Stanford, New York (1853)
- *Album Quilts*, Baltimore, Maryland (circa 1840s)

SAMPLE ACTIVITIES AND ASSESSMENTS

Note: This unit could be taught in three parts. First, start with "bridges" so that students see the bridge as both an architectural structure and a symbolic metaphor coming together. Students will then see how children are able to bridge cultural gaps through friendship. Then read the fictional works to further the theme of Unlikely Friends. Students will think about differences in characters such as Charlotte and Wilbur and the way they become friends. Finally, writing a friendly letter to a book character will help the students to think deeply about the fictional characters.

1. INFORMATIONAL READING AND INFORMATIVE/EXPLANATORY WRITING

Introduce a chapter from *Bridges: Amazing Structures to Design, Build & Test*. This is an informational book, but it is also a how-to book. It will teach how to build bridge structures in the classroom or at home. Read the text to the children and allow them to note that the how-to section is set up as a series of steps to follow. Gather the supplies and allow the students to follow the directions to experiment with building a bridge. Discuss how diagrams help to explain the directions. *Writing prompt:* "After building a bridge in the classroom or at home, write an explanatory paragraph telling someone else how you made your bridge." (SL.2.6, W.2.2, RI.2.3, RI.2.6, RI.2.7)

2. INFORMATIONAL READING AND INFORMATIVE/EXPLANATORY WRITING

Begin a class discussion by asking the students: "If a real hippopotamus had no other companions, what other kind of animal could you imagine her having for a friend?" Be sure to require good reasons for their opinions as they answer. Read the book *Owen and Mzee: The True Story of a Remarkable Friendship* (Isabella Hatkoff) aloud. When you are finished reading, have the students discuss what the author (a six-year-old girl) wanted to accomplish by publishing the book, using questions such as:

"What did she want to explain? Describe? What questions did she want to answer? Why are there so many photographs?" Ask students to write a paragraph explaining how the two animals in the story became friends. *Writing prompt:* "After reading about these unlikely friends (i.e., Owen and Mzee), write a paragraph explaining how the two animals in the story became friends." (SL.2.6, W.2.2, RI.2.3, RI.2.6, RI.2.7)

3. LANGUAGE ACTIVITY

After reading about bridges, have students predict the meaning of compound words that contain the word *bridge*: *footbridge, drawbridge, flybridge,* and *bridgework*. Repeat the activity using another root word such as *water: waterbed, watercolor, watermelon, waterlog, watershed, waterproof, watertight, rainwater, waterway,* and *waterspout*. Extend this lesson by discussing idioms using the word *bridge* such as "We'll cross that bridge when we come to it," "that's water under the bridge," and "don't burn your bridges." (L.2.4d)

4. CLASS DISCUSSION/LITERATURE

Introduce the idea of a bridge as a metaphor by reading the book *Pop's Bridge* (Eve Bunting). (Help the students think of more metaphors to reinforce the meaning of this important term.) In this book, a group of boys experience the sacrifice involved in bridge building and the joy that comes with friendship. Discuss the literal bridge in the book and the way the bridge served as a link not only between two places, but also between two people. Introduce the following Isaac Newton quotation: "We build too many walls and not enough bridges." Discuss what Isaac Newton may have meant by his comment. (RL.2.7)

5. CLASS DISCUSSION/LITERATURE

Introduce a book such as *Snow in Jerusalem* (Deborah da Costa, Ying-Hwa Hu, and Cornelius Van Wright) by reviewing how unlikely friends become friends by finding something in common. Tell the students that they are going to read a book about two children who were not friends, but who found something in common anyway. As they read the story, have the students focus on how the children find something in common to make a friendship. Talk about how these two characters faced a challenge and made a hard choice. (RL.2.3, RL.2.7)

6. LITERATURE/LETTER WRITING

Read aloud the book *Charlotte's Web* (E. B. White) to the class. After you have finished the book, have the students connect with the characters in the book by writing friendly letters. Students should choose one of the characters in *Charlotte's Web* and write the character a letter. You may say, "Write a letter to one of the characters in *Charlotte's Web*. Explain why you chose the character, what you like about him or her, and ask the character a question." Require proper use of punctuation and form for the letters. Revise the letters and edit for spelling and punctuation. Then, have the students trade letters and write back to a classmate as if they were the classmate's chosen character. For example, if a child receives a letter addressed to Wilbur, she would write a letter back as if she were Wilbur and answer the question asked. (L.2.2b, RL.2.7, W.2.5)

7. WRITING/DIGITAL COMMUNICATION

To encourage communication among unlikely friends, arrange for your students to communicate with students from another class in a place far away. Begin an e-mail or pen-pal correspondence with students from another class in a contrasting location. Setting parameters for what can be shared, ask students to write letters introducing themselves and asking the other student about him-/herself.

The purpose of this activity would be to find ways the students are similar and the ways the students are different from one another. This writing activity could also be done writing from whole class to whole class instead of students writing to one another. (W.2.5, W.2.6, L.2.2b)

8. CLASS DISCUSSION/LITERATURE

As students read the *Henry and Mudge* books, challenge them to look closely at the characters. Before the first chapter, ask the students to be ready to describe Henry and Mudge. Using sticky notes or whiteboards, require each student to write down two characteristics of each character. Although one of the characters is a dog and one is a boy, they have a wonderful friendship. Have students share at least two words to describe Henry and two words to describe Mudge. Discuss what can be learned about friendship through these stories. (RL.2.7, L.2.5b)

9. CLASS DISCUSSION/POETRY/LANGUAGE

As you read from the poetry collection *If Not for the Cat* (Jack Prelutsky), explain to students the Haiku style of poetry. Point out to the students that these poems are very short, but they make you think. As you read a poem, keep the accompanying illustration hidden until students try to guess the animal being described. These poems are filled with words that may be new to your students. When you are finished reading (reciting) each poem, ask students to choose one new word to save in the word bank. (L.2.4e, L.2.5, RL.2.4)

10. ART/CLASS DISCUSSION

Use the Maryland Historical Society's interactive website to explore the tradition of album quilts. Discuss with students the reasons behind making such quilts. How would quilting build strong friendships? What types of images do you see in these quilts? What do the images tell us about the people who made these quilts? (SL.2.4)

11. ART/CLASS DISCUSSION

Using paper squares and cut-out images, divide the class into (unlikely) groupings of three to four students. Have them discuss what type of album quilt they would like to produce as a group—what event should they commemorate? Using teamwork, each group should produce a small "quilt" of images. (SL.2.1, SL.2.5)

READING FOUNDATIONS: A PACING GUIDE FOR READING INSTRUCTION

See Grade Two, Level Three, of the Pacing Guide for Reading Instruction for a complete pacing guide for this unit.

ADDITIONAL RESOURCES

- *Friendly Letter Mini-Lesson* (L.2.2b)
- *Letter Generator* (ReadWriteThink) (W.2.6, L.2.2b)
- *Build A Bridge* (RI.2.3)
- *Fun and Learning About Bridges* (RI.2.3)
- Brooklyn Bridge Website
- Maryland Historical Society Website

TERMINOLOGY

Body	Editing	How-to books
Capitalization	Informative/explanatory writing	Idiom
Closing	Figurative	Literal
Compare	Friendly letter	Metaphor
Compound word	Greeting	Revision
Contrast	Haiku	

MAKING INTERDISCIPLINARY CONNECTIONS

This unit teaches:

Art: Structural art (e.g., architecture and symmetry), quilts
Geography: World geography (e.g., as related to settings such as Jerusalem)
Science: Animals (e.g., habitats)

This unit could be extended to teach:

Science: Animals (e.g., classifications)

Grade Two, Unit Three Sample Lesson Plan

The Fire Cat by Esther Averill

In this series of four lessons, students read *The Fire Cat* by Esther Averill, and they:

Explore the adventures of Pickles, the Fire Cat (RL.2.1, RL.2.3)

Examine the power of friendship (RL.2.3)

Learn the meaning of responsibility (RL.2.3)

Examine the concept of happiness (RL.2.3)

Summary

Lesson I: Meet Pickles

Identify and chart the characteristics of Pickles, Mrs. Goodkind, and fireman Joe (RL.2.1, RL.2.5)

Explore the meanings of the names of the leading characters (RL.2.1)

Investigate the main conflict in the first chapter (RL.2.5, RL.2.6)

Recognize the use of foreshadowing (RL.2.5)

Lesson II: Pickles, the Fire Cat

Examine the role that the fire chief plays in Pickles's evolving character (RL.2.1, RL.2.6, RF.2.4)

Trace the steps that Pickles takes in his desire to become a "good firehouse cat" (RL.2.1, RL.2.5, RF.2.4, SL.2.1)

Compare Pickles's life living with Mrs. Goodkind with his life in the firehouse (RL.2.6, SL.2.1)

Note the power of persistence (W.2.1, W.2.2, RF.2.3)

Lesson III: Pickles the Hero

Explore Pickles's new life (RL.2.1, SL.2.1)

Articulate the lessons that Pickles learns and the actions that he takes (RL.2.1, SL.2.1)

Discuss Pickles's courage (RL.2.1, SL.2.1)

Examine the statement that Pickles "rode home … a proud and happy cat." (RL.2.1)

Lesson IV: Learning from Pickles

Revisit the Pickles story (RL.2.1, SL.2.1, SL.2.2)

Examine the meaning of responsibility that Pickles's story reveals (RL.2.5, SL.2.1)

Explore the ways that Pickles's story teaches the meaning of friendship (SL.2.1)

Lesson II: Pickles, the Fire Cat

Objectives

Examine the role that the fire chief plays in Pickles's evolving character (RL.2.1, RL.2.6, RF.2.4)

Trace the steps that Pickles takes in his desire to become a "good firehouse cat" (RL.2.1, RL.2.5, RF.2.4, SL.2.1)

Compare Pickles's life living with Mrs. Goodkind with his life in the firehouse (RL.2.6, SL.2.1)

Note the power of persistence (W.2.1, W.2.2, RF.2.3)

Required Materials

☐ A class set of *The Fire Cat* by Esther Averill

Procedures

1. Lead-In:

Quietly, students read Chapter Two of *The Fire Cat.*

2. Step by Step:

   a. Students will reread *The Fire Cat* (the whole book) aloud with partners.

   b. In a class discussion (where students provide evidence from the text) the students trace Pickles's actions once the fire chief tells him that he will be permitted to stay "IF" he learns "to be a good firehouse cat."

   Pickles does not give up when he falls "with a BUMP." He continues to practice sliding down the pole.

   He says to himself, "I must keep on learning everything I can." He also tells himself that he "must learn to help the firemen with their work."

   He learns how to sit in the fire truck.

   He holds on to the hose.

   c. A discussion about the fire chief follows several prompts:

   How many times does the narrator say, "The chief did not say anything"? Why?

   How does the fire chief help Pickles become a responsible fire cat?

   d. In order to understand Pickles's character, compare his life with Mrs. Goodkind with his life in the firehouse. Students are likely to conclude that Pickles does not search for physical comfort; instead, he wants to have challenges.

3. Closure:

In preparation for the writing assignment (homework), the students explore how Pickles's persistence and determination help him become a fire cat.

Differentiation

Advanced

- In a small group, explore the meaning of the word *persistence* by using a cube. Use each face of the cube to do one of the following: write the word, illustrate it, write two synonyms for it, write two antonyms for it, write the name of a person you know who exemplifies it, and write a strong sentence using the word as related to a character in a different book.

Struggling

- Offer the option of also listening to a recording of *The Fire Cat*.
- Support the students in writing a paragraph by writing the first two sentences of the paragraph together before the students leave school.

Homework/Assessment

Students write a paragraph that discusses how Pickles's determination helps him become a firehouse cat.

Grade 2 ▶ *Unit 4*

A Long Journey to Freedom

In this fourth six-week unit of second grade, students read informational text and fictionalized accounts of the African American journey to freedom.

ESSENTIAL QUESTION

? What is challenging about writing a narrative?

OVERVIEW

Building on Unit Three's building bridges focus, students recognize the long and multifaceted effort to break down barriers to racial equality in the United States. By reading the true stories of Henry "Box" Brown, Rosa Parks, Ruby Bridges, the Greensboro Four, and others, students see the links between historical events. Each student writes a narrative "from a box," (i.e., in the style of *Henry's Freedom Box*). They also write an opinion piece that is published digitally in a class presentation and possibly online.

FOCUS STANDARDS

These Focus Standards have been selected for the unit from the Common Core State Standards.

RL.2.6: Acknowledge differences in the points of view of characters, including by speaking in a different voice for each character when reading dialogue aloud.

RI.2.3: Describe the connection between a series of historical events, scientific ideas or concepts, or steps in technical procedures in a text.

RI.2.9: Compare and contrast the most important points presented by two texts on the same topic.

W.2.1: Write opinion pieces in which they introduce the topic of book they are writing about, state an opinion, supply reasons that support the opinion, use linking words (e.g., *because, and, also*) to connect opinion and reasons, and provide a concluding statement or section.

W.2.3: Write narratives in which they recount a well-elaborated event or short sequence of events, include details to describe action, thoughts, and feelings, use temporal words to signal event order, and provide a sense of closure.

W.2.6: With guidance from adults, use a variety of digital tools to produce and publish writing, including in collaboration with peers.

SUGGESTED STUDENT OBJECTIVES

- Write a narrative imagining that you are a character in one of the stories.
- Select the correct verb form, particularly of irregular verbs, to show past tense in narrative writing.
- Note links between historical events, including parallel connections and sequential connections.
- Analyze narrative poetry to understand its elements, meaning, and the use of formal and informal English.
- Compare two texts (a biography and an autobiography) on the life of a famous person.
- Write an opinion piece, citing evidence for the opinion.
- Express an opinion by creating and displaying a PowerPoint slide.
- Record the opinion piece being read aloud to use for a class presentation or online web page.

SUGGESTED WORKS

(E) indicates a CCSS exemplar text; (EA) indicates a text from a writer with other works identified as exemplars.

LITERARY TEXTS

Note: The date or time period that is captured or discussed in each of these works is included in parentheses for your reference.

Stories

- *The Other Side* (1950s) (Jacqueline Woodson and E.B. Lewis)
- *Freedom Summer* (1964) (Deborah Wiles and Jerome Lagarrigue)

Stories (Read Aloud)

- *Freedom on the Menu: The Greensboro Sit-Ins* (1960) (Carole Boston Weatherford and Jerome Lagarrigue)
- *Dear Mr. Rosenwald* (1920) (Carole Boston Weatherford)
- *Finding Lincoln* (1951) (Ann Malaspina and Colin Bootman)
- *A Sweet Smell of Roses* (1963) (Angela Johnson and Eric Velasquez)

Poem

- "Words Like Freedom" (Langston Hughes) (EA)

Poems (Read Aloud)

- "Rosa" (Rita Dove)
- "Merry-Go-Round" (Langston Hughes) (EA)
- "Harriet Tubman" (Eloise Greenfield)
- "Lincoln" (Nancy Byrd Turner)

INFORMATIONAL TEXTS

Informational Books

- *Henry's Freedom Box: A True Story from the Underground Railroad* (1849) (Ellen Levine and Kadir Nelson)
- *Rosa Parks* (Rookie Biographies) (1955) (Wil Mara)
- *Ruby Bridges Goes to School: My True Story* (1960) (Ruby Bridges)
- *Martin Luther King Jr. and the March on Washington* (1963) (Frances E. Ruffin and Stephen Marchesi) (E)
- *Martin's Big Words: The Life of Dr. Martin Luther King Jr.* (1963) (Doreen Rappaport and Bryan Collier)
- *Sit-In: How Four Friends Stood Up by Sitting Down* (1960) (Andrea D. and Brian Pinkney)

Informational Books (Read Aloud)

- *Moses: When Harriet Tubman Led Her People to Freedom* (c.1820–1913) (Carole Boston Weatherford and Kadir Nelson)
- *Lincoln: A Photobiography* (1809–1865) (Russell Freedman) (E)
- *A Picture Book of Jesse Owens* (1935) (David A. Adler and Robert Casilla)
- *The Story of Ruby Bridges* (1960) (Robert Coles and George Ford) (E)

ART, MUSIC, AND MEDIA

Art

- Norman Rockwell, *The Problem We All Live With* (1963)
- *Working Photograph of Ruby Bridges* (artist and date unknown)
- *Photograph of Ruby Bridges* (AP Photo, 1963)

Film

- Euzhan Palcy, dir., *Disney's Ruby Bridges: A Real American Hero* (1998)

SAMPLE ACTIVITIES AND ASSESSMENTS

Note: The books in this unit can be taught in chronological order, beginning in the middle 1800s with the Underground Railroad, Tubman, and Lincoln; moving to Jesse Owens, and then Rosenwald (1920), Rosa Parks (1955), Ruby Bridges and the Greensboro Sit-In (1960); and, finally, Martin Luther King Jr. The connections between historical events (RI.2.3) will be seen as a long journey if each book is linked to the other as related stories.

1. LANGUAGE

As you have the students read the literature of this unit, look for words that might lend themselves to a discussion of affixes and roots. Teach the students that by knowing the root word, you can approximate the meaning of another word that they may not know. For example, if the children have learned the meaning of *prejudice* and then come across the word *prejudicial,* they may have an idea of its meaning, especially if they see *prejudicial* in context as they read. Encourage students to use dictionaries to determine accurate meanings and to check spelling while writing. (L.2.4b, L.2.4c)

2. CLASS DISCUSSION/INFORMATIONAL TEXT

Read and discuss the book *Henry's Freedom Box* (Ellen Levine), a true story of a slave's journey to freedom. Be sure to discuss the characters, setting, plot, and message of the book. Students may enjoy listening to the author read the story, noting the way she changes her voice with the different characters. (RL.2.6, RI.2.3, SL.2.2, W.2.)

3. NARRATIVE WRITING

After reading about Henry's journey to freedom (in *Henry's Freedom Box*), introduce this narrative prompt: "Write a story as if you are in the box headed for freedom. Begin your story as you get into the box and end the story as the box is opened at your destination. Be sure to describe the action in the story, your thoughts, and feelings. Use words to show time order and end with a strong wrap-up." To help prepare students for writing strong paragraphs, plan the writing using a sequential graphic organizer (flow map or trifold paper) showing a beginning, middle, and end. To help the students with thoughts and feelings, you may want to have them journal after spending several minutes in a well-ventilated, open box. (W.2.3)

4. LANGUAGE ACTIVITY

Revise the "stories from inside a box" (see Narrative Writing; / activity 3) by focusing on action words. Discuss the present tense and past tense of verbs, focusing particularly on irregular verbs such as "I hide, I hid" and "I sit, I sat." (L.2.1d)

5. CLASS DISCUSSION/POETRY

The poems about Harriet Tubman ("Harriet Tubman," Eloise Greenfield) and Abraham Lincoln ("Lincoln," Nancy Byrd Turner) are narrative poems that tell a story. Read (recite) the poems. Use these questions to discuss the poems:

How are the poems similar and how are they different?

What poetic elements (e.g., alliteration, repetition, regular beats, and rhyme) do you hear/see in the poetry?

What is the message of each poem? Are they similar or different?

Which of the poems uses formal English and which one uses more informal English? (L.2.3a, RL.2.4)

6. CLASS DISCUSSION/INFORMATIONAL TEXT

Read aloud the two supplied texts about Ruby Bridges (*Ruby Bridges Goes to School* and *The Story of Ruby Bridges*). Before reading, explain that one of the books is an autobiography (*Ruby Bridges Goes to School: A True Story*) that Bridges wrote about her own experiences. Explain that the other book, *The Story of Ruby Bridges,* is biographical, which means that an author wrote the book about Bridges's life. When you finish reading each book aloud, have the students choose the most important parts of the story. Then, have them compare how the books are similar and how they are different. (There are several other opportunities to do this compare/contrast activity, or assessment, with the Greensboro Sit-In and Martin Luther King Jr. texts.) (RI.2.3, RI.2.9, SL.2.3)

7. ART/CLASS DISCUSSION

While the class is focused on Ruby Bridges, show the students some photographs of Bridges and the Rockwell, which was painted after a photograph of her. What can you learn about Bridges and the time in which she lived by looking at these works? Compare the photo of Bridges walking to school with that section of Rockwell's painting. What has Rockwell added or subtracted (e.g., the lunchbox, graffiti)? What tells us more about Bridges's character, the photograph or Rockwell's depiction of her? (*Note:* You should look for adjectives and character vocabulary in the conversation.) (L.2.5b, L.2.6, SL.2.3)

8. OPINION WRITING

Give the students this writing prompt: "Choose one of the people studied in this unit who you think is the greatest hero in this long journey to freedom. Give two or three strong reasons for choosing this person." Students should be moving toward writing paragraphs. Remind them to introduce the person and give strong reasons why the person was chosen using words like *because* and *also* to link ideas. Encourage the addition of details to strengthen the writing and a strong statement to close. (W.2.1, L.2.1f)

9. WRITING/MEDIA

Students can publish their opinion pieces by scanning the drawing and putting it into a slide. Opinion pieces should be recorded and played as the drawing is projected. These slides and recordings could be posted on a web page to be viewed by friends and relatives. Arrange the slides chronologically to reinforce the linking of ideas in this long journey to freedom. (W.2.6, SL.2.5)

READING FOUNDATIONS: A PACING GUIDE FOR READING INSTRUCTION

See Grade Two, Level Four, in the Reading Foundations section for a complete pacing guide for this unit.

ADDITIONAL RESOURCES

- *Inside and Outside: Paradox of the Box* (LearnNC) (RL.2.3)
- *Ellen Levine Reads Henry Freedom's Box* (Scholastic, Author Interviews) (RL.2.6)
- *A Class of One* (PBS, an interview with Ruby Bridges Hall, 1997) (SL.2.2)
- Martin Luther King Jr.'s "I Have a Dream" speech (American Rhetoric: Top 100 Speeches) (SL.2.3)

TERMINOLOGY

Action	Conclusion	Opinion piece	Time order words
Autobiography	Linking words	Record	
Biography	Narrative	Scan	

MAKING INTERDISCIPLINARY CONNECTIONS

This unit teaches:

Art: Photography, Norman Rockwell
Geography: Southern states and Canada
History: Slavery (e.g., Lincoln, Tubman), Civil Rights Movement (e.g., Ruby Bridges, Martin Luther King Jr.)

This unit could be extended to teach:

History: Civil War (e.g., slavery, states' rights), Civil Rights (e.g., Susan B. Anthony)

Grade Two, Unit Four Sample Lesson Plan

"Words Like Freedom" by Langston Hughes
Langston Hughes, edited by David Roessel and Arnold Rampersad

In this series of three lessons, students read "Words Like Freedom" by Langston Hughes, and they:

Explore the life and legacy of Langston Hughes (RI.2.1, RI.2.2, RI.2.3, RI.2.6, SL.1.1, SL.1.2)

Explore the theme of "Words Like Freedom" (RL.2.4, SL.1.1, SL.1.2)

Examine a collection of Hughes's poems (RL.2.4, RL.2.10, RF.2.4, SL.1.1, SL.1.2)

Summary

Lesson I: Meet Langston Hughes

Meet Langston Hughes – an introduction

Recall key ideas from the introduction (RI.2.1, RI.2.2, RI.2.3, RI.2.6, SL.1.1, SL.1.2)

Explore the role that poets can play in society (RI.2.3)

Lesson II: "Words Like Freedom"

Examine the use of repetition in the poem (RL.2.4)

Note the use of italics in the poem (RL.2.4)

Explore the theme of the poem (RL.2.4, SL.1.1, SL.1.2)

Lesson III: The Poems of Langston Hughes

Select (in groups) a different poem from *Langston Hughes*, edited by David Roessel and Arnold Rampersad (RL.2.4, RL.2.10, RF.2.4)

Explore the theme of the new poem (RL.2.4, SL.1.1, SL.1.2)

Note the possible similarities of the new poem and "Words Like Freedom" (RL.2.4, SL.1.1, SL.1.2)

Lesson I: Meet Langston Hughes

Objectives

Meet Langston Hughes — an introduction

Recall key ideas from the introduction (RI.2.1, RI.2.2, RI.2.3, RI.2.6, SL.1.1, SL.1.2)

Explore the role that poets can play in society (RI.2.3)

Required Materials

☐ Class set of "Words Like Freedom," by Langston Hughes

☐ A poster-size copy of "Words Like Freedom"

☐ *Langston Hughes*, edited by David Roessel and Arnold Rampersad

☐ A map of the Unites States

Procedures

1. Lead-In:

Teacher reads aloud the poem "Words Like Freedom." Students can read along from the poster-size copy of poem. After the reading, the teacher tells the students that they will return to this and other poems after they learn about the poet and his life.

2. Step by Step:

a. Before you begin to read excerpts from *Langston Hughes* to the students, tell them to note details about the life of Hughes and his place in the literary history of the United States. (You may choose to use other sources as you introduce Hughes.)

b. Read excerpts from the "Introduction" to *Langston Hughes*.

c. Lead a discussion about Langston Hughes, his life, and his legacy. Some important facts to highlight are:

- Hughes was born in Missouri in 1902. (Students locate Missouri on the map of the United States.)
- He was an important African American poet.
- He wrote about the African American experience.
- He lived most of his adult life in New York City. (Students locate New York City on the map of the United States.)
- In the 1920s, Hughes lived and worked in Harlem.
- This period was known as the Harlem Renaissance.
- Many artists lived and worked in Harlem at that time.
- Hughes incorporated traditions of African American music into his work.
  (This list includes only a few important facts. You may choose to expand this part of the lesson.)

3. Closure:

Together, the students read "Words Like Freedom" aloud.

Differentiation

Advanced

- Students read through a variety of Hughes's poetry with a partner, noting his craft in creating poetry.
- Students choose another work of art from the Harlem Renaissance period and describe it in writing. After studying the artwork, students create original poetry based on what they see in the art.

Struggling

- Pre-teach the meaning and discuss the powerful connotations of the words *freedom* and *liberty*.
- Students work through the poem, line-by-line in a small group, looking for connections to the Civil Rights movement and illustrating each line or stanza.

Homework/Assessment
N/A

Grade 2 ▶ *Unit 5*

Hand-Me-Down Tales from Around the World

In this fifth six-week unit of second grade, students practice opinion and narrative writing as they read the poetry of Robert Louis Stevenson and a wide variety of legends, folktales, and informational books from around the world.

ESSENTIAL QUESTION

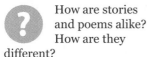 How are stories and poems alike? How are they different?

OVERVIEW

Building on previous units, students write opinions and narratives related to the folktale/world theme of this unit. Students discuss text features as a part of reading informational text. Although students have compared versions of tales in unit two, they will now compare a narrative version of a story to a poetry version, using the story of the Pied Piper. Students develop independent reading skills as they read texts on grade level (and beyond) throughout this unit.

FOCUS STANDARDS

These Focus Standards have been selected for the unit from the Common Core State Standards.

RL.2.2: Recount stories, including fables and folktales from diverse cultures, and determine their central message, lesson, or moral.

RI.2.7: Explain how specific images (e.g., a diagram showing how a machine works) contribute to and clarify a text.

W.2.3: Write narratives in which they recount a well-elaborated event or short sequence of events, include details to describe action, thoughts, and feelings, use temporal words to signal event order, and provide a sense of closure.

SL.2.3: Ask and answer questions about what a speaker says in order to clarify comprehension, gather additional information, or deepen understanding of a topic or issue.

SL.2.4: Tell a story or recount an experience with appropriate facts and relevant, descriptive details, speaking audibly in coherent sentences.

SUGGESTED STUDENT OBJECTIVES

- Read poetry, informational text, and literature on grade and stretch levels.
- Retell folktales from diverse cultures, determining their central message or lesson.
- Write imaginative narratives in which they tell a well-elaborated story.
- Ask and answer questions of a guest speaker.
- Use text features in nonfiction to aid comprehension of the text.
- Compare a variety of versions of the same story (e.g., versions of *Stone Soup*), contrasting the differences in story elements and key details.
- Compare a poetry version and a prose version of the same story (e.g., the Pied Piper legend).
- Learn the irregular forms of plural nouns.
- Memorize a poem and record it.

SUGGESTED WORKS

(E) indicates a CCSS exemplar text; (EA) indicates a text from a writer with other works identified as exemplars.

LITERARY TEXTS

Stories

- *The Treasure* (Uri Shulevitz) (E)
- *Itching and Twitching: A Nigerian Folktale* (Patricia C. McKissack, Robert L. McKissack, and Laura Freeman)
- *The Girl Who Wore Too Much: A Folktale from Thailand* (Margaret Read McDonald and Yvonne Lebrun Davis)
- *Caps for Sale: A Tale of a Peddler* (Esphyr Slobodkina)
- *The Enormous Turnip* (Alexei Tolstoy and Scott Goto)
- *Liang and the Magic Paintbrush* (Demi)
- *Stone Soup* (Ann McGovern and Winslow Pinney Pels)
- *Cuckoo/Cucú: A Mexican Folktale* (Lois Ehlert and Gloria De Aragon Andujar)
- *Moon Rope/Un lazo a la luna: A Peruvian Folktale* (Lois Ehlert and Amy Prince)
- *The Pied Piper's Magic* (Steven Kellogg)
- *Stone Soup* (Marcia Brown)
- *Stone Soup* (Jon J. Muth)
- *The Real Story of Stone Soup* (Ying Chang Compestine)
- *Stone Soup* (Tony Ross)
- *Some Friends to Feed: The Story of Stone Soup* (Pete Seeger, Paul Dubois Jacobs, and Michael Hays)
- *Stone Soup* (Heather Forest and Susan Gaber)
- *Bone Button Borscht* (Aubrey Davis and Dušan Petričić)

Stories (Read Aloud)

- *The Thirteen Clocks* (James Thurber and Marc Simont) (E)
- *Martina the Beautiful Cockroach: A Cuban Folktale* (Carmen Agra Deedy and Michael Austin) (EA)

- "How the Camel Got His Hump" in *Just So Stories* (Rudyard Kipling) (E)
- *The Village of Round and Square Houses* (Ann Grifalconi)
- *The Lost Horse: A Chinese Folktale* (Ed Young and Tracey Adams) (EA)
- *The Five Chinese Brothers* (Claire Huchet Bishop and Kurt Wiese)
- *Not One Damsel in Distress: World Folktales for Strong Girls* (Jane Yolen and Susan Guevara)

Poems

- "The Land of Counterpane" (Robert Louis Stevenson)
- "Foreign Lands" (Robert Louis Stevenson)
- "The Land of Story Books" (Robert Louis Stevenson)
- "At the Seaside" (Robert Louis Stevenson)
- "Where Go the Boats?" (Robert Louis Stevenson)
- "My Bed is a Boat" (Robert Louis Stevenson)

Poem (Read Aloud)

- "The Pied Piper of Hamelin" (Robert Browning) (E)

INFORMATIONAL TEXTS

Informational Books

- *Art Around the World* (Discovery World) (Heather Leonard) (E)
- *Shoes, Shoes, Shoes* (Around the World Series) (Ann Morris)
- *On the Go* (Around the World Series) (Ann Morris and Ken Heyman)
- *Loving* (Around the World Series) (Ann Morris and Ken Heyman)
- *Bread, Bread, Bread* (Around the World Series) (Ann Morris and Ken Heyman)
- *Houses and Homes* (Around the World Series) (Ann Morris and Ken Heyman)

Informational Books (Read Aloud)

- *If the World Were a Village: A Book about the World's People* (David Smith and Shelagh Armstrong) (E)
- *Hungry Planet: What the World Eats* (Peter Menzel and Faith D'Aluisio)
- *How I Learned Geography* (Uri Shulevitz) (EA)

ART, MUSIC, AND MEDIA

Art

- Edgar Degas, *The Dancing Class* (1870)
- Giovanni Domenico Tiepolo, *A Dance in the Country* (1755)
- Edgar Degas, *The Little Fourteen-Year-Old Dancer* (1879–1880)

Music

- Sergei Prokofiev, "Peter and the Wolf" (1936)

Film

- "Peter and the Wolf," Suzie Templeton, dir. (2006)

Dance

- *Peter and the Wolf* (Royal Ballet School, 1995)
- *A Folk Tale (Et Folkesagn)* (Royal Danish Ballet, 2011)
- *The Firebird* (Northwest Ballet, 2008)

SAMPLE ACTIVITIES AND ASSESSMENTS

1. CLASS DISCUSSION/POETRY

Introduce the unit by asking students about using their imaginations to go places. Introduce a poet who lived over one hundred years ago and also loved to go places in his imagination: Robert Louis Stevenson. As a child, he was sometimes sick. While confined to his bed, he created imaginary lands in his head, such as The Land of Counterpane. He also loved the sea. As students read (recite) his poems, have them think about his imagination and how he loved to wonder about the world. (You may want to read and reread his poetry throughout this unit, encouraging the students to look for poetic elements. Most of all, direct children to enjoy the idea of going places in their minds as you read folktales from around the world. Having a large world map to mark the place from which the story comes will give this unit a stronger geography focus.) (RL.2.4)

2. CLASS DISCUSSION/POETRY

Introduce the poem "The Pied Piper of Hamelin" by Robert Browning. This poem is a narrative based on a legend that is thought to have happened in Hamelin, Germany. Remind students that a legend is a story in which some things really happened and other things have been exaggerated over time as the story was passed down through generations. Ask the students which parts of the legend are probably true and which events have been exaggerated over time. Read the poem to the children. Give the students an opportunity to retell the story, confirming that they understand the main events of the story. Using a program such as "Comic Life," allow students to create a comic strip of "The Pied Piper" story told in the narrative poem. (The language in this poem is quite sophisticated. Reading the Kellogg book first will scaffold student comprehension of the poem. It will also provide another opportunity to compare versions.) Ask questions such as:

- How many of you think this story could have really happened?
- What was the story teaching? (RL.2.2, SL.2.4. L.2.4)

3. LANGUAGE ACTIVITY

After reading "The Pied Piper of Hamelin," do a word activity based on the poem. Collect some plural nouns from the poem. Talk about the singular for each word and how it is made plural (e.g., *rats, babies, vats, children, tongues, shoes,* and *mice*). Extend this activity by collecting the plurals of irregular nouns in particular. (L.2.1b)

4. CLASS DISCUSSION/LITERATURE

Introduce the characteristics of folktales by reading one or two and asking students what the tales have in common. Then, invite speakers to read folktales from home countries. For example, invite someone from Cuba or the Caribbean to read *Martina the Beautiful Cockroach: A Cuban Folktale* (Carmen Agra Deedy). As the visitor reads the story, have students consider what message the folktale might teach. When the story is over, the speaker could share some information about the country from which the folktale comes. Give an opportunity for students to ask questions about the folktale and the country. (SL.2.3, RL.2.2)

5. CLASS DISCUSSION/LITERATURE

Read the book *Stone Soup* (Marcia Brown) aloud to the students. Introduce other versions of the book (e.g., by Muth, Seeger, and Davis). Compare and contrast the versions of the story, using a teacher-created graphic organizer that addresses *who, what, where, why, when,* and *how* questions or a graphic organizer that addresses *character, setting, plot,* and *conclusion* categories. Encourage student participation by handing each child three sticky notes to use to post information on the graphic organizers. (RL.2.2, RL.2.9)

6. LITERARY RESPONSE

Have students select a folktale to read. Provide each student with a piece of plain white paper. Then, give these instructions:

Read a folktale with a partner [a stronger reader can read to a weaker reader, or they can take turns or read chorally]. When you are finished reading the folktale, follow these directions:

- Fold your paper into fourths.
- Draw a picture of the main characters in one square.
- Draw the setting in another square.
- Draw your favorite part of the plot in another square.
- In the last part, write a few sentences describing what you think the folktale is teaching.

Each time the students do this activity, substitute one more square with writing instead of drawing. As a student reads the last book independently, have them use the four-square outline to write a retelling of the folktale. Ask them to describe why they know it is a folktale (i.e., elicit common characteristics of folktales). (RL.2.2, RL.2.5, RL.2.7, RL.2.10, W.2.7, SL.2.2)

7. CLASS DISCUSSION/INFORMATIONAL TEXT

The informational books in this unit are based on themes like shoes or bread. For example, the author of these books, Ann Morris, studied interesting shoes from all around the world, had photographs taken of them, and then published them in a book, *Shoes, Shoes, Shoes.* As students read the books, ask them to look at the way the book is organized and locate the information about each photograph by using the index. As they study the book, challenge them to find the location on a world map from where those shoes came. To link to geography, give each pair of students a world map to mark as the text moves from one place to another. (After the students have had an opportunity to study multiple books in this series, ask them why they think the author wrote these books for children.) (RI.2.5, RI.2.6, RI.2.10)

8. CLASS DISCUSSION/INFORMATIONAL TEXT

If the World Were a Village: A Book about the World's People (David Smith) is an informational book packed with rich facts about the world. One of the interesting things about this book is that it shows the world as if it were a village of just one hundred people. Although you may have time for just a few pages, focus on how much information can be learned from the illustrations and text. Keep a list of the information that the students glean from the pages as you read. (RI.2.3, RI.2.6, RI.2.7)

9. NARRATIVE WRITING

Give the students this prompt: "Write an imaginary narrative telling about a time you passed through a mysterious door and ended up in a different country. The country may be from the folktale unit, from a book you have read, or just a place you want to visit. Be sure to say where you find the door, the country where the door leads, and how you arrive back where you began. Include details to describe action, thoughts, and feelings. Be sure to end your story well, thinking about how authors wrap up stories." Remind the students that their sentences should have subjects, verbs, and proper end punctuation. (W.2.3, L.2.2a)

10. MUSIC APPRECIATION

Explain to the students that Sergei Prokofiev is a Russian musical composer who wrote a musical rendition of the folktale called "Peter and the Wolf." Explain that he used different musical instruments to represent the characters in the story. Compare and contrast different productions of this piece (e.g., animated version, music-only CD, video of the ballet). (RL.2.2, RL.2.6, RL.2.9, SL.2.2)

11. ART/CLASS DISCUSSION

How can we view folktales in an artistic way? Have students view clips of the ballets provided. After viewing clips of each folktale ballet, discuss with students: "Can you see the storytelling clearly in these works? If so, how? If not, how would you, as a dancer or choreographer, make this clearer for the viewer? Does viewing a folktale, rather than reading it, change the meaning for the viewer? How so?" For background on ballet, see the essay titled "The Ballet" at the Metropolitan Museum. It may be helpful to introduce concepts of ballet through the artworks listed previously. (SL.2.5)

12. DRAMATIZATION/FLUENCY

Revisit the Robert Louis Stevenson poems, reminding students how they have used their imaginations to visualize the folktale being read and the places being read about (see Class Discussion/Poetry, activity 1). Discuss how repeated readings may deepen a poem's meaning, and challenge the students to memorize one of the poems to share in front of the class. Record the students' poetry performances with a video camera. (RL.2.4, SL.2.5)

13. LITERATURE/OPINION WRITING

Give the students this prompt: "All of the stories we read in this unit were folktales of some kind. Why do you think stories are handed down from one group of people to another? Be sure to support your opinion with strong reasons." Remind the students that their sentences should have subjects, verbs, and proper end punctuation. (W.2.1)

READING FOUNDATIONS: A PACING GUIDE FOR READING INSTRUCTION

See Grade Two, Level Five, in the Reading Foundations section for a complete pacing guide for this unit.

ADDITIONAL RESOURCES

- *A Collection of Folktales from Around the World* (Oak Terrace Elementary School, Highwood, IL) (RL 2.2)
- PBS musical version of *The Pied Piper* (Part One and Part Two)
- North American and Central American folklore
- Essay on "The Ballet" (The Metropolitan Museum)

TERMINOLOGY

Character	Index	Noun	Setting
Conclusion	Legend	Plot	
Folktale	Narrative poem	Plural	

MAKING INTERDISCIPLINARY CONNECTIONS

This unit teaches:

Music and Dance: Sergei Prokofiev, ballet

History and Geography: World geography (e.g., places of origin for folktales: Nigeria, Thailand, Mexico, Peru, etc.; cultural comparisons)

This unit could be extended to teach:

History and Geography: (e.g., *e pluribus unum,* Ellis Island, etc.)

Grade Two, Unit Five Sample Lesson Plan

"How the Camel Got His Hump" by Rudyard Kipling

In this series of two lessons, students listen to the teacher read "How the Camel Got His Hump" by Rudyard Kipling, and they:

Consider the moral of "How the Camel Got His Hump" by Rudyard Kipling (RL.2.1, RL.2.2, SL.2.1)

Provide and evaluate an artistic interpretation of the tale (SL.2.1)

Summary

Lesson I: "How the Camel Got His Hump": A Story and Its Moral

Explore the plot of "How the Camel Got His Hump" (RL.2.1, RL.2.3, RL.2.5, SL.2.1)

Identify the characters of the story (RL.2.1)

Note the setting and the time that the story takes place (RL.2.1)

Examine Camel and his actions (RL.2.1, RL.2.3, SL.2.1)

Consider the moral of the story (RL.2.1, RL.2.2, SL.2.1)

Lesson II: Illustrating "How the Camel Got His Hump" by Rudyard Kipling

Reread "How the Camel Got His Hump," by Rudyard Kipling (RL.2.1, RL.2.5)

Identify sections in the story (RL.2.1, RL.2.5)

Draw illustrations interpreting the story

Display and evaluate the illustrated stories (SL.2.1)

Revisit the moral of the story (RL.2.1, RL.2.2, SL.2.1)

Lesson I: "How the Camel Got His Hump": A Story and Its Moral

Objectives

Explore the plot of "How the Camel Got His Hump" (RL.2.1, RL.2.3, RL.2.5, SL.2.1)

Identify the characters of the story (RL.2.1)

Note the setting and the time that the story takes place (RL.2.1)

Examine the Camel and his actions (RL.2.1, RL.2.3, SL.2.1)

Consider the moral of the story (RL.2.1, RL.2.2, SL.2.1)

Required Materials

☐ Copies of "How the Camel Got His Hump," by Rudyard Kipling (The copies contain only the text, no illustrations.)

Procedures

1. Lead-In:
   Read "How the Camel Got His Hump" aloud.
2. Step by Step:
   a. Lead a brief discussion of the plot of the story.
   b. Discuss the characters next. Students will identify:

   - Man
   - Camel
   - Horse
   - Dog
   - Ox
   - *Djinn* (genie)

   c. Students explore the setting of the story ("a Howling Desert" and "the beginning of years").
   d. Students continue their discussion, evaluating Camel's behavior and the consequences of his acts.
3. Closure:
   Prompt the students to consider the moral of the story.

Differentiation

Advanced

- Students will read (or listen to) more "Just So Stories" by Kipling that focus on the "how the . . ." theme. Each student chooses one of the other stories to illustrate. Use the illustrations and recorded narration to create a multimedia presentation of "Just So Stories" for the other students.

Struggling

- Following the reading of the story and brief discussion of plot, assign the students a character. As you read the story again, students will act out the parts of each of the characters. Students watching should echo the repeated word "HUMPH" on cue. Continue the lesson as described with step c.

Homework/Assessment
N/A

Taking Care of Ourselves

In this sixth six-week unit of second grade, students will enjoy a wide range of reading and practice informative/explanatory writing while studying human body systems.

ESSENTIAL QUESTION

? Why should we support our opinions with reasons?

OVERVIEW

Examining still life paintings of food for detail, students describe what they see, and arrange and paint a still life of healthy snacks. Building on the painting experience in this unit and the bridge writing in Unit Three, students write informative/explanatory pieces. They read informational texts on body systems in the grade 2 to grade 3 reading range with fluency. As they discover a range of food-related titles, students independently read fiction and poetry, looking for an underlying message.

FOCUS STANDARDS

These Focus Standards have been selected for the unit from the Common Core State Standards.

RL.2.4: Describe how words and phrases (e.g., regular beats, alliteration, rhymes, [and] repeated lines) supply rhythm and meaning in a story, poem, or song.

RL.2.10: By the end of the year, read and comprehend literature, including stories and poetry, in the grades 2 through 3 text complexity band proficiently, with scaffolding as needed at the high end of the range.

SL.2.5: Create audio recordings of stories or poems; add drawings or other visual displays to stories or recounts of experiences when appropriate to clarify ideas, thoughts, and feelings.

RI.2.8: Describe how reasons support specific points the author makes in a text.

RI.2.10: By the end of year, read and comprehend informational texts, including history/social studies, science, and technical texts, in the grades 2 through 3 text complexity band proficiently, with scaffolding as needed at the high end of the range.

W.2.1: Write opinion pieces in which they introduce the topic of the book they are writing about, state an opinion, supply reasons that support the opinion, use linking words (e.g., *because, also*) to connect opinion and reasons, and provide a concluding statement or section.

SUGGESTED STUDENT OBJECTIVES

- Write an informative/explanatory piece describing the experience of painting.
- Use descriptive words (adjectives) to describe food they taste.
- Consult a dictionary on the spelling of descriptive words.
- Read to understand more on a specific topic (e.g., the systems of the body in a narrative informational text, *The Magic School Bus Inside the Human Body*).
- Read texts independently and fluently in both literary and informative genres, on grade level and into the stretch 2 through 3 level of text.
- Read books with a common theme (e.g., food) to explore the treatment of themes in literature.
- Sing songs about a given topic, noting how the rhythm and rhyme of the music and lyrics might help understanding of the topic.
- Use reference books to research a scientific topic (e.g., names of bones in the human body).
- Write a paragraph with an introductory sentence, at least one supporting sentence, and a conclusion.
- Write an opinion piece about a given topic (e.g., an important thing to do to stay healthy).
- Use reflexive pronouns (e.g., *myself, yourself,* and *ourselves*) correctly.

SUGGESTED WORKS

(E) indicates a CCSS exemplar text; (EA) indicates a text from a writer with other works identified as exemplars.

LITERARY TEXTS
Stories

- *Yoko* (Rosemary Wells)
- *Tar Beach* (Faith Ringgold)
- *In the Night Kitchen* (Maurice Sendak) (EA)
- *Gregory the Terrible Eater* (Mitchell Sharmat, Jose Aruego, and Ariane Dewey)
- *Cloudy with a Chance of Meatballs* (Judi and Ron Barrett)
- *Dim Sum for Everyone* (Grace Lin)
- *Thunder Cake* (Patricia Polacco)
- *How My Parents Learned to Eat* (Ina R. Friedman and Allen Say)
- *Everybody Serves Soup* (Norah Dooley and Peter J. Thornton)
- *Everybody Brings Noodles* (Norah Dooley and Peter J. Thornton)

Stories (Read Aloud)

- *The Magic School Bus Inside the Human Body* (Joanna Cole and Bruce Degan)
- *Something's Happening on Calabash Street* (Judith Ross)

- *Strega Nona* (Tomie de Paola)
- *Chato's Kitchen* (Gary Soto and Susan Guevara)
- *Too Many Tamales* (Gary Soto and Ed Martinez)
- *Everybody Cooks Rice* (Norah Dooley and Peter J. Thornton)
- *Everybody Bakes Bread* (Norah Dooley and Peter J. Thornton)
- *My Mom Loves Me More Than Sushi* (Filomena Gomes and Ashley Spires)
- *The Sweetest Fig* (Chris Van Allsburg)

Poems
- "Sick" (Shel Silverstein)
- "The Pizza" (Ogden Nash)
- "Bananas and Cream" (David McCord)
- *Chicken Soup with Rice: A Book of Months* (Maurice Sendak) (EA)

Poems (Read Aloud)
- "Turtle Soup" (Lewis Carroll) (EA)
- *Eats: Poems* (Arnold Adoff and Susan Russo)
- "Boa Constrictor" (Shel Silverstein)

INFORMATIONAL TEXTS
Informational Books
- *What Happens to a Hamburger?* (Paul Showers and Edward Miller)
- *The Digestive System* (Rebecca L. Johnson)
- *Good Enough to Eat: A Kid's Guide to Food and Nutrition* (Lizzy Rockwell)
- *The Nervous System* (Joelle Riley)
- *The Skeleton Inside You* (Philip Balestrino and True Kelley)

Informational Books (Read Aloud)
- *Muscles: Our Muscular System* (Seymour Simon) (EA)
- "Muscles" (Kids Discover Magazine)
- *The Mighty Muscular and Skeletal Systems: How Do My Muscles and Bones Work?* (John Burstein)
- *Bones: Our Skeletal System* (Seymour Simon) (EA)
- "Bones" (Kids Discover Magazine)
- "Nutrition" (Kids Discover Magazine)
- Healthy Eating Series (Susan Martineau and Hel James)
- *Eat Your Vegetables! Drink Your Milk!* (Alvin Silverstein, Virginia B. Silverstein, and Laura Silverstein Nunn)
- *The Food Pyramid* (Christine Taylor-Butler)
- *Showdown at the Food Pyramid* (Rex Barron)
- *Guts: Our Digestive System* (Seymour Simon) (EA)
- *Break It Down: The Digestive System* (Steve Parker)
- *Digestive System* (Cheryl Jakab)

- *The Digestive System* (Christine Taylor-Butler)
- *The Digestive System* (Kristin Petrie)
- "Brain" (Kids Discover Magazine)
- *The Astounding Nervous System: How Does My Brain Work?* (John Burstein)
- *The Nervous System* (Christine Taylor-Butler)

ART, MUSIC, AND MEDIA

Art

- Annibale Carracci, *The Beaneater* (1584–1585)
- Michelangelo Merisi da Caravaggio, *Basket of Fruit* (circa 1599)
- Willem Claesz Heda, *Still Life on a Table* (1638)
- Pieter Claesz, *Still Life with Two Lemons* (1629)
- William Bailey, *Still Life with Rose Wall and Compote* (1973)
- Wayne Thiebaud, *Cakes* (1963)
- Claes Oldenburg, *Two Cheeseburgers, with Everything* (1962)
- Guiseppe Arcimboldo, *Vertumnus* (1590–1591)

Music and Songs

- "Dry Bones" (Traditional)
- "I'm Being Swallowed by a Boa Constrictor" (Traditional)
- "Food, Glorious Food" (from *Oliver,* by Lionel Bart)

SAMPLE ACTIVITIES AND ASSESSMENTS

1. CLASS DISCUSSION

Why do our brains need good food? To begin this unit, students will need to think about the relationship between good food and brain function—how to nurture a healthy body. Encourage the students to look at the figurative meaning of the term *good food*. (SL.2.1)

2. ART/CLASS DISCUSSION/ART MAKING

Introduce the genre of still life to the students. As students view the paintings, talk about the details, objects, and positions of objects that they notice. Closely examine the works by Heda and Claesz. Explain that these artists did "high-definition" work almost two hundred years before photography was invented. They called it *trompe l'oeil,* which is French for "deceive the eye." Students should notice how these paintings are "realer than real." Put cut fruit, a basket, or metalware on the table and have students try to draw one of the objects precisely. (SL.2.1, SL.2.2)

3. ART/CLASS DISCUSSION

Look at the Thiebaud versus the Bailey. How are the colors different? Are we looking at the objects from above, below, or straight on? Did the artists place the objects close together or far apart? Why do you think Bailey chose to space the objects in his painting asymmetrically, versus the symmetry of the Thiebaud? Introduce the Arcimboldo painting into the discussion. Continue to talk about color, perspective, symmetry, and detail and the many different ways in which artists choose to paint, even when they are all painting a still life. (SL.2.1, SL.2.2)

4. INFORMATIVE/EXPLANATORY WRITING

After students have painted the still life (see Art/Class Discussion/Art Making, activity 2), extend the activity by writing. Give the students this prompt: "Write an explanatory how-to piece focused on how you created your painting. Include a description of your still life, the steps of setting up the display through creating your painting, and a strong conclusion." (W.2.2)

5. WORD ACTIVITY

Have the students taste-test healthy snacks, fruits, and vegetables. Encourage them to use adjectives by challenging them to come up with at least three descriptive words between each new taste. For example, "This apple is tangy, sweet, and crunchy!" Encourage students to use a dictionary to check the spelling of the words as needed. (L.2.2e, L.2.5a)

6. CLASS DISCUSSION/LITERATURE

Introduce the book *The Magic School Bus Inside the Human Body* (Joanna Cole). Remind the students that this book is a fantasy but contains information that is true. Use this book to introduce the body systems for the informational side of this unit: skeletal, muscular, digestive, and nervous systems. Begin a chart for each of the body systems to add content learning from other read-aloud and student-read books. Students can post information from their own reading on a chart by using index cards or sticky notes. (RI.2.4)

7. STUDENT READING/INFORMATIONAL TEXT

Have students independently read informational books to learn about each body system. Students should record new learning about each of the body systems in a notebook. They should look for the ways the author supports the main idea. For example, when reading a book about nutrition, ask students to find reasons in the text for why a person should eat healthy foods. (RI.2.8, RI.2.10)

8. TEACHER READ ALOUD/CLASS DISCUSSION

Introduce the book *Everybody Cooks Rice* (Norah Dooley and Peter J. Thornton), which is about a girl who lives in an ethnically diverse neighborhood. She makes a very interesting discovery about her neighbors when she sees what each one is cooking. Read the book aloud. When you are finished, ask the children questions such as:

- What do you think the author wanted you to learn in this book?
- What are the clues from the text that helped you come to that conclusion? (RL.2.2)

9. STUDENT READING/FICTION

In order to stretch students' reading skills and test for comprehension and fluency, have students read a variety of fictional texts independently. Although the books share the common theme of food, they have very different messages. For example, *Tar Beach* (Faith Ringgold), which includes a picnic scene, is literally about rising above prejudice. *Gregory the Terrible Eater* (Mitchell Sharmat, Jose Aruego, and Ariane Dewey) is a funny book about a goat, but carries a message about healthy eating. These books offer a range of reading in the 2 through 3 band of grade level and stretch texts. (RL.2.2, RL.2.10)

10. LANGUAGE ACTIVITY

The title of this unit is Taking Care of Ourselves. Ask students what other words they know that end with -*self* or -*selves*. (Possible answers: *myself, himself, herself, themselves, yourself,* and *yourselves*.)

Practice using these special kinds of pronouns in sentences: "I can do it _____." "She climbed the monkey bars by _____." "They went to the playground by _____." (L.2.1c, SL.2.6)

11. SONG AND CONTENT VOCABULARY ACTIVITY

Explore text, rhythm, and rhyme in the song "Dry Bones." Discuss how bones are connected in the song. It's fun, though not necessarily accurate (e.g., the "toe bone" is not connected directly to the "heel bone"). Then have the students research the scientific names of the bones. Assign each pair of students one of the bones in the song to research online or in an encyclopedia. They should be sure to find out how the bones are actually attached and note the real names for each of the bones mentioned. For example, the twenty-six bones in the foot and the toes are actually called "phalanges." Extend this activity to the stretch level by having the students sing the song with the scientific names. (RL.2.4, RI.2.7)

12. OPINION WRITING

Ask the students to choose one thing that they think is most important to do in order to stay healthy. Tell them to support their opinions with facts that they learned from one of the books they read. Remind them to stay on topic, include details, use appropriate linking words between ideas, and provide a strong conclusion. (W.2.1)

READING FOUNDATIONS: A PACING GUIDE FOR READING INSTRUCTION

See Grade Two, Level Six, in the Reading Foundations section for a complete pacing guide for this unit.

ADDITIONAL RESOURCES

- *General Nutrition* (North Dakota State University)
- *Health Smart Virginia: Second Grade Curriculum Resources* (Virginia Department of Education)

TERMINOLOGY

Adjectives	Explanatory writing	Opinion writing
Dictionary	Fantasy	Reflexive pronouns

MAKING INTERDISCIPLINARY CONNECTIONS

This unit teaches:

Art: Seventeenth-century Dutch still life painting, William Bailey, Wayne Thiebaud
Science: Body systems (e.g., digestive, nervous, muscular, and skeletal)
Nutrition (e.g., foods to eat and healthy living)

This unit could be extended to teach:

Science: Healthy living (e.g., teeth, safety, and environmental hazards)

Grade Two, Unit Six Sample Lesson Plan

In the Night Kitchen by Maurice Sendak

In this series of two lessons, students read *In the Night Kitchen* by Maurice Sendak, and they:

Explore Mickey and his night adventures in the kitchen (RL.2.1, RL.2.3, SL.2.1, SL.2.4)

Explore the significance of rereading texts (RL.2.1, RL.2.3, SL.2.1, SL.2.4)

Summary

Lesson I: Mickey's Adventures in the Night Kitchen

Closely study Sendak's illustrations (RL.2.7)

Note the minimal use of words

Chronicle Mickey's adventures (RL.2.1, RL.2.3, SL.2.1, SL.2.4)

Examine Mickey's character (RL.2.1, RL.3, SL.2.1)

Lesson II: Rereading *In the Night Kitchen*

Revisit Mickey's adventures (RL.2.1, RL.2.3, SL.2.1, SL.2.4)

Reassess (Lesson I) assumptions about Mickey's character (RL.2.1, RL.2.3, SL.2.1, SL.2.4)

Explore the significance of rereading *In the Night Kitchen* (SL.2.1, SL.2.4, RL.2.10)

Examine Mickey's night (W.2.1, RL.2.3, RL.2.5)

Lesson II: Rereading *In the Night Kitchen*

Objectives

Revisit Mickey's adventures (RL.2.1, RL.2.3, SL.2.1, SL.2.4)

Reassess (Lesson I) assumptions about Mickey's character (RL.2.1, RL.2.3, SL.2.1, SL.2.4)

Explore the significance of rereading *In the Night Kitchen* (SL.2.1, SL.2.4, RL.2.10)

Examine Mickey's night (W.2.1, RL.2.3, RL.2.5)

Required Materials

☐ Class set of *In the Night Kitchen* by Maurice Sendak

Procedures

1. Lead In:
   Students (quietly) reread *In the Night Kitchen* by Maurice Sendak.

2. Step by Step:
   a. In a class discussion, students revisit Mickey's adventures.
   b. Students reassess their understanding of Mickey and his actions.
   c. Student volunteer rereads the final page of the book, "And that's why, thanks to Mickey, we have cake every morning."

3. Closer:
   Students discuss how this passage changes the way that they reread the book.

Differentiation

Advanced

- Students are asked to give an opinion about Mickey's character *and* his adventure, supporting each with evidence from the text.

Struggling

- Students prepare for the homework by writing the first sentence together in a small group. Students orally review their opinions about Mickey's character or adventures and find support in the text. Students discuss the conclusion of the paper.

Homework/Assessment

Students write a paragraph in which they express their view of Mickey's night. The paragraph should have:

- A sentence introducing the topic, the text, and the author
- A sentence expressing an opinion about Mickey (his character or his adventures)
- Evidence from the text to support their view
- A concluding sentence

READING FOUNDATIONS: A PACING GUIDE FOR READING INSTRUCTION

The Pacing Guide for Reading Instruction begins at a level appropriate for students who do not already know how to read. This will be the majority of students in most school systems, including those who enter school with limited language and/or literary experience and those who simply lack the phonological, decoding, and encoding skills needed for beginning reading and spelling. The pacing of code-emphasis instruction and the amount of time allotted to it will vary according to student skill levels, as measured on early screening, diagnostic, and progress-monitoring assessments. Nevertheless, all students need to master these essential building blocks.

Some students enter school having already learned the alphabetic principle and basic word recognition and are reading above expectation for these early grades. Those students should be allowed to progress more quickly through the foundational skills sequence, as long as they demonstrate mastery of the concepts. It is conceivable that in the same class, one group of students may just be finishing Level One at the end of the first kindergarten unit, but another group of students could be finishing Level Three if the pace is accelerated.

At times, the content maps might seem incongruent with the skills in the Reading Foundations. An important fact about our maps is that the activities are simply sample activities. They represent a *range* of activities. Also, in keeping with the Common Core State Standards, we continually use developmental options for writing such as "using a combination of drawing, dictating, and writing."

Differentiated instruction is at the heart of effective classroom management. Teachers may need to deliver the literature-focused and content-focused part of the lesson by reading to and dialoguing with the students, taking care to ensure that they also teach a code-emphasis, explicit, and systematic program to all those who need it.

Kindergarten	Level One	Level Two	Level Three
Reading Objectives for Print Concepts (RF.K.1a,b,c,d)	Identify and track single-syllable printed words in short sentences; identify examples of *word*, *sentence*, and *letter* on a printed page. (RF.K.1a,b,c) Match letters to templates; match manipulative upper- and lowercase letters; and point to letters that the teacher names. (RF.K.1d)	Listen for word length; identify longer and shorter words in print. (RF.K.1b,c) Using a printed alphabet template, match plastic or wooden letters to the model and name them in sequence. (RF.K.1d) Identify capital letter, period, and specific printed words on sentence strips. (RF.K.1b)	Listen and point to (track) printed words from left to right, top to bottom, and page by page as text is read aloud. (RF.K.1a) Identify features of a book (title page, author, illustrator, left to right, and top to bottom arrangement of print). (RF.K.1a) Independently match upper- and lowercase letters while naming them. (RF.K.1d)
Model Activities for Print Concepts	As you read a short nursery rhyme (or poem) from a chart, ask students to point to words as they are read. (RF.K.1a,b,c) With movable letters, word cards, and sentence strips, demonstrate the meaning of *letter*, *word*, and *sentence*. Then, ask students to identify examples of each in a printed phrase from a familiar rhyme. (RF.K.1a,b,c) Students trace letters in sand trays, carpet squares, or sandpaper while naming them; trace letter shapes written in large font on a chalkboard; or match manipulative upper- and lowercase letters or letters written on cards until they can point to any letter you name. (RF.K.1d)	Write two words, one long and one short. Ask children to guess which one is a match for the word you say: *Ann, Anthony; Kate, Katherine; ball, basketball; elf, elephant; hip, hippopotamus.* (RF.K.1b,c) Write a four- to five-word sentence from a familiar rhyme or story. Ask students to point to each word as they read aloud with you, and point to and name the end punctuation and the capital letter(s). (RF.K.1a,b,c)	Using a big book, point to words as text is read; then, ask students to point to words going left to right and top to bottom, matching voice to print. (RF.K.1a,b,c) After explaining *author* and *illustrator*, have students point to names on book covers and explain the role of each in making the book. (RF.K.1a,b,c) Using individual alphabet mats with uppercase letters printed in order, have students match lowercase plastic letters to the uppercase, in order, and name them. (RF.K.1d)

Kindergarten	Level One	Level Two	Level Three
Reading Objectives for Phonological Awareness (RF.K.2a,b,c,d)	Listen to and participate in recitation of nursery rhymes, rhyming books, finger plays, songs, and poems. (RF.K.2a) Listen for specific words embedded in rhymes or stories. (RF.K.2a)	Orally identify rhyming words and understand that rhymes have the same last rime (i.e., the vowel and any consonants that follow). (RF.K.2a,c) Count, segment, and delete parts of compound words and words with two and three syllables. (RF.K.2b) Identify the distinguishing features of voiced and voiceless consonant phonemes; orally produce individual consonant phonemes after correct teacher modeling of the voicing distinction: /p/ /b/; /k/ /g/; /t/ /d/; /f/ /v/; /sh/ /zh/; /th/ /th/; /ch/ /j/; /s/ /z/ (RF.K.2d) Classify vowel sounds as open sounds and consonants as closed sounds; locate the vowel sound in every syllable. (RF.K.2d) With teacher modeling and a picture or gestural cue from a key word, pronounce the short vowel sounds and the long vowel sounds (orally—no print!). (RF.K.2d)	Recite familiar rhymes and poems; play with alliteration; create words with sound substitutions (e.g., "silly" words). (RF.K.2a) Orally segment, delete, and substitute syllables in compound words and multisyllable words. (RF.K.2b) Explore the way related groups of phonemes are pronounced: stops /p/, /b/, /t/, /d/,/k/, /g/; hissy sounds /f/, /v/, /th/, /th/, /s/, /z/, /sh/; nasals /m/, /n/, /ng/; glides /h/, /w/, /wh/, /y/; and liquids /l/ and /r/. (RF.K.2d) Blend onsets and rimes; orally match the first phonemes in spoken words; delete an initial phoneme from a word; substitute an initial phoneme. (Begin with continuants: /m/, /s/, /f/, /r/, /l/, /v/, /th/, /th/, /z/, /sh/). (RF.K.2c) Attend to short vowel-sound placement in the mouth, with the jaw dropping for /ĭ/, /ĕ/, /ă/, /ŭ/, /ŏ/. Identify whether the short vowel sounds in spoken words are the same or different. (RF.K.2d) Orally blend two or three phonemes into simple words and segment two- to three-phoneme words by moving tokens into sound boxes while the phonemes are being pronounced. (RF.K.2d)

Kindergarten	Level One	Level Two	Level Three
Model Activities for Phonological Awareness	While reading (reciting) "Humpty Dumpty," snap your fingers on a word at the end of a line (e.g., *wall*). The children will snap when they hear the word that rhymes with it (i.e., *fall*). Continue with various rhymes and poems. (RF.K.2a) After recitation of a favorite rhyme or song, present a puppet that has trouble remembering his words. Students hold up their thumbs if they hear the puppet make a mistake: "Jack and Jill went up the **pill**." Call on individuals to say the right word. (RF.K.2a) Using felt rectangles to represent four to five spoken words (e.g., "Jack went up the hill"), ask students to change the color of the rectangle standing for the word that is changed in a spoken sentence (e.g., "Jill went up the hill." "Jill climbed up the hill." "Jill climbed up the ladder."). (RF.K.2a)	Using different colored index cards representing three common rimes (/-ill/, /-ock/, /-ate/) and other colored cards for first sounds (/l/, /d/, /m/), show in a pocket chart that the first sound(s) might change, but if the last part is the same, the words rhyme (d-ock, l-ock do rhyme; l-ock and l-ate do not rhyme). (RF.K.2a,c) Say a word slowly in syllables and have students say the whole word: *tooth-paste; bath-tub; but-ter-fly; ba-na-na-bread*. (RF.K.2b) With students looking in mirrors and putting their hands over their ears to hear vocal resonance, model and describe the difference between /p/ and /b/; /f/ and /v/; /k/ and /g/; and so forth; with students, classify spoken consonant sounds as voiced or unvoiced. (RF.K.2d) Describe vowels as open sounds and consonants as closed off by the lips, teeth, and tongue; categorize the first sounds of spoken words as vowels (open sounds) or consonants (closed sounds): *o-ver; m-ouse; sh-ower; a-lligator*. (RF.K.2d)	Play "Willaby Wallaby Woo" with students' names. (RF.K.2a) With a picture cue, ask students to help a puppet who only says words in parts. After the puppet speaks the syllables, students blend them into a whole word: *Sep-tem-ber; di-no-saur; cin-na-mon; tel-e-vis-ion*. (RF.K.2b) Play the speech sound guessing game. Students imitate the sounds and/or look in a mirror to answer questions such as, "Which sound is made with the lips—/p/ or /k/? Which sound is made with the mouth wide open—/ŏ/ or /w/? Which sound is made with the tongue between the teeth—/f/ or /th/?" and so forth. (RF.K.2d) Show three picture cards, such as *milk, bed, and moose, or fan, feather, and thimble*. Students say the words, match the pictures that start with the same sound, isolate the target sound, and then find the sound-symbol card with that sound. Vary the difficulty by monitoring the confusability of the first sounds (i.e., /m/ and /n/ are harder to discriminate than /m/ and /t/). (RF.K.2d)

Reading Foundations: A Pacing Guide for Reading Instruction (Kindergarten, Levels One Through Three)

Kindergarten	Level One	Level Two	Level Three
		With puppets, pictures, or gestures, associate each short vowel sound with its keyword and letter name: /ĭ/ - itch – i /ĕ/ - edge – e /ă/ - apple – a /ŏ/ - octopus – o /ŭ/ - up – u (RF.K.2d) With puppets, pictures, or gestures, practice associating a long vowel sound with its keyword and letter name: /ā/ - apron – a /ē/ - eagle – e /ō/ - oval – o /ū/ - unicorn – u /ɹ/ - ice cream – i (RF.K.2d)	Ask students to listen carefully for a specific vowel sound in the words you say. They repeat the sound only if they hear it in the word: /ē/ —me, eat, sleep, pie, snow, east, team, fast. (RF.K.2d)
Reading Objectives for Phonics and Word Recognition (RF.K.3a,b,c)	With the teacher leading, recite an alphabet song that includes the letter name, and a key word (picture or gesture) and sound associated with each letter. (RF.K.3a,b) Note: A set of sound-symbol cards that includes most of the forty-four speech sounds of English should be displayed and learned in segments.	Name the key word that goes with a letter; say the sound that goes with a key word; and say the letter(s) that represent a sound. Given a sound-symbol card, say the keywords and consonant phonemes that are represented with two letters: th, sh, ch, ng, wh. (RF.K.3a,b)	Say the alphabet song (as described in Unit 1) and a short vowel song or rhyme, with minimal teacher prompting. (RF.K.3a,b) Demonstrate accuracy and fluency in sound — key word—symbol association for most consonants and short vowels. (RF.K.3a,b)

Kindergarten	Level One	Level Two	Level Three
	High-frequency symbols (graphemes) for each of the consonant and vowel phonemes that are only represented by letter combinations (such as /sh/, /th/, /ch/, /ng/, and /aw/) can be gradually introduced before the end of the kindergarten year.		Identify the letters c and k as both representing /k/; c and s as both representing /s/; qu as a team that represents /kw/; and final x as the symbol for /ks/ (as in "box"). (RF.K.3a,b) Read common words such as *I, the, a.* (RF.K.3c)
Model Activities for Phonics and Word Recognition	Teach an alphabet song or rhyme by daily repetition. As you lead recitation of the alphabet song, point to the sound-symbol cards, and pause on occasion so that students can fill in a known letter name/keyword/sound (e.g., "r," rabbit, /r/) on their own. (RF.K.3a,b)	Play the sound-symbol game with known vowels and consonants: You say a keyword (or make a gesture); students say the sound. Or, you say the sound, and students make the gesture and say the letter name. (RF.K.3a). [Suggested order for introduction and mastery through a 12–18 week period: /m/, /s/, /f/, /a/, /t/, /p/, /n/, /i/, /h/, /k/ spelled c, /l/, /b/, /j/ spelled j, initial /r/, /o/, /k/ spelled k, /d/, /g/ spelled g, /e/, /y/ spelled y, /z/, /ks/ spelled x, /u/, /kw/ spelled qu, /v/, /w/.] Once the students have practiced the sound-symbol associations by recitation, hand out sound-symbol cards to students seated in a circle. Toss a beanbag to students randomly, and have them say the letter name, keyword, and/or sound on their card. (RF.K.3a, b)	Play a sound-symbol guessing game, focusing on end of alphabet, lower frequency letter-sound correspondences, and subtle contrasts: *I'm thinking of a letter that stands for the sound combination /ks/; I'm thinking of a sound that's made with the lips closed and the voice off* (/p/), etc. (RF.K.3a,b) Make a few simple words with letter tiles (no blends) and leave off the first letter. Say the whole word and ask students what sound is missing. Students find the missing sound in the sound-symbol cards and then supply the missing letter for the beginning of each word: (b)ear; (w)ent; (s)ing. Shift to ending sounds as students become proficient with first sounds: we(t), mu(d), su(n). (RF.K.3a,b) Encourage students to read first-step books with rebuses for content words by pointing to each

Kindergarten	Level One	Level Two	Level Three
Reading Objectives for Fluency (RF.K.4)	n/a	n/a	word. Ask students to identify high-frequency irregular words *I, the, a,* in the text. (RF.K.3c) Recognize a few familiar words as wholes. (RF.K.4)
Model Activities for Fluency			Students can collect favorite words with a specific consonant sound (/s/, /b/, or /r/, for example) and illustrate each word in a word book. Reread the word books many times to pick up fluency. (RF.K.4)
Writing, Handwriting, and Spelling Objectives (LK.1a,c,d)	Demonstrate pencil grip and posture for writing; trace, copy, and write lines, circles with large motor and small motor control. (LK.1a)	Copy and write first name; write circle letters (a, c, o, d, g, q) within lines. (LK.1a)	Form letters that are made with a downward line first: b, f, h, i, j, k, l, m, n, p, r, t, u. (L.K.1a) Directed writing: Write letters for sounds given by the teacher; write high-frequency words *I, the, a.* (L.K.2c) Attempt phonetic spellings of unknown words; copy and/or complete words in simple printed sentences (e.g., "I like to ——."). (L.K.2d)
Model Activities for Writing, Handwriting, and Spelling	Draw large shapes (circle; horizontal line; cross, etc.) on the chalkboard. Count or provide a rhythm as students trace the shape with the whole arm and pointer fingers on the board or in the air. "Trace" with eyes open and closed. (L.K.1a)	As a "writing warm-up," transfer rhythmic writing of shapes and lines to paper with lines; then combine circles and lines for first letters. (L.K.1a)	Before students practice tracing and copying, number the pencil strokes and draw arrows to show how the pencil moves. (L.K.1a) Encourage students to pay attention to what their mouths are doing when they spell by sound, and to look at the sound-symbol cards to remember the letters as they try to spell new words. (L.K.2d)

Reading Foundations: A Pacing Guide for Reading Instruction (Kindergarten, Levels Four Through Six)

Kindergarten	Level Four	Level Five	Level Six
Reading Objectives for Print Concepts (RF.K.1d)	Increase fluency in naming randomly ordered upper- and lowercase letters to benchmark level. (RF.K.1d)	Increase fluency in accurately naming randomly ordered upper- and lowercase letters. (RF.K.1d)	n/a
Model Activities for Print Concepts	Devote a few minutes of classroom time to simple speed drills several times weekly. Create or find letter naming practice sheets with randomly ordered upper- and lowercase letters on a page. Have students work in pairs to practice naming the letters as quickly as they can until they can name approximately twenty-seven letters in one minute. Re-teach any letters students are missing. (RF.K.1d)	Screen students for letter naming accuracy and fluency. Re-teach unknown letters to students who are making errors. Have students who still need practice spend a few minutes daily on speed drills until they can name approximately thirty-five letters in one minute. (RF.K.1d)	Students should be able to name randomly distributed upper- and lowercase letters at a rate of at least forty correct per minute. (RF.K.1d)
Reading Objectives for Phonological Awareness (RF.K.2c,d,e)	Delete and substitute initial sounds and final sounds in spoken words; segment one-syllable words with three to four phonemes, using sound boxes. Isolate and pronounce the vowel sound. (RF.K.2d) Identify and recite the long vowel sounds; learn a long vowel song or rhyme for mnemonic support. (RF.K.2d)	Blend four-phoneme words orally, including words with the most transparent consonant blends (-st, -lk, -ft). (RF.K.2c) Classify phonemes as consonants (closed sounds) and vowel sounds (open phonemes), and syllables as closed (ending in a consonant) or open (ending in a long vowel).	With modeling and support, orally segment and blend any single syllable word with three to four phonemes, including any of the forty-four vowel sounds and consonants of English. (RF.K.2c)
		Make new consonant-vowel-consonant (CVC) words by substituting an initial phoneme, medial vowel, or final phoneme. (RF.K.2e)	

Kindergarten	Level Four	Level Five	Level Six
		Match spoken single-syllable words by the medial vowel sound, including all eighteen vowel sounds of English. (RF.K.2d)	
Model Activities for Phonological Awareness	Use a picture clue and a puppet who can't say his last sounds. Ask students to help him say a whole word correctly: peanu(t), butt(er), sandwi(ch); chicke(n) McNugge(ts); vanill(a) i(ce) crea(m). (RF.K.2d) Use a grid (sound box template) in which each box stands for one speech sound. Students work with movable tiles or chips. Say a word with two (*zoo*), three (*fog*), or four (*fast*) phonemes. Model, then lead students as they segment each sound, moving a chip into a box as they say the sounds in order. Say the whole word after it is segmented. Ask, which is the first sound? The second sound? The last sound? And so forth. (RF.K.2d) Ask students to listen for two long vowels (e.g., /ā/ or /ū/) in the words you say. After you say a word, students say the vowel sound: *cape, soon, say, blue, stew, sail*, etc. Or ask students to hold up the sound-symbol card with the correct sound. (RF.K.2d)	Model blending words with four sounds. Hold up your fist; raise a finger as you say each sound (e.g., /m/, /a/, /s/, /k/), then blend the whole word (i.e., mask) as you sweep your hand from left to right. Students follow your lead. (RF.K.2c) Create "vowel houses" where words with the same vowel sound live together. Using picture cards for one-syllable words with three or four different vowel sounds, students find the house where they live (e.g., *saw, paw, dawn; blue, moon, chew; snow, bow, oak; star, art, mark*). (RF.K.2d) Explain that consonant sounds are closed off by the lips, teeth, and tongue, and vowel sounds are open and sustained. Say a sound and ask students to hold up a response card: V for vowel and C for consonant. Using colored squares to represent speech sounds, show which sound has changed when a spoken word is changed, one sound at a time: *sun, ton, shun, shut, shout, out, oat, own, shown*. (RF.K.2e)	Continue matching spoken words to "vowel houses" and be sure that all the vowel houses have some words living in them, even the less frequent: *toy, boy, oil; book, hoof, bush; cow, brow, ouch*. (RF.K.2d) Segment three- and four-phoneme spoken words by tapping head, shoulders, waist, and toes as you say the sounds (/h/ /ou/ /se/, etc.). Then ask, what was the waist sound? What was the head sound? And so forth. (RF.K.2c) Ask students to help you blend words you are reading in a story. As you read aloud, say a short word in phonemes and have students blend the whole word (e.g., "Because the rabbit ran so /f/ /ă/ /s/ /t/, the /f/ /ŏ/ /k/ /s/ fell way behind."). (RF.K.2c)

Kindergarten	Level Four	Level Five	Level Six
Reading Objectives for Phonics and Word Recognition (RF.K.3a,b,c,d)	Using manipulative cards, blend initial letter-sounds /f/, /l/, /m/, /n/, /r/, /s/, final sounds /d/, /g/, /p/, /t/, and short vowels /a/, /i/, /o/ into VC and CVC combinations. (RF.K.3a,b)	Build simple short vowel (closed) syllables with letter-sounds used in Unit 4, plus vowels /ŭ/ and /ĕ/, and consonant grapheme cards including b, sh, h, j, c, k, ck, v, w (as in wet), x (as in fox), y (as in yes), z, ch, th, qu, and wh. (RF.K.3a,b)	Increase fluency and accuracy in reading any CVC syllable that uses the letter-sound correspondences practiced in Themes 4 and 5. (RF.K.3a,b)
	Read up to ten of the most common words by sight, using multi-sensory or manipulative props as necessary. (RF.K.3c)	Read up to twenty of the most common words by sight. (RF.K.3c)	Read twenty-five or more of the most common words by sight. (RF.K.3c)
		Recognize the change of meaning when plural -s is added to a noun. (RF.K.3d)	Recognize some common words with the VCe (vowel-consonant-silent "e") long vowel spelling pattern (*like, ate, home, cute*). (RF.K.3a,b,d)
		Read long vowel (open) syllables *he, she, we, so, no, hi, my*. (RF.K.3c,d)	
Model Activities for Phonics and Word Recognition	Teach blending of simple words with letter tiles or letter cards. Students watch and follow: For example, with the word *sat*, 1) point to the spelling of the first sound[s] and say "sound" as you point to it; 2) point to the second spelling [a] and say "sound" as you point to it; 3) sweep your hand from left to right under the letters as you say "blend it;" 4) point to the third spelling [t] and say "sound" as you point to it; 5) sweep your hand from left to right under the letters as you say "blend it." Then say, "What's the word?" Quickly use it in a sentence. (RF.K.3a,b)	Teach blending of simple words with three to four sounds—on a chalkboard or whiteboard—as students watch and follow: For example, with the word *fox*, 1) write the spelling of the first sound [f] and say "sound" as you point to it; 2) write the second spelling [o] and say "sound" as you point to it; 3) sweep your hand from left to right under the letters as you say "blend it;" 4) write the third spelling [x] and say "sound" as you point to it; 5) sweep your hand from left to right under the letters as you say "blend it." Then say, "What's the word?" Quickly use it in a sentence. (RF.K.3a,b)	Using a pocket chart or letter tiles, introduce students to the VCe long vowel pattern by adding "magic e" to familiar CVC words and noting the change of vowel sound: Hop—hope Cap—cape Hat—hate Pin—pine Shin—shine Can—cane Cut—cute (RF.K.3a,b,d) Practice reading phrases with the learned VCe words, plus *like, home,* and *came*. (RF.K.3a,b,d)

Reading Foundations: A Pacing Guide for Reading Instruction (Kindergarten, Levels Four Through Six)

Kindergarten	Level Four	Level Five	Level Six
	Give students letter cards or tiles with a few consonants and one or two short vowels. Model, then lead them in building words with two to three sounds. (RF.K.3a,b) Progress to sound substitution: Change *at* to *an*; *an* to *man*; *mat* to *man*, *man* to *fan*, *fan* to *fin*, and so forth. (RF.K.3a,b) Explain that some words in English do not play fair or follow the rules. Introduce up to five to ten of the most frequent irregular words.	Give students letter cards or tiles with more consonants and two or three short vowels. Model, then lead them in building words with three to four sounds. Continue sound substitution games. (RF.K.3a,b) To a familiar word (e.g., *rock, zip, jam*) have students add *s*, pronounce the new word, and use it in a sentence. (RF.K.3d) Practice new irregular or "red" words by tracing them, saying the letters, and saying the whole word before reading in context. (RF.K.3c)	Underline all irregular words as you read phrases and beginner texts. Ask students to tell you why they are underlined. (RF.K.3c)
Reading Objectives for Fluency (RF.K.4)	After previewing, read simple, decodable texts with words and sound-symbol correspondences that have been taught. (RF.K.4)	After previewing, read simple, decodable texts with words and sound-symbol correspondences that have been taught. (RF.K.4)	After previewing, read simple, decodable texts with words and sound-symbol correspondences that have been taught. (RF.K.4)
Model Activities for Fluency	Use simple "first step" stories with high-frequency words and decodable words that have been taught and practiced. Preview the book: What (who) is it about? Where is the title? What might happen? Let students read to a partner and then retell the story. (RF.K.4) Have students revisit their predictions. If the prediction was incorrect, explain what was different.	Continue with "first step" stories with high-frequency words and decodable words that have been taught and practiced. Preview the book: What (who) is it about? Where is the title? What might happen? Let students read to a partner and then retell the story. Check predictions and explain any discrepancies. Choral read for variety. (RF.K.4) With phonetically regular, unknown words, encourage students to blend each sound into the whole word. (RF.K.4)	Continue with pre-primer stories with high-frequency words and decodable words that have been taught and practiced. Preview the book: What (who) is it about? Where is the title? What might happen? Why? Let students read to a partner and then retell the story. (RF.K.4) Encourage rereading of familiar texts, with emphasis on phrasing and expression. (RF.K.4) With phonetically regular, unknown words, encourage students to blend each sound into the whole word. (RF.K.4)

Kindergarten	Level Four	Level Five	Level Six
Writing, Handwriting, and Spelling Objectives (LK.1a,b, LK.2a,c, RF.K.2d)	Form letters with horizontal lines and diagonals: e, s, v, w, x, y, z. (L.K.1a) Write the consonant letters, including digraphs th, ch, wh, sh when the sounds are dictated. Write CVC words to dictation; write simple sentences using CVC words and five to ten of the highest-frequency words in written text. (RF.K.2d, L.K.1f, L.K.2a, L.K.2c)	Write short, dictated sentences with a capital letter and end punctuation, using a word wall or other reference for high-frequency irregular words. (L.K.2a,b) Create short sentences with known words; attempt spellings of unknown/unusual words. (L.K.2c,d)	Using learned words and sound-symbol associations, formulate and transcribe several sentences that tell a narrative sequence or that describe an object, event, or activity. (W.K.3, L.K.1, L.K.2)
Model Activities for Writing, Handwriting, and Spelling	Play the sound-symbol game, but with a written response. You say a letter, key word, and/or sound, and students write the symbol. Provide individual sound-symbol cards for reference as necessary. (L.K.1a, RF.K.3a,b) Dictate a simple sentence for completion, with unknown words provided and lines for missing words: (He) will (hit) (the) ball; (I) (got) (a) car. Help students segment the phonetically regular words as they write. (RF.K.2d, L.K.1.1f, L.K.2a, L.K.2c)	Dictate a simple sentence with a line provided for each word: *I hit the pin. He hit his chin.* Help students segment the phonetically regular words as they write, referring to sound-symbol cards as necessary. (RF.K.2d, L.K.1.1f, L.K.2a, L.K.2c) Develop a word wall for easy indexing of irregularly spelled words and encourage correct spelling of words that have been practiced. (L.K.2c,d) In shared writing, as students volunteer words for retelling or creating stories, encourage them to provide letters for sounds as you write. (W.K.3, W.K.7, L.K.2d)	After following a storyboard and rehearsing a story orally, encourage students to write several sentences connected by a narrative sequence. Encourage phonetic spelling of unknown words and correct spelling of the highest-frequency words that have been practiced. (W.K.3, L.K.1, L.K.2)

Reading Foundations: A Pacing Guide for Reading Instruction (Grade One, Levels One Through Three)

Grade One	Level One	Level Two	Level Three
Reading Objectives for Print Concepts (RF.1.1a)	On a printed page, identify examples of first and last letters in a word, first and last words on a page, and first and last words in a sentence. (RF.1.1a) Track print from left to right and top to bottom as the teacher reads the words aloud. (RF.1.1a) On a printed page, point to capital letters and end punctuation in sentences, and match periods, question marks, and exclamation points to sentence types. (RF.1.1a)	Pause and adapt phrasing in response to periods at the ends of sentences. (RF.1.1a)	While orally reading beginning text, notice and respond to all end punctuation by adjusting vocal intonation. (RF.1.1a)
Model Activities for Print Concepts	Give students pretend (or real) magnifying glasses to play detective with a simple book they are reading. After each term has been directly taught, play "I Spy" to find examples of first (initial), last (final), middle (medial), top, bottom, left, right, and capital letters, and periods, question marks, and exclamation points. (RF.1.1a) Using a big book or chart with familiar language, ask students to take turns pointing to printed words as the teacher says them.	Before students read sentences or pages aloud, ask them to point to end punctuation. Model vocal phrasing indicated by each mark. Lead the group in choral reading of short sentences, and then call on individuals to reread sentences with appropriate phrasing and intonation. (RF.1.1a)	To practice the inflection required by punctuation, insert punctuation into the alphabet sequence and ask students to choral read: A, B, C! D, E, F, G, H, I? J, K, L, MNO. PQ? R S T. U, V, W! X, Y, Z. (RF.1.1a)
Reading Objectives for Phonological Awareness	Orally segment, delete, and substitute syllables in multisyllable words. (RF.1.2a)	Orally blend the first part of a word with a final consonant. (RF.1.2b)	Within the context of a simple story, blend two- and three-phoneme words, without consonant blends, that have been orally segmented. (RF.1.2b)

Reading Foundations: A Pacing Guide for Reading Instruction (Grade One, Levels One Through Three)

Grade One (RF.1.2a,b,d)	Level One	Level Two	Level Three
(RF.1.2a,b,d)	Listen for two or three widely contrasting vowel sounds (e.g., /ō/ and /ē/) in a series of spoken words; isolate and repeat a target sound when it is heard (RF.1.2a) Say the short vowel sounds in order of placement in the mouth; feel the jaw dropping for /ĭ/, /ĕ/, /ă/, /ŭ/, /ŏ/ and match a word to another with the same short vowel sound. (RF.1.2a)	Substitute an initial or final consonant in a word and blend it into a new word. (RF.1.2b)	Given a two- or three-phoneme word, segment and pronounce the sounds in sequence. (RF.1.2d)
Model Activities for Phonological Awareness	Using colored rectangles or cards (distinguished from any manipulative used to mark phonemes), ask students to decide how many rectangles are needed to mark the syllables of a spoken word: *detective; investigator; mystery; pilot; adventure.* Students put out a card for each syllable, while saying the syllables slowly. Then ask, "Which one is this?" Or ask, "What is left if I take this one away?" (RF.1.2a) Create "vowel houses" where words with the same vowels live. Using picture cards or spoken words, ask students to listen for and pronounce the vowel in the word, and then place it in the right vowel house. Start with two vowels per activity; progress to more as the students become skilled. (RF.1.2a)	Using the puppet that has trouble finishing his words (introduced in Kindergarten), pronounce words or names (preferably from the stories the students are reading) without the last sound. Ask students to help the puppet say the whole word *and* say the missing sound clearly in isolation. (RF.1.2b) Play this listening game: The word is _____ (shop). If I change /sh/ to /ch/, what's the new word? <u>Chop!</u> The word is _____ (bake). I f I change /k/ to /s/, what's the new word? <u>Base!</u> (RF.1.2b)	Selecting sentences from stories you've read aloud, segment some words as you read, asking for students' help in putting them together: "This is story about a town /m/ /ou/ /s/ (_____) [pause—let students supply whole word] and a country mouse." (RF.1.2d) Using spoken words with all medial vowel sounds (long, short, diphthong, r-controlled), build segmentation fluency with this routine: Say a word. Students repeat. Segment the sounds orally as a finger is raised for each phoneme. Sweep the hand from left to right as the word is blended.

Grade One	Level One	Level Two	Level Three
	After demonstrating the jaw dropping as each short vowel is articulated, and providing a visual chart for reference, select the five short vowel sound-symbol cards and give them to students to hold. Say a word with a short vowel. The student with that card holds it up while everyone says the vowel sound and its key word, feeling how open or closed their mouth is and looking in the mirror if necessary. (RF.1.2a)		(*Note*: At this stage, students should be fluent and proficient with segmentation of one-syllable words.) (RF.1.2b,d)
Reading Objectives for Phonics and Word Recognition (RF.1.3a,b,c,g)	With reference to sound-spelling cards containing a keyword and major spellings for each sound, learn sound-spelling associations by means of a see/hear/say/and write sequence: /m/, /ă/, /t/, /h/, /p/, /n/, /k/ spelled c, /d/, /s/, /ĭ/, /b/. (RF.1.3a,b,c)

Blend and read simple words containing the taught sound-spellings, in isolation and in connected text. (RF.1.3a,b,c)

Using a tracing, oral-spelling, and visual imagery routine, learn approximately three to five common **irregular** new words per week. (Note: Many of the most common words in English do follow regular patterns of phonics and are no longer "irregular" once the patterns have been taught.) (RF.1.3g) | Learn sound-spelling associations by means of a see/hear/say/and write sequence: /r/, /f/, /g/, /ŏ/, /ks/ spelled x, /ar/, /k/ spelled -ck, /ŭ/, /z/, /l/, /ĕ/ spelled e and ea, /y/, /w/, /hw/ spelled wh, /er/ spelled ir, ur, or er. (RF.1.3a,b,c)

Blend and read simple words containing the taught sound-spellings, in isolation and in connected text. (RF.1.3a,b,c)

Read regular plural nouns formed with "s" and pronounced /s/ or /z/ (e.g., cats, dogs) and explain the meaning of the plural. (RF.1.3g) | Learn sound-spelling associations by means of a see/hear/say/and write sequence: /sh/ spelled sh, /th/, /ch/, /k/ spelled k, /ā/ spelled a_e, and a_e, /j/ spelled j and –dge, /j/ spelled ge, gi, /ī/ spelled i, i_e, /s/ spelled ce, ci, /ō/ spelled o, o_e, /z/ spelled s, /v/, /ū/ spelled u, u_e, /ē/ spelled e, e_e, /ē/ spelled ee, ea, /kw/ spelled qu, long vowels + r, /ē/ spelled y, _ie_, /ā/ spelled ai, ay, /ī/ spelled igh, /ī/ spelled y, ie, /ng/ spelled -ng (RF.1.3a,b,c)

Apply associations to blending and reading simple words in isolation and in connected text. (RF.1.3a,b,c)

Read plural nouns with –s and –es and verbs with -ing. (RF.1.3g) |

Grade One	Level One	Level Two	Level Three
Model Activities for Phonics and Word Recognition	(*Note:* Introduce about two new sounds per week.) As each new sound-symbol card is introduced, teach a simple story or rhyme about the sound (e.g., "This is Leo the Lion; he loves to lick lollipops . . ."). With learned associations, play "I'm thinking of . . . " (e.g., the letter that represents /h/; a sound that letter c can represent; a vowel that begins the word *apple* . . .). (RF.1.3a,b,c) Teach sound-by-sound blending of simple words with two to four sounds on a chalkboard or whiteboard, as students watch and follow: For example, with the word *pin*, 1) write the spelling of the first sound [p] and say "sound" as you point to it; 2) write the second spelling [i] and say "sound" as you point to it; 3) sweep your hand from left to right under the letters as you say "blend it"; 4) write the third spelling [n] and say "sound" as you point to it; 5) sweep your hand from left to right under the letters as you say "blend it." Then say, "What's the word?" Quickly use it in a spoken sentence. (RF.1.3a,b,c)	(*Note:* Introduce about two to three new sounds per week.) Conduct daily quick drills with learned sound-symbol associations: You say the sound, students say the letter(s); you say the letter(s), students say the sound; you say the sound, students write the letter(s). Automaticity is the goal. (RF.1.3a,b,c) Teach blending of whole words with three to four sounds, as students watch and follow: 1) write the whole word—*f a s t*; 2) point to each letter-sound and say "sound", cuing students to say the sounds in order—/f/ /a/ /s/ /t/; 3) sweep your hand from left to right under the letters, saying "blend it"; students say the whole word. Quickly use the word in a sentence. (RF.1.3a,b,c) Blend fifteen to thirty words per day with sound-symbol associations that have been taught; then read in phrases, sentences, and books. Include nouns with the non-syllabic plural -s. (RF.1.3a,b,c,g)	(*Note:* Introduce about two to three new sounds per week.) Conduct daily quick drills with learned sound-symbol associations. Give students letter (or grapheme) tiles, including digraphs and vowel teams (*ng, th, ck, ee,* etc.) written on one tile. Students can practice one-minute speed drills in pairs, naming the sounds for the graphemes. (RF.1.3a,b,c) To teach the VCe pattern for long vowels, use letter tiles to show how "magic e" changes words: *mad-made, hop-hope, pet-Pete, cut-cute, hid-hide*. (RF.1.3a,b,c) Ask students to underline target letter combinations before blending whole words with a new letter pattern: <u>close</u>, <u>cent</u>, ni<u>ce</u>; do<u>dge</u>; <u>high</u>. (RF.1.3a,b,c) With letter (grapheme) tiles, construct whole words with three to four learned sounds. You say a word; students repeat the word, build it, blend it, and use it in a sentence. (RF.1.3a,b,c)

Grade One	Level One	Level Two	Level Three
	Blend fifteen to thirty words per day with sound-symbol associations that have been taught; then read in phrases, sentences, and books. Underline or color code the irregular words" that don't follow the learned patterns. (RF.1.3a,b,c,g)		Use a pocket chart to add inflections -ing, -s, and -es to base words that do not require doubling or dropping silent e (walk-ing, shout-s, pick-ing; pass-es, fox-es). Challenge students to use inflected word in spoken sentences, and discuss how the ending changes the word's meaning. (RF.1.3g)
Reading Objectives for Fluency (RF.1.4a,b,c)	Discriminate between sense and nonsense, and expect that printed words (if accurately read) will generally make sense. (RF.1.4c)	After teacher or partner modeling, reread phrases and sentences to improve phrasing and intonation. (RF.1.4a,b,c)	By mid-year, read twenty to thirty words correctly per minute in unrehearsed grade level text with 96% accuracy or better, and demonstrate comprehension through retelling. (RF.1.4a) Given printed phrases or phrase markers, reread a familiar passage, adjusting intonation and expression to convey meaning. (RF.1.4b) On encountering an unknown word, the reader a) looks carefully at the letter sequence, b) sounds out the word, and c) checks the sense within the whole sentence or passage. If it does not make sense, he or she rereads or asks for assistance. (RF.1.4c)

Grade One	Level One	Level Two	Level Three
Model Activities for Fluency	Play with "sense" and "nonsense." Read a sentence, deliberately changing a key word or two. Ask students if it makes sense; if not, ask them to say why. (RF.1.4c) Categorize words as "sense" or "nonsense." Explain that reading, in general, should make sense. (RF.1.4c)	Tell students that reading aloud should sound like talking. After they have read a sentence or passage for accuracy, ask them to read with you and follow your voice. (RF.1.4a,b,c)	Using an overhead projector or large print book, mark the phrases and read them aloud as you sweep your hand under the groups of words. Encourage students to sweep their fingers under the groups of words as they "smush" them together. (RF.1.4a,b,c) Structure partner reading: Assign one person to be "reader" and the other to be "coach." The coach can say, "Try that again" if an error is made. At the end of the book, coach asks the reader to tell what each page or part of the book was about. Students then change roles for the next book reading. (RF.1.4a,b,c)
Writing, Handwriting, and Spelling Objectives (L.1.1a,j, L.1.2b,d,e, W.1.3)	Form the upper- and lowercase versions of the letters m, a, t, h, p, n, c, d, s, i, b; spell one-syllable words with those letters and twenty of the most often used words in writing. (L.1.1a, L.1.2d) Complete sentences in which one part of the "who" "is doing/did what" "to whom or what" is missing. (L.1.1j) Identify, then generate, words or phrases that answer the questions *who, what, where, when, or how.* (L.1.1j)	Form the upper- and lowercase versions of the letters r, f, g, o, x, k u, z, l, e, y, w; spell one-syllable words with sound-spellings that have been taught. (L.1.1a, L.1.2d,e) Change statements into questions and questions into statements, with end punctuation. (L.1.1j, L.1.2b)	Recall and write all the alphabet letters with accuracy. (L.1.1a) Spell one-syllable words with sound-spellings that have been taught. (L.1.2d,e) Elaborate "bare bones" sentences by describing the subject (the who/what part) and saying more about the predicate (the doing part). (L.1.1j) Write several sentences telling events in a narrative sequence. (L.1.1j, W.1.3)

Grade One	Level One	Level Two	Level Three
Model Activities for Writing, Handwriting and Spelling (L.1.1a,j, L.1.2b,d,e, W.1.3)	Given directional arrows, lined spaces, and verbal cues, students trace and then write the letters they are learning to read. (L.1.1a)	Given directional arrows, lined spaces, and verbal cues, students trace and then write the letters they are learning to read. (L.1.1a)	Challenge students to write the alphabet accurately and fluently from memory, including j, q, and v. (L.1.1a)
	Explain that each complete sentence must have basic parts. With a sentence frame representing who or what - is doing or did - to whom or what, where, when or how, students write words to create a complete sentence: *Sid hid the mat.* (L.1.1j)	As you dictate words and sentences for writing, say the whole sentence and have students make a line for each word. Then, help students segment the sounds in each word as they write, checking against the sound-spelling cards. (L.1.2d,e)	Use a grid to map graphemes to phonemes during spelling practice; one box contains the letters for one sound: sh-a-ck; d-o-dge; th-i-ng; ch-i-ll. (L.1.2d,e)
	Given a simple statement, such as "The bat hit Sid on his cap," students identify which words answer the basic questions *who, what, when, where,* and *how,* as they write the sentence in the sentence frame. (L.1.1j)	Pass out question word cards to students. Give a simple statement, then call on students to create questions with their question words (*who, what, when, where, how*). Enlist their help as you transcribe the words onto a chart or board. (L.1.1j, L.1.2b)	Expand kernel sentences by answering any three of the question words: *who, what, when, where, why, how.* (For example, "She rode" becomes "Tina rode her bike into the shrub.") (L.1.1j)
			Provide a visual frame marked *beginning, middle,* and *end,* with sequence words such as *first, then, next,* and *finally;* ask students to write a simple narrative with one or more illustrations. (L.1.1j, W.1.3)

Reading Foundations: A Pacing Guide for Reading Instruction (Grade One, Levels Four Through Six)

Grade One	Level Four	Level Five	Level Six
Reading Objectives for Print Concepts (RF.1.1)	While orally reading beginner text, adjust intonation and phrasing in response to all punctuation used at first grade level. (RF.1.1)	n/a	n/a
Model Activities for Print Concepts	Extract a passage from a mid-first-grade reader; omit end punctuation and commas, and place on an overhead or chart. Read aloud, pausing where punctuation occurs. Ask students to supply what is missing. Or, mix up the punctuation and see how it changes meaning. (RF.1.1)	n/a	n/a
Reading Objectives for Phonological Awareness (RF.1.2c,d)	After segmenting a word, isolate and pronounce the first, second, third, or fourth phoneme. (RF.1.2c) Given a word with up to four phonemes, segment and pronounce the sounds in sequence. (RF.1.2d)	Using sound-spelling cards for reference, match any isolated phoneme with its sound-spelling card. (RF.1.2c) Given a word with up to five phonemes, segment and pronounce the sounds in sequence. (RF.1.2d)	Demonstrate phoneme segmentation fluency and accuracy with any one-syllable word. (RF.1.2d)
Model Activities for Phonological Awareness	Give students about six colored squares, including two of the same color. Say a word with a blend: "clock." Students move a square for each sound—/k/ /l/ /ŏ/ /k/—into sound boxes or a grid. Ask, what was the second sound? (/l/) What was the vowel sound? (/ŏ/) And so forth. Finish by blending the whole word and checking its meaning. (RF.1.2c,d)	Hand out the sound-spelling cards to the whole group. Conduct a quick drill: You say a sound, and the student with the right card holds it up or stands up. Then, you say four to five sounds that will build a word: "sleeps" — /s/ /l/ /ē/ /p/ /s/ — and students with those cards stand in order to create the word. (RF.1.2c,d) Delete a sound (remove the card holder) and ask students to make the new word: "seeps," "sleep," or "leap." (RF.1.2c,d)	If students are accurate, emphasize fluency with those who are still slow. As students segment a word, have them raise a finger for each sound they say, then sweep the whole hand left to right as they blend the word. (RF.1.2d)

Grade One	Level Four	Level Five	Level Six
Reading Objectives for Phonics and Word Recognition (RF.1.3a,b,c,e,f,g)	Learn sound-spelling associations by means of a see/hear/say/write sequence: /ō/ spelled oe, /ō/ spelled ow, /ō/ spelled oa, /ū/ spelled ew or ue, /ow/ spelled ow, /ow/ spelled ou, /aw/ spelled aw or au, /ū/ spelled oo, ue, u_e, u, orew, /oo/ spelled oo, /n/ spelled kn, /oi/ spelled oi or oy. (RF.1.3a,b,c)	Learn sound-symbol associations for /r/ spelled wr and /f/ spelled ph. (RF.1.3a,b,c)	Read two-syllable words with learned syllable patterns and compound words with recognizable base words (e.g., *backpack, flashlight*) by first identifying the vowel in each syllable, and then decoding the words. (RF.1.3f)
	Apply sound-symbol associations to blending and reading simple words in isolation and in connected text. (RF.1.3a,b,c)	Apply associations to blending and reading simple words in isolation and in connected text. (RF.1.3a,b,c)	Apply word-reading skills out of context and in the context of connected text. (RF.1.3f)
	Identify the vowels in words with two simple closed syllables (e.g., *rabbit, humbug, basket, catnip, napkin, webcast, hobnob*) before sounding out the words. (RF.1.3e)	Count the vowels in words with two open, closed, vowel-r, or VCe syllables (e.g., *robot, wiper, compete, dateline*) before sounding out the words. (RF.1.3f)	Identify learned inflectional word forms in connected text, reading them with accuracy and fluency. (RF.1.3g)
	Apply word-reading skills out of context and in the context of connected text. (RF.1.3e)	Apply word-reading skills out of context and in the context of connected text. (RF.1.3f)	
	Read comparative adjective forms with -er and -est and illustrate the effect on meaning. (RF.1.3g)	Identify the base word and ending in inflected forms with no orthographic change in the base word (e.g., *wish + ed, wish + ing, wish + es; dark + er, dark + est*). (RF.1.3g)	
	Read verbs with -ed and illustrate or explain the meaning of the past tense. Pronounce the three sounds of the -ed inflection: /d/, /t/, and /ed/ (*spelled; missed; mended*). (RF.1.3g)		

Grade One	Level Four	Level Five	Level Six
Model Activities for Phonics and Word Recognition	Continue sound-symbol drills and whole word blending as before, incorporating new sounds into the repertoire. (RF.1.3a,b,c) Explain that closed syllables have short vowels spelled with one letter and end in one or more consonants; the consonants close off the syllable and keep the vowel contained. Using a pocket chart and/or syllable cards, play a matching game with sets of closed syllables. Start with compounds (*back + pack*; *back + log*; *hot + dog*) and then work with two-syllable words (*bas + ket*; *nap + kin*; *rab + bit*; *hum + ming*) and longer words for those who are ready (*fan + tas + tic*; *ac + com + plish + ment*). (RF.1.3e) Put roughly fifteen to twenty words with different spellings for the same long vowel (e.g., /ō/) on index cards. Sort words by the spelling for the sound (i.e., *snow, blow, know, flow; vote, home, chose; boat, moan, load; toe, floe, doe; no, so, go*). Then complete written sentences with the words. (RF.1.3a,b,c) With the class, create verbal and/or pictorial illustrations of comparative forms of descriptive words: *green, greener, greenest; fast, faster, fastest.*	Continue blending words with all learned sound-spellings, but delete "sound-by-sound" cues; just sweep hand under the word from left to right. After reading single words, read phrases, sentences, and decodable texts that use the words. (RF.1.3a,b,c,f) Explain that open syllables end in a vowel letter that is free to sing its name. Explain also that vowel-r syllables have vowel sounds affected by "bossy" r. With manipulative word cards, sort single-syllable words by vowel spelling and syllable type: open (*so*), closed (*drop*), VCe (*slope*), and vowel-r (*fork*). (RF.1.3f) As students approach unknown longer words, have them identify or underline the vowel in each syllable, using knowledge of syllable spelling patterns, before sounding out the word. Then use meaning and context to adjust pronunciation as necessary. (RF.1.3a,b,c,f) Construct a flip chart with two parallel parts: base words (e.g., *dark, fight, peep*) and inflections (e.g., -*ing*, -*ed*, -*est*, -*er*, -*s*). Combine items from the two columns and ask students to judge if the word makes sense before they try to use it in a sentence. (Note: At this point, avoid base words that require spelling changes. (RF.1.3g)	Sort sets of single-syllable words by vowel spelling and syllable type: open (*so*), closed (*drop*), VCe (*slope*), vowel-r (*fork*), and vowel team (*boat*). Students highlight or color code the vowel before sorting. (RF.1.3f) To decode unknown longer words, use a routine: Underline the vowel in each syllable, say the vowel sound, and underline familiar endings. Sweep a pointer or finger under each syllable as you sound out the word, then use meaning and context to adjust pronunciation as necessary. (RF.1.3f,g) Conduct daily one-minute speed drills on irregular words. Distribute six to eight irregular words, repeated randomly over a page, and challenge students to read them accurately at a rate of forty to sixty per minute. (RF.1.3f)

Grade One	Level Four	Level Five	Level Six
	Point out that -ed has meaning, is added to verbs, and is pronounced three ways. Write the sounds /d/, /t/, and /ed/ above three columns. As you read past tense words extracted from reading material, ask students to decide in which column a word's past tense ending belongs (e.g., mended = /ed/; picked = /t/; filled = /d/). (RF.1.3g)		
Reading Objectives for Fluency (RF.1.4a,b,c)	With text at the instructional level (90-95% accuracy), reread to improve accuracy, phrasing, and intonation. (RF.1.4a,b,c) On encountering an unknown word, the reader a) looks carefully at the letter sequence, b) sounds out the word, and c) checks the sense within the whole sentence or passage. If it does not make sense, he or she rereads or asks for assistance. (RF.1.4c)	Read aloud a familiar text to a peer partner or adult so that the listener will comprehend the text. (RF.1.4a,b,c) On encountering an unknown word, the reader a) looks carefully at the letter sequence, b) sounds out the word, and c) checks the sense within the whole sentence or passage. If it does not make sense, he or she rereads or asks for assistance. (RF.1.4c)	By year's end, read fifty to sixty words correct per minute in unrehearsed grade level text with 97% accuracy or better and demonstrate comprehension through retelling. (RF.1.4a) Read aloud a familiar text to a peer partner or adult so that the listener will comprehend the text. (RF.1.4a,b,c) On encountering an unknown word, the reader a) looks carefully at the letter sequence, b) sounds out the word, and c) checks the sense within the whole sentence or passage. If it does not make sense, he or she rereads or asks for assistance. (RF.1.4c)

Grade One	Level Four	Level Five	Level Six
Model Activities for Fluency	Using a text the students have read once, revisit it for some "detective work." Ask students to read a sentence or page to find words that tell why something happened; who did something; how something was done; and so forth. When students have pointed to those words in their books, choral read that section with appropriate phrasing. (RF.1.4a,b,c) Remind students of the "look at the whole word, sound it out, and check it" routine for unknown words. If they are stuck on a sound, ask them to check the sound-symbol cards—which should be posted in a place easy to see—to solve the problem. (RF.1.4c)	Model an alternate oral reading procedure for students to use as partners. Students sit facing opposite directions, shoulder to shoulder. The first reader reads a page; then the second reader reads the same page (for the less skilled) or reads the next page. After reading, students take turn retelling what was read. (RF.1.4a,b,c) Remind students of the "look at the whole word, sound it out, and check it" routine for unknown words. (RF.1.4c)	Conduct daily one-minute speed drills on irregular words. Distribute six to eight irregular words randomly repeated over a page, and challenge students to read them accurately at a rate of forty to sixty words per minute. (RF.1.4a) Ask students to keep reading logs, recording about twenty minutes daily of time spent reading with a peer, parent, or other volunteer. (RF.1.4a,b,c)
Writing, Handwriting, and Spelling Objectives (L1.1j, L1.2d,e L1.4c, W1.2)	Spell accurately and in context sixty to seventy of the most often-used words in writing. (L.1.2d) Write sentences with compound subjects and compound predicates. (L.1.1j) Given a topic, write several sentences that tell about the same thing. (L.1.1j; W.1.2)	Spell one-syllable words with inflections in a structured context. (L.1.4c) Use simple and compound sentences in writing and vary the position of adverbial phrases. (L.1.1j)	Spell accurately and in context 100 of the most often used words in writing. (L.1.2d) Spell one-syllable, regular pattern words with long and short vowels. (L.1.2d,e) Recognize the difference between topic sentences and details. (W.1.2)
Model Activities for Writing, Handwriting and Spelling	Rehearse mnemonic cues and sentences for irregular, high-frequency words: *Mom said, "Sally's apple is delicious."* (L.1.2d)	Complete written sentences with the correct inflected forms of nouns and verbs: *The (tree/trees) are (grow, growing) on the steep slope. That is the (taller, tallest) of three (pine, pines).* (L.1.4c)	To commit the most common 100 words to memory, students can make an index card for each word they need to practice. If they can write the word quickly and accurately three days in a row, the word can be "retired" to a word bank. (L.1.2d)

Grade One	Level Four	Level Five	Level Six
	Model, then lead students in combining simple sentences: The hungry snake ate the rat. The snake ate the chipmunk. *The hungry snake ate the rat and the chipmunk.* (L.1.1j) After selecting a topic for description, brainstorm with students the kinds of descriptive words that could be used in writing about that topic. Encourage them to formulate sentences orally before writing. Provide the target words in a word bank, and ask students to write several sentences using those words and others they know to write their descriptions. (L.1.1f, L.1.1j, W.1.2)	Complete compound sentences using the connectives *and, but, so, because:* *"I liked that book because . . . "* *"I liked that book, but . . . "* *"I liked that book, so . . . "* (L.1.1j, W.1.1) Lift sentences with adverbial clauses from familiar text or student writing. Ask students to rewrite them, moving the adverbial clause if appropriate, and adding a comma if needed: *We went home after the play and ate supper.* *After the play, we went home and ate supper.* *We went home and ate supper after the play.* Encourage students to change phrase position when they revise their own writing. (L.1.1j)	Play "What Pattern Am I?" Given three columns for long vowel syllable types—open (*me, she, no, so, hi*), VCe (*spoke, slime, robe, quake*) and vowel team (*seem, sail, play, boat, right, meat*)—write words in the correct category. (L.1.2d) Write three to five sentences on sentence strips, including a topic and a few details. Mix them up and give them to pairs of students to put in a sensible order. Then, ask students to suggest edits or revisions to the passage, including word choice, elaboration, or word order, as they rewrite the paragraph. (W.1.2, W.1.5, L.1.1j)

Reading Foundations: A Pacing Guide for Reading Instruction (Grade Two, Levels One Through Three)

Grade Two	Level One	Level Two	Level Three
Reading Objectives for Phonics and Word Recognition (RF.2.3,a,b,c,d,e,f)	Generate symbols (graphemes) for sounds (phonemes) and sounds for symbols, with accuracy and fluency, including short vowels and all common consonant correspondences. (RF.2.3a)	Accurately associate symbols (graphemes) with sounds (phonemes), and sounds with symbols, including those in Unit One and most common spellings for long vowels (/ē/ = e, ee, ea, e_e; /ɪ/ = i, y, i_e, igh; /ā/ = a, ai, ay, a_e; /ō/ = o, o_e, oa, ow; /ū/ = u, u_e, oo, ew, ue; /yū/ = u, u_e, ew, eu, ue) (RF.2.3a,b)	Fluently and accurately associate symbols (graphemes) with sounds (phonemes), and sounds with symbols, including those in Unit One and Unit Two, diphthongs (/ou/ = ou, ow; /oi/ = oi, oy), and vowel + r correspondences (er, ar, or). (RF.2.3a,b)
	Identify the syllable units in spoken words; know that each syllable must have a vowel; and when the vowel is short, the syllable will be closed. (RF.2.3c)	Identify and pronounce the vowel sounds in written closed, open, and VCe syllables (hit, hi, hide). (RF.2.3c)	Identify, sort, and pronounce the vowel sounds in closed, open, VCe, vowel team, and vowel + r syllables. (RF.2.3c).
	Add and delete common inflectional suffixes (-s, -es, -ed, -ing, -er, -est) from base words that do not require a change of spelling, and recognize how meaning is changed by the suffix. (RF.2.3d)	Add and delete common inflectional suffixes beginning with vowels (-es, -ed, -ing, -er, -est) from base words that require doubling of a final consonant (running, wettest), and recognize how meaning is changed by the suffix. (RF.2.3d)	Add and delete common suffixes beginning with vowels (-es, -ed, -ing, -er, -est, -y) from base words that require deletion of a final silent e (slimy, hoping), and recognize how meaning is changed by the suffix. (RF.2.3d)
	Read words with common spelling variations for consonants: double f, l, s, z after short vowels; -ck, -tch, and -dge after short vowels; soft c and g. (RF.2.3.e)	Read words with the -ild, ind, old, ost pattern (finding, kindest, most, unfold) and the -all, -al patterns (fallen, recall; calm, palm, talk). (RF.2.3e)	Read and pronounce words with silent letter spellings (knee, wrong, gnaw, comb, ghost) and wo (word, work) and wa (warp, warm; water, was, waffle) patterns (RF.2.3e)
	Read accurately twenty additional high-frequency, irregular words from the 300 most common words in written English (e.g., there, where, any, many). (RF.2.3.f)	Read accurately twenty additional high-frequency, irregular words from the 300 most common words in written English. (RF.2.3.f)	Read accurately twenty additional high-frequency, irregular words from the 300 most common words in written English. (RF.2.3.f)

Grade Two	Level One	Level Two	Level Three
Model Activities for Phonics and Word Recognition	Consolidate students' automatic command of basic sound-symbol associations by including one-minute drills: You say a sound, students write the common spelling(s); or, students look at a series of randomly ordered graphemes and say the sounds. (RF.2.3a)	Using manipulative grapheme tiles, create columns for each spelling of one long vowel (i, igh, i_e, y); then, have students pronounce and sort single-syllable words with those spellings (*my, sight, wipe, pi*). (RF.2.3a,b)	First teach that /er/ has three common spellings: er, ir, ur. Note that /er/ can be treated as one phoneme, because the vowel and consonant are welded together. Also, /ar/ and /or/ are partly welded. (RF.2.3a,b)
	Explain that every syllable has a vowel, and the jaw drops open as the vowel is spoken. Ask students to look in a mirror and repeat words with one to four syllables, holding their hand under their chin to feel the jaw drop. To hear the accented syllable, students can pretend the word is a dog's name. As they "call the dog," they will hold the accented syllable longer. (SUM mer; WIN ter, AU tumn, fan TAS tic) (RF.2.3c)	With sets of closed, VCe, and open syllables on cards, ask students to identify the type of syllable and the pronunciation of each syllable; then, they can arrange the syllables into words, read and use them in a sentence: *prin-cess; grace-ful; life-less; ex-pose; com-pute; e-ven; se-cret; mu-sic; si-lent.* (RF.2.3c)	Adding vowel + r syllables into the mix (*stor-y; black-bird; turn-stile; churn-ing*). Practice reading two- and three-syllable words by scooping under each syllable with a pencil, identifying the syllable type, coding the vowel as o (open), c (closed), r (vowel-r), or e (VCe) if necessary. Then play a question game with the words: Which word means _____? (RF.2.3c)
	Line three students up with large letter cards – *h, i, t* or *b, e, d*. Ask the class to read the word and identify the last letter as short. Point out that the last letter is a consonant (a closed sound) that closes in the syllable and keeps the vowel short. Then ask the "last letter" to turn away, leaving an open syllable (hi, be) where the vowel is free to sing its name. Show how two closed syllables can combine: *mas-cot; cac-tus; mag-net; ban-dit.* (RF.2.3c)	Practice adding and deleting common suffixes beginning with vowels (-y, -es, -ed, -ing, -er, -est, -ish) to base words that require doubling of a final consonant (*running, wettest, fatter, reddish*). Explain and illustrate the formula: *If the word has one syllable, and ends in one consonant, preceded by one vowel, double the consonant before adding a suffix that begins with a vowel.* Create cloze sentences to be completed with the correctly suffixed word. Example: fatter = fat + (t) + er. (RF.2.3d)	Practice adding and deleting common suffixes beginning with vowels (-y, -es, -ed, -ing, -er, -est, -ish) to base words that require deletion of a final silent e (*writing, hoping, skated*). Explain and illustrate the formula: *If a word ends in a final silent e, and the added suffix begins with a vowel, delete the silent e.* Create cloze sentences to be completed with the correctly suffixed word. Example: slime + y = slimy. (RF.2.3d)

Grade Two	Level One	Level Two	Level Three
	Starting with base words that do not require a spelling change (wind, melt, mist, backpack), ask students to combine base words and common inflections, pronounce the result, and use the words in sentences. (RF.2.3d) Provide word cards that demonstrate a pattern such as hard and soft c. Ask students to sort the words by the sound of letter c (/s/ or /k/) and see if they can find the pattern. Confirm that c usually has the sound /s/ before e, i, and y, but the sound /k/ before a, o, and u. (RF.2.3e) To introduce an irregular word (does, what, where), contrast the spelling pronunciation and the actual pronunciation. Explain that the oldest words in English have changed their pronunciation over hundreds of years. (RF.2.3f)	Collect words with -ild, -ind, -old, -ost patterns (finding, kindest, most, unfold, postal). Ask students to underline the base word's vowel, pronounce the words, and describe why the words break the pattern of regular closed or open syllables. (RF.2.3e) As students learn an irregular word, provide a written model for the students to trace, copy, and then write from memory. During each step, students say the letter names—not the sounds. Say the word before and after writing. (RF.2.3f)	Collect "wo" words (work, worse, worm, word, worth, worthy, won, wonder) and "wa" words (water, warm, want, was, wash). After explicitly contrasting the expected sound of the vowel with its actual pronunciation, ask students to say what's true about vowels that follow w: *W often changes the following vowel.* (RF.2.3e) Construct one-minute speed drills for centers in which students practice accurate and fluent reading of problematic irregular and/or high-frequency words (because, through, there, where, laugh). Choose six words for each speed drill, randomly distributing them in a 5 × 6 grid. Partners can time one another. (RF.2.3f)
Reading Objectives for Fluency (RF.2.4a,b,c)	Orally read grade-appropriate connected text, with demonstrated comprehension, at sixty words correct per minute. (RF.2.4a,b,c)	Orally read grade-appropriate connected text with accuracy and demonstrated comprehension, at sixty-five words correct per minute. (RF.2.4a,b,c)	By mid-year, orally read grade-appropriate text with 96% accuracy and demonstrated comprehension, at seventy words correct per minute. (RF.2.4a,b,c)

Grade Two	Level One	Level Two	Level Three
Model Activities for Fluency	Using an overhead projector or large print book, mark phrases and read them aloud as you sweep your hand under the groups of words. Encourage students to sweep their fingers under the groups of words as they "smush" them together. (RF.2.4a,b,c) Structure partner reading: Assign one person to be "reader" and the other to be "coach." The coach can say, "Try that again" if an error is made. At the end of the book, coach asks the reader to tell what each page or part of the book was about. Students then change roles for the next book reading. (RF.2.4a,b,c)	Select a story or poem that students read with 95% accuracy. Practice reading the text in unison until everyone can read it as a chorus. Ask smaller groups of students to perform the reading for other groups or classes. (RF.2.4a,b,c)	Encourage repeated readings of stories that students can read with 95% accuracy. Use a tape-recorded model for students to read along with in a listening center. Then ask individual students to read the same story aloud to a partner, who times them, records words correct per minute, and charts the results. (RF.2.4a,b,c)

Reading Foundations: A Pacing Guide for Reading Instruction (Grade Two, Levels Four Through Six)

Grade Two	Level Four	Level Five	Level Six
Reading Objectives for Phonics and Word Recognition (RF.2.3,a,b,c, d,e,f)	Identify the consonant-le final syllable pattern, and accurately read two-syllable words ending in a consonant-le syllable (*cradle; paddle; bible, bumble; google, gurgle; steeple, settle*). (RF.2.3a,b,c) Add and delete common suffixes (-ly, -less, -es, -ed, -ing, -er, -est) from base words with final y (*bunnies, penniless, babying*), and recognize how meaning is changed by the suffix. (RF.2.3d) Read and decompose contractions into their constituent base words (*they'd = they would; should've = should have*). (RF.2.3e) Read accurately twenty additional high-frequency, irregular words from the most common words in written English. (RF.2.3.f)	Read two-syllable words with an ambiguous VCV syllable juncture (e/ven, ev/ery; ra/dar, rad/ish) adapting pronunciation to make a meaningful word. Identify common prefixes on base words (un, mis, re, pre); recognize how addition or deletion of the prefix changes the word's meaning. (RF.2.3d) Associate spellings of common homophone pairs with their major meanings (*for, four; wear, where; their, there*). (RF.2.3e) Read accurately twenty additional high-frequency, irregular words from the most common words in written English. (RF.2.3.f)	Fluently and accurately read two-syllable base words comprising any of the six regular syllable patterns (RF.2.3a,b,c). Read grade-level base words with the most common prefixes (in-, un-, mis-, dis-, re-, de-, a-) and suffixes (-ly, -er, -ion, -less, -ness) and recognize how meaning of the base is changed by the suffix. (RF.2.3d) Read less common (but predictable) patterns for vowels, such as *eigh* for /ā/ (*neighbor*), *ough* for /ō/ (*though, dough*), and *ei* for /ē/ (*ceiling*). (RF.2.3e) Read accurately twenty additional high-frequency, irregular words from the most common words in written English. (RF.2.3.f)

Grade Two	Level Four	Level Five	Level Six
Model Activities for Phonics and Word Recognition	Give small groups of students sets of cards with closed, vowel-r, vowel team, and open syllables that will combine with a set of -cle final syllables to make words. Have students read the syllables before combining them with the -cle syllables. Give a point for each real word created, and discuss any unknown meanings. (*un-cle; bu-gle; pur-ple; sim-ple; si-dle; nee-dle; net-tle; chor-tle; wad-dle; waf-fle,* etc.) (RF.2.3a,b,c)	Lead students as they practice a routine for reading unknown big words. Find the known parts: Circle a prefix and box a suffix. Identify the vowel(s) in the base word using syllable identification. Scoop under each part as it is pronounced, and then blend the whole word. (RF.2.3a,b,c,d)	Practice the most common syllable division principles: VC/CV (*rab/bit*); VC/CCV (*com/plete*); V/CV (*si/lent*) or VC/V (*mag/ic*) and follow the "big word" routine outlined in Unit Five. (RF.2.3a,b,c)
	Introduce the "y rule" by comparing word pairs with and without suffixes. Can students determine what happened to the "y"? *baby – babies dirty - dirtiest* *cry – cried jumpy - jumpier* *fry – frier story – stories* (RF.2.3d)	Explain to students that prefixes and suffixes have meaning and change meaning of a base word. Define a few of the most common prefixes (*un, re, mis*). Play a question-answer game with the most common prefixes: *If "usable" means you can use an item, what does "unusable" mean? What does "reusable" mean? Misused?* Then write the words, circling the prefixes and boxing any suffixes. (RF.2.3d)	Practice using affixed words in cloze exercises (incomplete sentences) where the meaning of the prefix and/or suffix must fit the given context. (*She [remade/remaking/unmade] her bed in the morning.*) (RF.2.3d)
	Collect examples of contractions from the texts students are reading. Enlist students' assistance in decomposing the contractions into their base words. Explain that the apostrophe kicks out letters and replaces them when the words are contracted. (RF.2.3e)	With the class, gradually create an illustrated homophone dictionary. First introduce the most common and most regular word in a homophone pair or group, insuring that students have practiced its use in context. Introduce the homophone partner only when students are sure of the most common word of the pair (e.g., *base* before *bass; there* before *their; plane* before *plain*). (RF.2.3e)	After identifying a less common spelling for a vowel ($\bar{a}$ = eigh), ask students to sort a group of words with several spelling patterns for that vowel: /$\bar{a}$/ = *eigh, ai, ay, a_e.* Then, read decodable passages with a heavy concentration of words that contain the spelling patterns just practiced. (RF.2.3e)
			Continue the irregular word study routine, with emphasis on automatic recognition in the speed drills described in Unit Three. (RF.2.3f)

Grade Two	Level Four	Level Five	Level Six
	If students have not automatized recognition of common irregular words that have been taught through tracing, copying, and writing, sequence practice so that it moves from single word recognition, to reading the words in phrases, to reading in sentences and text. Practice only a few words at one time. (RF.2.3f)	Continue study of irregular words, about four to five per week, by first presenting the words out of context. Ask students to trace, say the letters, copy, and write the words, examining the parts that are irregular. Then, read the words in text that affords many opportunities for practice. (RF.2.3f)	
Reading Objectives for Fluency (RF.2.4a)	Orally read grade-appropriate connected text, with demonstrated comprehension, at seventy-five words correct per minute. (RF.2.4a)	Orally read grade-appropriate connected text with accuracy and demonstrated comprehension, at eighty words correct per minute. (RF.2.4a)	By year's end, orally read grade-appropriate text with 97% accuracy and demonstrated comprehension, at ninety words correct per minute. (RF.2.4a)
Model Activities for Fluency	Take a simple sentence from a text and change its punctuation. Model accurate reading with a change in prosody indicated by the punctuation. Then, ask students to practice similar sequences, explaining the difference in meaning: *Was she lazy! Was she lazy?* (RF.2.4a,b,c)	Including independent reading, partner reading, choral reading, and reading with a taped book, students should document in a reading log that they are spending at least twenty minutes daily with text they can read with sufficient accuracy and comprehension. (RF.2.4a,b,c) Students at risk should have their progress measured and charted every few weeks. (RF.2.4a)	Encourage students to read several books by the same author, once they discover a series they enjoy. (RF.2.4a,b,c)

GRADE 3

When students enter third grade, they should be confident readers, able to sound out words, read with expression, and make meaning of what they read. They should be familiar with a repertoire of poems, stories, fables, folktales, myths, biographies, artistic and musical works, and historical and scientific texts. During this year, students continue to make connections between literature and other subjects. They read stories inspired by the sea while learning about oceans. They study myths from ancient Greece, learn about the branches of government in the United States, read about artists, musicians, and inventors, find common themes in trickster tales across many cultures, come to recognize the beauty of poetic language, and more. Throughout the units, they write reports, letters, stories, poems, and descriptions; they continue to work on grammar and punctuation. They participate in structured class discussions and learn how to take notes and conduct basic research. By the end of third grade, students should be ready to start writing simple essays and speeches. They are able to write on a range of topics and have background knowledge that will help them with the challenges of upper elementary school and beyond.

Standards Checklist for Grade Three

Standard	Unit 1	Unit 2	Unit 3	Unit 4	Unit 5	Unit 6
Reading—Literature						
1		FA	FA			
2	FA					FA
3	FA	A				
4					FA	
5		A			FA	
6						FA
7	A			A		
8 n/a						
9	A	A				
10						FA
Reading—Information Text						
1	A		A	A		
2		FA	A		A	A
3		A	FA			
4				FA		
5	A	A	A		A	A
6		A		A		
7	A		A		FA	
8				FA		
9		FA		A		
10			A			FA
Writing						
1			A		FA	A
1a			A		A	A
1b			A		A	A
1c			A		A	A
1d			A		A	A
2		A	FA	A	A	
2a		A	A	A	A	
2b		A	A	A	A	
2c		A	A	A	A	
2d		A	A	A	A	
3	FA	F	A			A
3a	A		A			A
3b	A	F	A			A
3c	A		A			A
3d	A		A			A
4	A				A	
5	A	A	A	A	A	
6	A				A	A
7	A		A	FA	A	A
8	A		A		A	
9 n/a						
10		A	A	A	A	A
Speaking and Listening						
1	FA	FA	FA	A	A	A
1a		FA	FA	A	A	A
1b	A	A	A	A	A	A
1c	FA	A	A	A	A	A

Standard	Unit 1	Unit 2	Unit 3	Unit 4	Unit 5	Unit 6
1d	A	A	A	A	A	A
2	A	A			A	A
3	A	A	A	FA	A	A
4	A	A	A			A
5			A			FA
6	A	A				
Language						
1	FA	FA	FA	A	A	A
1a	FA	FA	A	A	A	A
1b	A	A	A	A	A	A
1c	A	A	A	A	A	A
1d	A	A	A	A	A	A
1e	A	A	A	A	A	A
1f	A	A	A	A	A	A
1g	A	A	A	A	A	A
1h	A	A	FA	A	A	A
1i	A	A	FA	A	A	A
2	A	A	A	A	A	A
2a	A	A	A	A	A	A
2b	A	A	A	A	A	A
2c	A	A	A	A	A	A
2d	A	A	A	A	A	A
2e	A	A	A	A	A	A
2f	A	A	A	A	A	A
2g	A	A	A	A	A	A
3	A	A	A	A	A	A
3a	A	A	A	A	A	A
3b	A	A	A	A	A	A
4				F		
4a					A	
4b			A	A	FA	
4c			A			
4d				FA		
5					A	
5a					A	
5b		A	A	A	A	
5c			A		A	
6		A		A		
Reading Foundations						
1 n/a						
2 n/a						
3			A		F	
3a			A	A		
3b			A		FA	
3c			A	A		
3d			A			
4			A		FA	F
4a			A	A		
4b	A		A	FA	A	
4c			A	A	A	FA

F = Focus Standards; A = Activity/Assessment

Stories Worth Telling Again and Again

In this first six-week unit of third grade, students read stories that are worth telling and retelling.

OVERVIEW

Students read the tales of grandparents and they become familiar with the tradition of "trickster stories" across multiple cultures. They read a Langston Hughes poem, and review the parts of speech through Ruth Heller's *World of Language* books. The students engage the texts in multiple ways: They write stories they want to preserve; they also build upon their knowledge of geographical settings of folktales from previous grades as they research the cultural backgrounds of the trickster tales. They dramatically interpret a poem by Langston Hughes.

FOCUS STANDARDS

These Focus Standards have been selected for the unit from the Common Core State Standards.

RL.3.2: Recount stories, including fables, folktales, and myths from diverse cultures; determine the central message, lesson, or moral, and explain how it is conveyed through key details in the text.

RL.3.3: Describe characters in a story (e.g., their traits, motivations, or feelings) and explain how their actions contribute to the sequence of events.

SL.3.1: Engage effectively in a range or collaborative discussions (one-on-one, group, and teacher-led) with diverse partners on grade 3 topics and texts, building on others' ideas and expressing their own clearly.

SL.3.1(c): Ask questions to check understanding of information presented, stay on topic, and link their comments to the remarks of others.

W.3.3: Write narratives to develop real or imagined experiences or events using effective technique, descriptive details, and clear event sequences.

L.3.1: Demonstrate command of the conventions of Standard English grammar and usage when writing or speaking.

L.3.1(a): Explain the function of nouns, pronouns, verbs, adjectives, and adverbs in general and their functions in particular sentences.

SUGGESTED STUDENT OBJECTIVES

- Tell stories from personal experiences and write narratives telling those stories.
- Revise and edit narratives with the help of peers and adults.
- Determine and analyze characters' traits and motivations in realistic fiction such as *The Stories Julian Tells*.
- Distinguish nouns, pronouns, and verbs from each other, understanding the role of each in a sentence.
- Perform a poem dramatically, (e.g., a Langston Hughes poem) with expression and appropriate phrasing for meaning.
- Compare and contrast the message and characters in two books with the same theme (e.g., "grandparent" books).
- Determine the trickster, the fool, the problem, and the solution in various cultures' trickster tales.
- Research one of the trickster tale's cultures, as part of responding to class-generated questions.
- Create a class book or a multimedia presentation based on the culture research.
- Discuss artists' contributions to the preservation of the Native American culture through art.

SUGGESTED WORKS

(E) indicates a CCSS exemplar text; (EA) indicates a text from a writer with other works identified as exemplars.

LITERARY TEXTS

Stories

Our stories:

- *The Stories Julian Tells* (Ann Cameron and Ann Strugnell) (E)
- *More Stories Julian Tells* (Ann Cameron and Ann Strugnell) (EA)
- *The Stories Huey Tells* (Ann Cameron and Roberta Smith) (EA)
- *Gloria's Way* (Ann Cameron and Lis Toft) (EA)

Grandparents' stories:

- *Grandfather's Journey* (Allen Say) (EA)
- *Tea with Milk* (Allen Say) (EA)
- *Song and Dance Man* (Karen Ackerman and Stephen Gammell)
- *Snowed in with Grandmother Silk* (Carol Fenner and Amanda Harvey)
- *Annie and the Old One* (Miska Miles and Peter Parnall)
- *Through Grandpa's Eyes* (Patricia MacLachlan and Deborah Kogan Ray) (EA)
- *Knots on a Counting Rope* (Bill Martin Jr., John Archambault, and illustrated by Ted Rand)
- *The Memory String* (Eve Bunting and Ted Rand)

Cultural trickster stories:

- *Tops & Bottoms* (Janet Stevens) (E)
- *Bruh Rabbit and the Tar Baby Girl* (Virginia Hamilton and James Ransome)
- *Love and Roast Chicken: A Trickster Tale from the Andes Mountains* (Barbara Knutson)

- *Iktomi and the Buzzard* (Paul Goble)
- *Iktomi and the Coyote* (Paul Goble)
- *Iktomi and the Boulder* (Paul Goble)
- *Iktomi and the Berries* (Paul Goble)
- *Iktomi Loses His Eyes* (Paul Goble)

Stories (Read Aloud)

- *The Apple and the Arrow* (Mary Buff and Conrad Buff)
- *Sign of the Beaver* (Elizabeth George Speare)

Poems

- "Grandpa's Stories" (Langston Hughes) (E)
- "Aunt Sue's Stories" (Langston Hughes) (EA)
- "Mother to Son" (Langston Hughes) (EA)
- "By Myself" (Eloise Greenfield)

Poems (Read Aloud)

- "Your World" (Georgia Douglas Johnson) (E)
- "The Telephone" (Robert Frost) (EA)
- "Nani" (Alberto Rios)
- "You Are Old, Father William" (Lewis Carroll) (EA)
- "For want of a nail, the shoe was lost . . . " (Traditional)

INFORMATIONAL TEXTS

Informational Books

Students will do Internet research on a culture related to a favorite trickster tale:

- African American slave culture
- European culture (choose a specific country)
- Native American (Plains) culture
- Andes Mountain culture

Informational Books (Read Aloud)

- *Throw Your Tooth on the Roof: Tooth Traditions Around the World* (Selby Beeler and G. Brian Karas) (E)
- *Merry-Go-Round: A Book About Nouns* (World of Language) (Ruth Heller)
- *Mine, All Mine: A Book About Pronouns* (World of Language) (Ruth Heller)
- *A Cache of Jewels and Other Collective Nouns* (World of Language) (Ruth Heller)
- *Kites Sail High: A Book About Verbs* (World of Language) (Ruth Heller)

ART, MUSIC, AND MEDIA

Art

- Jan van Eyck, *Arnolfini Portrait* (1434)
- Pablo Picasso, *Guernica* (1937)
- Jacopo Pontormo, *Descent from the Cross* (1528)
- *Trajan's Column*, in Rome, Italy (completed 113 CE) (detail)

SAMPLE ACTIVITIES AND ASSESSMENTS

Note: This unit is a natural fit for inviting grandparents or older family friends into the classroom to tell their own stories or to read the stories under the Grandparent Story section. At the beginning of the school year, you may see some unique opportunities to engage the grandparents with their own grandchildren's learning or to volunteer in the classroom. A Grandparents' Day would be a perfect celebration to include in this unit.

1. CLASS DISCUSSION/LITERATURE

Introduce the unit by asking students if they have family stories they love to tell. Allow students to share favorite family stories for a few minutes. Introduce that day's new chapter book: *The Stories Julian Tells* (Ann Cameron and Ann Strugnell). As students read the first chapter of the book, "The Pudding Like a Night on the Sea," ask them to examine Julian as a character. You might post these leading questions and discuss their meaning by having your students ask you the questions as their new teacher:

- How would you describe Julian?
- What are his character traits?
- Why does he do what he does?

Tell students to cite evidence from the text as they answer the questions. Read the chapter aloud to the students as they follow along. Continue reading the subsequent chapters in the days that follow, encouraging as much independent reading as possible. Continue to focus on character traits and motivation. As students finish this book, allow them to choose to move to other character stories in this series or to continue with Julian. This provides the opportunity to compare and contrast books and/or characters by the same author. (RL.3.3, RL.3.9, SL.3.1b, SL.3.4, SL.3.6)

2. NARRATIVE WRITING

Students have been sharing favorite family stories, so shift the discussion to how stories are passed down from grandparents specifically. Then, assign the following: "Interview one of your family members (e.g., a parent, grandparent, aunt, or uncle) to learn a family story. Save the story by taking notes or by recording it digitally. Use the story you record to write a narrative." This writing project should be worked on over an extended period of time, focusing on elaboration, revision, and editing, using the standards as guidance. Create a word wall to gather words used most often in writing and word families. (W.3.3, W.3.4, W.3.5, L.3.1, L.3.2, L.3.3)

3. CLASS DISCUSSION/LANGUAGE

Ruth Heller has written a series of informational books that teach parts of speech. Remind students they learned about nouns in second grade. As you read the book *Merry-Go-Round: A Book About Nouns* (Ruth Heller), have the students listen for more information about nouns. Pause as you read to allow the students to share what they are learning or to ask questions. Review nouns, pronouns, and verbs using the Ruth Heller series. Create word banks for each part of speech and add vocabulary from class work to reinforce the application. (RI.3.1, L.3.1a)

4. POETRY PERFORMANCE

Give the students this prompt: "Choose one of Langston Hughes's poems to memorize or read interpretively. Be sure to communicate the meaning of the poem in the way you recite or read it."

Demonstrate fluent reading to the children, being sure to show how meaningful phrasing and expression guide the dramatic interpretation of a poem. (RF.3.4b)

5. LITERARY RESPONSE

After reading *Knots on a Counting Rope* (Bill Martin Jr., John Archambault, and illustrated by Ted Rand), review the character traits of the boy and his grandfather. Have the students partner and list three characteristics for each. Introduce another story that honors grandparents: *Through Grandpa's Eyes* (Patricia MacLachlan and Deborah Kogan Ray). As students finish reading the new book, have them work with the same partner to list at least three characteristics of each character in the new story.

- How are the grandparents similar and different?
- How are the grandchildren similar and different?
- What is the message of each book? What do you think the author might have wanted you to learn? (RL.3.3)

6. LITERARY RESPONSE

Lead a discussion with the students to introduce the genre of trickster tales, using questions such as these:

One of the types of folk stories handed down in cultures is the "trickster tale."

- What root word do you hear in *trickster*?
- Have you ever played a trick on someone?
- Have you ever had a trick played on you?

Tell students that trickster tales are stories that involve playing tricks to solve problems, and—to make these stories even more interesting—that they are from different cultures. As students read, encourage them to think about characters and their traits. Remind them that the story is not just in the text, but also in the illustrations. The illustrations help to tell the story and to give hints about the culture or origin. Use the following questions to guide discussions after they (or you) read the trickster stories. Eventually require students to answer these questions independently.

- Who is the trickster?
- Who is the fool who gets tricked?
- What was the problem in the story?
- How did the trick solve the problem?

Think about what the message of the story might be and why these stories have been told for hundreds of years. (RL.3.2, RL.3.3, RL.3.7)

7. SHARED RESEARCH

Students have read a variety of trickster tales from various cultures. Now it is time to focus on one of the cultures. You could, for example, choose to focus on the Plains Native American culture by first reading the Iktomi tales by Paul Goble and then assigning a short class research project on it. In small groups, have students generate open-ended questions that can be answered about the culture. Assign each small group a question to answer. To answer the questions, help students create a list of resources such as the Internet, encyclopedias, and informational books. As students read and research, circulate to help them select the most relevant and useful information. When the small groups have finished their information gathering and organization, they should create a class book or multimedia presentation to show what they have learned about the culture. When they are finished, ask "Why did the Plains Indians create trickster stories to tell to their children?" This activity can be repeated and extended with any of the cultures from which trickster stories came by giving small groups of students the following prompt: "Research a culture that tells trickster tales. Generate questions related to the culture and assign a person to research each question. Create a book or multimedia presentation to communicate your findings." (RI.3.1, RI.3.5, W.3.4, W.3.5, W.3.6, W.3.7, W.3.8, SL.3.1, SL.3.4)

8. ART/CLASS DISCUSSION

In each of these images, see if you can identify a story or event that has been passed down through generations. These might be stories for a civilization to remember or perhaps just a family. Discuss how these images also serve as records. What does the artist do to document the importance of an event (e.g., include unique elements or details)? How might these stories be retold because of these images? (SL.3.1c, SL.3.1d, SL.3.2, SL.3.3)

9. ART/CLASS DISCUSSION

Closely examine the van Eyck image, noticing the work's many unique and peculiar details. Why is there only one candle in the chandelier? Is that the artist's signature in the center of the painting? Can you see other figures reflected in the mirror at center? Discuss how close examination of a painting, like a literary work, often reveals hidden or deeper meaning. (SL.3.1c, SL.3.2, SL.3.3)

ADDITIONAL RESOURCES

- Dylan Pritchett: Storyteller (cuesheet) (The Kennedy Center) (SL.3.4, W.3.3)
- *Fables and Trickster Tales Around the World* (National Endowment for the Humanities) (RL.3.2)
- *Dynamite Diamante Poetry* (ReadWriteThink) (L.3.1a) *Note:* This is an activity on nouns.
- *Composing Cinquain Poems with Basic Parts of Speech* (ReadWriteThink) (L.3.1a)
- *Using Picture Books to Teach Characterization in Writing Workshop* (ReadWriteThink) (RL.3.3)
- *Maps of United States Indians by State* (Native Languages of the Americas) (RI.3.7)
- *Native American Informational Chart* (Mountain City Elementary School, Mountain City, TN) (RI.3.5)
- *A Collection of Trickster Tales* (AmericanFolklore.Net) (RL.3.2)

TERMINOLOGY

Author	The fool	Noun	Solution
Character motivation	Generational stories	Problem	The trickster
Character traits	Illustrator	Pronoun	Trickster tales
Collective noun	Internet search	Revising	Verb
Editing	Narrative writing	Shared research	Verb tenses

MAKING INTERDISCIPLINARY CONNECTIONS

This unit teaches:

Art: Artists as historians and documentarians (e.g., Jan van Eyck)
Geography: Cultures (e.g., Plains Native Americans and Andes Mountain tribes)

This unit could be extended to teach:

Music: Music of featured cultures (e.g., spirituals and Quechua songs)
Geography: U.S. geography (as related to Native Americans)
History: Native American Nations (e.g., the Bering land bridge theory, Southwest, Eastern "Woodland")

Grade Three, Unit One Sample Lesson Plan

The Stories Julian Tells by Ann Cameron

In this series of four lessons, students read *The Stories Julian Tells* by Ann Cameron, and they:

Explore the tales of *The Stories Julian Tells* (RL.3.3.1, RL.3.3.2, RL.3.3, RL.3.9, SL.3.1, SL.3.2)

Identify memoir as a genre

Compose memoirs (W.3.3a, W.3.4, W.3.5)

Summary

Lesson I: Reading Julian's Stories

Revisit Julian's stories (RL.3.1, RL.3.2, RL.3.3, RL.3.9)

Select one of Julian's stories for close analysis

Identify the use of first-person narrative (RL.3.6)

Identify the elements of the short story (plot, characters, setting, conflict, and theme) in the selected story (RL.3.1, RL.3.2, RL.3.3, RL.3.9)

(In groups, begin to) identify personal stories to retell (SL.3.4)

Lesson III: Revising Memoirs

Read memoirs critically

Identify areas that need revisions (W.3.3a, W.3.4, W.3.5)

Who are the characters?

Is the plot clear?

Is the setting described in detail?

Does the lead character in the story have a conflict?

Does the story have a theme?

Revise memoirs (W.3.5)

Lesson II: Memoirs—Writing Personal Narratives (Memoirs)

Identify memoir as a literary genre

Note the similarities between Julian's stories and memoirs (SL.3.1, SL.3.2)

Recall details of personal stories (SL.3.4)

Compose the first draft of a memoir, incorporating elements of the short story (W.3.3)

Lesson IV: Telling Stories

Record strengths of peers' memoirs (SL.3.1, SL.3.2)

Reflect on the similarities between the fictional tales of Julian and the memoirs (SL.3.4)

Lesson III: Revising Memoirs

Objectives

Read memoirs critically

Identify areas that need revisions (W.3.3a, W.3.4, W.3.5)

- Who are the characters?
- Is the plot clear?
- Is the setting described in detail?
- Does the lead character in the story have a conflict?
- Does the story have a theme?

Revise memoirs (W.3.5)

Required Materials

☐ Class set of *The Stories Julian Tells* by Ann Cameron

☐ First drafts of memoirs

Procedures

1. Lead-In:

   Students read their own memoirs quietly.

2. Step by Step:

   a. Students' revision process focuses on the elements of the short story that were identified earlier. Your prompts may include questions like:
   - What are the details that describe the setting?
   - If the setting is the bedroom, is it large, small, or perhaps messy with candy wrappers on the floor?
   - Who is the leading character of the memoir — perhaps a grandmother?
   - Does she speak with an accent? Does she love cooking?
   - And, what is the story about? Is it about a missing baseball card?
   - Or is it really about friendship and the missing card is part of the story?

   You may choose to select passages from Julian's stories to explain the type of revisions expected. On page two of *The Stories Julian Tells*, for example, Ann Cameron dedicates a paragraph to describe Julian's father: "My father is a big man . . ."

   b. Students revise their work.

3. Closure:

   At the end of the lesson, remind the students to complete their revisions at home.

Differentiation

Advanced

- Supplied with a list of the revision prompting questions, students work with a partner to do revisions.

Struggling

- Pre-teaching: As you read the Julian story, use the same list of prompting questions to analyze the setting, characters, plot, and theme.
- Students read their story drafts to an adult. As the adult prompts the child for revision, the adult takes dictation from the child.
- Students write their newly revised story on a computer, making use of spell check.

Homework/Assessment

Conclude revisions.

Inspired by the Sea

In this second six-week unit of third grade, students read stories, poetry, and informational texts that are inspired by a love of or curiosity about the sea.

ESSENTIAL QUESTION

? Why does the sea inspire writers?

OVERVIEW

Students read about characters who long for or live near the sea. They become familiar with the wide range of informational texts on the topic of oceans and water. They continue to review the parts of speech by comparing two poems written about oysters. The students engage the texts in several ways. For example, they write stories modeled after the haystack scene in *Sarah, Plain and Tall* (Patricia MacLachlan), showing action, thoughts, and feelings. They also build their knowledge of ocean animals as they research their favorite sea creature.

FOCUS STANDARDS

These Focus Standards have been selected for the unit from the Common Core State Standards.

RI.3.2: Determine the main idea of a text; recount the key details and explain how they support the main idea.

RI.3.9: Compare and contrast the most important points and key details presented in two texts on the same topic.

RL.3.1: Ask and answer such questions to demonstrate understanding of a text, referring explicitly to the text as the basis for the answers.

L.3.1: Demonstrate command of the conventions of Standard English grammar and usage when writing or speaking.

L.3.1(a): Explain the function of nouns, pronouns, verbs, adjectives, and adverbs in general and their functions in particular sentences.

W.3.3: Write narratives to develop real or imagined experiences or events using effective technique, descriptive details, and clear event sequences.

W.3.3(b): Use dialogue and descriptions of actions, thoughts, and feelings to develop experiences and events or show the response of characters to situations.

SL.3.1: Engage effectively in a range of collaborative discussions (one-on-one, group, and teacher-led) with diverse partners on grade 3 topics and texts, building on others' ideas and expressing their own clearly.

SL.3.1(a): Come to discussions prepared, having read or studied required material; explicitly draw on that preparation and other information known about the topic to explore ideas under discussion.

SUGGESTED STUDENT OBJECTIVES

- Cite textual evidence to support an interpretation of characters' motivations.
- Write imaginary narratives using dialogue and descriptions of actions, thoughts, and feelings.
- Explain the function of adverbs and adjectives in speech, literature, and writing.
- Compare and contrast two poems written about oysters.
- Compare and contrast two informational books about the same topic (e.g., a drop of water).
- Determine the main idea and supporting details of informational text.
- Research a favorite sea animal.
- Write a short informative piece about a favorite thing (e.g., a sea animal); apply growing understanding of what makes a strong, focused paragraph.

SUGGESTED WORKS

(E) indicates a CCSS exemplar text; (EA) indicates a text from a writer with other works identified as exemplars.

LITERARY TEXTS

Stories

- *Sarah, Plain and Tall* (Patricia MacLachlan) (E)
- *The Storm* (The Lighthouse Family series) (Cynthia Rylant and Preston McDaniels) (E)
- *The Whale* (The Lighthouse Family series) (Cynthia Rylant and Preston McDaniels) (EA)
- *The Raft* (Jim LaMarche) (E)
- *Amos & Boris* (William Steig) (E)
- *Canoe Days* (Gary and Ruth Wright Paulsen)
- *Three Days on a River in a Red Canoe* (Vera B. Williams)

Stories (Read Aloud)

- "The River Bank" in *The Wind in the Willows* (Kenneth Grahame)
- *Paddle-to-the-Sea* (Holling Clancy Holling)
- *Minn of the Mississippi* (Holling Clancy Holling)

Poems

- "At the Seaside" (Robert Louis Stevenson)
- "Sleepy Pearl" (Frances Gorman Risser)
- "Do Oysters Sneeze?" (Jack Prelutsky)

- "Undersea" (Marchette Chute)
- "Beach Stones" (Lilian Moore)
- "The Waves" (Gertrude M. Jones)
- "A Sand Witch for a Sandwich" (Emily Sweeney)
- "A Wave" (Gussie Osborne)

Poems (Read Aloud)
- "The Jumblies" (Edward Lear) (E)
- "From the Shore" (Carl Sandburg) (EA)
- "Seal Lullaby" (Rudyard Kipling) (EA)
- "Song of a Shell" (Violet L. Cuslidge)
- "The Barracuda" (John Gardner)

INFORMATIONAL TEXTS
Informational Books
- *Whales* (Smithsonian) (Seymour Simon) (EA)
- *Life in a Kelp Forest* (Mary Jo Rhodes and David Hall)
- *Sea Turtles* (Mary Jo Rhodes and David Hall)
- *Partners in the Sea* (Mary Jo Rhodes and David Hall)
- *Octopuses and Squids* (Mary Jo Rhodes and David Hall)
- *Seahorses and Sea Dragons* (Mary Jo Rhodes and David Hall)
- *Disasters at Sea* (DK Readers) (Andrew Donkin)
- *Titanic: Disaster That Rocked the World* (DK Readers) (Mark Dubowski)
- *Journey of a Humpback Whale* (DK Readers) (Caryn Jenner)
- *Shark Attack!* (DK Readers) (Cathy East Dubowski)

Informational Books (Read Aloud)
- *A Drop of Water: A Book of Science and Wonder* (Walter Wick) (E)
- *A Drop Around the World* (Barbara Shaw McKinney and Michael S. Maydak)
- *John Muir: America's Naturalist* (Images of Conservationists) (Thomas Locker)
- *Rachel Carson: Preserving a Sense of Wonder* (Thomas Locker and Joseph Bruchac)
- *The Lamp, the Ice, and the Boat Called Fish: Based on a True Story* (Jacqueline Briggs Martin and Beth Krommes)
- *The Cod's Tale* (Mark Kurlansky and S. D. Schindler) excerpts (e.g., informative illustrations/text features)
- *Swimming with Hammerhead Sharks* (Kenneth Mallory)
- *Survival Secrets of Sea Animals* (Mary Jo Rhodes and David Hall)
- *Predators of the Sea* (Mary Jo Rhodes and David Hall)
- *Life on a Coral Reef* (Mary Jo Rhodes and David Hall)
- *Dolphins, Seals, and Other Sea Mammals* (Mary Jo Rhodes and David Hall)
- *Crabs* (Mary Jo Rhodes and David Hall)
- *Many Luscious Lollipops: A Book About Adjectives* (World of Language) (Ruth Heller)
- *Up, Up and Away: A Book About Adverbs* (World of Language) (Ruth Heller)

ART, MUSIC, AND MEDIA
Art
- Edward Hopper, *Ground Swell* (1939)
- Joseph Turner, *Margate, from the Sea* (1835–1840)
- Katsushika Hokusai, *Mount Fuji Seen Below a Wave at Kanagawa* (1826–1833)
- Richard Diebenkorn, *Horizon: Ocean View* (1959)
- Claude Monet, *Garden at Sainte-Adresse* (1867)

SAMPLE ACTIVITIES AND ASSESSMENTS

Note: This unit can be tailored to meet science or social studies standards. By filling your class library with books about food chains, ecosystems, and/or nature preservation, you have a rich science unit. By focusing on the geography of and the people who live near lakes, rivers, and oceans, you have a strong social studies unit.

1. CLASS DISCUSSION/LITERARY

Review characters and character motivation from the first unit. Introduce the book *Sarah, Plain and Tall* (Patricia MacLachlan) as historical fiction: a fictional story from the days of settling the prairies. Introduce also the name of the unit: Inspired by the Sea. As you read the first chapter of this book, challenge students to look for specific places in the text where they can prove that a character in the story is "inspired by the sea." Ask students to give you a thumbs-up when they hear/see a line in the text that talks about a character "inspired by the sea." Students should easily detect Sarah as the character motivated by her love of the sea. One of her letters reads, "I have always loved to live by the sea." Create a chart and write down any evidence of Sarah's motivation. Discuss what motivates the other characters. Each day, as students come together to discuss the reading, instruct them to be prepared to give textual evidence of Sarah's motivation and the motivation of at least one other character. (RL.3.1, RL.3.3, SL.3.1a, SL.3.4)

2. NARRATIVE WRITING/LITERARY ACTIVITY

Chapter Five of *Sarah, Plain and Tall* contains a narrative about haystacks. Prepare students to write well-developed narratives and guide a discussion of the way Patricia MacLachlan wrote the haystack section by asking them the following questions about the narrative in the chapter:

- How many of you wanted to try sliding down a haystack after reading that scene?
- What was it in her writing that made you feel like you were there?
- How did you know what the characters were feeling?
- How did the dialogue help you to "be there"?
- How did she communicate action? Thoughts? Feelings?
- How did she order the events?
- How did she close the scene?

Then give the students this prompt: "Write a personal narrative about something similar to the haystack slide, such as riding a roller coaster, sledding down a snowy hill, or sliding down a hill. Be sure to show your actions, your thoughts, and your feelings through dialogue and description." (RL.3.1, W.3.3, W.3.4, W.3.5, W.3.10, L.3.1, L.3.2, L.3.2c, L.3.3, L.3.3a, L.3.6)

3. CLASS DISCUSSION/LANGUAGE ACTIVITY

Many Luscious Lollipops (Ruth Heller) teaches about adjectives through several language lessons. Read this book to the class, covering a few pages a day so that students may incorporate what they learn each day into conversation and writing. Use the adjectives and adverbs (which are covered in another Heller book, *Up, Up and Away*) to build interesting sentences about the sea and in students' own narratives. Be sure students can explain the function of each part of speech (adjectives and adverbs) and its use in literature, speech, and writing. (L.3.1a, L.3.2d, L.3.5b)

4. CLASS DISCUSSION/POETRY

Encourage the dramatic interpretation and recitation of poetry in this unit. Read two poems aloud that have similar topics such as: "Sleepy Pearl" (Frances Gorman Risser) and "Do Oysters Sneeze?" (Jack Prelutsky). Ask the students the following questions:

- What do you think is the message of each poem? Cite evidence from the poem, by stanza and line, that hints at the meaning.
- How are these poems similar? How are they different?
- Which of the poems do you think is better? Why? (RL.3.5, RL.3.9, SL.3.1a,d)

5. CLASS DISCUSSION/INFORMATIONAL TEXT

Read aloud two books with similar topics, such as: *A Drop of Water: A Book of Science and Wonder* (Walter Wick) and *A Drop Around the World* (Barbara Shaw McKinney). As you read the books, discuss the following questions:

- What is the main idea of the book? Of each section?
- What are the key points used to create the main idea?
- How are the two books similar?
- How are they different?
- What are the text features used by the authors/illustrators to teach more about a drop of water?
- Do these books have the same purpose?
- Does one of the books teach more than the other?
- How could one of the books be improved? (SL.3.1d, SL.3.2, RI.3.2, RI.3.9, RI.3.6)

6. INFORMATIONAL TEXT

Choose a book that has good examples of text features (e.g., cross-section diagram, table) such as *The Cod's Tale* (Mark Kurlansky). Create a list of all the text features the students will see in the book. Display the text as you read, instructing students to look for text features as you turn each page. Give each student one sticky note. As they spot a text feature, have them write the page number on the sticky note and put it by the name of the text feature on the list. Discuss the purpose of each text feature in general and in the text you are reading. (RI.3.5)

7. WRITING/INFORMATIONAL TEXT

Give the students this prompt: "You have read books about animals that live in the sea. Think about which animal has been most interesting to you. Write a paragraph about what you have learned about a specific sea animal: its habitat, its adaptations, and its diet. You may want to do more research on the Internet, in encyclopedias, or in a library book to add to your learning." Some students will need guidance in generating open-ended questions about their specific animal, a plan for locating the most relevant and useful information, and organizing their information into focused paragraphs. (SL.3.1a, W.3.2, W.3.10, RI.3.2)

8. LANGUAGE ACTIVITY

Choose an interesting sea animal from the books you have read together as a class. Ask the students to come up with five adjectives each to describe the animal. Generate a list of adjectives from the list of student ideas. Then have students come up with movements the animal makes and five adverbs to go with the movements. Create short sentences using the adjectives and adverbs (e.g., "*Huge* whales glide *gracefully*."). After students write several of the sentences on a chart, have them practice making new sentences with comparative or superlative adjectives and adverbs (e.g., "This huge whale glides *more gracefully* than that one.") To extend this activity in a different form, ask pairs of students to choose a sea animal. Gather strong adjectives, verbs, and adverbs to describe the animal and its movements. Use the words to create a Wordle with the name of the animal as the center. (L.3.1g, SL.3.6)

9. ART/CLASS DISCUSSION

Continue with class discussion about the title of the unit, Inspired by the Sea. What do you see in each artwork—can you see the sea? Cover the part of the work that is not part of the sea. What changes about the sea? What do you notice in the water? Why did the artist choose those colors? Is it obvious that this detail is a picture of the sea? What else could it be? Closely compare the Diebenkorn image with the Hopper. Discuss the differences in color, line, texture, and shape of each seascape. Discuss the ideas of abstraction and realism by contrasting these works. (SL.3.1, SL.3.3)

10. ART/CLASS DISCUSSION/WRITING

Review all of the artworks. Ask students to describe differences among the works. Which one depicts the sea most accurately? Is it realistic or abstract? What would you create if you painted or drew your own image of the sea? Describe your "ideal" sea image in words. (W.3.3, SL.3.4, SL.3.5)

ADDITIONAL RESOURCES

- "Ocean Poems" (Kaunakakai Multiage Primary School, Kaunakakai, HI) (RL.3.5)
- Patricia MacLachlan (1938–), *Biography* (JRank Encyclopedia) (RI.3.3)
- *Reading and Writing About Pollution to Understand Cause and Effect* (ReadWriteThink) (RI.3.3)
- *History of America "On the Water"* (Smithsonian, National Museum of American History) (RI.3.3)
- *Blue Planet: Seas of Life* (five-disc box set, BBC, 2008)

TERMINOLOGY

Adjectives	Dialogue	Poet	Text features
Adverbs	Illustrator	Quotation marks	
Author	Line	Stanza	
Comma	Poem	Text evidence	

MAKING INTERDISCIPLINARY CONNECTIONS

This unit teaches:

Art: Edward Hopper
Geography: Rivers of North America (e.g., the Mississippi River and the St. Lawrence River)
Science: Aquatic life (e.g., animals, habitats, and environmental conservation)

This unit could be extended to teach:

Geography: Exploration (e.g., search for the Northwest Passage)
History: Life on the prairie (e.g., related to *Sarah, Plain and Tall*)
Science: Animal classifications (e.g., amphibians, reptiles, birds, and mammals) and ecology (e.g., interdependence, ecosystems, and environmental conservation)

Grade Three, Unit Two Sample Lesson Plan

Sarah, Plain and Tall by Patricia MacLachlan

In this series of four lessons, students read *Sarah, Plain and Tall* by Patricia MacLachlan, and they:

Explore Sarah and her love for the sea (RL.3.2)
Examine Sarah's ability to share her love (RL.3.1, RL.3.2)

Summary

Lesson I: Caleb, Anna, Papa, and Sarah (Ch. 1–3)

Identify the main characters in *Sarah, Plain and Tall* (RL.3.1, RL.3.3)

Explore the narrator's point of view (RL.3.6)

Examine the cause of sadness in the family (RL.3.1)

Explore the content of the letters (RL.3.1, RL.3.5, SL.3.1)

(Begin to) note Sarah's feeling for the sea (RL.3.1, RL.3.3, SL.3.1)

Lesson II: Life on the Farm (Ch. 4–6)

(Begin to) explore Sarah's personality (RL.3.3, SL.3.1)

Explore Sarah's new life (RL.3.1, RL.3.3, SL.3.1)

Examine Sarah's relationship with Caleb and Anna (RL.3.1, RL.3.3)

(Continue to) note Sarah's life by the sea (RL.3.1, RL.3.3)

Lesson III: Sarah's Ways (Ch. 7–end)

Explore Sarah's ways (RL.3.1)

Examine Papa's attitude toward Sarah (RL.3.1, RL.3.3)

Analyze Caleb's words: "Papa, come quickly! Sarah has brought the sea!" (RL.3.1)

Revisit Sarah's story and give the chapters of the book titles (SL.3.1)

Lesson IV: Sarah's Sea

Identify Maine on a map

Explore the ways that Sarah manages to keep the sea close to her (RL.3.1, RL.3.3, W.3.1a,b,c,d; SL.3.1)

Select passages that depict Sarah's feelings for the sea (RL.3.1, RL.3.3)

Analyze the means by which Sarah shares the sea with others (RL.3.1, RL.3.3, W.3.1a,b,c,d)

Lesson IV: Sarah's Sea

Objectives

Identify Maine on a map

Explore the ways that Sarah manages to keep the sea close to her (RL.3.1, RL.3.3, W.3.1a,b,c,d; SL.3.1)

Select passages that depict Sarah's feelings for the sea (RL.3.1, RL.3.3)

Analyze the means by which Sarah shares the sea with others (RL.3.1, RL.3.3, W.3.1a,b,c,d)

Required Materials

☐ Class set of *Sarah, Plain and Tall*, by Patricia MacLachlan

☐ Map of the United States

☐ Sticky notes

Procedures

1. Lead-In:

Students identify Sarah's home state, Maine, on a map of the United States. They note that Maine is in the northeast of the United States, along the Atlantic Ocean.

2. Step by Step:

a. In groups, students discuss what they know so far about Sarah and the sea.

b. Students independently go back to the text and, using sticky notes as markers, select passages that depict Sarah's feeling for the sea.

c. Lead a class discussion. Students, referring to specific passages from the book (marked by the sticky notes), analyze Sarah's ways of keeping the sea close to her and her new family.

3. Closure:

Introduce the students to the homework assignment.

Differentiation

Advanced

- Following the completion of the opinion paragraph, students will build on their knowledge of the Maine coastline. Students will choose a feature (geographic or biological) of the Maine coastline to research. Students will create informational posters about the feature they study.

Struggling

- Before leaving school, students will meet in a small group with the teacher to draft their first sentence.
- Students will create a list of evidence from the text and from the sticky notes to support an opinion related to Sarah and the sea.
- Students will complete the assignment at home.
- Students will work with the teacher the following morning to review (and revise) the work completed.

Homework/Assessment

In paragraph form, students discuss Sarah and the sea. The paragraph will have:

- A sentence introducing the topic, the text, and the author
- A sentence introducing an opinion
- Several sentences that support the point of view and provide evidence from the text
- A concluding sentence

Creative, Inventive, and Notable People

In this third six-week unit of third grade, students read biographies about musicians, artists, and inventors of the early twentieth century.

ESSENTIAL QUESTION

? How are the words *creative* and *inventive* similar? How are they different?

OVERVIEW

Students read fiction that shows the passion of an artist; poetry that shows a different way of thinking; and biographies of creative people living and working in the same time period. They also read about conjunctions and use them while composing sentences that describe what they learned about the inventors. They create a slide presentation and build upon the word work on conjunctions by writing an opinion piece about a favorite person in the unit. Finally, they record themselves fluently reading a poem, illustrate the poem, and post the work on the Internet for parents to enjoy.

FOCUS STANDARDS

These Focus Standards have been selected for the unit from the Common Core State Standards.

RI.3.3: Describe the relationship between a series of historical events, scientific ideas or concepts, or steps in technical procedures in a text, using language that pertains to time, sequence, and cause/effect.

RL.3.1: Ask and answer such questions to demonstrate understanding of a text, referring explicitly to the text as the basis for the answers.

SL3.1: Engage effectively in a range of collaborative discussions (one-on-one, group, and teacher-led) with diverse partners on grade 3 topics and texts, building on others' ideas and expressing their own clearly.

SL.3.1(a): Come to discussions prepared, having read or studied required material; explicitly draw on that preparation and other information known about the topic to explore ideas under discussion.

W.3.2: Write informative/explanatory texts to examine a topic and convey ideas and information clearly.

L3.1: Demonstrate command of the conventions of Standard English grammar and usage when writing or speaking.

L.3.1(h): Use coordinating and subordinating conjunctions.

L.3.1(i): Produce simple, compound, and complex sentences.

SUGGESTED STUDENT OBJECTIVES

- Define and apply words such as "creative" and "inventive" to describe artists, musicians, and inventors.
- Work with base words to create new words by adding prefixes and suffixes.
- Read biographies (e.g., of artists, musicians, and inventors) and explain the characteristics of a biography.
- Take simple research notes while reading biographies.
- Design and create five slides for a presentation on a notable person (e.g., an inventor).
- Learn about conjunctions and use them to create simple, compound, and complex sentences.
- Write an opinion piece based on the three key words in this unit (e.g., *creative, inventive,* and *notable*).
- Record themselves reading a poem.
- Create an accompanying illustration that captures a poem's meaning and display it on a class Internet page.

SUGGESTED WORKS

(E) indicates a CCSS exemplar text; (EA) indicates a text from a writer with other works identified as exemplars.

LITERARY TEXTS
Stories
- *Emma's Rug* (Allen Say) (EA)
- *Rocks in His Head* (Carol Otis Hurst and James Stevenson)

Story (Read Aloud)
- *The Sign Painter* (Allen Say) (E)

Poems
- "Paper I" (Carl Sandburg) (EA)
- "Paper II" (Carl Sandburg) (EA)
- "The Folk Who Live in Backward Town" (Mary Ann Hoberman)
- "Jimmy Jet and his TV Set" (Shel Silverstein)

Poems (Read Aloud)
- *The Pot That Juan Built* (Nancy Andrews-Goebel and David Diaz)
- *No One Saw: Ordinary Things Through the Eyes of an Artist* (Bob Raczka)

INFORMATIONAL TEXTS
Informational Books
- *My Name is Georgia: A Portrait* (Jeanette Winter)
- *Vincent van Gogh: Sunflowers and Swirly Stars* (Brad Bucks and Joan Holub)

- *The Yellow House: Vincent van Gogh and Paul Gauguin Side by Side* (Susan Goldman Rubin)
- *Picasso and the Girl with a Ponytail* (Laurence Anholt)
- *When Marian Sang: The True Recital of Marian Anderson* (Pam Munoz Ryan and Brian Selznick)
- *Ella Fitzgerald: The Tale of a Vocal Virtuoso* (Andrea Davis Pinkney and Brian Pinkney)
- *Thomas Edison: A Brilliant Inventor* (TIME for Kids Biographies) (Editors of TIME for Kids with Lisa DeMauro)
- *Henry Ford: Putting the World on Wheels* (TIME for Kids Biographies) (Editors of TIME for Kids with Dina El Nabli)
- *Alexander Graham Bell: Inventor of the Telephone* (TIME for Kids Biographies) (Editors of TIME for Kids with John Micklos Jr.)
- *Amelia and Eleanor Go For a Ride* (Pam Munoz Ryan and Brian Selznick)
- *Hooray for Inventors!* (Marcia Williams)

Informational Books (Read Aloud)

- *The Museum Book: A Guide to Strange and Wonderful Collections* (Jan Mark and Richard Holland) (E)
- *Ah, Music!* (Aliki) (E)
- *Paul Gauguin* (Getting to Know the World's Greatest Artists) (Mike Venezia)
- *Van Gogh* (Getting to Know the World's Greatest Artists) (Mike Venezia)
- *Here's Looking at Me: How Artists See Themselves* (Bob Raczka)
- *Inventing the Future: A Photobiography of Thomas Alva Edison* (Marfe Ferguson Delano and Jennifer Emmett)
- *To Fly: The Story of the Wright Brothers* (Wendie Old and Robert Andrew Parker)
- *Hidden Worlds: Looking Through a Scientist's Microscope* (Stephen Kramer and Dennis Kunkel)
- *Fantastic! Wow! And Unreal! A Book About Interjections and Conjunctions* (Ruth Heller)

ART, MUSIC, AND MEDIA

Visual Artists

- Pablo Picasso, *Gertrude Stein* (1906–1906)
- Vincent van Gogh, *Self-Portrait* (1887–1888)
- Alice Neel, *Faith Ringgold* (1976)
- Andy Warhol, *Self-Portrait* (1967)
- Paul Gauguin, *Self-Portrait* (1889)

Musicians

- Richard Avedon, *Marian Anderson, Contralto, New York* (1955)
- World-Telegram staff photographer, *Louis Armstrong* (1953)
- Arnold Newman, *Igor Stravinsky* (1946)

Writers

- Winold Reiss, *Portrait of Langston Hughes* (no date)
- Edoardo Gelli, *The Last Portrait of Mark Twain* (1904)
- Artist unknown, *Helen Keller with Anne Sullivan* (1888)

SAMPLE ACTIVITIES AND ASSESSMENTS

Note: Although the fiction titles are more contemporary, the artists, musicians, and inventors are all from the twentieth century. You may want to study the artists and musicians in the first half of the unit and then spend the last three weeks on the inventors.

1. CLASS DISCUSSION

Begin this new unit with a discussion of its title: Creative, Inventive, and Notable People. Use some of the following questions to guide the conversation, and ask students first to write answers in complete sentences in their journals before the class discussion begins:

- What does it mean to be *creative*? (base word: *create*)
- Whom do you know that is creative?
- What other words can we make from the base word *create*? (Possible answers: *creation, created, creating, recreate, uncreative,* and *recreation*)
- What does it mean to be *inventive*? (base word: *invent*)
- Whom do you know that is inventive?
- What does it mean to be *notable*? (base word: *note*)
- Whom do you know that is notable?
- How are the words *creative* and *inventive* similar?
- How are they different? (RF.3.3c, L3.2e, L.3.4c, L.3.4b, L.3.5b, L.3.5c)

2. CLASS DISCUSSION/LITERARY

Introduce *The Sign Painter,* written and illustrated by Allen Say (who also wrote *Grandfather's Journey,* from Unit Two). In this book about a man and a boy who paint billboards, the illustrations play an important role in telling the story. While you read it aloud, challenge the students to question and think, and ask them to jot down questions. Read at a leisurely pace so that students have the opportunity to ask questions about specific illustrations, words, or pages of the book where they might lose focus or struggle with understanding the story. (RL.3.1)

3. INFORMATIONAL READING/NOTE TAKING

Reading biographies of artists and musicians provides an opportunity for students to focus on noting important information in the text. Teach students about the title of a biography and how it is sometimes the name of the person and how it is sometimes a description of the person's main contribution. Tell students that while they are reading or listening to someone else read a biography, they should note the key events that occur in the subject's life. Have students recall and generate a list of the key question words to consider, such as *who, where, when, why, what,* and *how.* Divide students into small groups and assign each group a question stem. Have students create a chart with the questions down the left-hand column of the chart. Then create a similar chart on the board or a notepad in the front of the room. Using the key question words to guide comprehension, read aloud a biography of a famous person such as the singer Marian Anderson. As students hear answers to their questions, have them raise their hands. Write answers on a class chart and have the students write the information on their own charts. As you repeat this activity with other biographies, ask students to generate more open-ended research questions. (RI.3.1, RI.3.3, RI.3.7, W.3.8, L.3.2a)

4. RESEARCH AND INFORMATIVE/EXPLANATORY WRITING

Have students choose an age-appropriate biography to read from a series, such as the *TIME for Kids* series of biographies. Instruct the students to take notes based on the key questions (as described in the previous activity) while reading the biographies. If there is time, students should generate one open-ended question to research after finishing the biography. After students have located a few additional sources and answered their last question, partner the students to share information and create a short series of slides to answer each of the questions (*who, where, when, why, what,* and *how*), as well as to highlight three to five key events in the person's life. Have students combine multiple questions on one slide such as *where* and *when*. Limit each pair to a total of five slides, with the last slide showing the key events in the inventor's life. Combine the slides into one presentation and present it to an audience such as the students' parents or another class. You might also choose to give students this writing prompt: "Choose a famous person's biography to read. Write about the person. Be sure to answer the questions *who, where, when, why, what,* and *how* and highlight three to five key events in the person's life." Make sure that students cite their main source properly. Following this research, a class could present a "Wax Museum," where each student dresses as their assigned person and tells about her/his life. (SL.3.1a, SL.3.4, RI.3.3, W.3.2, W.3.5, W.3.8, W.3.10, L.3.1, L.3.2, L.3.3)

5. RESEARCH/INFORMATIONAL TEXT/ORAL PRESENTATION

Have each student choose an invention that they love (e.g., a bicycle, an MP3 player). Or students can choose a painting or song listed in the Art, Music, and Media section. Students will then formulate open-ended questions using the question stems (*who, where, when, why, what,* and *how*) to guide the research about who invented or created the item they selected. Have students create a presentation of the information they discover about the inventor of their favorite object. Require students to use the guiding question stems as an organizational tool in their presentations. Allow students to photograph the object so that they can display an image of it while they tell about the history of their invention. If students picked an artwork or a song, display the work or play a recording as the student shares their research. You may choose to give the students the assignment in the form of a research prompt: "Choose an invention, an artwork, or song that you love. Research to find out who invented it, created it, or wrote it. Photograph the object or artwork, or record the song to use for an oral presentation of your research results." Make sure that students cite their source properly. (RI.3.5, W.3.7, W.3.8, SL.3.4)

6. LANGUAGE ACTIVITY/GRAPHIC ORGANIZER

Using Ruth Heller's book *Fantastic! Wow! And Unreal! A Book About Interjections and Conjunctions*, teach the coordinating conjunctions (*and, but, or, nor, for, yet, so*) and subordinating conjunctions (*after, before, when, while, since, until*). Apply conjunctions by creating simple, compound, and complex sentences from a cause-and-effect graphic organizer. For example, consider the invention of the assembly line by Henry Ford.

- What caused him to invent it?
- What were the effects of the invention?

Have students create cause-and-effect-related sentences orally, and then have them write the sentences down. Teach about the use of coordinating and subordinating conjunctions in their work. (L.3.1h, L.3.1i, RI.3.3)

7. FLUENCY/POETRY ACTIVITY

The poems in this unit show how poets look at the world in a different way. Students should choose one of the poems and then practice reciting it in the way that best exemplifies the meaning of the poem. With a video camera, record the students reading (reciting) poems. Then, have students create an accompanying illustration to display while you play the recording of their poetry reading. Alternatively, both the recording and the illustration can be posted on the Internet for parents to listen to and see. (SL.3.5, RF.3.4b)

8. REFLECTIVE/OPINION WRITING

Give the students this prompt: "You began this unit with a discussion about three words: *creative, inventive,* and *notable.* Choose the person from this unit that you believe to be the most creative, inventive, and notable. Write about the person you choose, and give reasons why you believe they are creative, inventive, and notable." (W.3.1, L.3.2)

9. ART/CLASS DISCUSSION

Select two works to compare in a large-group discussion—for instance, the Warhol self-portrait and the photograph of Louis Armstrong. Discussion should focus on choices that the artist made to communicate the importance of the subject, including the subject's unique creative sensibility in art, music, or writing. In the above example, students might explore why the trumpet is the focal point of the photograph—does the photographer want the viewer to focus mainly on the music or on the man? How is the self-portrait of Warhol different? What details does he give us, and what remains ambiguous? How did the painter or photographer choose to depict the artist (or musician or writer) and portray his or her talents? (SL.3.1, SL.3.3)

10. ART/NARRATIVE WRITING

Examine again one of the portraits that you most admire. If you were to create either a self-portrait or a portrait of someone you respect, what features would you include? What aspects of these artists' works would you use in your own interpretations? Write a brief narrative describing your imagined portrait. (W.3.3)

ADDITIONAL RESOURCES

- "When Marian Sings" (RF.3.4)
- *Biocube Biography Summarizer* (ReadWriteThink) (RI.3.2)
- *Spark Lab Inventor Profiles* (Smithsonian, The Lemelson Center for the Study of Invention & Innovation) (RI.3.10)
- *Rooting Out Meaning: Morpheme Match-Ups in the Primary Grades* (ReadWriteThink) (RF.3.3)

TERMINOLOGY

Biographies	Coordinating conjunction	Presentation	Subordinating conjunction
Complex sentence		Research questions	
Compound sentence	Note taking	Simple sentence	

MAKING INTERDISCIPLINARY CONNECTIONS

This unit teaches:

Art: Andy Warhol, Pablo Picasso, Alice Neel
Music: Jazz (e.g., Louis Armstrong, Ella Fitzgerald) and opera (e.g., Marian Anderson)

History: Inventors (e.g., Thomas Edison and Alexander Graham Bell)

Science: Inventions (e.g., the assembly line, light bulb, and telephone) and flight (e.g., the Wright Brothers and Amelia Earhart)

This unit could be extended to teach:

History: Inventors (e.g., before and after the twentieth century)

Science: Light/optics (e.g., light, reflection, and lenses), sound (e.g., sound waves, the human voice, and the human ear), and vision/hearing (i.e., how they work in the human body)

Grade Three, Unit Three Sample Lesson Plan

Emma's Rug by Allen Say

In this series of four lessons, students read *Emma's Rug* by Allen Say, and they:

Explore the power of artists' inspiration (RL.3.2)

Examine an individual's ability to overcome a crisis (RL.3.1, RL.3.2)

Consider the role that illustrations play in telling Emma's story (RL.3.7, SL.3.1)

Summary

Lesson I: Emma's World

Explore the story line of *Emma's Rug* (RL.3.1, RL.3.2)

Identify the characters in the story (RL.3.3)

List key events in the story (RL.3.5)

Lesson II: Emma's Rug

Reread Emma's story (through p. 19) (RF.3.4)

Describe the rug (RL.3.1, SL.3.1)

List Emma's activities (RL.3.1, RL.3.3, W.3.2)

Identify the source of Emma's inspiration (RL.3.1, SL.3.1)

Analyze Emma's response to the attention that she receives (RL.3.1, SL.3.1)

Note the use of illustrations in the story (RL.3.7)

Lesson III: A Crisis

Reread the rest of the story (p. 20–end of story) (RF.3.4)

Explore the reasons for Emma's scream (RL.3.1, RL.3.3)

Consider the act of Emma's mother (RL.3.1, RL.3.3)

Examine Emma's response to the crisis (RL.3.1, RL.3.3)

Lesson IV: Inspiration

Revisit the ending of the story

Analyze the meaning of the narrator's words: "She saw eyes watching her and then the faces of creatures all around." (RL.3.1, RL.3.4)

Consider the importance of the illustration at the end of the story (RL.3.7)

Discuss the following question: Where does inspiration come from? (SL.3.1)

Lesson II: Emma's Rug

Objectives

Reread Emma's story (through p. 19) (RF.3.4)

Describe the rug (RL.3.1, SL.3.1)

List Emma's activities (RL.3.1, RL.3.3, W.3.2)

Identify the source of Emma's inspiration (RL.3.1, SL.3.1)

Analyze Emma's response to the attention that she receives (RL.3.1, SL.3.1)

Note the use of illustrations in the story (RL.3.7)

Required Materials

☐ Class set of *Emma's Rug* by Allen Say

Procedures

1. Lead-In:
   Reread *Emma's Rug* through page 19.
2. Step by Step:
   a. Students discuss the description of the rug. They use specific examples from the text: It is "shaggy," "plain," and it "keeps the feet warm."
   b. Students look at the illustrations of the rug and note that it is indeed "plain" (i.e., there are no pictures on it).
   c. Students, citing the text, note Emma's relationship to the rug (p. 6).
   d. Students note the way that Emma stares into the rug as if she sees something in it (illustration on p. 7).
   e. Students analyze Emma's response to the attention she receives.
3. Closure:
   Student volunteers summarize the details of the discussion.

Differentiation

Advanced

- Students will write a paragraph about the illustration on page 7 of the book, discussing the way Emma stares into the rug and what she might see in it.

Struggling

- Read the story aloud to the students, as they "whisper read" along with you. Each time the rug is described in the text, ask the students to chorally read aloud the sentences. Using a real rug, show the students the meaning of "shaggy," "plain," and "keeps the feet warm."

Homework/Assessment
Students reread the ending of the story.

Grade 3 ▶ *Unit 4*

The People, the Preamble, and the Presidents

In this fourth six-week unit of third grade, students read about the people, the Preamble (to the Constitution), and the presidents of the United States.

OVERVIEW

Building on knowledge of the notable people in the last unit, students read informational texts about the people who came to America and established a new government in the eighteenth century. They read about the lives of presidents, research a president of interest, and write a "bio-poem" (a biography in poem form). Finally, students create and perform a cumulative choral reading of the Preamble to the U.S. Constitution and memorize it for an oral recitation.

ESSENTIAL QUESTION

❓ Why is it important to choose words carefully?

FOCUS STANDARDS

These Focus Standards have been selected for the unit from the Common Core State Standards.

RI.3.4: Determine the meaning of general academic and domain-specific words and phrases in a text relevant to a grade 3 topic or subject area.

RI.3.8: Describe the logical connection between particular sentences and paragraphs in a text (e.g., comparison, cause/effect, [and] first/second/third in a sequence).

SL.3.3: Ask and answer questions about information from a speaker, offering appropriate elaboration and detail.

RF.3.4: Read with sufficient accuracy and fluency to support comprehension.

RF.3.4(b): Read on-level prose and poetry orally with accuracy, [at the] appropriate rate, and [with] expression on successive readings.

W.3.7: Conduct short research projects that build knowledge about a topic.

L.3.4: Determine or clarify the meaning of unknown and multiple-meaning words and phrases based on grade 3 reading and content, choosing flexibly from a range of strategies.

L.3.4(d): Use glossaries and beginning dictionaries, both print and digital, to determine or clarify the precise meaning of key words and phrases.

SUGGESTED STUDENT OBJECTIVES

- Ask and answer questions of a speaker (e.g., a visitor invited to discuss immigration).
- Sequence the events in an informational text (e.g., *Coming to America: The Story of Immigration*).
- Define key words in the Preamble to the U.S. Constitution.
- Create an acrostic poem for a key word in the Preamble demonstrating study of the definition.
- Dramatically read the Preamble in collaboration with classmates through a cumulative choral reading.
- Orally recite the Preamble.
- Study the illustrations in *We the Kids: The Preamble to the Constitution* (David Catrow) and explain the role of the illustrator in illuminating the meaning of a text.
- Compare and contrast two similar books on the same topic (e.g., the presidents).

SUGGESTED WORKS

(E) indicates a CCSS exemplar text; (EA) indicates a text from a writer with other works identified as exemplars.

LITERARY TEXTS

Stories

- *Woodrow for President: A Tail of Voting, Campaigns, and Elections* (Peter J. and Cheryl Shaw Barnes)
- *Arthur Meets the President: An Arthur Adventure* (Marc Brown)
- *Otto Runs for President* (Rosemary Wells)
- *The Garden on Green Street* (Meish Goldish)
- *Vote!* (Eileen Christelow)
- *Lily and Miss Liberty* (Carla Stevens and Deborah Kogan Ray)
- *In America* (Marissa Moss)
- *The Dream Jar* (Bonnie Pryor and Mark Graham)
- *Annushka's Voyage* (Edith Tarbescu and Lydia Dabcovich)
- *The Long Way to a New Land* (Joan Sandin)
- *Molly's Pilgrim* (Barbara Cohen and Daniel Mark Duffy)
- *Make a Wish Molly* (Barbara Cohen and Jan Naimo Jones)
- *When Jesse Came Across the Sea* (Amy Hest and P.J. Lynch)
- *Hannah's Journal: The Story of An Immigrant Girl* (Marissa Moss)
- *Oranges on Golden Mountain* (Elizabeth Partridge)
- *The Memory Coat* (Elvira Woodruff and Michael Dooling)
- *Together in Pinecone Patch* (Thomas F. Yezerski)
- *Hope in My Heart: Sofia's Immigrant Diary, Book 1* (Kathryn Lasky)
- *In the Year of the Boar and Jackie Robinson* (Bette Bao Lord and Marc Simont)
- *The Orphan of Ellis Island* (Elvira Woodruff)

Poems (Read Aloud)

- "The Star-Spangled Banner" (Francis Scott Key)
- *The Star-Spangled Banner* (Francis Scott Key, illustrated by Peter Spier)

- "The Flag Goes By" (H. H. Bennett)
- "George Washington" (Rosemary and Stephen Vincent Benet)
- "Washington Monument by Night" (Carl Sandburg) (EA)
- "A Nation's Strength" (Ralph Waldo Emerson)

INFORMATIONAL TEXTS

Informational Books

- *So You Want to Be President?* (Judith St. George and David Small) (E)
- *14 Cows for America* (Carmen Agra Deedy, Thomas Gonzalez, and Wilson Kimeli Naiyomah) (E)
- *Ellis Island* (Elaine Landau)
- *Smart About the Presidents* (Smart About History) (Jon Buller, Susan Schade, Maryann Cocca-Leffler, Dana Regan, and Jill Weber)

Informational Books (Read Aloud)

- *Coming to America: The Story of Immigration* (Betsy Maestro and Susannah Ryan)
- *We the Kids: The Preamble to the Constitution* (David Catrow)
- *Shh! We're Writing the Constitution* (Jean Fritz and Tomie dePaola)
- *. . . If You Were There When They Signed The Constitution* (Elizabeth Levy and Joan Holub)
- *James Madison: Fourth President 1809–1817* (Mike Venezia)
- *The Presidency* (True Books) (Patricia Ryon Quiri)
- *The Presidency* (True Books) (Christine Taylor-Butler)
- *Lives of the Presidents: Fame, Shame (and What the Neighbors Thought)* (Kathleen Krull and Kathryn Hewitt)
- *Remember the Ladies: 100 Great American Women* (Cheryl Harness)

ART, MUSIC, AND MEDIA

Art

- Emanuel Leutze, *Washington Crossing the Delaware* (1851)
- Gilbert Stuart, *George Washington* (1796)
- John Trumbull, *John Adams* (1792–1793)
- Jean Antoine Houdon, *Bust of Thomas Jeffersona* (1789)
- Daniel Chester French, *Lincoln Memorial* (1922)
- Aaron Shikler, *Oil Portrait of John F. Kennedy* (official portrait) (1970)
- Robert Rauschenberg, *Retroactive 1* (1964)
- Artist unknown, *Reagan Inaugural Parade* (1981)
- Chuck Close, *Portrait of Bill Clinton* (2005)

SAMPLE ACTIVITIES AND ASSESSMENTS

Note: For the people part of this unit, bring in as many immigration stories, through texts and speakers (especially parents and grandparents), as you can, to represent the students in your class. (SL.3.3)

1. CLASS DISCUSSION/LANGUAGE

Introduce the unit by writing the three key words on the board: *people, preamble,* and *presidency.* As you work through each word (possibly over a few days/class periods), give students a copy of a *semantic map* and display yours (on an overhead projector, document camera, or an interactive whiteboard, for example). Using dictionaries for reference, begin with the word *people*. To ensure full participation, require each student to turn to a partner and talk about each part of the map before filling in the spaces. Maps such as these create a richer understanding of a word they already know (e.g., *people*) by looking at parts of speech and the word's synonyms. (L.3.1b,c, L.3.4b, L.3.4d, L.3.6, RF.3.3a)

2. LANGUAGE/VOCABULARY

Divide students into groups of three or four and give them one of the key words (*people, preamble,* or *presidency*). Ask them to write the word on a poster in large bold print. Then have them use their semantic maps to create symbols, pictures, and words (synonyms) that illustrate the rich meaning of each word. Hang the posters around the room to refer to throughout the unit. (L.3.1b,c, L.3.4b, L.3.6, RF.3.3a)

3. DRAMATIC READING/FLUENCY

Divide the class into eight groups to perform a cumulative choral reading of the Preamble to the U.S. Constitution. Have the first group read to the first comma, the second group read to the next comma, and so on. Continue adding voices/phrases until the whole class is reading the Preamble. Students will quickly and naturally memorize the Preamble and can perform it independently as an oral recitation. (RF.3.3c, RF.3.4)

4. LANGUAGE ACTIVITY/ACROSTIC POEM

Using the formatted Preamble text below, give students the following writing prompt: "Choose a key word (in bold) from the Preamble. Use defining phrases, simple similes, or synonyms to show that you understand the key word." You may want to do one as a class example and then have the students work independently or with partners to complete the task. (RI.3.4, W.3.2b, W.3.10, L.3.2g, L.3.4d, SL.3.1)

> We the People of the United States, in Order to form a more perfect **Union**, establish **Justice**, insure domestic **Tranquility**, provide for the common **defense**, promote the general **Welfare**, and secure the Blessings of **Liberty** to ourselves and our **Posterity**, do ordain and establish this **Constitution** for the United States of America.

5. CLASS DISCUSSION/LITERATURE

Using the book *We the Kids: The Preamble to the Constitution* (David Catrow), discuss the role of an illustrator in telling a story. Showing only the illustrations (by, for example, covering the text with sticky notes), have the students concoct a story aloud and together. After the students have created a story, show them that the text for the book is actually the Preamble to the U.S. Constitution. Together, read the book again to see how each illustration illustrates the meaning of a phrase. (RL.3.7, SL.3.1)

6. CLASS DISCUSSION/INFORMATIONAL TEXT

Choose two books about presidents for the students to compare and contrast, such as *So You Want to Be President?* and *Lives of the Presidents*. Ask students the following questions:

- In what ways are the two books similar?
- How are they different?
- Did you feel that any of the humorous comments made about the presidents were inappropriate? (*Note:* Be sure they quote from the text to back up their opinion.) (RI.3.6, RI.3.1, RI.3.9, SL.3.1)

7. RESEARCH AND INFORMATIVE/EXPLANATORY WRITING

Give the students this research prompt: "From the books we've read about the presidents, choose the president who interests you most. Research that president using online sources, an encyclopedia, and a biography of him." Teachers will want to remind the students to generate research questions before they begin locating sources. When they have completed the research, challenge them with this writing prompt: "Write an informative bio-poem based on the American president you chose to research." Students may use the format described below to organize the poem. Students should use the process of revising and editing before publishing their work. (*Note:* The example about George Washington that follows is for the teacher, though you may decide to share it with the class to explain the activity.) To help struggling students, the teacher may want to create a graphic organizer to aid with gathering the necessary information for the bio-poem. (W.3.2, W.3.5, W.3.6, W.3.7, W.3.10, L.3.1, L.3.2, L.3.3)

Formatting Guidelines

Line 1: First, middle, and last name

Line 2: Four jobs held by the man during his life (other than presidency)

Line 3: Birthplace, child of

Line 4: Lover of

Line 5: Educated

Line 6: Resident of

Line 7: Three contributions

Line 8: Number order of president (ordinal number)

Line 9: Nickname

Sample Poem

George Washington
Surveyor, planter, soldier, commander
Born in Virginia, son of Mary
Lover of Martha, math, and farming
Educated in elementary school
Resident of Mount Vernon
Revolutionary commander, government creator, humble leader
First president
Father of our country

8. ART/CLASS DISCUSSION

Select one of the following comparisons: *Washington Crossing the Delaware* (Leutze) versus *Reagan Inaugural Parade* (photographer unknown) or *George Washington* (Stuart) versus *Oil Portrait of John F. Kennedy* (Shikler). Discuss how the style of depicting presidents has changed over time—and how it has remained the same. What elements can you identify in each painting that have remained? Subjects, details, themes? (SL.3.1, SL.3.3)

9. ART/CLASS DISCUSSION

What have modern artists chosen to omit or add in more recent portraits—such as the portrait of Bill Clinton by Chuck Close or Rauschenberg's portrait of John F. Kennedy? How do these images differ from previous presidential portraits? (SL.3.1, SL.3.3)

10. CLASS DISCUSSION/LITERATURE

Introduce the book *Coming to America: The Story of Immigration* (Betsy Maestro and Suzannah Ryan) as telling the story of immigration. Tell students that America is unique because its people have come from so many different backgrounds. To understand how all of these people came to the same place, challenge students to think about the sequence of events in America's history. Define *chronological order* and relate it to something like your daily schedule or school calendar. As you read the book aloud, have students jot down important events on sticky notes, keeping them in chronological order. Ask them also to be thinking about why we might need to have rules to guide our government. (You can extend this lesson to discuss those government rules by pausing on page 14, where students will notice how many people were living together in the growing cities of New York, Boston, Philadelphia, Charleston, Baltimore, and New Orleans. As the page turns, students will see how people started moving west and the growing need for different laws. Use this to launch a discussion of the need for a central government.) (RI.3.4, RI.3.8, SL.3.1, L.3.5b)

11. CLASS DISCUSSION/LITERATURE

Introduce a collection of historical fiction books based on the topic of immigration. Allow students to choose a book that interests them. As students read, ask them to use sticky notes to respond to questions such as:

- Who came to America?
- When did they come?
- Why did they come?
- From where did they come?
- Where did they settle in America?
- Note examples of the adjustments they made in America.
- Note a passage in the book that shows challenges faced by the main character in a strange new country.

Use these guiding questions to conduct whole-group discussions about the people who came previously and continue to come to America. Require students to show evidence of their findings from their books. Extend these discussions by assigning students to craft a well-developed paragraph about the book's main character and that character's greatest challenge. (RL.3.1, RL.3.3, RL.3.5, RL.3.9, RL.3.10, RF.3.4, W.3.10)

ADDITIONAL RESOURCES

- *The Preamble to the Constitution: How Do You Make a More Perfect Union?* (National Endowment for the Humanities) (RI.3.4)
- *Voting! What's It All About?* (ReadWriteThink) (RI.3.9)
- *Hands-On Presidential Activity: Children Write to the President* (Smithsonian, National Museum of American History) (W.3.4)
- *What Happens in the White House?* (National Endowment for the Humanities)
- *A President's Home and the President's House* (National Endowment for the Humanities)
- *How Was the White House Designed?* (National Endowment for the Humanities)
- "Preamble," *Schoolhouse Rock* (1976)

TERMINOLOGY

Bio-poem

Chronological order

Cumulative choral
reading

Dictionary

Sequence

Synonyms

MAKING INTERDISCIPLINARY CONNECTIONS

This unit teaches:

Art: portraiture, Gilbert Stuart, Emanuel Leutze, Chuck Close, Robert Rauschenberg
Geography: U.S. geography (e.g., as related to immigration and migration)
History: U.S. Constitution (e.g., James Madison and the Preamble), immigration, and the presidency

This unit could be extended to teach:

Geography: Early American settlements
History: Colonial times (e.g., focus on life before the first presidency)

Grade Three, Unit Four Sample Lesson Plan

"The Flag Goes By" by H. H. Bennett

In this series of three lessons, students read "The Flag Goes By" by H. H. Bennett, and they:

Examine the imagery in "The Flag Goes By" (RL.3.1, RL.3.4, RL.3.5, RL.3.10, SL.3.2)
Probe the patriotic message of "The Flag Goes By" (RL.3.5, RL.3.9, SL.3.2)
Explore the history of "Old Glory" (RI.3.5, W.3.7)

Summary

Lesson I: "The Flag Goes By" by H. H. Bennett

Examine the visual description of the flag and the people in the poem (RL.3.1, RL.3.4, RL.3.5, RL.3.10, SL.3.2)

Explore the repeated use of the words *Hats off!* (RL.3.4, SL.3.1)

Probe the patriotic theme of "The Flag Goes By" (RL.3.5, RL.3.9, SL.3.2)

Lesson II: Researching the History of "Old Glory"

Investigate the story of "Old Glory" (RI.3.5, W.3.7)
   History of the flag
   Origins of the name "Old Glory"
   Gradual transformation of the flag

Record findings (W.3.2, W.3.8)

Lesson III: Reporting the History of "Old Glory"

Recall findings (W.3.8)
Lay out findings (SL.3.2)
Share results (SL.3.4)

Lesson II: Researching the History of "Old Glory"

Objectives

Investigate the story of "Old Glory" (RI.3.5, W.3.7)
- History of the flag
- Origins of the name "Old Glory"
- Gradual transformation of the flag

Record findings (W.3.2, W.3.8)

Required Materials

- ☐ Class set of "The Flag Goes By," by H. H. Bennett
- ☐ Computers with Internet access
- ☐ Printers
- ☐ Paper
- ☐ Poster boards

Procedures

1. Lead-In:
   Explain the research project to the students. Introduce the students to the "Step by Step" process.

2. Step by Step:
   a. In small groups, students will conduct online research. (A resource is www.usflag.org.) They will investigate the:
      - History of the flag
      - Origins of the name "Old Glory"
      - Gradual transformation of the flag

   b. Students record their findings. The format may be decided by you or by the groups themselves.

3. Closure:
   Students will tour their class exhibits.

Differentiation

Advanced

- Students in each group may want to use a shared spreadsheet as they research, so they can compile their information into one document.
- In subsequent class times, students could pull the organized information from the document to create a multimedia presentation on the flag, set to patriotic music and introduced by a dramatic reading of the poem.

Struggling

- In advance of this lesson, students will work together to perform the poem "The Flag Goes By," focusing on reading fluency and on internalizing the ideas in the poem.
- Work with students to create a graphic organizer on which to record their research findings.

Homework/Assessment

Reread the findings in preparation for communicating them to the class.

A Feast of Words on a Planet Called Earth—and Beyond

In this fifth six-week unit of third grade, students read stories, poems, and informational text full of rich language, a "feast of words."

ESSENTIAL QUESTION

? What makes a word or phrase the "right" word or phrase?

OVERVIEW

Students read fiction that demonstrates the use of idioms and exhibits careful diction. They read poems that focus on a simple topic such as corn or grass to see how the topics are developed line by line and stanza by stanza. They write to express their own opinions about the idea of having laws that legislate what people can and cannot eat. Working with Latin suffixes, they will see the way suffixes transform one part of speech into another. Students illustrate an idiom to express their own interpretation of its meaning and then write a note to Amelia Bedelia about the idiom. Finally, the students will stretch beyond this world to read and research about other planets.

FOCUS STANDARDS

These Focus Standards have been selected for the unit from the Common Core State Standards.

RI.3.7: Use information gained from illustrations (e.g., maps [and] photographs) and the words in a text to demonstrate understanding of the text (e.g., where, when, why, and how key events occur).

RF.3.3: Know and apply grade-level phonics and word analysis skills in decoding words.

RF.3.3(b): Decode words with common Latin suffixes.

L.3.4: Determine the meaning of the new word formed when a known affix is added to a known word.

RL.3.4: Describe the meaning of words and phrases as they are used in a text, distinguishing literal from nonliteral language.

RL.3.5: Refer to parts of stories, dramas, and poems when writing or speaking about a text, using terms such as *chapter, scene,* and *stanza;* describe how each successive part builds on earlier sections.

W.3.1: Write opinion pieces on topics or texts, supporting a point of view with reasons.

SUGGESTED STUDENT OBJECTIVES

- Independently read stories, poems, and informational text.
- Use dictionaries and thesauruses, both in print and online, to look up words and to consider varied shades of meaning.
- Decode and analyze words with Latin suffixes.
- Collect words from poems, both from read-aloud selections and from independent reading.
- Comprehend poems by seeing how each stanza or line builds on its predecessor for meaning (e.g., "Eating While Reading," Gary Soto).
- Listening to a read-aloud novel such as *The Search for Delicious* (Natalie Babbitt), note how each chapter builds on earlier sections, requiring careful reading/listening for comprehension.
- Write an opinion piece based on one's own thinking (e.g., about food legislation); apply growing understanding of strong, focused paragraphs.
- Dramatically read a poem (or recite it from memory).
- Learn the meaning of idioms both within stories and in books about idioms.
- Research and write a report about a planet, using the key questions (*who, where, when, why, what,* and *how*) to guide research.

SUGGESTED WORKS

(E) indicates a CCSS exemplar text; (EA) indicates a text from a writer with other works identified as exemplars.

LITERARY TEXTS
Stories
- *Amelia Bedelia* (Peggy Parish and Fritz Siebel)
- *Thank You, Amelia Bedelia* (Peggy Parish and Barbara Siebel Thomas)
- *Amelia Bedelia, Rocket Scientist* (Herman Parish and Lynn Sweat)
- *Dog Breath! The Horrible Trouble with Hally Tosis* (Dav Pilkey)
- *My Momma Likes to Say* (Denise Brennan-Nelson and Jane Monroe Donavan)
- *Even More Parts: Idioms from Head to Toe* (Tedd Arnold)

Stories (Read Aloud)
- *The Search for Delicious* (Natalie Babbitt) (E)
- *Frindle* (Andrew Clements and Brian Selznick)

Books About Idioms
- *In a Pickle and Other Funny Idioms* (Marvin Terban and Giulio Maestro)
- *Mad as a Wet Hen! And Other Funny Idioms* (Marvin Terban and Giulio Maestro)
- *Punching the Clock: Funny Action Idioms* (Marvin Terban and Thomas Huffman)

- *Raining Cats and Dogs: A Collection of Irresistible Idioms and Illustrations to Tickle the Funny Bones of Young People* (Will Moses)
- *There's a Frog in My Throat: 440 Animal Sayings a Little Bird Told Me* (Loreen Leedy and Pat Street)
- *Why the Banana Split: Adventures in Idioms* (Rick Walton and Jimmy Holder)
- *Ve Lo Que Dices/See What You Say: Modismos en Espanol e Ingles/ Spanish and English Idioms* (Nancy Maria Grande Tabor)
- *Birds of a Feather: A Book of Idioms* (Vanita Oelschlager and Robin Hegan)

Poems
- "Eating While Reading" (Gary Soto) (E)
- *Candy Corn: Poems* (James Stevenson)
- *Popcorn: Poems* (James Stevenson)
- *Sweet Corn: Poems* (James Stevenson)
- "Catch a Little Rhyme" (Eve Merriam) (EA)
- "Barefoot Days" (Rachel Field)
- "The City" (Langston Hughes) (EA)
- "Skyscrapers" (Rachel Field)

Poems (Read Aloud)
- "I Wandered Lonely as a Cloud" (William Wordsworth)
- "The Grass" (Emily Dickinson)
- "Spring Grass" (Carl Sandburg) (EA)
- "The Grass on the Mountain" (Paiute American Indian, transcribed by Mary Austin)

INFORMATIONAL TEXTS
Informational Books
- *A Medieval Feast* (Aliki) (E)
- *The Planets* (Gail Gibbons) (EA)
- *Moonshot: The Flight of Apollo 11* (Brian Floca) (E)
- *Planets!* (TIME for Kids) (Editors of TIME For Kids with Lisa Jo Rudy)
- *The Solar System* (Gregory Vogt)
- *Our Solar System (Revised Edition)* (Seymour Simon)
- *Mercury* (News Nonfiction Readers) (Christine Taylor-Butler)
- *Venus* (News Nonfiction Readers) (Melanie Chrismer)
- *Mars: The Red Planet* (All Aboard Science Reader) (Patricia Brennan Demuth)
- *Mars* (News Nonfiction Readers) (Melanie Chrismer)
- *Jupiter* (News Nonfiction Readers) (Christine Taylor-Butler)
- *Saturn* (True Books) (Elaine Landau)
- *Uranus* (News Nonfiction Readers) (Christine Taylor-Butler)
- *Uranus* (True Books) (Elaine Landau)
- *Neptune* (News Nonfiction Readers) (Melanie Chrismer)

- *Discover the Planets* (Kids Can Read) (Cynthia Pratt Nicolson and Bill Slavin)
- *Pluto: From Planet to Dwarf* (True Books) (Elaine Landau)
- *Mercury* (A True Book: Space) (Larry Dane Brimner)
- *Venus* (A True Book: Space) (Larry Dane Brimner)
- *Mars* (A True Book: Space) (Larry Dane Brimner)
- *Jupiter* (A True Book: Space) (Larry Dane Brimner)
- *Saturn* (A True Book: Space) (Larry Dane Brimner)
- *Uranus* (A True Book: Space) (Larry Dane Brimner)
- *Neptune* (A True Book: Space) (Larry Dane Brimner)
- *Earth* (A True Book: Space) (Larry Dane Brimner)

Informational Books (Read Aloud)

- *What the World Eats* (Faith D'Aluisio and Peter Menzel) (E)
- *It's Disgusting and We Ate It! True Food Facts from Around the World and Throughout History* (James Solheim and Eric Brace)
- *11 Planets: A New View of the Solar System* (David A. Aguilar)
- *When Is a Planet Not a Planet? The Story of Pluto* (Elaine Scott)
- *Next Stop Neptune: Experiencing the Solar System* (Alvin Jenkins, illus. by Steve Jenkins)

Resources for Students

- Dictionaries
- Online dictionaries
- Thesaurus
- Online thesauruses
- *Scholastic Dictionary of Idioms (Revised)* (Marvin Terban)

ART, MUSIC, AND MEDIA

Art

- Jackson Pollock, *One: Number 31, 1950* (1950)
- Jackson Pollock, *Number 1, 1950 (Lavender Mist)* (1950)
- Morris Louis, *Number 182* (1961)
- Sam Gilliam, *Red Petals* (1967)
- Helen Frankenthaler, *Canyon* (1965)
- Helen Frankenthaler, *Wales* (1966)

SAMPLE ACTIVITIES AND ASSESSMENTS

Note: You may want to do the planets in science at the same time you are doing fiction/poetry in language arts. The two parts of the unit will come together in the research project at the end of the unit.

1. LANGUAGE/LATIN SUFFIXES

Display this list of words with a common Latin suffix (e.g., *-able, -ible, -ation, -fy, -ify, -ment, -ty, -ity*): *likeable, readable, drivable, laughable,* and *teachable.* Ask students:

What does each word have in common with the rest? (*Answer:* the same Latin suffix, *-able*)

Then explain that this is an example of a Latin suffix. Have students use whiteboards to write the root word for each (i.e., *like, read, drive, laugh,* and *teach*). Then ask students:

What part of speech is *read*? (*Answer:* verb)

Explain that when we add the suffix *-able,* it becomes a different part of speech (i.e., an adjective). Then use the new word in a sentence so that students see the part of speech change. For example, "I was surprised to find this thick book was very readable." Then explain that *readable* describes the book, which means it's an adjective. Extend this lesson by continuing to collect words that end in *-able* or *-ible*. (RF.3.3b, L.3.2e, L.3.4b)

2. VOCABULARY/THESAURUS

Have students look up the word *know* in an online thesaurus. Create a horizontal line on the board with *wonder* at one end and *know* at the other. To show shades of meaning, discuss the placement of other state-of-mind words (i.e., the synonyms and antonyms of *know*) on the scale. Repeat this activity with verbs and/or adjectives (such as *warm*) that come up in student reading. (L.3.5c)

3. LANGUAGE/POETRY

As you and the students read (recite) poems throughout this unit, ask them to collect words that they like in their journals. Read aloud a poem such as "I Wandered Lonely as a Cloud" (William Wordsworth) several times, modeling fluent reading. Choose an evocative word from the poem because, for example, of the way it sounds, or what it means. Every time the class reads a poem, either together or individually, give the students a few minutes to choose one or two words that they like and then use them in a sentence. (RF.3.4c)

4. POETRY/COMPREHENSION

Use a poem such as "Eating While Reading" (Gary Soto) to illustrate how each new line builds meaning on the preceding lines. Have students read multiple poems aloud to each other, explaining their understanding of the poem, line by line and stanza by stanza. (RL.3.5)

5. LANGUAGE/WRITING

Read several books that use idioms in the story (e.g., the *Amelia Bedelia* series) or a book that uses idioms as the text (e.g., Terban's work). Then assign the students this prompt: "Choose an idiomatic saying. Draw a picture of the literal and figurative meaning of the saying. Write a short paragraph to explain to someone like Amelia Bedelia why it is important to know what the saying really means." Find examples of more idioms on the Internet. (RL.3.4, RI.3.5, L.3.4a, L.3.5a)

6. FLUENCY/POETRY

Give the students this prompt: "Choose one of the poems in this unit's collection. Memorize it (or read it) and perform it for the class. Be sure to use your best expression as you read." To add a twist to the poetry performance, pair up the students and have them choose a poem with personification such as "Skyscrapers" (Rachel Field). As one student reads, have the other student play the role of the skyscraper (or the personified object in the poem of choice). (RF.3.4b)

7. CLASS DISCUSSION/LITERATURE

Before this lesson, gather some cubes or building blocks to use as a visual representation. Using a chapter book such as *The Search for Delicious* (Natalie Babbitt) or *Frindle* (Andrew Clements and Brian Selznick), use the building blocks to show how the author of a book builds meaning. At the end of each chapter, have students write on sticky notes what they believe is the main idea of the chapter. Place the sticky notes on the board and look to see how well the students comprehended the text, discussing as you read them aloud. After the class comes to consensus, write down the main idea of the chapter on another sticky note and place it on the block. Do this with each chapter (or in reading session if you do not finish a chapter in one sitting) to show how events build upon each other. If, later in the book, the class realizes (with your guidance) that they have forgotten something important in a previous chapter, go back and revise the building blocks. This will teach the students that good readers tailor their thinking—rethinking the importance of events and ideas—as they read. (RL.3.5, SL.3.2)

8. CLASS DISCUSSION/INFORMATIONAL TEXT/OPINION WRITING

Using a book such as *What the World Eats* (Faith D'Aluisio and Peter Menzel), discuss the differences in the way people eat around the world. Challenge the students to think critically about nutrition, their eating habits, and the way other cultures look at food. Use the following questions to guide the discussion:

What do you think the authors were trying to say in this text?

Can you support your opinion with evidence from the text?

How did the illustrations support the ideas in the print part of the text?

Do you think the authors fairly described the way people in the United States eat?

Finally, assign an opinion writing piece: "In your opinion, do you think there should be laws passed to tell people what they can and cannot eat? Support your answer with strong reasons." (RI.3.2, RI.3.7, SL.3.1a, SL.3.1c, SL.3.1d, SL.3.1b, SL.3.2, W.3.1, L.3.1i, L.3.2)

9. INFORMATIVE/EXPLANATORY WRITING (INFORMATIONAL TEXT)

Writing Prompt: "Generate questions to answer about a planet other than Earth. Write a report based on the research." Assign to the students a research project on a planet other than Earth. Create a display of many books on the planets and have students choose a book with which to start their research. Using the key words *where, when, why, and how key events occur,* students should begin by creating a list of open-ended questions they want to answer through their research. The generating of questions could happen as a class if students need modeling of the process. To help students with organizing information, give students large index cards with each question on one side and have them write the answers on the other side. When they are finished finding the answers, have them use these cards to help them write a report on the planet. As students revise, they should focus on word choice to make their reports as literary and interesting as possible. Students should create one prop to help explain their most interesting finding about the planet. (L.3.1, L.3.2, L.3.3, L.3.5, W.3.2, W.3.7, W.3.8, W.3.10)

10. ART/CLASS DISCUSSION

Building on the use of verbs, idioms, and dramatic reading, show the students *Number 31* (Pollock) and *Canyon* (Frankenthaler). Ask students: What words come to mind when you see these paintings? What words might you use to describe the colors? The texture? What forms do you see? Is there action in the paintings? How so? Define any of the words used (i.e., *texture, shape, form,* etc.). Review the difference between realism and abstraction. (L.3.1, L.3.3, L.3.5, SL.3.1, SL.3.3)

11. ART/OPINION WRITING

Now, compare Gilliam with Louis. Both artists were concerned with and interested in truly combining paint with canvas. Why do you think each artist chose these colors? Do you think he or she meant to make it look like this, or is it random? How do these paintings make you feel? Write a brief paragraph answering these questions. (W.3.1)

ADDITIONAL RESOURCES

- *Figurative Language: Teaching Idioms* (ReadWriteThink) (L.3.5a)
- *Dancing Minds and Shouting Smiles: Teaching Personification through Poetry* (ReadWriteThink) (RL.3.5)
- *Delicious, Tasty, Yummy: Enriching Writing with Adjectives and Synonyms* (ReadWriteThink) (W.3.5)
- *Martian Real Estate: A Good Investment?* (National Geographic) (W.3.7)

TERMINOLOGY

Idiom	Latin suffixes	Thesaurus	Word roots

MAKING INTERDISCIPLINARY CONNECTIONS

This unit teaches:

Art: abstract painting (e.g., Jackson Pollock, Helen Frankenthaler, Sam Gilliam, Morris Louis)
Geography: World geography (e.g., continents and countries)
Science: the solar system (i.e., the planets)

This unit could be extended to teach:

Science: Astronomy (e.g., the universe, galaxies, orienteering, and exploration of space)

Grade Three, Unit Five Sample Lesson Plan

"Eating While Reading" by Gary Soto

In this series of three lessons, students read "Eating While Reading" by Gary Soto, and they:

- Examine the form of the poem (RL.3.5)
- Explore the content of the poem (RL.3.1, RL.3.2)
- Write poems triggered by Soto's "Eating While Reading" (W.3.3)
- Explore the use of a poem as an inspiration to write another poem (SL.3.6)

Summary

Lesson I: "Eating While Reading"

- Explore the form of the poem (RL.3.5)
- Note the use of punctuation (RL.3.5)
- Examine the purpose of the repetitions (RL.3.5)
- Examine the change between the first and the second question (RL.3.1, SL.3.2, SL.3.3)
- Consider the title of the poem (SL.3.2)
- Discuss the message of the speaker (RL.3.3)

Lesson II: Writing Triggered Poems

- Revisit "Eating While Reading" (RL.3.1)
- Initiate ideas for personal poems using Soto's opening lines as a trigger: ("What is better/than this song/And a walk in the park …") (SL.3.6)
- Compose a poem (W.3.3)
- Rewrite the poem (W.3.5)

Lesson III: Sharing Poems

- Revisit personal poems
- Share results (SL.3.6)
- Explore the use of a poem as an inspiration to write another poem (SL.3.6)

Lesson I: "Eating While Reading"

Objectives

Explore the form of the poem (RL.3.5)

Note the use of punctuation (L.3.2)

Examine the purpose of the repetitions (RL.3.5)

Examine the change between the first and the second question (RL.3.1, SL.3.2, SL.3.3)

Consider the title of the poem (SL.3.2)

Discuss the message of the speaker (RL.3.3)

Required Materials

☐ Copies of the poem "Eating While Reading," by Gary Soto

☐ Large copy of "Eating While Reading," by Gary Soto

☐ (*Recommended*: Add numbers to the lines of the poem.)

Procedures

1. Lead-In:
After the students receive copies of the poem "Eating While Reading" by Gary Soto, student volunteers read the poem aloud. The poem should be read at least twice.

2. Step by Step:
   a. Prompt the students as they explore the form of the poem:
      - There is only one stanza; when you read the poem, what is the impact of a single stanza?
      - Are there different parts of the poem, even though there are no stanzas?
      - The line "What is better" repeats. Why?
      - The list that follows "Or the ..." occurs five times. What is its purpose?
      - There are two question marks; why?
      (During the class discussion, students refer to the text. The numbered lines and the large copy on the board facilitate the reading.)
   b. The final prompt offers a transition to the next step, which is a close examination of the beginning of the two questions:
      "What is better

      Than this book ...?"

      and the second:

      "What is better than this sweet dance

      On the tongue ...?"

      Students discuss the difference between the two questions ("book"/"sweet dance").

c. The final two lines of the poem present a transition to a discussion about the content of the poem. Students then consider the title of the poem and ask, "What is the poem about?"

3. Closure:
Students volunteer to reread the poem aloud.

Differentiation

Advanced

- Using a thesaurus, students think of new and challenging words that would fit in Gary Soto's poem (i.e., words to be substituted for "churn," "crack," "swig," "twist," "slither," and "sticky"). Students create a "revised" poem using their newly discovered words. Students share the poem with the rest of the class.

Struggling

(Following the Lead-In for this lesson, do this activity with a small group or the whole class.)

- Focus on the vivid words in this poem by allowing different students to experience them (i.e., the "churn" of a chewy candy, the "balloon" of bubble gum, the "crack" of sunflower seeds).
- Display favorite class books. Students discuss the feelings they had when it was time to read the next chapter.

Homework/Assessment
N/A

Grade 3 ▶ *Unit 6*

Fantastic Adventures with Dragons, Gods, and Giants

In this sixth six-week unit of third grade, students read fantasies, adventure poetry, mythology, and informational texts about ancient Greece and ancient Rome.

OVERVIEW

Beginning with fantasy stories and poems about dragons, students learn to summarize and illustrate chapters, seeing how they are building blocks to the ending. They record themselves reading fluently an assigned chapter (i.e., with a video camera or tape recorder). They combine the recording with their illustrated chapter summaries to create a multimedia presentation. They will also hear a variety of myths, both Greek and Roman, and read a book based on Homer's *The Odyssey*. Finally, students will research an Olympic sport and compare it to an Olympic sport in the days of ancient Greece.

ESSENTIAL QUESTION

Why is it important to know mythology?

FOCUS STANDARDS

These Focus Standards have been selected for the unit from the Common Core State Standards.

RI.3.10: By the end of year, read and comprehend informational texts, including history/social studies, science, and technical texts, at the high end of the grades 2–3 text complexity band independently and proficiently.

RF.3.4: Read with sufficient accuracy and fluency to support comprehension.

RF.3.4(c): Use context to confirm or self-correct word recognition and understanding, rereading as necessary.

RL.3.2: Recount stories, including fables, folktales, and myths from diverse cultures; determine the central message, lesson, or moral and explain how it is conveyed through key details in the text.

RL.3.6: Distinguish their own point of view from that of the narrator or those of the characters.

RL.3.10: By the end of the year, read and comprehend literature, including stories, dramas, and poetry, at the high end of the grades 2–3 text complexity band independently and proficiently.

SL.3.5: Create engaging audio recordings of stories or poems that demonstrate fluid reading at an understandable pace; add visual displays when appropriate to emphasize or enhance certain facts or details.

SUGGESTED STUDENT OBJECTIVES

- Independently read books in the grade 2 through 3 stretch text range with fluency and comprehension.
- Summarize and illustrate the chapters of a book (e.g., *My Father's Dragon).*
- Create an audio recording of a dramatic reading of a chapter in a challenging chapter book.
- Create a multimedia presentation (e.g., a set of slides) of the recording and the illustrations for the book summaries.
- Write an opinion piece describing the "most interesting" mythical character.
- Retell myths with key details, noting the message of each.
- Quote from the text to support the main idea of a nonfiction book.
- Read a variety of informational books on ancient Greece and ancient Rome.
- Research a current Olympic sport, comparing and contrasting it to a sport in the days of ancient Greece.
- Write a short fantasy narrative.

SUGGESTED WORKS

(E) indicates a CCSS exemplar text; (EA) indicates a text from a writer with other works identified as exemplars.

LITERARY TEXTS
Stories
- "Adventures of Isabel" (Ogden Nash)
- "A Dragon's Lament" (Jack Prelutsky)
- "The Dragons are Singing Tonight" (Jack Prelutsky)
- "Life Doesn't Frighten Me At All" (Maya Angelou)

Stories (Read Aloud)
- *Greek Myths for Young Children* (Heather Amery and Linda Edwards)
- *D'Aulaires' Book of Greek Myths* (Ingri d'Aulaire and Edgar Parin d'Aulaire)
- *The Gods and Goddesses of Olympus* (Aliki)
- *Favorite Greek Myths* (Mary Pope Osborne and Troy Howell)
- *Classic Myths to Read Aloud: The Great Stories of Greek and Roman Mythology* (William F. Russell)
- *The Orchard Book of Roman Myths* (Geraldine McCaughrean and Emma Chichester)
- *My Father's Dragon* (Ruth Stiles Gannett and Ruth Chrisman Gannett)
- *The One-Eyed Gant* (Mary Pope Osborne and Troy Howell)
- *Could Be Worse!* (James Stevenson)

Poem (Read Aloud)
- "The Tale of Custard the Dragon" (Ogden Nash)

INFORMATIONAL TEXTS

Informational Books

- *Boy, Were We Wrong About Dinosaurs!* (Kathleen V. Kudlinski and S. D. Schindler) (E)
- *If I Were a Kid in Ancient Greece* (Ken Sheldon, ed.)
- *Ancient Greece and the Olympics: A Nonfiction Companion to Hour of the Olympics* (Magic Tree House Research Guide 10) (Mary Pope Osborne, Natalie Pope Boyce, and Sal Murdocca) (EA)
- *Ancient Rome and Pompeii: A Nonfiction Companion to Vacation Under the Volcano* (Magic Tree House Research Guide 14) (Mary Pope Osborne, Natalie Pope Boyce, and Sal Murdocca) (EA)
- *Rome: In Spectacular Cross Section* (Andrew Solway and Stephen Biesty)

Informational Books (Read Aloud)

Greece
- *Ancient Greece* (DK Eyewitness Books) (Anne Pearson)
- *I Wonder Why Greeks Built Temples and Other Questions About Ancient Greece* (Fiona MacDonald)
- *If I Were a Kid in Ancient Greece: Children of the Ancient World* (Ken Sheldon, ed.)

Rome
- *If I Were a Kid in Ancient Rome: Children of the Ancient World* (Ken Sheldon, ed.)
- *Tools of the Ancient Romans: A Kid's Guide to the History & Science of Life in Ancient Rome* (Rachel Dickinson)
- *Science in Ancient Rome* (Jacqueline L. Harris)
- *Ancient Rome* (DK Eyewitness Books) (Simon James)

ART, MUSIC, AND MEDIA

Art

- Greek and Roman Art Collection (The Metropolitan Museum of Art)
- The Colosseum, Rome, Italy (80 AD)
- The Parthenon, Athenian Acropolis, Greece (438 BCE)

SAMPLE ACTIVITIES AND ASSESSMENTS

Note: If you choose to begin with *My Father's Dragon* (Ruth Stiles Gannett and Ruth Chrisman Gannett), it will create a transition to the adventures in *The One-Eyed Giant* (Mary Pope Osborne and Troy Howell). Because there is so much literature in the mythology of ancient Greece, you may want to spend a week or two on the Gannetts' book and then move on to the mythology for the remainder of the unit. Since this may be the first time students are introduced to myths, it is helpful to keep a list of the mythological gods, creatures, and characters as you read. By focusing on the outstanding characteristic (e.g., Heracles—Greek, Hercules—Roman—strength) or domain (Poseidon—the sea) of each, students will begin to see the foundational role played by these names and places in word derivations.

1. CLASS DISCUSSION/LITERARY AND INFORMATIVE/EXPLANATORY WRITING

Writing prompt:"While reading a chapter book such as *My Father's Dragon*, write a summary of each chapter and illustrate it. Compile the chapter summaries for an abridged version of the book." As students read the book *My Father's Dragon* (Ruth Stiles Gannett and Ruth Chrisman Gannett), focus on how each chapter builds on the last to tell the story. As students finish each chapter, have them write down a short summary of what happened and illustrate it with a drawing. Have the students turn this into a mini-book of the larger book. As students write their summaries in this activity, you could teach a strategy for writing succinct summaries such as "Somebody-Wanted-But-So." (RL.3.10, RF.3.4c, L.3.1, L.3.2, L.3.3)

2. FLUENCY/AUDIO RECORDING

As a class, create a set of audio recordings of the book *My Father's Dragon* (Ruth Stiles Gannett and Ruth Chrisman Gannett). Using the illustrations from the chapter summaries (see the preceding Class Discussion/Literary section), assign to each student a chapter to rehearse reading aloud. With a video camera or tape recorder, have students record themselves reading a chapter in their best reading voice, interpreting the parts of each character. To extend this fluency activity, choose poems to read (recite) interpretively and record. (SL.3.5, RL.3.10, RF.3.4c)

3. LITERARY/OPINION WRITING

Give the students this prompt: "Choose the most interesting mythical character. Support your opinion with strong evidence from the texts you have read and connect your writing to specific parts of the myth. Be sure also to use linking words and phrases (e.g., *because, therefore, since,* and *for example*) to connect your opinion and reasons. Provide a concluding statement." (RL.3.2, W.3.1, L.3.1)

4. CLASS DISCUSSION/LITERARY

After reading each of the myths, have students retell the story with as many key details as they can. Have them partner to retell, helping the partner when he/she forgets what came next. Discuss the following prompts/questions as a class, or have them write down their thoughts for more independent thinking and accountability before discussing as a group.

- As we read the myth and as we retell the stories, let's think about the message in the myth.
- Why was the myth told during the time of the ancient Greeks?
- Why is it still told today? (RL.3.2, SL.3.2, L.3.1, L.3.2, L.3.3)

5. CLASS DISCUSSION/INFORMATIONAL TEXT

Introduce the book *Boy, Were We Wrong About Dinosaurs!* (Kathleen V. Kudlinski and S. D. Schindler) by explaining that this book will teach them how scientists sometimes change their thinking after new evidence is collected. Tell students that in the discussion after reading, they should be prepared to share two different specific places in the book where this happened. Have them write down their thoughts on a whiteboard or a sticky note. (RI.3.2, RI.3.10, RF.3.4c, SL.3.1a)

6. RESEARCH/INFORMATIONAL TEXT AND INFORMATIVE/EXPLANATORY WRITING

Read a variety of nonfiction readings on the first Olympic games in ancient Greece. Then give the students this prompt: "Using online resources, research one sport from the most recent summer Olympics. Tell how it is similar and how it is different from the first games. Create a teaching poster or multimedia slide and report orally on your learning." (RI.3.5, W.3.6, W.3.7, SL.3.4, L.3.2, L.3.3)

7. CLASS DISCUSSION/LITERARY/WRITING

Lead a class discussion based on *Could Be Worse!* (James Stevenson) using the following prompts/questions:

- How do you think the children felt when they tried to tell the grandfather of an adventure and he always topped it with a fantastic tale?

- If you were the grandfather, what story would you have told?
- Write a fantastic grandfather response to this: "I fell off the monkey bars on the playground and scraped my knee." (RL.3.6, W.3.3, W.3.10, L.3.1, L.3.2, L.3.3)

8. ART/CLASS DISCUSSION

Introduce some of the art held in the Greek and Roman collections at the Metropolitan Museum of Art. Then lead a discussion about how the students see the mythology influencing ancient Greek and Roman art. In particular, discuss the relationship between the stories of the people (myths) and the inspiration for artistic pieces. (RL.3.2)

9. ART/CLASS DISCUSSION

Compare images of the Colosseum and the Parthenon. Explain that one of these buildings was used for contests, battles, and dramas based on mythology. The other was used as a place of worship as well as a treasury, dedicated to a special goddess known as Athena. Can you tell which building was which, just by looking at them? What would you need to know in order to tell the difference? (SL.3.1, SL.3.3)

10. ART/CLASS DISCUSSION

Ask students what they notice first about the architecture of each building. What features do the buildings have in common? The Parthenon was built many years before the Colosseum—what traditions were carried into Roman society in terms of architectural style? What didn't the Romans do that the Greeks did on their colossal building? (SL.3.1, SL.3.3)

ADDITIONAL RESOURCES

- *Powerful Writing: Description in Creating Monster Trading Cards* (ReadWriteThink) (L.3.1a, RL.3.2)
- *It Came from Greek Mythology* (National Endowment for the Humanities) (RL.3.2)
- Folklore and mythology electronic texts

TERMINOLOGY

Fantasy	Mythology	Narrative poem	Summary

MAKING INTERDISCIPLINARY CONNECTIONS

This unit teaches:

Art: Ancient Greek and Roman Art (e.g. the Colosseum, the Parthenon)

History: Ancient Greece (e.g., the Olympics and life in ancient Greece) and ancient Rome (e.g., Roman mythology, government, and life)

This unit could be extended to teach:

History: Vikings (e.g., Norse mythology, Norsemen, and Leif Ericson)

Grade Three, Unit Six Sample Lesson Plan

"Adventures of Isabel" by Ogden Nash

In this series of three lessons, students read "Adventures of Isabel" by Ogden Nash, and they:

Identify the stanzas of the poem (RL.3.5, SL.1.1)

Explore the story in each stanza (RL.3.1, RL.3.5, SL.3.1)

Visualize the adventures of Isabel (SL.3.5)

Illustrate the adventures of Isabel (SL.3.5)

Summary

Lesson I: "Adventures of Isabel"

Consider the content of the four stanzas (RL.3.1, RL.3.5, SL.3.1)

(In groups) select one of the four stanzas

(In groups) examine the progression of the stanza (RL.3.1, RL.3.5, SL.3.1)

Lesson III: "Adventures of Isabel" Illustrated

Display the illustrations (from Lesson II)

Examine the illustrations (RL. 3.7)

Reflect on the process (SL.3.4)

Lesson II: Illustrating the Poem

(In groups) recall the details of the assigned stanza (RL.3.1, RL.3.5, SL.3.1)

(In groups) note specific scenes in the stanza (RL.3.5)

Illustrate a select scene (SL.3.5)

Lesson II: Illustrating the Poem

Objectives

(In groups) recall the details of the assigned stanza (RL.3.1, RL.3.5, SL.3.1)

(In groups) note specific scenes in the stanza (RL.3.5)

Illustrate a select scene (SL.3.5)

Required Materials

☐ Copies of "Adventures of Isabel" by Ogden Nash (not illustrated)
☐ Colored pencils and markers
☐ Drawing paper

Procedures

1. Lead-In:
   Reread "Adventures of Isabel."

2. Step by Step:
   a. In groups from the previous lesson, students revisit the stanza that they were assigned. They explore the specific details that they will illustrate. For example: The first stanza depicts the bear as "enormous" and says that it has a "cavernous" "mouth." Isabel "wash[es] her hands" and she "straighten[s] her hair up."
   b. Students draw select scenes from their assigned stanza.

3. Closure:
   Student volunteers read "Adventures of Isabel" aloud.

Differentiation

Advanced

- In a small group, students explore the use of the thesaurus by choosing five new vocabulary words from the poem.
- Each student looks up one word, finding five new similar words for each of the original five words.
- If time allows, students could take one of those new words and create a scale showing the words in order of intensity. For example, a scale for *scurry* might look like this: – scamper – bustle – hasten – tear – zip

Struggling

- Students will focus on vocabulary by comparing/contrasting vocabulary words. For example, the description of the bear's hunger in stanza one uses *hungry* and then *ravenous*.
- Teacher writes both words on a whiteboard.
- Students discuss how the words are the same and how they are different.
- Words and/or phrases to compare could include *cruel/cavernous, scream/scurry, rage/rancor, hairy/horrid, punched/poked, coughs/chills.*

Homework/Assessment
N/A

GRADE 4

Fourth grade is an important time of transition in elementary school. At this point, students have learned the fundamentals of reading and writing, have read and listened to many stories and poems from a range of cultures, and have learned about a variety of historical and scientific topics, as well as myths. They now begin to consider the nature of literature—its forms, themes, and relation to nonfiction—as they write essays, speeches, reports, and stories. In the unit on Tales of the Heart, students consider how stories reveal what we have in common. Next, students look at geography as it relates to seasons and weather, and how these settings are represented in literature. Later in the year, students compare fictional and nonfictional portrayals of animals; investigate the scientific aspects of science fiction; read literature from America's past, in particular the American Revolution; compare narratives and informational texts about earth and sky; and consider what heroes have in common. The units draw connections among literature and other subjects, including history, science, geography, and art. Conducting research in libraries and online, students prepare and deliver persuasive speeches and compare differing accounts of historical events. Throughout the year, they study vocabulary from different subject areas and begin to learn about word roots. By the end of fourth grade, students can explain how fictional and nonfictional accounts reveal different aspects of reality. They have learned to draw connections between literary form and meaning, identify common themes in stories from many cultures, and write short essays on a variety of topics.

Standards Checklist for Grade Four

Standard	Unit 1	Unit 2	Unit 3	Unit 4	Unit 5	Unit 6	Standard	Unit 1	Unit 2	Unit 3	Unit 4	Unit 5	Unit 6
Reading—Literature							Speaking and Listening						
1	A	FA	A	A	A		1	FA	FA	A	A	A	A
2	FA	A	A	A	A	A	1a	FA	A	A	A	A	A
3	A	FA	A	A	A	A	1b	FA	A	A	A	A	A
4	A	A	A	A	A	FA	1c	A	FA	A	A	A	A
5	A	A	FA	A	A	A	1d	A	FA	A	A	A	A
6	A		A	FA		A	2					A	FA
7	A	A		A			3				FA	A	A
8 n/a							4	A	A		A	FA	A
9			A	A	FA	A	5	A	A	FA	A	A	A
10						A	6						A
Reading—Informational Text							Language						
1	FA	A	A	A	A	A	1					A	A
2			FA	A			1a	A	A	A	A	A	A
3		FA			A		1b			A	A	A	A
4		A	A			A	1c		A	A	A	A	A
5		A	A	FA			1d		A	A	A	A	A
6	A	A		FA			1e				A	A	A
7		A	A	A	FA		1f					A	A
8	A				A	FA	1g	A	A	A	A	A	A
9	A	A	A	A	A	A	2				A	A	A
10						A	2a	A	A	A	A	A	A
Writing							2b			A	A	A	A
1			FA	FA	A	A	2c			A	A	A	A
1a			A	A	A	A	2d			A	A	A	A
1b			A	A	A	A	3				A	FA	A
1c			A	A	A	A	3a	A			A	A	A
1d			A	A	A	A	3b				A	A	A
2	FA	FA			A	A	3c				A	A	A
2a	FA	A	A	A	A		4	F			FA	A	A
2b	FA	A	A	A	A		4a	FA	A	A	A	A	A
2c	A	A	A	A	A		4b				A	A	A
2d	A	A			A	A	4c				A	A	A
3		A			FA	A	5		F	FA	A	A	A
3a	A				A	A	5a	A	FA	A	A	A	A
3b	A	A			A	A	5b			FA	A	A	A
3c		A			A	A	5c			FA	A	A	A
3d		A			A	A	6						FA
3e		A			A	A	Reading Foundations						
4	A	A	A	A	A	A	1 n/a						
5	A		A	A	A	A	2 n/a						
6			A	A	A	A	3	FA					
7	A	A	A	A	A	FA	3a	A					
8			A	A	A	A	4			F	F		
9	A	A	A	A	A		4a		FA				
9a	A	A	A	A	A		4b		FA				
9b	A	A	A	A	A		4c			FA			
10						A							

F = Focus Standards; A = Activity/Assessment

Tales of the Heart

This four-week unit invites students to explore the mixture of emotions that accompany the transition to fourth grade, as well as to learn from informational text about the body.

ESSENTIAL QUESTION

? How do stories reveal what we have in common?

OVERVIEW

Students examine emotions, beginning with a traditional favorite, Judy Blume's *Tales of a Fourth Grade Nothing*, and continuing with Sharon Creech's *Love That Dog,* Grace Nichols's poem, "They Were My People," and the traditional "Monday's Child Is Fair of Face." *Harriet the Spy* (Louise Fitzhugh) is the suggested read aloud for this unit because, just as Harriet writes everything down in her journal, students keep a journal of what they learn throughout the year. Nonfiction text about body systems is supplemented with nonfiction biographies of doctors. Students summarize fiction and nonfiction texts, write informative/explanatory pieces, and engage in collaborative discussions—all skills that will be used throughout the fourth-grade year. Finally, this unit ends with a class discussion and paragraph response to the essential question.

FOCUS STANDARDS

These Focus Standards have been selected for the unit from the Common Core State Standards.

RL.4.2: Determine a theme of a story, drama, or poem from details in the text; summarize the text.

RI.4.1: Refer to details and examples in a text when explaining what the text says explicitly and when drawing inferences from the text.

RF.4.3: Know and apply grade-level phonics and word analysis skills in decoding words.

RF.4.3(a): Use combined knowledge of all letter-sound correspondences, syllabication patterns, and morphology (e.g., roots and affixes) to read accurately unfamiliar multisyllabic words in context and out of context.

W.4.2: Write informative/explanatory texts to examine a topic and convey ideas and information clearly.

W.4.2(a): Introduce a topic clearly and group related information in paragraphs and sections; include formatting (e.g., headings), illustrations, and multimedia when useful to aid comprehension.

W.4.2(b): Develop the topic with facts, definitions, concrete details, quotations, or other information and examples related to the topic.

SL.4.1: Engage effectively in a range of collaborative discussions (one-on-one, group, and teacher-led) with diverse partners on grade 4 topics and texts, building on others' ideas and expressing their own clearly.

SL.4.1(a): Come to discussions prepared, having read or studied required material; explicitly draw on that preparation and other information known about the topic to explore ideas under discussion.

SL.4.1(b): Follow agreed-upon rules for discussions and carry out assigned roles.

L.4.4: Determine or clarify the meaning of unknown and multiple-meaning words and phrases based on grade 4 reading and content, choosing flexibly from a range of strategies.

L.4.4(a): Use context (e.g., cause/effect relationships and comparisons in text) as a clue to the meaning of a word or phrase.

SUGGESTED STUDENT OBJECTIVES

- Find similarities and differences in story characters, and how they change over the course of a story.
- Write a variety of responses to stories and poems using coherent paragraphs.
- Research a famous doctor or scientist and write a bio-poem (i.e., a biography in poem form) about him/her.
- Recite poetry for classmates.
- Become more fluent in the use of terminology related to poetry.
- Begin to make connections between poetic/literary devices and the theme of a story, drama, or poem.

SUGGESTED WORKS

(E) indicates a CCSS exemplar text; (EA) indicates a text from a writer with other works identified as exemplars.

LITERARY TEXTS

Stories

- *Love That Dog* (Joanna Cotler Books) (Sharon Creech) (EA)
- *Tales of a Fourth Grade Nothing* (Judy Blume)
- *Clarice Bean Spells Trouble* (Lauren Child)
- *Fourth Grade Rats* (Jerry Spinelli)
- *Just Juice* (Karen Hesse and Robert Andre Parker)
- *Red Ridin' in the Hood: and Other Cuentos* (Patricia Santos Marcantonio and Renato Alarcáo)
- *Porch Lies: Tales of Slicksters, Tricksters, and Other Wily Characters* (Patricia McKissack and Andre Carrilho)

Poems

- "They Were My People" (Grace Nichols) (E)
- "Monday's Child Is Fair of Face" (Mother Goose)

- "Dreams" (Langston Hughes) (EA)
- "Humanity" (Elma Stuckey)
- "On the Way to School" (Charles Ghigna)
- "The Drum" (Nikki Giovanni)
- *Honey, I Love: And Other Love Poems* (Eloise Greenfield and Leo and Diane Dillon)

Stories (Read Aloud)

- *Harriet the Spy* (Louise Fitzhugh)

INFORMATIONAL TEXTS

Informational Books

- *The Heart: Our Circulatory System* (Seymour Simon)
- *The Heart and Circulation* (Exploring the Human Body) (Carol Ballard)
- *The Circulatory System* (Kristin Petrie)
- *The Amazing Circulatory System: How Does My Heart Work?* (John Burstein)
- *The Circulatory System* (A True Book) (Darlene R. Stille)
- *Lungs: Your Respiratory System* (Seymour Simon)
- *The Respiratory System* (Susan Glass)
- *The Respiratory System* (Kristin Petrie)
- *The Remarkable Respiratory System: How Do My Lungs Work?* (John Burstein)
- *The Respiratory System* (A True Book) (Darlene R. Stille)
- *The ABCs of Asthma: An Asthma Alphabet Book for Kids of All Ages* (Kim Gosselin and Terry Ravanelli)
- *The Endocrine System* (Rebecca Olien)
- *The Exciting Endocrine System: How Do My Glands Work?* (John Burstein)
- *Grossology and You: Really Gross Things About Your Body* (Sylvia Branzei and Jack Keely)
- *What Makes You Cough, Sneeze, Burp, Hiccup, Blink, Yawn, Sweat, and Shiver?* (My Health) (Jean Stangl)
- *I Wonder Why I Blink: And Other Questions About My Body* (Brigid Avison)

Book About Poetry Terms

- *Skin Like Milk, Hair of Silk: What Are Similes and Metaphors?* (Words Are Categorical) (Brian P. Cleary)

Biographies

- *Elizabeth Blackwell: Girl Doctor* (Childhood of Famous Americans) (Joanne Landers Henry)
- *Clara Barton* (History Maker Bios) (Candice F. Ransom)
- *100 African Americans Who Shaped History* (chapter on Daniel Hale Williams) (Chrisanne Beckner)

Biographies (Advanced Readers or Read Aloud)

- *The Mayo Brothers: Doctors to the World* (Community Builders) (Lucile Davis)
- *Charles Drew: Doctor Who Got the World Pumped Up to Donate Blood* (Getting to Know the World's Greatest Inventors and Scientists) (Mike Venezia)

ART, MUSIC, AND MEDIA

Art

- *Dying Gaul*, in Rome, Italy (230 BCE–220 BCE)
- Alexander Calder, *Untitled* (1976)
- Pablo Picasso, *Guernica* (1937)
- Vincent van Gogh, *Portrait of Dr. Gachet* (1890)
- Giotto di Bondone, *Lamentation* (1305–1306)
- Jean-Honoré Fragonard, *The Swing* (1766)
- Vincent van Gogh, *Portrait of a Dog* (1862) (*Note*: this was drawn when the artist was nine years old)

SAMPLE ACTIVITIES AND ASSESSMENTS

1. LITERARY GRAPHIC ORGANIZER

As a class, we will keep a chart with the categories listed below of the stories and poems we read. As the chart is filled in, we will use the information to talk about what we learned from literature.

- Title and author
- Type of literature (story or poem)
- Main character(s)
- Problem
- Solution
- Summary (using the "Somebody-Wanted-But-So" strategy)

Write your own response on a sticky note, on a whiteboard, or in your journal and share it with a partner before each section of the class chart is filled in. (RF.4.3a, RL.4.1, RL.4.2, RL.4.5, L.4.4a)

2. CLASS DISCUSSION

Let's compare and contrast what is the same and what is different about characters, problems, and solutions in literature. Does any of this remind you of experiences you've had? Turn and talk about your ideas with a partner. Then, look back for specific lines or paragraphs from the stories and poems read that describe what you mean. (SL.4.1a, SL.4.1b, RL.4.2)

3. INFORMATIONAL TEXT/GRAPHIC ORGANIZER

As a class, keep a chart of information about the respiratory, circulatory, and endocrine systems. As the chart is filled in, use open-ended research questions to select the most useful and relevant information to include in a discussion about related information in nonfiction books.

- The body system
- What does it do?
- What are its parts?
- What are some interesting facts?
- What are the words we should know? (e.g., cardiology, pulmonology, etc.)

Write your own response on a sticky note, on a whiteboard, or in your journal and share it with a partner before each section of the class chart is filled in. (RF.4.3a, RI.4.1, RL.4.2, RL.4.4, RI.4.9, L.4.4a)

4. INFORMATIVE/EXPLANATORY WRITING

As a follow-up to completing the Informational Text Graphic Organizer on the respiratory, circulatory, and endocrine systems as a class, choose a system about which to write a well-developed essay that includes at least two supporting details and a summary of how these systems are interrelated. Before turning in your essay, edit your work for correct capitalization, use of relative pronouns and adverbs, and homophones (see Standards for more details). (W.4.9a, W.4.4, L.4.1a,g, L.4.2a)

5. JOURNAL RESPONSE

Following a class discussion of each body system and the similarities and differences between them, be ready to write in your journal about each system and how they work together, citing evidence from what you have read. (SL.4.1.a,b, W.4.2a,b, W.4.4, W.4.7, L.4.1a, L.4.1g, L.4.2a)

6. LITERATURE RESPONSE

Jack changes from the beginning to the end of *Love That Dog* (Sharon Creech). Create a two-column chart in your journal with two headings: "Beginning of School Year" and "End of School Year." Under each heading, list examples of the things Jack does, thinks, and says in the beginning of the year compared to the end of the year. What do you think Jack can teach you about yourself? (RL.4.1, RL.4.3)

7. POETRY RESPONSE

Not only do poets use a variety of verses, rhyme schemes, and meters, but they use specific techniques to make their poems unique. Find examples of rhyme schemes, alliteration, similes, and metaphors in *Love That Dog* (Sharon Creech) and other poems read in this unit. As a class, create a T-chart that includes the name of the technique and examples of each. Mark your poems with sticky notes so you can easily reference the examples you found when it's time for class discussion. Finally, try to write your own poem that imitates a poet of choice. (RL.4.4, L.4.5a, W.4.4)

8. NARRATIVE WRITING

How do Peter's experiences in *Tales of a Fourth Grade Nothing* (Judy Blume) remind you of your family? Talk with a partner and share your ideas. Then, write a short story about a family member, and share it with the same partner. Ask your partner to tell you what they like and what could be improved (i.e., if a specific section needs more details to be clear). Your teacher may ask you to type your story and possibly draw and scan an illustration for publication on the class web page. (W.4.3a,b, W.4.4, W.4.5)

9. RESEARCH PROJECT/BIO-POEM

Read a biography and other informational text about famous doctors and scientists. Generate several open-ended research questions to guide your research. Write a bio-poem about the person that includes important facts you think your classmates should know. Include audio or visual displays in your presentation, as appropriate. Share your poem with your class. Before turning in your poem, edit your work for correct capitalization, use of relative pronouns and adverbs, and homophones (see Standards for more details). Your teacher may ask you to type your poem and insert a picture of the person from the Internet for publication on the class web page. (RI.4.1, RL.4.6, RI.4.8, RI.4.9, W.4.2d, W.4.7, SL.4.4, SL.4.5, L.4.1a,g, L.4.2a)

10. DRAMATIZATION/FLUENCY

Choose one of the poems from this unit, such as "They Were My People" (Grace Nichols), to read and discuss with a partner. Perform the poem as a duet with a classmate. Record the readings using a video camera for future reference and to see how your fluency improves during the course of the year. (RF.4.3a)

11. WORD STUDY

Words that share roots are related in their meanings. As an individual and as a class, keep an index card file of new words learned in this unit (i.e., *cardiovascular, cardiac, cardiology, pulmonology, pulmonologist,* etc.). Keeping the words on index cards will allow you to use and sort the words by meaning and spelling features. (*Note:* This will be an ongoing activity all year long.) You may also be asked to work in groups to create *semantic maps* of the body systems in order to explore your understanding of the interconnectedness of the body systems. (L.4.4a, RI.4.6)

12. ART/CLASS DISCUSSION

View each of the images and try to identify the emotion that the artist wanted to impart to the viewer. Compare the *Dying Gaul* with the *Lamentation*. What did the artists want you to feel? Next, look at *The Swing*. How is this different? What elements of the artists' painting styles, color palettes, or details did they include that help to convey these emotions? Is it the subject matter that mostly conveys the emotions, or is it the artists' way of presenting it? (SL.4.1)

13. ART/CLASS DISCUSSION

Review the elements of form in art (e.g., line, color, texture, form). Identify and describe these in Picasso's *Guernica* and van Gogh's *Portrait of Dr. Gachet*. How did these artists use formal elements to convey emotion in these works? (SL.4.1)

14. CLASS DISCUSSION/REFLECTIVE ESSAY

As a class, summarize what was learned in this unit as it relates to the essential question: How do stories reveal what we have in common? Following the class discussion, write your response in your journal. Edit your work for correct capitalization, use of relative pronouns and adverbs, and homophones (see Standards for more details) before sharing it with your teacher. Your teacher may ask you to type your essay and respond to a poll about the unit on the classroom blog. (W.4.4, W.4.9a,b, L.4.1a,g, L.4.2a)

15. GRAMMAR AND USAGE

Your teacher will teach mini-lessons on the individual language standards. For example, he/she will explain relative pronouns to the class, and then you will practice some cloze activities as a class: (i.e., The story was about a girl _____ [who, what, which] wanted a dog of her own.) Select a piece of your own writing, circle the relative pronouns, and ensure the correct ones were used. (L.4.1a)

16. MECHANICS/GRAMMAR WALL

As a class, create a Mechanics/Grammar bulletin board where, throughout the year, you will add to a checklist of editing topics as they are taught through targeted mini-lessons (e.g., proper use of punctuation and capitalization). Once skills are taught in a mini-lesson and listed on the bulletin board, you are expected to edit your work for the elements before publication. (L.4.1, L.4.2, L.4.3)

17. MECHANICS

Your teacher will teach mini-lessons on the individual language standards. For example, as a class you will make a list of times when capitalization is used (i.e., first word of a sentence, proper nouns, important words in a title of a book or article, and abbreviations). Then, you will choose a piece of your own writing and underline words that should be capitalized in your own rough draft (using appropriate editing marks). Check your work with a partner. (L.4.2a)

18. VOCABULARY/WORD WALL

As a class, create a Vocabulary Word Wall bulletin board where, throughout the year, you will add and sort words as you learn them in each unit of study. (L.4.4)

ADDITIONAL RESOURCES

- *Today is Native American Writer Leslie Marmon Silko's Birthday* (ReadWriteThink) (RL.4.6)
- *Judy Blume Author Study* (Scholastic) (RI.4.9)
- *Dr. Christian Barnard Performed the First Human Heart Transplant* (ReadWriteThink) (W.4.7)
- *Question and Answer Books—From Genre Study to Report Writing* (ReadWriteThink) (W.4.2)
- *Poems about Family and Childhood* (Inquiry Unlimited)
- *Circulatory System Lesson* (Instructor Web)
- *Lessons for Grade 4* (Texas Heart Institute)
- *The Human Heart* (The Franklin Institute)
- *Guide to Cardiovascular Health* (The Nemours Foundation) (PDF)
- "Somebody-Wanted-But-So" strategy (West Virginia Department of Education)

TERMINOLOGY

Bio-poem	Graphic organizer	Poetic terms: stanza, line, verse
Characters	Metaphor	Problem and solution
Dramatization	Poetic devices: rhyme scheme, meter, alliteration	Semantic map
Fluency		Simile

MAKING INTERDISCIPLINARY CONNECTIONS

This unit teaches:

Science:

Body systems: circulatory (e.g., chambers of the heart, four blood types, etc.), respiratory (e.g., parts of the lungs, carbon dioxide/oxygen exchange, dangers of smoking, asthma, etc.), endocrine (e.g., pituitary, adrenal, thyroid glands, etc.)

Doctors (e.g., Elizabeth Blackwell, Benjamin Banneker, Charles Drew, etc.) and their contributions to science

Art: form in art, Vincent van Gogh, Giotto di Bondone, Jean-Honoré Fragonard, Pablo Picasso

This unit could be extended to teach:

Music: elements of music (e.g., steady beat, rhythmic patterns, accents, downbeats, etc.)

Mathematics:

Graphing (e.g., heart beats per minute at rest vs. during exercise, etc.)

Measurement (e.g., liters [blood], pounds [weight], inches/centimeters [height], peak flow meter [lung capacity], etc.)

Physical education/health: Ways to keep the heart and lungs healthy (e.g., cardiovascular exercise, healthy diet, etc.)

Grade Four, Unit One Sample Lesson Plan

Love That Dog by Sharon Creech

"The Red Wheelbarrow" by William Carlos Williams

"Stopping by Woods on a Snowy Evening" by Robert Frost

"The Tyger" by William Blake

"dog" by Valerie Worth

"The Pasture" by Robert Frost

"Street Music" by Arnold Adoff

"The Apple" by S. C. Rigg

"Love That Boy" by Walter Dean Myers

In this series of ten lessons, students read *Love That Dog* by Sharon Creech, and they:

Identify the speaker of the novel/poem (RL.4.2, RL.4.6)

Infer missing details (RL.4.1, RL.4.3)

Explore poetry along with the speaker (RL.4.2, RL.4.5, RL.4.6, RL.4.10, RF.4.4)

Note the speaker's evolving view of poetry (RL.4.3, RL.4.6)

Examine the function of the subplot in the novel (RL.4.1, RL.3.3)

Record responses to poems (RL.4.1, RL.4.2, RL.4.5, RL.4.6, L.4.4)

Challenge their views of poetry (RL.4.2, W.4.9)

Lesson I: Meet Jack, Room 105, Miss Stretchberry, and "The Red Wheelbarrow"

Identify key components of the unit *Love That Dog* (RL.4.5, SL.4.1)

Record impressions to the reading of "The Red Wheelbarrow" (RL.4.2, RL.4.10, RF.4.4, W.4.9)

Explore responses to "The Red Wheelbarrow" (SL.4.1, RL.4.5)

Examine Jack's reflections when he reads "The Red Wheelbarrow" (RL.4.1, RL.4.2, RL.4.5, RL.4.6, L.4.4)

(Begin to) probe the missing details between Jack's entries (RL.4.1, RL.4.3)

Lesson II: The Woods and a Blue Car

(Continue to) probe the missing details between Jack's entries (RL.4.1, RL.4.3, SL.4.1)

Record responses to "Stopping by Woods on a Snowy Evening" (RL.4.2, RL.4.5, RL.4.10, RF.4.4, W.4.9)

Explore Jack's responses to "Stopping by Woods on a Snowy Evening" (RL.4.1, RL.4.2, RL.4.3)

Note Jack's reference to the blue car (RL.4.3)

Lesson III: "The Tyger" and a Blue Car

(Continue to) probe the missing details between Jack's entries (RL.4.1, RL.4.3)

Record responses to "The Tyger" (RL.4.2, RL.4.5, RF.4.3, RL.4.10, RF.4.4, W.4.9)

Probe why Jack says that "The Tyger" "sounded good" (RL.4.2)

Trace Jack's evolving description of the blue car

Lesson IV: "dog"

Consider the details in "dog" (RL.4.2)

(Along with Jack) describe a pet (even a pretend one) (SL.4.1)

Explore why Jack likes "dog" (RL.4.1, RL.4.3)

(Continue to) probe the missing details between Jack's entries (RL.4.1, RL.4.3)

Note the emergence of a subplot (RL.4.1, RL.4.3)

Lesson V: "The Pasture"

Consider Jack's views of poetry following his reading of "The Pasture" (RL.4.2, RL.4.6)

Explore and record personal views of poetry (RL.4.5, RL.4.10, RF.4.4, W.4.9)

Note the significance of Jack's January 24 entry (RL.4.1, RL.4.3)

Continue to trace the novel's subplot (RL.4.1)

Lesson VI: "Street Music," "The Apple," and "My Yellow Dog"

Consider the form of "Street Music" and "My Yellow Dog" (RL.4.2, RL.4.5, RL.4.6)

Explore Jack's response to "Street Music" (RL.4.2, RL.4.5, RL.4.10, RF.4.4)

Note the return of a car to Jack's reflections (RL.4.1, RL.4.3)

Reflect on Jack's decision to identify himself as the poet of "My Yellow Dog" (RL.4.3)

Revisit personal reflections

(Begin to) identify topics for writing own poems (W.4.9)

Lesson VII: "Love That Boy" and Sky

Explore Jack's March 14 entry and the revelation of a new name, Sky (RL.4.1)

Record personal reflection in response to Jack's excitement (RL.4.10, RF.4.4, W.4.9)

(Following the reading of March 22 entry, return to folders and begin to) compose drafts of personal poems (W.4.9, W.4.10, L.4.1, L.4.2, L.4.3, L.4.5)

Lesson VIII: Walter Dean Myers

Examine Jack's letter to Walter Dean Myers (RL.4.3)

Conduct research and record facts about the life and writing of Myers (RI.4.1, W.4.7)

Explore the life of Myers (based on findings) (RI.4.1)

(Continue to) work on personal poems (W.4.9, W.4.10, L.4.1, L.4.2, L.4.3, L.4.5)

Lesson IX: Miss Stretchberry and "My Sky"

Explore Miss Stretchberry's contribution to Jack's evolving understanding of poetry (RL.4.3, RL.4.5, RL.4.6)

Examine "My Sky" and note how Jack integrates what he has learned into his own composition (RL.4.2, RL.4.3, RL.4.5, RL.4.10, RF.4.4)

Revise personal poems (W.4.4, W.4.5, W.4.10, L.4.1, L.4.2, L.4.3, L.4.5)

Lesson X: Love That Dog

Revisit Jack's story (RL.4.1, RL.4.3)

Explore and share select entries from folder (W.4.10)

Share personal poem (RL.4.5, SL.4.4)

Reflect on the idea of inspiration (L.4.4, SL.4.1)

Lesson I: Meet Jack, Room 105, Miss Stretchberry, and "The Red Wheelbarrow"

Objectives

Identify key components of the unit Love That Dog (RL.4.5, SL.4.1)

Record impressions to the reading of "The Red Wheelbarrow" (RL.4.2, RL.4.10, RF.4.4, W.4.4, W.4.9)

Explore responses to "The Red Wheelbarrow" (SL.4.1, RL.4.5)

Examine Jack's reflections when he reads "The Red Wheelbarrow" (RL.4.1, RL.4.2, RL.4.5, RL.4.6, L.4.4)

(Begin to) probe the missing details between Jack's entries (RL.4.1, RL.4.3)

Required Materials

☐ Class set of Love That Dog by Sharon Creech

☐ Pocket folders with fasteners (contents below)

Procedures

1. Lead-In:

Distribute folders and instruct students to study their contents. They will find:

• "The Red Wheelbarrow" by William Carlos Williams

- "Stopping by Woods on a Snowy Evening" by Robert Frost
- "The Tyger" by William Blake
- "dog" by Valerie Worth
- "The Pasture" by Robert Frost
- "Street Music" by Arnold Adoff
- "The Apple" by S. C. Rigg
- "Love That Boy" by Walter Dean Myers
- Loose-leaf paper

2. Step by Step:
   a. Introduce the structure of the unit on *Love That Dog* by Sharon Creech. Tell them that:

   The folders they just looked through will be used *only* for this unit

   All the poems that they will read are in the folder

   The loose-leaf will be used to record their responses to the poems and to the novel *Love That Dog* by Sharon Creech

   b. Ask a student to volunteer to read "The Red Wheelbarrow" aloud.
   c. Instruct the students to reread "The Red Wheelbarrow" in the folder. Tell them to record their initial responses to the poem in the space around the poem.
   d. Lead a discussion exploring the students' responses.
   e. Introduce *Love That Dog* by Sharon Creech. Tell the students to read Jack's first three entries.

3. Closure:
   Using prompts, guide a discussion in which the students compare Jack's response to the "The Red Wheelbarrow" to their own.

Differentiation

Advanced

- Students will conduct research on a poet of choice from this unit and study three more of his or her poems.
- At the close of the unit (or as each poet is featured), students will share their research with the rest of the class through a multimedia or creative video presentation. Students should include commentary on the style of the poet's work.

Struggling

- Make recordings of poems available to students in a listening center, freeing them to focus on meaning instead of the actual decoding of the poems.
- Encourage students to draw pictures to go with stanzas of poetry as a first step in responding to the poems. As they try to visualize the poet's ideas, it may lead to a deeper understanding of the poem.

Homework/Assessment

Students will write (in the unit folder) a brief poem, emulating "The Red Wheelbarrow."

Grade 4 ▶ *Unit 2*

Literature Settings: Weather or Not

This six-week unit invites students to explore geography as it relates to seasons and weather. Students discover how these settings are represented in—and affect events in—literature.

OVERVIEW

Students read contrasting styles of poems about weather, including Carl Sandburg's "Fog" and Robert Frost's "Dust of Snow," and discuss how poetic techniques affect the interpretation of poems. Then students read informational texts, such as "Kenya's Long Dry Season" by Nellie Gonzalez Cutler, and apply the information learned to their appreciation of the setting of *Safari Journal* by Hudson Talbott. Students learn about geography and weather through a variety of informational texts. Class discussions will focus on the back-and-forth relationship between information gleaned from the informational texts and the insights they develop from literature.

ESSENTIAL QUESTION

? How does the author's use of setting affect the plot of a story?

FOCUS STANDARDS

These Focus Standards have been selected for the unit from the Common Core State Standards.

RL.4.1: Refer to details and examples in a text when explaining what the text says explicitly and when drawing inferences from the text.

RL.4.3: Describe in depth a character, setting, or event in a story or drama, drawing on specific details in the text (e.g., a character's thoughts, words, or actions).

RI.4.3: Explain events, procedures, ideas, or concepts in a historical, scientific, or technical text, including what happened and why, based on specific information in the text.

RF.4.4: Read with sufficient accuracy and fluency to support comprehension.

RF.4.4(a): Read on-level text with purpose and understanding.

RF.4.4(b): Read on-level text orally with accuracy, appropriate rate, and expression on successive readings.

W.4.7: Conduct short research projects that build knowledge through investigation of different aspects of a topic.

SL.4.1: Engage effectively in a range of collaborative discussions (one-on-one, group, and teacher-led) with diverse partners on grade 4 topics and texts, building on others' ideas and expressing their own clearly.

SL.4.1(c): Pose and respond to specific questions to clarify or follow up on information, and make comments that contribute to the discussion and link to the remarks of others.

SL.4.1(d): Review the key ideas expressed and explain their own ideas and understanding in light of the discussion.

L.4.5: Demonstrate understanding of figurative language, word relationships, and nuances in word meanings.

L.4.5(a): Sort words into categories (e.g., colors, clothing) to gain a sense of the concepts the categories represent.

SUGGESTED STUDENT OBJECTIVES

- Find similarities and differences in story settings, and note how the author's use of setting affects a story.
- Explain how having factual knowledge of a topic (e.g., weather) can increase your appreciation of literature about the topic.
- Track information and take notes on a topic studied over time (e.g., weather).
- Write a question-and-answer report that includes audio and/or visual aids to communicate research findings about different aspects of a topic (e.g., a particular weather phenomenon).
- Identify similes and metaphors in texts read.
- Recite poetry written in different styles about the same topic.

SUGGESTED WORKS

(E) indicates a CCSS exemplar text; (EA) indicates a text from a writer with other works identified as exemplars.

LITERARY TEXTS

Stories

- *Safari Journal* (ASPCA Henry Bergh Children's Book Awards) (Hudson Talbott)
- *Owen and Mzee: The True Story of a Remarkable Friendship* (Isabella Hatkoff, Craig Hatkoff, Paula Kahumbu, and Peter Greste)
- *Time of Wonder* (Robert McCloskey)
- *Strawberry Girl* (Lois Lenski)
- *The Long Winter (Little House)* (Laura Ingalls Wilder) (EA)
- *One Day in the Prairie* (Trophy Chapter Book) (Jean Craighead George)
- *A Prairie Alphabet (ABC Our Country)* (Jo Bannatyne-Cugnet)
- *Rainbow Crow* (Nancy Van Laan)
- *Hurricane Book and CD (Read Along)* (David Wiesner)
- *Hurricane* (Jonathan London and Henri Sorensen)

Poems

- "Dust of Snow" (Robert Frost) (E)
- "Fog" (Carl Sandburg) (E)
- *A Visit to William Blake's Inn: Poems for Innocent and Experienced Travelers* (Nancy Willard)
- "Clouds" (Christina Rossetti)
- *The Storm Book* (Charlotte Zolotow)

INFORMATIONAL TEXTS

Informational Books

- "Kenya's Long Dry Season" (Nellie Gonzalez Cutler) (E)
- *W is for Wind: A Weather Alphabet* (Pat Michaels and Melanie Rose)
- *Hurricanes: Earth's Mightiest Storms* (Patricia Lauber) (E)
- *Hurricanes* (Seymour Simon) (EA)
- *The Everything Kids' Weather Book* (Joseph Snedeker)
- *Do Tornadoes Really Twist? Questions and Answers About Tornadoes and Hurricanes* (Melvin and Gilda Berger) (EA)
- *Weather Whys: Questions, Facts And Riddles About Weather* (Mike Artell)
- *Let's Investigate Marvelously Meaningful Maps* (Madelyn Wood Carlisle and Yvette Santiago Banek) (E)
- *If You're Not from the Prairie* (David Bouchard)
- *Can It Rain Cats and Dogs? Questions and Answers About Weather* (Scholastic Question and Answer Series) (Melvin and Gilda Berger) (EA)
- *Storms* (Seymour Simon) (EA)
- *Cloud Dance* (Thomas Locker)
- *The Cloud Book: Words and Pictures* (Tomie dePaola) (EA)
- *The Snowflake: A Water Cycle Story* (Neil Waldman)
- *It Figures! Fun Figures of Speech* (Marvin Terban and Giulio Maestro)
- *National Geographic World Atlas for Young Explorers*

Informational Book (Read Aloud)

- *The Weather Wizard's Cloud Book: A Unique Way to Predict the Weather Accurately and Easily by Reading the Clouds* (Louis D. Rubin Sr., Jim Duncan, and Hiram J. Herbert)

ART, MUSIC, AND MEDIA

Art

- John Constable, *Seascape Study with Rain Cloud* (1827)
- Claude Monet, *Rouen Cathedral: The Portal (Sunlight)* (1893)
- Thomas Hart Benton, *July Hay* (1943)
- Édouard Manet, *Boating* (1874)
- Wassily Kandinsky, *Cemetery and Vicarage in Kochel* (1909)
- Gustave Caillebotte, *Paris Street, Rainy Day* (1877)
- Claude Monet, *Bridge over a Pond of Water Lilies* (1899)
- Kazimir Malevich, *Morning in the Village after Snowstorm* (1912)

SAMPLE ACTIVITIES AND ASSESSMENTS

1. LITERARY GRAPHIC ORGANIZER

As a class, we will keep a chart (with the categories listed here) of the stories and poems we read. As the chart is filled in, we will use the information to talk about what we learned from literature.

- Title and author
- Type of literature (story or poem)
- Main character(s)
- Setting (geography, season, and/or weather)
- Summary (using the "Somebody-Wanted-But-So" strategy)

Write your own response on a sticky note, whiteboard, or in your journal and share it with a partner before each section of the class chart is filled in. (RF.4.4a,b, RL.4.1, RL.4.2, RL.4.3, RL.4.5)

2. CLASS DISCUSSION

Let's compare and contrast the effect that the poem or story's setting has on its events. How are similar settings portrayed similarly and differently? Look back for specific lines or paragraphs in order to find explicit details from the stories and poems we've read. What would happen if the setting of the story or poem were changed? (SL.4.1, RL.4.2)

3. INFORMATIONAL TEXT GRAPHIC ORGANIZER

As a class, keep a chart of information with the categories listed below learned about seasons and weather, at home and far away. As the chart is filled in, use the information to talk about related information in nonfiction books and/or online, either explicitly read or inferred.

- Type of weather
- How is it caused?
- What positive effects does this weather have?
- What negative effects can this weather have?
- What do we need to do to prepare for this kind of weather?
- What parts of the world experience this weather?
- What are the weather words we should know? (e.g., *meteorology, prediction, forecast*, etc.)

Write your own response on a sticky note, on a whiteboard, or in your journal and share it with a partner before each section of the class chart is filled in. (RF.4.4a,b, RI.4.1, RL.4.2, RL.4.4, RI.4.9, L.4.4a)

4. INFORMATIVE/EXPLANATORY WRITING

Following a class discussion of weather and climate, be prepared to write about the positive and negative effects of weather on real life and life in literature. Your response should be a well-developed essay that includes at least two supporting details. Before turning in your essay, edit your work for modal auxiliaries, order of adjectives, and commas and quotation marks (see Standards for more details). (W.4.2, L.4.1a,c,d,g; L.4.1g, L.4.2a,b)

5. JOURNAL RESPONSE

Following a class discussion of weather and climate, be prepared to write in your journal about the positive and negative effects of this weather on real life and life in literature. (SL.4.1, W.4.2a,b, W.4.4, W.4.7, L.4.1a,c,d,g; L.4.2a,b)

6. READING FLUENCY

Here is a page from *W is for Wind* by Pat Michaels. Find the highlighted line on your page—this is your cue line. When you hear that line read by a classmate, it is your cue to read the next passage aloud. Take two minutes to practice your passage to yourself, and then we will read the text as a class and discuss the information learned from it. (RI.4.3, RI.4.9, RF.4.4a,b)

7. CLASS DISCUSSION

How is reading a book similar to, and different from, predicting the weather? Write your own response on a sticky note, on a whiteboard, or in your journal and share it with a partner. Cite specific examples from the text and from the experience of reading stories. (SL.4.1, RL.4.3)

8. LITERATURE RESPONSE

What impact does weather have on stories such as *The Long Winter* (Laura Ingalls Wilder), *Time to Wonder* (Robert McCloskey), or *Hurricane Book* (David Wiesner)? What if the setting were changed (i.e., from winter to summer, from the sea to the desert, or from a hurricane to a snowy day)? How would that change the story? Turn and talk about your ideas with a partner, then write a first draft of a scene for a modified story of choice. (RL.4.3, W.4.3)

9. POETRY/LITERATURE RESPONSE

Read *It Figures! Fun Figures of Speech* by Marvin Terban as a class, and talk about the sections on similes and metaphors. Then, use sticky notes to mark where you find examples of similes and metaphors about weather in poems and stories from this unit. Continue the T-chart started in Unit One (name of the technique and examples of each). (RL.4.4, RL.4.5, L.4.5a)

10. CLASS DISCUSSION

After studying meteorology and weather (specifically clouds) in informational texts, read the poems "Clouds" by Christina Rossetti and "Fog" by Carl Sandburg. How does your understanding of cloud formation increase your appreciation for these poems (or not)? Write your own response on a sticky note, on a whiteboard, or in your journal and share it with a partner before discussing as a class. (SL.4.1, RL.4.1, RL.4.3)

11. DRAMATIZATION/FLUENCY

Choose one of the poems from this unit, such as "Dust of Snow" by Robert Frost, to read and discuss with a partner. Memorize and/or recite the poem for your classmates. Record the readings using a video camera for future reference and to see how your fluency improves during the course of the year. (RF.4.4a,b, RL.4.5)

12. RESEARCH PROJECT/WRITE A WEATHER FORECAST (OPTION 1)

Read at least two informational texts, in print or online, about a specific season in a geographical region of choice. Watch a meteorologist presenting a weather forecast online or on TV, and outline what makes that style of presenting unique. Then, write a weather forecast that describes at least two aspects of weather. Be sure to edit your work for modal auxiliaries, order of adjectives, and commas and quotation marks (see Standards for more details). Your teacher may ask you to type your forecast, and possibly even record it as a podcast or using a video camera, for publication on the class web page. (RI.4.1, RI.4.3, RI.4.4, RI.4.7, RI.4.9, W.4.2, W.4.7, SL.4.4, SL.4.5, L.4.1a,c,d,g; L.4.2a,b)

13. RESEARCH PROJECT/Q&A REPORT (OPTION 2)

Read at least two informational texts, in print or online, about a season or weather phenomenon of choice. Write a report in question-and-answer format that includes at least four logically ordered open-ended questions and the answers. Be sure to edit your work for modal auxiliaries, order of adjectives, and commas and quotation marks (see Standards for more details) before sharing with the class. Your teacher may ask you to type your forecast and insert a relevant picture from the Internet, or one taken with a digital camera, for publication on the class web page. (RI.4.1, RI.4.3, RI.4.4, RI.4.7, RI.4.9, W.4.2, W.4.7, SL.4.4, SL.4.5, L.4.1a,c,d,g; L.4.2a,b)

14. CLASS DISCUSSION

Look at the variety of maps available in books such as *Let's Investigate Marvelously Meaningful Maps* by Madelyn Wood Carlisle. Why is it helpful to use different types of weather maps? How is reading a map similar to and different from reading a book? Write your own response on a sticky note, on a whiteboard, or in your journal and share it with a partner before discussing as a class. (RI.4.7, SL.4.1)

15. WORD STUDY

As an individual and as a class, keep an index card file of new words learned in this unit (i.e., *meteorology, prediction, forecast, catastrophic, catastrophe,* etc.). How does the context of the word help you understand its meaning? Keeping the words on index cards will allow you to use and sort the words by meaning and spelling features. (*Note:* This will be an ongoing activity all year long.) In addition, you may be asked to create an individual semantic map of related words in order to help you explore understanding of the interconnectedness of weather and story events. (L.4.4a, RI.4.6)

16. ART/NARRATIVE WRITING

Look at how weather is portrayed in the various art selections. What adjectives would you use to describe the weather? Are there any similes, metaphors, or figurative language that you think work best? Write down your own response and compare your answer with others in the class. Choose your favorite artwork and find a partner who chose the same piece. Together, write an opening scene from a story that would have that weather as its setting, using at least one metaphor or simile. (RL.4.7, W.4.3b, L.4.5a)

17. CLASS DISCUSSION AND INFORMATIVE/EXPLANATORY WRITING

As a class, summarize what was learned in this unit as it relates to the essential question ("How does the author's use of setting affect the plot of a story?"). Write your own response on a sticky note, on a whiteboard, or in your journal and share it with a partner before discussing as a class. Following the class discussion, write your response in your journal. Be sure to edit your work for modal auxiliaries, order of adjectives, and commas and quotation marks (see Standards for more details) before sharing it with your teacher. Your teacher may ask you to type your essay and respond to a poll about the unit on the classroom blog. (W.4.4, W.4.9a,b, L.4.1a,c,d,g; L.4.2a,b)

18. ART/CLASS DISCUSSION

Examine the Constable, Benton, and Malevich pieces and discuss how the formal elements (e.g., color, line, texture, and shapes) in these works relate to the weather being shown. Ask questions such as: How do the color and texture of the sky help to convey the weather? What lines lead you to understand this is a specific type of weather? How do the shapes that define the figures and landscape signal particular weather conditions? (SL.4.1, SL.4.3)

19. GRAMMAR AND USAGE

Your teacher will teach mini-lessons on the individual language standards. For example, he/she will explain modal auxiliaries to the class, and then you will practice some cloze activities as a class: (i.e., The clouds seem to be getting lighter, so I think the rain _____ [can, may, must] stop soon.) Select a piece of your own writing, circle *can, may,* and *must,* and ensure the correct one was used. (L.4.1c)

20. MECHANICS/GRAMMAR WALL

As a class, continue adding to the Mechanics/Grammar bulletin board started in Unit One. Remember—once skills are taught in a mini-lesson and listed on the bulletin board, you are expected to edit your work for these elements before publication. (L.4.1, L.4.2, L.4.3)

21. VOCABULARY/WORD WALL

As a class, continue adding to the Vocabulary Word Wall bulletin board where, throughout the year, you will add and sort words as you learn them in each unit of study. (L.4.4)

ADDITIONAL RESOURCES

- *Weather Detectives: Questioning the Fact and Folklore of Weather Sayings* (ReadWriteThink) (W.4.7)
- *Literature as a Jumping Off Point for Nonfiction Inquiry* (ReadWriteThink) (RL.4.2)
- *The Tropical Storm that Became Katrina Formed Over the Bahamas in 2005* (ReadWriteThink) (RI.4.3)
- *Exploring Cause and Effect Using Expository Texts About Natural Disasters* (ReadWriteThink) (RI.4.5)
- *Using Snowflake Bentley as a Framing Text for Multigenre Writing* (ReadWriteThink) (RI.4.9)
- *Using Picture Books to Teach Setting Development in Writing Workshop* (ReadWriteThink) (W4.3)
- *How To Read Weather Maps* (Discovery Channel, Discovery Education)
- *Strawberry Girl Lesson Plan* (Lesson plan for *Strawberry Girl* by Lois Lenski) (Scholastic)
- Weather Channel for Kids
- Weather Metaphors (Knowgramming.com)
- Idioms Category: Weather (UsingEnglish.com)
- Music Meteorology (Weather Dude)
- Photographs of storms
- Animated interpretation of Robert Frost's "Dust of Snow"
- "Somebody-Wanted-But-So" strategy (West Virginia Department of Education)

TERMINOLOGY

Context	Poetic devices: rhyme scheme, meter, simile, metaphor	Poetic terms: stanza, line, verse	Setting
Explicit information			
Inference		Prediction	

MAKING INTERDISCIPLINARY CONNECTIONS

This unit teaches:

Art: texture, form in art, John Constable, Thomas Hart Benton, Kazimir Malevich

Geography:

United States/local geography (e.g., coastal areas, plains, mountains, etc.)

African geography (e.g., Sahara Desert, tropical rain forests, coastal plains, grassy flatlands, etc.)

Science:

Weather: (e.g., snow, fog, wind, cold and warm fronts, air movement and air pressure, effects of altitude on weather, hurricanes, tornadoes, etc.)

Meteorology and weather prediction (e.g., cloud formation, weather maps, weather stations, satellite maps, etc.)

This unit could be extended to teach:

Geography: Map reading (e.g., climate, physical, political, topographical, etc.)

Science: Weather prediction tools and how to read them (e.g., barometer, anemometer, psychrometer, thermometer, rain gauge, Doppler radar, etc.)

Grade Four, Unit Two Sample Lesson Plan

"Dust of Snow" by Robert Frost

"Fog" by Carl Sandburg

In this series of four lessons, students read "Dust of Snow" by Robert Frost and "Fog" by Carl Sandburg, and they:

> Note the use of poetic devices in their analysis of poetry (RL.4.1, RL.4.5)
>
> Analyze the role that nature plays as a source of inspiration for poets (RL.4.1, RL.4.2, RL.4.3, RL.4.6)
>
> Reflect upon the power of poems to capture special moments (SL.4.1)

Summary

Lesson I: "Dust of Snow"

Identify the rhyming scheme of the poem "Dust of Snow" (RL.4.1, RL.4.5)

Examine the impact that the rhyming scheme has on the meaning of the poem (RL.4.1, RL.4.5)

Analyze the relationship between the form of the poem and its content (RL.4.1, RL.4.3)

Note the shift in content from the first to the second stanza

Reflect on the speaker's perspective (RL.4.2, RL.4.6)

Explore the theme of the poem (RL.4.2)

Lesson II: "Fog"

Identify the metaphor in the poem

Annotate the poem for words that relate to the metaphor (RL.4.1, RL.4.5)

Explicate the use of the metaphor (RL.4.1)

Explore the mood of the poem (RL.4.2, RL.4.3)

Consider the speaker's perspective (RL.4.6)

Note the differences in form between "Dust of Snow" and "Fog" (RL.4.5)

Analyze the differences in the speakers' point of view (in "Dust of Snow" and "Fog") (RL.4.6)

Lesson IV: Critiquing Personal Poems

Note the use of nature in classmates' poems

Identify metaphors

Explore the poems' forms (RL.4.5)

Identify the setting of the poems (RL.4.3)

Note the emergence of mood in the poems (SL.4.1)

Reflect upon the use of poetry to depict special moments (SL.4.1)

Lesson III: Writing Poetry

Reread the poems "Dust of Snow" and "Fog"

Analyze the role that nature plays in both poems (RL.4.1)

Select a special moment (similar to the moments depicted in "Dust of Snow" and "Fog") to write about (W.4.3)

Identify the use of nature to depict the moment (RL.4.4)

Create a web of words that captures the moment (W.4.4, W.4.5)

Group select words in poetic form (W.4.4, W.4.5)

Refine the poems (W.4.4, W.4.5)

Lesson III: Writing Poetry

Objectives

Reread the poems "Dust of Snow" and "Fog"

Analyze the role that nature plays in both poems (RL.4.1)

Select a special moment (similar to the moments depicted in "Dust of Snow" and "Fog") to write about (W.4.3)

Identify the use of nature to depict the moment (RL.4.4)

Create a web of words that captures the moment (W.4.4, W.4.5)

Group select words in poetic form (W.4.4, W.4.5)

Refine the poems (W.4.4, W.4.5)

Required Materials

☐ Copies of "Dust of Snow," by Robert Frost, and "Fog," by Carl Sandburg

Procedures

1. Lead-In:
Student volunteers will reread "Dust of Snow" and "Fog."

2. Step by Step:
   a. A class discussion notes the different ways that the poets use nature to capture a moment. In "Dust of Snow," it is a crow that "shook down" a "dust of snow" that impacts the speaker's mood. In "Fog," the speaker uses a metaphor, "little cat feet," to depict the movement of the fog. The speaker seems not to be involved in that moment.

b. Collectively, the students work on a sample; included below is one for "Wave."

<pre>
                                            crawl

                            tickling   surprisingly

                  purrs   **wave**   beneath

                  bubbles   dreams

                             gray
</pre>

c. With the students' help, highlight groupings of words, such as *surprising purr, tickling crawl, bubbling wave,* or *gray dream.*

d. Included is a possible grouping of words into a poem:

Wave

The wave that crawled
Beneath my feet
Surprised my morning
Dreams.

e. Students individually select a moment that they wish to capture.

f. Students, either individually or in pairs, create a web of verbs, adjectives, and adverbs around the word that represents their chosen moment.

g. Students group select words in poetic form.

h. Students refine their poems.

3. Closure:
Student volunteers read their poems aloud.

Differentiation

Advanced

- Encourage students to create a digital slide presentation or screenshot that documents the process the class used to write the poem. Alternately, students can record the process using a video camera.

- Allow students to set up a class web page to post all poems and record them as podcasts.
- Encourage students to create poems using richer language and more poetic devices (i.e., repetition, alliteration, simile, and metaphor) than their peers.

Struggling

- Orally and/or visually remind students what verbs (action words) and adjectives (describing words) are before beginning.
- Provide students with photos of nature moments from which to generate their list of adjectives and verbs. (For example, the sun setting or the downpour of a rainstorm.) Or, provide students with digital cameras to take photos in preparation for this lesson. Students write groups of words on sentence strips, read their phrases to their group members, and, as a group, assemble them in order. Students copy the poem they created together, practice reading together, and recite chorally for the class. The teacher may record the students reading with a video camera so they can see and hear themselves in order to improve their fluency.

Homework/Assessment
N/A

Grade 4 ▶ *Unit 3*

Animals Are Characters, Too: Characters Who Gallop, Bark, and Squeak

This eight-week unit invites students to compare how horses, dogs, and mice are portrayed in fiction and nonfiction.

ESSENTIAL QUESTION

? How do we portray animals in writing?

OVERVIEW

Students study how animals and their traits are personified in literature and film. The teacher may choose to have students read varied texts about the same animals to facilitate a whole-group discussion, or may choose to encourage students to read in small groups about different animals and share what they learn with each other. Students choose an animal to research and compare the research with how animals are portrayed in literature. After reading selections from *Scranimals* by Jack Prelutsky or from *The Book of Nonsense* by Edward Lear, students also try their hand at writing a poem or limerick about an unusual animal. Students also begin writing their own narratives that incorporate the techniques and vocabulary learned with animal characters. If time permits, students may have the opportunity to compare how film and print versions of texts are similar and different from each other. This unit ends with a class discussion and informative/explanatory essay response to the essential question.

FOCUS STANDARDS

These Focus Standards have been selected for the unit from the Common Core State Standards.

RL.4.5: Explain major differences between poems, drama, and prose, and refer to the structural elements of poems (e.g., verse, rhythm, meter) and drama (e.g., casts of characters, settings, descriptions, dialogue, stage directions) when writing or speaking about a text.

RI.4.2: Determine the main idea of a text and explain how it is supported by key details; summarize the text.

RF.4.4: Read with sufficient accuracy and fluency to support comprehension.

RF.4.4(c): Use context to confirm or self-correct word recognition and understanding, rereading as necessary.

W.4.3: Write narratives to develop real or imagined experiences or events using effective technique, descriptive details, and clear event sequences.

SL.4.5: Add audio recordings and visual displays to presentations when appropriate to enhance the development of main ideas or themes.

L.4.5: Demonstrate understanding of figurative language, word relationships, and nuances in word meanings.

L.4.5(b): Define words by category and by one or more key attributes (e.g., a *duck* is a bird that swims; a *tiger* is a large cat with stripes).

L.4.5(c): Identify real-life connections between words and their use (e.g., note places at home that are *cozy*).

SUGGESTED STUDENT OBJECTIVES

- Discuss and interpret poetic techniques and forms, such as rhyme scheme and limericks.
- Compare the structures of poems and their use of poetic devices.
- Find similarities and differences in how animal characters are personified in fiction.
- Collaborate with classmates in order to publish a story.
- Read informational texts about a topic (e.g., animals) and compare the factual information with fictional portrayals.
- Compare print and film versions of stories (e.g., *The Black Stallion).*
- Explain major differences among poetry, drama, and prose.
- Shape a journal response into an informative/explanatory essay; use several well-constructed paragraphs.

SUGGESTED WORKS

(E) indicates a CCSS exemplar text; (EA) indicates a text from a writer with other works identified as exemplars.

LITERARY TEXTS

Stories

General

- *James Herriot's Treasury for Children: Warm and Joyful Tales by the Author of All Creatures Great and Small* (James Herriot)
- *It's Raining Cats And Dogs: Making Sense of Animal Phrases* (Jackie Franza and Steve Gray)
- *Every Living Thing* (Cynthia Rylant and S. D. Schindler)
- *Nacho And Lolita* (Pam Munoz Ryan and Claudia Rueda)
- *The Mayor of Central Park* (Avi and Brian Floca)
- *Tacky the Penguin* (Helen Lester and Lynn Munsinger) (easier)

Horses

- *The Black Stallion* (Walter Farley) (E)
- *Black Beauty: The Greatest Horse Story Ever Told* (DK Readers Level 4) (Anna Sewell and Victor Ambrus)
- *Paint The Wind* (Pam Munoz Ryan)
- *San Domingo: The Medicine Hat Stallion* (Marguerite Henry and Robert Lougbeed)
- *Gift Horse: A Lakota Story* (S. D. Nelson)
- *The Girl Who Loved Wild Horses* (Paul Goble)
- *Misty of Chincoteague* (Marguerite Henry and Wesley Dennis) (advanced)

Dogs

- *Because of Winn-Dixie* (Kate DiCamillo)
- *Shelter Dogs: Amazing Stories of Adopted Strays* (Peg Kehret and Greg Farrar)
- *Lewis and Clark and Me: A Dog's Tale* (Laurie Myers and Michael Dooling)
- *The Trouble with Tuck: The Inspiring Story of a Dog Who Triumphs Against All Odds* (Theodore Taylor)
- *Three Names* (Patricia MacLachlan and Alexander Pertzoff)
- *A Dog's Life: Autobiography of a Stray* (Ann M. Martin)
- *Marley: A Dog Like No Other—A Special Adaptation for Young Readers* (John Grogan)
- *Lassie Come-Home* (Eric Knight's original 1938 classic; Rosemary Wells and Susan Jeffers)
- *Shiloh* (Phyllis Reynolds Naylor and Barry Moser) (advanced)

Mice

- *Tale of Despereaux: Being the Story of a Mouse, a Princess, Some Soup, and a Spool of Thread* (Kate DiCamillo and Timothy Basil Ering)
- *Ben and Me: An Astonishing Life of Benjamin Franklin by His Good Mouse Amos* (Robert Lawson)
- *Ralph S. Mouse* (Beverly Cleary and Tracy Dockray)
- *The Mouse and the Motorcycle* (Beverly Cleary)
- *The Bookstore Mouse* (Peggy Christian and Gary A. Lippincott)
- *Ragweed* (The Poppy Stories) (Avi Floca and Brian Floca)
- *Poppy* (The Poppy Stories) (Avi Floca and Brian Floca)
- *The Race Across America No. 37* (Geronimo Stilton) (or any of the Geronimo Stilton series)
- *The Story of Jumping Mouse: A Native American Legend* (John Steptoe)
- *Mrs. Frisby and the Rats of NIMH* (Robert C. O'Brien)

Poems

- "A Bird Came Down the Walk" (Emily Dickinson) (E)
- "The Rhinoceros" (Ogden Nash)
- "The Erratic Rat" (traditional limerick)
- *The Complete Nonsense of Edward Lear* (Edward Lear)
- *Scranimals* (Jack Prelutsky and Peter Sis)
- *The Beauty of the Beast: Poems from the Animal Kingdom* (Jack Prelutsky)
- *Poetry for Young People: Animal Poems* (John Hollander and Simona Mulazzani)

INFORMATIONAL TEXTS

Informational Books

General
- "Seeing Eye to Eye" (*National Geographic Explorer!*) (Leslie Hall) (E)
- "Good Pet, Bad Pet" (*Ranger Rick*, June 2002) (Elizabeth Schleichert) (E)
- *National Geographic Encyclopedia of Animals* (Karen McGhee and George McKay)

Veterinarians
- *I Want to Be a Veterinarian* (Stephanie Maze)
- *Veterinarian* (Cool Careers) (William David Thomas)

Horses
- *Horses* (Seymour Simon) (E)
- *H is for Horse: An Equestrian Alphabet* (Michael Ulmer and Gijsbert van Frankenhuyzen)
- *Your Pet Pony* (A True Book) (Elaine Landau)
- *Horse Heroes: True Stories Of Amazing Horses* (DK Readers Proficient Readers, Level 4) (Kate Petty)
- *Panda: A Guide Horse For Ann* (Rosanna Hansen and Neil Soderstrom)
- *The Kids' Horse Book* (Sylvia Funston)

Dogs
- *Dogs* (Seymour Simon) (EA)
- *W is for Woof: A Dog Alphabet* (Ruth Strother and Gijsbert van Frankenhuyzen)
- *Everything Dog: What Kids Really Want to Know About Dogs* (Kids' FAQs) (Marty Crisp)
- *A Dog's Gotta Do What a Dog's Gotta Do: Dogs at Work* (Marilyn Singer)
- *Your Pet Dog* (A True Book) (Elaine Landau)
- *Why Are Dogs' Noses Wet? And Other True Facts* (Howie Dewin)

Mice
- *Outside and Inside Rats and Mice* (Sandra Markle)
- *The Mouse (Animal Life Stories)* (Angela Royston and Maurice Pledger)

ART, MUSIC, AND MEDIA

Media

- Carroll Ballard, dir., *Black Stallion* (1979)
- Caroline Thompson, dir., *Black Beauty* (1994)
- Max Nosseck, dir., *Black Beauty* (1946)
- Wayne Wang, dir., *Because of Winn Dixie* (2005)
- Sam Fell and Robert Stevenhagen, dir., *Tale of Despereaux* (2008)
- Chris Noonan, dir., *Babe* (1995)
- Brad Bird and Jan Pinkava, dir., *Ratatouille* (2007)

SAMPLE ACTIVITIES AND ASSESSMENTS

1. POETRY/LITERATURE RESPONSE

Read selections from *The Book of Nonsense* by Edward Lear aloud with a partner. Not only should you discuss what the poems mean, but also talk about how the poetic devices, structures, and vocabulary used are similar and different. As a class, we will define a limerick and its elements, and then talk about how Lear's poems exemplify these characteristics. We will continue the T-chart started in the first unit (name of the technique and examples). At a later time, you will read selections from *Scranimals* by Jack Prelutsky aloud with the same partner. Partners will again find examples of poetic techniques and mark them with a sticky note. Last, but not least, you will work with a partner to write your own animal limerick of a single animal (i.e., a lion) or an imaginary animal (i.e., such as the broccoli + lion = broccolion). (RL.4.4, RL.4.5, W.4.4, L.4.5a,c)

2. LITERARY GRAPHIC ORGANIZER

As a class, keep a chart of information (using the categories here) to track what is learned about animals such as horses, dogs, mice, or other animals of interest. Use the chart to generate research questions to help select the most useful and relevant information (for a research project later).

- Title and author
- Type of narration (first-person, third-person)
- Animal character(s)
- Character traits, and how they developed over time in the story
- Examples of personification (i.e., thoughts, words, and actions)
- Synonyms for the character
- Antonyms for the character
- Summary (using the "Somebody-Wanted-But-So" strategy:)

Write your response on a sticky note, on a whiteboard, or in your journal and share it with a partner before each section of the class chart is complete. (RF.4.4c, RL.4.1, RL.4.2, RL.4.3, RL.4.4, RL.4.5, RL.4.6, L.4.5c)

3. CLASS DISCUSSION

Let's compare and contrast how animals are personified. How is this personification portrayed in literature? If animals *could* talk and act like humans, which of the actions are most similar to generalizations about the animal (i.e., the "sly" fox, the "lazy" pig, etc.). Look back for specific lines or paragraphs in order to find explicit details from the stories and poems read. (SL.4.1, RL.4.3)

4. LITERATURE RESPONSE

Write a journal entry from an animal's perspective, being sure to give the animal human characteristics. Trade your journal entry with a partner to see if they can figure out your animal from your effort to "personify" it while still maintaining its unique animal characteristics. (W.4.4, W.4.9a,b, RL.4.3)

5. INFORMATIONAL TEXT GRAPHIC ORGANIZER

As a class, keep a chart of information using the categories here about animals such as horses, dogs, mice, or other animals of interest. Use the chart to generate open-ended research questions and to select the most useful and relevant information later for independent research.

- Name of animal
- Habitat
- Diet

- Protection/body facts
- Enemies
- Life expectancy
- Interesting facts

Write your response on a sticky note, on a whiteboard, or in your journal and share it with a partner before each section of the class chart is completed. (RF.4.4c, RI.4.1, RI.4.2, RI.4.4, RI.4.5, RI.4.7, RI.4.9)

6. JOURNAL RESPONSE

Following a class discussion of animals studied, write a journal response (or make a graphic representation such as a Venn diagram) that compares facts learned with how the animal is portrayed in literature. (W.4.2a,b,c; W.4.4, W.4.7, L.4.1a,b,c,d,g; L.4.2a,b,c)

7. RESEARCH AND INFORMATIVE/EXPLANATORY WRITING

Choose an animal or two that you would be interested in researching (see Activity 5; students may refer to their notes and research questions from that activity). Generate and make notes of (further) research questions. Find a classmate who is interested in the same animal. Together, research an animal of choice following the same categories as the graphic organizer (listed in Activity 5). Create a plan for researching your animal, using both online and print sources. Write a report—either in question-and-answer format where you write four questions and provide the answers—or in a well-developed informative/explanatory essay with at least two sources of information cited. Be sure to edit your work for the use of the progressive and commas before coordinating conjunctions in compound sentences (see Standards for more details). Your teacher may ask you to type your report and possibly draw and scan an illustration or insert a relevant photo from the Internet for publication on the class web page. (W.4.4, W.4.7, L.4.1a,b,c,d,g; L.4.2a,b,c)

8. NARRATIVE WRITING

As your class discusses animal stories and poems, begin outlining your own narrative about an original animal character by starting with filling in the categories listed in the graphic organizer above. Before you begin writing, reexamine the characters in stories and poems we've read in this unit, recalling how characters developed over the course of the story, examples of personification, and lists of synonyms and/or figurative language you want to use. Make sure to plan a sequence of events that makes sense and think about key details to include, using five new vocabulary words. You will have the opportunity to work with a partner to revise, edit, and improve your story (for the use of the progressive and commas before coordinating conjunctions in compound sentences—see Standards for more details), so that it can be published on a class web page for others to see. Once the story is written, you will be asked to type it and add audio recordings and visual displays to enhance it. (W.4.1, W.4.4, W.4.5, W.4.6, W.4.8, SL.4.5, L.4.5, L.4.1a,b,c,d,g; L.4.2a,b,c)

9. CLASS DISCUSSION/CREATE A CLASS BOOK

As a class, read and discuss *It's Raining Cats And Dogs: Making Sense of Animal Phrases* by Jackie Franza and Steve Gray. Illustrate the literal and figurative meaning of an animal idiom. Compile these illustrations into a class book to share with younger students, and try to incorporate phrases learned into your daily writing and speaking. An alternate class book idea is to make an ABC book of animal characters in a style similar to *W is for Woof* by Ruth Strother and Gijsbert Van Frankenhuyzen. Your teacher may ask you to create a slide of your section, including a scanned illustration or relevant photo from the web, before assembling into a class book (either electronic or in print). (RL.4.1, SL.4.1, L.4.5b)

10. CLASS DISCUSSION

Compare the film and print versions of a book such as *Black Beauty* or *Black Stallion*. You can also download and compare any animal film, such as *Babe*, to a script of the film. (Your teacher needs to check and approve the parts of the script you want to use.) Decide what you want to compare before viewing (e.g., characters, settings, descriptions, dialogue, and/or stage directions), and keep notes in your journal about similarities and differences as well as the major differences between drama and prose. (SL.4.1, RL.4.5)

11. DRAMATIZATION

After discussing the structural elements (e.g., casts of characters, settings, descriptions, dialogue, stage directions) that are unique to drama versus prose, add one or more of these elements to a Reader's Theater script of a fun animal story, such as *Tacky the Penguin* by Helen Lester and Lynn Munsinger. With at least two other classmates, add at least two scenes—one before the script begins and one after the script ends—to make it a one-act, three-scene play, and present it as a class. Record the presentations and edit them to create a movie to post on the class web page. (RL.4.5, W.4.4)

12. DRAMATIZATION/FLUENCY

Choose one of the poems from this unit, such as "A Bird Came Down the Walk" by Emily Dickinson or "The Rhinoceros" by Ogden Nash, to read and discuss with a partner. Recite the poem for your classmates. (RF.4.4c, SL.4.5)

13. WORD STUDY

As an individual and as a class, keep an index card file of new words learned in this unit. You may also have a nonsense word section where you make up words for animals (based on *Scranimals*) using new prefixes and suffixes learned until this point in the year. Each index card should include the word, a definition, the word in a sentence, and, for the nonsense words, an illustration. Keeping the words on index cards will allow you to use and sort the words by meaning and spelling features. (*Note:* This will be an ongoing activity all year long.) (L4.4a,b)

14. CLASS DISCUSSION AND INFORMATIVE/EXPLANATORY ESSAY

As a class, summarize what you learned in this unit as it relates to the essential question ("How is the portrayal of animals similar and different between fiction and nonfiction?") Following the class discussion, write a response in your journal. Work with a partner to revise and shape your response into an essay. Edit the essay for the use of the progressive and commas before coordinating conjunctions in compound sentences (see Standards for more details) before sharing with your teacher. Your teacher may ask you to post your essay and respond to a poll about the unit on the classroom blog. (W.4.4, W.4.5, W.4.9a,b, L.4.1a,b,c,d,g; L.4.2a,b,c)

15. GRAMMAR AND USAGE

Your teacher will teach mini-lessons on the individual language standards. For example, he/she will teach the class about the form and use of the progressive tense, and then you will practice some cloze activities as a class: (i.e., I _____ walking my dog down the street when my dad came home from work.) Next, your teacher will give you the start of a sentence (I was . . . I am . . . I will be . . .), and you will have the opportunity to finish the sentence with a partner. Select a piece of your own writing, find examples of the progressive tense, and ensure the correct forms were used. (L.4.1c)

16. MECHANICS/GRAMMAR WALL

As a class, continue adding to the Mechanics/Grammar bulletin board started in Unit One. Remember, once skills are taught in a mini-lesson and listed on the bulletin board, you are expected to edit your work for these elements before publication. (L.4.1, L.4.2, L.4.3)

17. MECHANICS

Select passages where animals are talking in your guided reading book. Highlight how commas and quotation marks are used to separate speaking parts from regular text. Then, choose a piece of your own writing and underline the dialogue of different characters included in your own writing. If two characters are talking, two different colors should be used. Edit your own writing, checking that you used a comma before a character speaks, and then quotation marks around each character's words. (L.4.2b)

18. VOCABULARY/WORD WALL

As a class, continue adding to the Vocabulary Word Wall bulletin board where, throughout the year, you will add and sort words as you learn them in each unit of study. (L.4.4)

ADDITIONAL RESOURCES

- *On Stage: Theater Games and Activities for Kids* (Lisa Bany-Winters) (RL.4.5)
- *Webcams in the Classroom: Animal Inquiry and Observation* (ReadWriteThink) (SL.4.1)
- *Black Beauty Author Anna Sewell was Born in 1820* (ReadWriteThink) (W.4.7)
- *Animal Inquiry* (ReadWriteThink) (W.4.7)
- *Celebrate Kate DiCamillo's Birthday Today* (ReadWriteThink) (RL.4.3)
- *Alaska Native Stories: Using Narrative to Introduce Expository Text* (ReadWriteThink) (RI.4.9)
- *Multimedia Responses to Content Area Topics Using Fact-"Faction"-Fiction* (ReadWriteThink) (RL.4.9)
- *How the Fourth Grade and I Wrote a Play* (Matt Buchanan) (W.4.6)
- *Author of the Month: Jack Prelutsky* (McGraw-Hill, Child Lit)
- *Writing with Writers: Poetry Writing with Jack Prelutsky* (Scholastic)
- *Limericks* (Old-Fashioned-American-Humor.Com)
- *Creative Drama Lesson Plans* (Creative Drama Classroom)
- *Reader's Theater K–3 Scripts* (Grandview Library, East Ramapo School District, NJ)
- *Horses in Art* (The Incredible Art Department)
- Movie scripts (script-o-rama.com)
- "Somebody-Wants-But-So" strategy (West Virginia Department of Education)

TERMINOLOGY

Character traits	Personification
First person	Poetic devices: rhyme scheme, meter, simile, metaphor
Limerick	
Narration	Third person

MAKING INTERDISCIPLINARY CONNECTIONS

This unit teaches:

History/Geography:
Importance of animals in Native American cultures (e.g., Lakota Indians)
Role of animals in historical events, such as exploration (e.g., Lewis and Clark)

Science: Animals (e.g., horses, mice, and dogs, etc.) and their traits (e.g., classification, habitat, diet, form(s) of protection, enemies, length of life, domesticated vs. wild, etc.); veterinarians

This unit could be extended to teach:

Science:
Senses of animals and people

Optics (e.g., examining ways that animals have adapted to interpret sensory information, etc.); parts of the eye in people and animals (e.g., optic nerve, cornea, lens, iris, pupil, retina, etc.) and the function of each part

Ears of animals and people; parts of the ear (e.g., outer ear, ear canal, ear drum, auditory nerve, etc.) and the function of each part

Music: How animals are portrayed in music (e.g., *Carnival of the Animals* by Camille Saint-Saëns, etc.)

Grade Four, Unit Three Sample Lesson Plan

The Black Stallion by Walter Farley

In this series of seven lessons, students read *The Black Stallion* by Walter Farley, and they:

Conduct a close reading of the novel *The Black Stallion* by Walter Farley (RL.4.1, RL.4.2, RL.4.3)

Perform preparatory tasks leading to a written discussion of the novel (RL.4.1, RL.4.2, RL.4.3)

Write analytical essays (W.4.1a,b,c,d; W.4.4)

Summary

Lesson I: Meet Alec and Black (Ch.1–3)

Identify the path of the Drake (RL.4.1)

Trace Alec's survival (RL.4.1, RL.4.3)

Investigate Alec's efforts to survive (RL.4.1, RL.4.3)

Explore Alec's personality (RL.4.1, RL.4.3, SL.4.1)

Probe Black's character (RL.4.1, RL.4.3)

Lesson II: Survival and Rescue (Ch. 4–6)

(Continue to) investigate Alec's acts of survival (RL.4.1, RL.4.3)

(Continue to) explore Alec's personality (RL.4.1, RL.4.3)

(Continue to) probe Black's character (RL.4.1, RL.4.3)

Examine the evolving relationship between the boy and the horse (RL.4.1, RL.4.2, RL.4.3, SL.4.1)

Trace Alec's rescue (RL.4.1, RL.4.3)

Lesson III: Home (Ch. 7–9)

Investigate Alec's and Black's early days at home (RL.4.1, RL.4.3)

(Continue to) examine the relationship between Alec and Black (RL.4.1, RL.4.2, RL.4.3, SL.4.1)

Note Napoleon's influence on Black (RL.4.1, RL.4.3)

Lesson IV: Challenges (Ch.10–12)

Explore Black's evolution (RL.4.1, RL.4.2, RL.4.3, SL.4.1)

Investigate Alec's role in Black's evolution (RL.4.1, RL.4.2, RL.4.3)

Examine Henry's contribution to Alec's relationship with Black (RL.4.1, RL.4.2, RL.4.3, SL.4.1)

Lesson VI: A Winner (Ch. 16–18)

Examine Henry's statement that "Alec isn't the same boy that you sent to India last summer" (p. 166) (RL.4.2, SL.4.1)

Closely review the race (RL.4.1, RL.4.2, RL.4.3)

Explore the meaning of Black's victory (RL.4.2, SL.4.1)

Lesson V: Progress (Ch. 13–15)

Probe the purpose of racing Black (RL.4.3, SL.4.1)

Explore the author's intent in shrouding Black's identity in a cloud of mystery (RL.4.3, SL.4.1)

Revisit earlier understanding of Alec's and Black's personalities (RL.4.1, RL.4.2, RL.4.3, SL.4.1)

Lesson VII: Preparing to Write Essays

Revisit the development of Alec's character (RL.4.1, RL.4.2, RL.4.3)

Interpret the power of friendship as it is portrayed in the novel (RL.4.1, RL.4.2, RL.4.3)

Analyze the complexity of Black's victory in the race (RL.4.1, RL.4.2, RL.4.3)

Provide a written analysis of a select objective (from above) (W.4.1a,b,c,d; W.4.4)

Lesson VII: Preparing to Write Essays

Objectives

Revisit the development of Alec's character (RL.4.1, RL.4.2, RL.4.3)

Interpret the power of friendship as it is portrayed in the novel (RL.4.1, RL.4.2, RL.4.3)

Analyze the complexity of Black's victory in the race (RL.4.1, RL.4.2, RL.4.3)

Provide a written analysis of a select objective (from above) (W.4.1a,b,c,d; W.4.4)

Required Materials

☐ Class set of *The Black Stallion* by Walter Farley

☐ Sticky notes

Procedures

1. Lead-In:

   Students read the three objectives that are written on the board.

2. Step by Step:

   a. In preparation for students' written analysis (homework), lead a discussion about the type of textual work that the three objectives involve.

   - *The first objective,* "revisit the development of Alec's character," calls for a step-by-step tracing of Alec's responses to his adventures and his evolution from a young boy to a mature young man.

   - *The second objective,* "interpret the power of friendship as it is portrayed in the novel," calls for a discussion of the developing friendship and trust between the boy and the horse.

   - *The third objective,* "analyze the complexity of Black's victory in the race" is the most advanced. Alec tries to stop Black once he sees his injury, but the horse races on despite the pain. How is this climax described? What message is conveyed by the author?

   b. Students select one of the objectives for further study.

   c. Using sticky notes, students skim through the novel and select passages that involve the objective that they selected.

3. Closure:

   Students who chose the same objective for written analysis discuss their findings in small groups.

Differentiation

Advanced

- Assign students the third objective, or allow them to create their own writing prompt.
- Give students an opportunity to talk through the meaning of the assignment with a partner to ensure understanding (before beginning the sticky note activity).

Struggling

- Group students who have chosen the same objective together, and allow them to choose either the first or second objective from step b.
- If the suggested objectives seem too difficult, create a simpler one such as: "Describe how Alec changed from the beginning of the novel to the end."
- Work closely with the students to skim the book, placing sticky notes throughout the text.
- Continuing to scaffold for success, students will work together on writing clear statements of opinion to begin their essays. Number the sticky notes to show how the passages support the opinion statements.
- As time allows, students will sketch out the rest of their essays while at school.

Homework/Assessment

Students write an essay (teachers determine the number of paragraphs) on the objective of their choice. Their essays must include an introduction, state a clear opinion, be soundly developed, provide textual support, and have a conclusion.

Grade 4 ▶ *Unit 4*

Revolutionaries from the Past

This eight-week unit invites students to read historical fiction and poetry from America's past—including works from the time of the American Revolution.

ESSENTIAL QUESTION

? What life lessons can we learn from revolutionaries in fiction and nonfiction?

OVERVIEW

While reading about America's past, not only do students highlight key information and supporting details about people and events in order to get a sense of chronology, but they spend time comparing and contrasting first- and third-person narratives. Students will read and discuss poetry, such as "Concord Hymn" by Ralph Waldo Emerson, and read speeches by revolutionaries including Patrick Henry and Sojourner Truth. Students read informational texts and study author Jean Fritz, who wrote books about the American Revolution, such as *Can't You Make Them Behave, King George?* After learning about revolutionary people of the past, students write their own speeches outlining their opinion on a current event, possibly taking a "revolutionary" position. This unit ends with a class discussion and essay response to the essential question.

FOCUS STANDARDS

These Focus Standards have been selected for the unit from the Common Core State Standards.

RL.4.6: Compare and contrast the point of view from which different stories are narrated, including the difference between first- and third-person narrations.

RI.4.5: Describe the overall structure (e.g., chronology, comparison, cause/effect, problem/solution) of events, ideas, concepts, or information in a text or part of a text.

RI.4.6: Compare and contrast a firsthand and secondhand account of the same event or topic; describe the differences in focus and the information provided.

W.4.1: Write opinion pieces on topics or texts, supporting a point of view with reasons and information.

SL.4.3: Identify the reasons and evidence a speaker provides to support particular points.

L.4.4: Determine or clarify the meaning of unknown and multiple-meaning words and phrases based on grade 4 reading and content, choosing flexibly from a range of strategies.

SUGGESTED STUDENT OBJECTIVES

- Describe the differences between firsthand accounts (primary sources) and secondhand accounts (secondary sources) in informational text.
- Order events in informational and literary text chronologically.
- Compare and contrast first- and third-person narrations.
- Discuss and interpret the literal and figurative meaning of idioms.
- Identify the reasons that speakers provide to support their positions (e.g., Patrick Henry and Sojourner Truth).
- Write opinion pieces about people and events explored in reading (e.g., American revolutionaries), supporting your point of view with at least two reasons.

SUGGESTED WORKS

(E) indicates a CCSS exemplar text; (EA) indicates a text from a writer with other works identified as exemplars.

LITERARY TEXTS

Stories

- *John Henry: An American Legend* (Ezra Jack Keats)
- *Navajo Long Walk* (The Council for Indian Education) (Nancy M. Armstrong and Paulette Livers Lambert)
- *Trail of Tears* (Step-Into-Reading, Step 5) (Joseph Bruchac)
- *Sleds on Boston Common: A Story from the American Revolution* (Louise Borden and Robert Andrew Parker)
- *The Secret of Sarah Revere* (Ann Rinaldi)
- *A Ride into Morning: The Story of Tempe Wick* (Ann Rinaldi)
- *Heroes of the Revolution* (David A. Adler and Donald A. Smith)
- *War Comes to Willy Freeman* (Arabus Family Saga) (James and Christopher Collier)
- *Yankee Doodle* (Gary Chalk)
- *The Madcap Mystery of the Missing Liberty Bell* (Real Kids, Real Places) (Carole Marsh) (advanced)
- *The Mystery on the Freedom Trail* (Real Kids, Real Places) (Carole Marsh)

Story (Read Aloud)

- *Poor Richard's Almanack* (Benjamin Franklin)

Poems

- "Concord Hymn" (Ralph Waldo Emerson)
- "George Washington" (Rosemary and Stephen Vincent Benet)
- "A Tragic Story" (William Makepeace Thackeray)
- "A Nation's Strength" (Ralph Waldo Emerson)
- "The Flag" (unknown)

INFORMATIONAL TEXTS

Informational Books

- *A is for America* (Devin Scillian and Pam Carroll)
- *O, Say Can You See? America's Symbols, Landmarks, And Important Words* (Sheila Keenan and Ann Boyajian)
- *If You Lived At The Time Of The American Revolution* (Kay Moore and Daniel O'Leary)
- *The Revolutionary War* (True Books: American History) (Brendan January)
- *Crispus Attucks: Black Leader of Colonial Patriots* (Childhood of Famous Americans) (Dharathula H. Millender and Gary Morrow)
- *Molly Pitcher: Young Patriot* (Childhood of Famous Americans) (Augusta Stevenson)
- *And Then What Happened, Paul Revere?* (Jean Fritz and Margot Tomes)
- *Will You Sign Here, John Hancock?* (Jean Fritz and Trina Schart Hyman)
- *Where Was Patrick Henry on the 29th of May?* (Jean Fritz and Margot Tomes)
- *Can't You Make Them Behave, King George?* (Jean Fritz and Margot Tomes)
- *Why Don't You Get a Horse, Sam Adams?* (Jean Fritz and Trina Schart Hyman)
- *The American Revolutionaries: A History in Their Own Words 1750–1800* (Milton Meltzer)
- *A History of US: From Colonies to Country* (Joy Hakim)

Biographies

- *Victory or Death! Stories of the American Revolution* (Doreen Rappaport, Joan Verniero, and Greg Call)
- *Paul Revere (In Their Own Words)* (George Sullivan)
- *The Secret Soldier: The Story Of Deborah Sampson* (Scholastic Biography) (Ann McGovern, Harold Goodwin, and Katherine Thompson)
- *How Ben Franklin Stole the Lightning* (Rosalyn Schanzer)
- *Now & Ben: The Modern Inventions of Benjamin Franklin* (Gene Barretta)
- *Susan B. Anthony: Champion of Women's Rights* (Childhood of Famous Americans Series) (Helen Albee Monsell)
- *Abigail Adams: Girl of Colonial Days* (Childhood of Famous Americans Series) (Jean Brown Wagoner)
- *Sojourner Truth: Ain't I a Woman?* (Scholastic Biography) (Patricia C. McKissack and Frederick McKissack)
- *In Their Own Words: Sojourner Truth* (Peter and Connie Roop)

Speeches

- Give Me Liberty or Give Me Death (March 23, 1775, Patrick Henry)
- Ain't I a Woman? (May 29, 1851, Sojourner Truth)
- On a Woman's Right to Vote (1873, Susan B. Anthony)

ART, MUSIC, AND MEDIA

Art

- John Singleton Copley, *Paul Revere* (1768)
- Grant Wood, *The Midnight Ride* (1931)

Media

- Rock and Revolution, "Too Late to Apologize" (2010)

SAMPLE ACTIVITIES AND ASSESSMENTS

1. LITERARY GRAPHIC ORGANIZER

As a class, keep a chart with the questions and categories listed here of the historical fiction stories and poems we've read. Use the information to talk about related information learned from literature.

- Title and author
- Text structure(s) used
- Type of narration (first-person, third-person)
- Character(s) (major and minor)
- Does this character remind you of other characters? Who/why?
- What information was changed that shows you this is historical *fiction*?
- What did you learn from the major characters?
- Summary

    Write your response on a sticky note, on a whiteboard, or in your journal and share it with a partner before each section of the class chart is filled in. (RL.4.1, RL.4.2, RL.4.3, RL.4.5, RL.4.6, RL.4.9)

2. CLASS DISCUSSION

Let's compare and contrast the points of view from which these stories and poems are narrated. Which clues/key words provide information about the point of view? How are the narratives different? Look back for specific lines or paragraphs in order to find explicit details from the stories and poems read. (SL.4.1, RL.4.6)

3. POETRY/LITERATURE RESPONSE

Choose a poem or story and change the point of view from which it is written. In other words, if the story is in first person, rewrite it in third, or if the story is in third person, rewrite it in first. Alternatively, choose a story to write in poetic form, or a poem to rewrite in story form. Discuss with a partner which style of writing you prefer and why. (RL.4.6, W.4.4, L.4.1a,b,c,d,e,g; L.4.2)

4. INFORMATIONAL TEXT GRAPHIC ORGANIZER

As a class, keep a chart using the categories and questions below of information learned about historical events from the American Revolution. Read informational texts about people and events that are both firsthand (primary sources) and secondhand (secondary sources), and talk about how the differences in point of view affect understanding. Does the overall structure of the text (chronology, cause/effect, etc.) affect your understanding of events as they are presented? As the chart is filled in, use the information to talk about what we learned from nonfiction books.

- Person or event
- Where this took place
- When this took place
- What is the historical significance of this event?
- From whose point of view is this account written?
- What other significant information do you want to remember about this person or event?
- Notes about text structure (chronology, cause/effect, etc.)

Write your response on a sticky note, on a whiteboard, or in your journal and share it with a partner before each section of the class chart is filled in. (SL.4.3, RI.4.1, RI.4.2, RI.4.5, RI.4.6, RI.4.7, RI.4.9)

5. TIMELINE

Following a class discussion of historical events, create a timeline of events that shows the chronology and cause/effect relationship among them. You may use a free online timeline generator or make your own. (W.4.2, W.4.4, W.4.7, L.4.1a,b,c,d,e,g; L.4.2)

6. CLASS DISCUSSION/AUTHOR STUDY

Select an author who writes nonfiction in the style of a story, such as Jean Fritz. Conduct research about him/her and why he/she chooses to write about historical topics; take notes in your journal. As you use online sources for your research, be sure to evaluate them for credibility. Share findings as a class. (SL.4.1, W.4.7)

7. CLASS DISCUSSION/CREATE A CLASS BOOK

Benjamin Franklin coined a number of phrases still used today, and they are found in *Poor Richard's Almanack*. Illustrate the literal and figurative meaning of two idioms that enhance understanding of the foundations of our country. What did Ben Franklin hope people would learn from these phrases? Compile these illustrations into a class book to share (e.g., with younger students), and try to incorporate the phrases you learned into your daily writing and speaking. Your teacher may ask you to create a slide of your page, including scanned illustrations or relevant photos from the Internet, before assembling them into a class book (either electronic or in print). (RL.4.1, SL.4.1, L.4.5b)

8. SPEECH APPRECIATION

Listen to your teacher read Sojourner Truth's "Ain't I a Woman?" and discuss the message. Then, look online to find Frances D. Gage's memories of listening to Sojourner Truth's speech. Compare the text of the speech with what Gage remembers. What are the similarities and differences? Do the points of view differ? How do Gage's memories enhance your understanding of the speech? Share your answers to these questions with a partner before participating in class discussion. (RI.4.6, SL.4.3)

9. CLASS DISCUSSION/LETTER WRITING (INFORMATIVE/EXPLANATORY)

With a partner, discuss the message of Patrick Henry's speech "Give Me Liberty or Give Me Death." Then, discuss the message of his speech as a class within the context of learning about the American Revolution. Does knowing historical information change your understanding of the message? Why or why not? Then, individually, write a letter to Patrick Henry, explaining your reactions to the message of his speech. Be sure to support your opinion by referring back to a specific line or quotation from his speech. Edit your work for the use of the prepositional phrases and spelling (see Standards for more details) before turning it in. (W.4.1, SL.4.1, SL.4.3, SL.4.4, L.4.1a,b,c,d,e,g; L.4.2)

10. SPEECH WRITING (OPINION)

Applying what you have learned from the speeches discussed in this unit, write your own speech expressing an opinion from the point of view of a revolutionary character. Think about the audience as well as the message when writing your speech. Be sure your opinion is supported by two pieces of evidence. Edit your work for the use of the prepositional phrases and spelling (see Standards for more details) before turning it in. You may also record your presentation using a video camera to compare the difference in impact between "seeing" and "hearing" the words. (W.4.1, W.4.7, SL.4.3, L.4.1a,b,c,d,e,g; L.4.2)

11. DRAMATIZATION (NARRATIVE)

After reviewing the structural elements (e.g., casts of characters, settings, descriptions, dialogue, stage directions, etc.) that are unique to drama (i.e., compared to prose), add these elements to a Reader's Theater script of a historical story. With at least two other classmates, add at least two scenes—one before the script begins and one after the script ends—to make it a one-act, three-scene play; present it as a class. You may record and create a movie from the presentations. (RL.4.5, W.4.4)

12. POETRY/CLASS DISCUSSION/PERFORMANCE

Read and discuss the meaning of "The Flag" by an unknown author. How does the first-person point of view influence your appreciation of the poem? Perform the poem with a classmate. (RL.4.6, SL.4.5)

13. POETRY/WRITING

Design and create a flag that simultaneously represents your family, your classroom, or your school. Explain the symbolism of the flag in your journal in a first-person narrative, similar to the presentation of "The Flag" (in Activity 12) and share it with a classmate. Be sure to edit your work for the use of the prepositional phrases and spelling (see Standards for more details). (RL4.4, SL.4.4, W.4.1a,c,d; L.4.1a,b,c,d,e,g; L.4.2)

14. SPEECH WRITING/OPINION

Revolutionaries aren't always popular during the time that they live, but they believe in something so passionately that they are willing to go out on a limb to express their beliefs. Think about a current event that you believe everyone should understand. Write a speech, supported by two pieces of evidence, about your thoughts and ideas, and present it to the class. Edit your work for the use of prepositional phrases and spelling (see Standards for more details) before turning it in. You may record your presentation using a video camera. (W.4.1, W.4.4, W.4.5, W.4.6, W.4.7, W.4.8, SL.4.5, L.4.1a,b,c,d,e,g; L.4.2, L.4.5)

15. MEDIA/CLASS DISCUSSION

Independently or as a class, view the video "Too Late to Apologize" (see Art, Music, and Media). The first time, talk about the meaning and historical significance of the words. Then view the video a second time, stopping to discuss the images used and how they represent America's past in a contemporary manner. *Optional extension:* Create or remix your own music video to accompany your speech (from Activity 14). (RL.4.7, RL.4.9, RI.4.7, RI.4.9, SL.4.1)

16. WORD STUDY

As an individual and as a class, keep an index card file of new words learned in this unit (i.e., *revolution, revolutionary, revolt,* etc.). Keeping the words on index cards will allow you to use and sort the words by spelling features, root words, prefixes, and suffixes. Find root words, and discuss how the prefixes and suffixes add clues to the meaning of the words. Consult reference materials to confirm pronunciations and clarify the meaning of the words and phrases. (*Note:* This will be an ongoing activity all year long.) (L.4.4a,b,c)

17. CLASS DISCUSSION/REFLECTIVE ESSAY

As a class, summarize what was learned in this unit as it relates to the essential question ("What life lessons can we learn from revolutionaries in fiction and nonfiction?"). Following the class discussion, individually write a response in your journal. Work with a partner to edit your work for the use of the prepositional phrases and spelling (see Standards for more details), and strengthen the content before turning it in to your teacher. Your teacher may ask you to type your essay and respond to a poll about the unit on the classroom blog. (W.4.9a,b, W.4.4, W.4.5, L.4.1a,b,c,d,e,g; L.4.2)

18. GRAMMAR AND USAGE

As a class, generate a list of the most common prepositions. Your teacher will give you a worksheet of sentences that contain prepositional phrases. (*Example:* The girl with the blue scarf sang first.) First, circle the preposition and underline the entire phrase. On the next day, your teacher will give you simple sentences (i.e., "The girl sang first.") and you will work with partners to create prepositional phrases to expand them. Finally, find simple sentences in your own writing and add prepositional phrases to add more details. (L.4.1e)

19. MECHANICS/GRAMMAR WALL

As a class, continue adding to the Mechanics/Grammar bulletin board started in Unit One. Remember, once skills are taught in a mini-lesson and listed on the bulletin board, you are expected to edit your work for these elements before publication. (L.4.1, L.4.2, L.4.3)

20. VOCABULARY/WORD WALL

As a class, continue adding to the Vocabulary Word Wall bulletin board where, throughout the year, you will add and sort words as you learn them in each unit of study. (L.4.4)

21. ART/CLASS DISCUSSION

Compare Copley's and Wood's portrayals of Paul Revere. How are they different? Do they have anything common—aside from both showing Revere? Students should think about what they know about Revere and his famous ride as they consider the works. What do you see first in each image? Is it Revere or something else? Each artist meant to tell a story through his painting—can you describe this story? (SL.4.1, SL.4.3, L.4.3)

22. ART/CLASS DISCUSSION

View the Copley and Wood paintings again. One work is a portrait painted while the person was living; the second, the artist's interpretation a hundred years later. Notice the differences in perspective (e.g., eye-level view vs. bird's-eye view). Why do you think the earlier image focuses more on the man and the later one on the event that made him famous? (SL.4.1, SL.4.3, L.4.3)

ADDITIONAL RESOURCES

- *Slave Narratives: Constructing U.S. History Through Analyzing Primary Sources* (National Endowment for the Humanities) (RI.4.6)
- *American Colonial Life in the Late 1700s: Distant Cousins* (National Endowment for the Humanities) (RI.4.7)
- *Learning About Research and Writing Using the American Revolution* (ReadWriteThink) (W.4.7)
- *Looking for the History in Historical Fiction: An Epidemic for Reading* (ReadWriteThink) (RI.4.9)
- *History Comes Alive: Using Fluency and Comprehension Using Social Studies* (ReadWriteThink) (RL.4.5)
- *Spotlight On America: Extraordinary Women* (Teacher Created Resources) (Robert W. Smith)
- *Readers Theatre for American History* (Anthony D. Fredericks)
- *In Their Own Words* series (Scholastic)

- *The American Revolution: Lighting Freedom's Flame* (National Parks Service)
- *African Americans in the American Revolution* (Buzzle.Com)
- "Indians in the American Revolution" (Wilcomb E. Washburn, speech) (AmericanRevolution.Org)
- *Featured Author: Jean Fritz* (Carol Hurst's Children's Literature Site)
- *Meet the Author: Jean Fritz* (Houghton Mifflin Reading)

TERMINOLOGY

Audience	Major character	Third-person point of view
Autobiography	Minor character	Writing style
Biography	Point of view	Speech
First-person point of view	Primary source	
Informational text structure	Secondary source	

MAKING INTERDISCIPLINARY CONNECTIONS

This unit teaches:

History/Geography:

Causes and provocations of the American Revolution (e.g., the Boston Massacre, Boston Tea Party, Intolerable Acts, Thomas Paine's *Common Sense*, etc.)

Biographies of Revolutionaries (e.g., Crispus Attucks, Molly Pitcher, Paul Revere, Deborah Sampson, King George, John Hancock, John Henry, etc.)

Introduction to the Trail of Tears (e.g., involuntary relocation, Cherokee Nation, Indian Removal Act, passive resistance, etc.)

Women's Rights advocates and legislation through history (e.g., Susan B. Anthony, Sojourner Truth, Fourteenth Amendment, etc.)

Art:

John Singleton Copley, Grant Wood

This unit could be extended to teach:

History/Geography:

The making of a constitutional government (e.g., the ideas behind the Declaration of Independence, the Constitution, levels and functions of government, etc.)

Biographies (e.g., Elizabeth Freeman, Phillis Wheatley, etc.)

Equal rights advocates through history (e.g., Eleanor Roosevelt, Mary McLeod Bethune, Rosa Parks, Martin Luther King Jr., Suraya Pakzad, etc.)

Grade Four, Unit Four Sample Lesson Plan

"Concord Hymn" by Ralph Waldo Emerson

A History of US: From Colonies to Country by Joy Hakim

In this series of five lessons, students read "Concord Hymn" by Ralph Waldo Emerson and passages from *A History of US: From Colonies to Country* by Joy Hakim, and they:

Explore the historical background of the battles of Lexington and Concord (RI.4.6)

Investigate the life and ideas of Ralph Waldo Emerson (RL.4.6, W.4.7)

Reflect upon the power of a poem to depict historical events (RL.4.2, RL.4.3, RL.4.5, RL.4.6, RL.4.9)

Probe the significance of events in the history of a people (RI.4.3)

Summary

Lesson I: Battles of Lexington and Concord	Lesson II: Ralph Waldo Emerson
Identify key events leading to the battles of Lexington and Concord (RI.4.1, RI.4.6)	Explore the life of Ralph Waldo Emerson (RI.4.9, W.4.7, SL.4.2)
Explore the battle of Lexington (RI.4.5)	Note important works by Emerson (RL.4.2, RL.4.6)
Explore the battle of Concord (RI.4.5)	Identify key ideas of Emerson (RL.4.6, RI.4.9)
Examine the significance of the two battles (SL.4.1, SL.4.4)	
Lesson III: "Concord Hymn" by Ralph Waldo Emerson	**Lesson IV: History in Art—Paintings of the Concord Bridge**
Read and reread "Concord Hymn" (RL.4.2, RL.4.10, RF.4.4, L.4.4)	Identify the location of the Concord Bridge
Annotate "Concord Hymn" for its historical details (RL.4.6)	Explore the artistic renditions of the battle of Concord (RL.4.6, RL.4.7, SL.4.5)
Note the event (completion of Concord Monument, April 19, 1836) that prompted the writing of the hymn (RI.4.1, RL.4.2)	Explore the artistic renditions of the Concord Bridge (RL.4.6, RL.4.7, SL.4.5)

Lesson V: Significance of Events in the History of a People

Recall the details of the battle of Concord (RI.4.1, RI.4.9)

Note the contribution of Emerson to immortalizing the event (RL.4.2, RL.4.6)

Reflect upon the power of a poem to depict historical events (RL.4.2, RL.4.6, RI.4.9)

Revisit the artistic works that depict the event (RL.4.6, RL.4.7, SL.4.5)

Explore the importance of the lingering memory of the battle of Concord (SL.4.1)

Lesson V: Significance of Events in the History of a People

Objectives

Recall the details of the battle of Concord (RI.4.1, RI.4.9)

Note the contribution of Emerson to immortalizing the event (RL.4.2, RL.4.6)

Reflect upon the power of a poem to depict historical events (RL.4.2, RL.4.6, RI.4.9)

Revisit the artistic works that depict the event (RL.4.6, RL.4.7, SL.4.5)

Explore the importance of the lingering memory of the battle of Concord (SL.4.1)

Required Materials

☐ "Concord Hymn" by Ralph Waldo Emerson
☐ Artwork and photos of the Concord Bridge
☐ Artwork depicting the Battle of Concord
☐ A History of US: From Colonies to Country by Joy Hakim
☐ Poster boards
☐ Markers

Procedures

1. Lead-In:
   Students will prepare the material of the previous four lessons.

2. Step by Step:
   a. Divide the class into several groups and assign each group one of the lessons' objectives. (Depending on the number of students in the class and the size of the groups, more than one group may be assigned to the same objective.) Using the information that the students gathered in the Lead-In, the groups will record their findings on a poster board.
   b. Each group will report their recalled findings to the rest of the class.

3. Closure:
   Lead a class discussion that probes the significance of events in the history of a people.

Differentiation

Advanced

- Extend this lesson by challenging students to explore the poet Henry Wadsworth Longfellow's role in Paul Revere's fame by reading the poem "Paul Revere's Ride."
- Challenge students to write an essay taking a position on the poet's role in communicating history. Students should argue whether the poet did more to preserve history or whether the poet did more to distort history. This could also take the form of a debate.

Struggling

- Creative groupings of students provide the support needed for this lesson. Students might be paired with a supportive partner who is strong in research and skilled at determining importance of the collected information. You may choose to work with a small group of students, taking on one of the objectives.
- Provide an outline or graphic organizer related to the information needed on the poster board, giving students the support they need to work in either a heterogeneous group or a homogeneous group.

Homework/Assessment
Students will write a one-page reflection about the significance of events in the history of a people.

Stories of the Earth and Sky

This four-week unit pairs Native American stories with informational text about the earth and sky.

ESSENTIAL QUESTION

? How are the earth and sky portrayed in fiction and nonfiction?

OVERVIEW

The unit begins with a discussion about stories that explain nature's mysteries, and how these stories are often passed down orally from generation to generation. Students are asked to share any personal stories about the earth and sky that they have been told. After a brief introduction to Native Americans' reverence and respect for the earth and sky, students read Native American stories and compare and contrast them as a genre. Students alternate reading stories, such as *The Earth Under Sky Bear's Feet* by Joseph Bruchac, and related informational texts, such as *Zoo in the Sky: A Book of Animal Constellations* by Jacqueline Mitton. Class discussions focus on how the informational text helps us to appreciate literature and how authors use artistic license to make a good story. Students also conduct and present research on constellations. After discussing Vincent van Gogh's *Starry Night* and El Greco's *View of Toledo*, students write their own story and publish it on a class web page. This unit ends with a class discussion and informative/explanatory essay in response to the essential question.

FOCUS STANDARDS

These Focus Standards have been selected for the unit from the Common Core State Standards.

RL.4.9: Compare and contrast the treatment of similar themes and topics (e.g., opposition of good and evil) and patterns of events (e.g., the quest) in stories, myths, and traditional literature from different cultures.

RI.4.7: Interpret information presented visually, orally, or quantitatively (e.g., in charts, graphs, diagrams, time lines, animations, or interactive elements on web pages) and explain how the information contributes to an understanding of the text in which it appears.

W.4.3: Write narratives to develop real or imagined experiences or events using effective technique, descriptive details, and clear event sequences.

SL.4.4: Report on a topic or text, tell a story, or recount an experience in an organized manner, using appropriate facts and relevant, descriptive details to support main ideas or themes; speak clearly at an understandable pace.

L.4.3: Use knowledge of language and its conventions when writing, speaking, reading, or listening.

SUGGESTED STUDENT OBJECTIVES

- Explain how knowledge of a topic (e.g., Native American mound builders, the earth, the sun, the moon, and the stars) increases understanding of literature that addresses the topics (e.g., Native American stories).
- Summarize information presented visually, orally, or quantitatively (e.g., in charts, graphs, diagrams, time lines, animations, or interactive elements on web pages) using appropriate facts and descriptive details.
- Write a story based on a painting (e.g., Vincent van Gogh's *Starry Night*; El Greco's *View of Toledo*) incorporating factual information and stylistic techniques used by authors.

SUGGESTED WORKS

(E) indicates a CCSS exemplar text; (EA) indicates a text from a writer with other works identified as exemplars.

LITERARY TEXTS

Stories

Myths and Legends

- *Children of the Earth and Sky: Five Stories About Native American Children* (Stephen Krensky and James Watling)
- *Keepers of the Night: Native American Stories and Nocturnal Activities for Children* (Michael J. Caduto and Joseph Bruchac)
- *Coyote Places the Stars* (Harriet Peck Taylor)
- *Star Boy* (Paul Goble)
- *The Girl Who Loved Wild Horses* (Paul Goble)
- *And Still the Turtle Watched* (Sheila MacGill-Callahan)
- *Thirteen Moons on Turtle's Back* (Joseph Bruchac)
- *The Earth Under Sky Bear's Feet* (Joseph Bruchac)
- *Keepers of the Earth: Native American Stories and Environmental Activities for Children* (Michael J. Caduto and Joseph Bruchac)
- *The Woman Who Outshone the Sun/La mujer que brillaba aún más que el sol* (Alejandro Cruz Martinez and Fernando Olivera)
- *A Pride of African Tales* (Donna L. Washington and James Ransome)
- *How the Stars Fell into the Sky: A Navajo Legend* (Jerrie Oughton and Lisa Desimini)
- *Ming Lo Moves the Mountain* (Arnold Lobel)
- *Moon Rope/Un lazo a la luna: A Peruvian Folktale* (Lois Ehlert and Amy Prince)
- *Moonstick: The Seasons of the Sioux* (Eve Bunting and John Sandford)

General

- *Common Ground: The Water, Earth, And Air We Share* (Molly Bang)
- *Butterfly Eyes and Other Secrets of the Meadow* (Joyce Sidman and Beth Krommes)
- *My Light* (Molly Bang)
- *Midnight on the Moon* (Magic Tree House Book 8) (Mary Pope Osborne and Sal Murdocca)
- *Follow the Moon* (Sarah Weeks and Suzanne Duranceau)
- *Space Explorers* (The Magic School Bus Chapter Book, No. 4) (Eva Moore and Ted Enik)

Stories (Read Aloud)

- *The Mission Possible Mystery at Space Center Houston* (Real Kids, Real Places) (Carole Marsh)
- *They Dance in the Sky: Native American Star Myths* (Ray A. Williamson, Jean Guard Monroe, and Edgar Stewart)

Poems

- "Indian Names" (Lydia Howard Huntley Sigourney)
- *A Pizza the Size of the Sun* (Jack Prelutsky)

INFORMATIONAL TEXTS

Informational Books

Native Americans

- *The Mound Builders of Ancient North America* (E. Barrie Kavasch) (E)
- *Mounds of Earth and Shell* (Native Dwellings) (Bonnie Shemie)

Space (Review from Grade Three)

- *Discovering Mars: The Amazing Story of the Red Planet* (Melvin Berger and Joan Holub) (E)
- *Can You Hear a Shout in Space? Questions and Answers About Space Exploration* (Scholastic Question and Answer) (Melvin Berger, Gilda Berger, and Vincent Di Fate) (EA)
- *Space: A Nonfiction Companion to Midnight on the Moon* (Magic Tree House Research Guide, No. 6) (Mary Pope, Wil Osborne, and Sal Murdocca)

Earth, Sun, Moon, and Stars

- *Earth: Our Planet in Space* (Seymour Simon)
- *Earth* (True Books) (Elaine Landau)
- *Earth* (Picture Reference) (World Book) (Christine Butler-Taylor)
- *G is for Galaxy* (Janis Campbell, Cathy Collison, and Alan Stacy)
- *Do Stars Have Points?* (Scholastic Question and Answer) (Melvin Berger) (EA)
- *I Wonder Why Stars Twinkle: And Other Questions About Space* (Carole Stott)
- *A Child's Introduction to the Night Sky: The Story of the Stars, Planets, and Constellations—and How You Can Find Them in the Sky* (Michael Driscoll and Meredith Hamilton)
- *Constellations* (True Books: Space) (Diane M. Sipiera and Paul P. Sipiera)
- *Find the Constellations* (H. A. Rey)
- *Zoo in the Sky: A Book of Animal Constellations* (Jacqueline Mitton and Christina Balit)
- *See the Stars: Your First Guide to the Night Stars* (Ken Croswell)
- *Constellations* (True Books) (Flora S. Kim)
- *The Moon* (Seymour Simon)

- *The Moon* (Starting with Space) (Paulette Bourgeois, Cynthia Pratt Nicolson, and Bill Slavin)
- *The Sun* (Seymour Simon)
- *The Sun* (True Books) (Elaine Landau)
- *The Sun* (Starting with Space) (Paulette Bourgeois and Bill Slavin)
- *Stars* (True Books: Space) (Paul P. Sipiera)
- *The Stars* (Starting with Space) (Cynthia Pratt Nicolson and Bill Slavin)

Informational Book (Read Aloud)

- *A Walk through the Heavens: A Guide to Stars and Constellations and their Legends* (Milton D. Heifetz and Wil Tirion)
- *Eats, Shoots & Leaves* (Lynne Truss)

ART, MUSIC, AND MEDIA

Art

Earth Images

- Louisa Matthíasdóttir, *Gul* (1990)
- Albert Pinkham Ryder, *Seacoast in Moonlight* (1890)
- Jean-Francois Millet, *Landscape with a Peasant Woman* (early 1870s)
- Piet Mondrian, *View from the Dunes with Beach and Piers* (1909)

Sky Images

- John Constable, *Study of Clouds* (1822)
- John Constable, *Hampstead Heath, Looking Towards Harrow at Sunset* (1823)
- El Greco, *View of Toledo* (c. 1595)
- Vincent van Gogh, *The Starry Night* (1889)
- Alfred Stieglitz, *Equivalents* (1923)
- Vija Celmins, *Untitled #3 (Comet)* (1996)

SAMPLE ACTIVITIES AND ASSESSMENTS

1. INTRODUCTORY ACTIVITY/CLASS DISCUSSION

Children of the Earth and Sky is a book about Native American traditions and cultures. While reading this book, notice instances in which the Native Americans' respect for the earth and sky is described or inferred. Your teacher will ask you to write, on sticky notes or in your journal, how the earth and sky are described in Native American literature and to compare the portrayals with what you already know about these topics. Do you have any stories about the earth or sky that you were told by your family when you were young? (RL.4.3, RL.4.9, SL.4.1, SL.4.2, L.4.3)

2. LITERARY GRAPHIC ORGANIZER

As a class, keep a chart with the categories listed here of the Native American and other stories the class read about the earth and sky. As the chart is completed, use the information to talk about what the class learned from literature.

- Title and author
- Which culture is this story from?
- What role does the earth or sky play in this story? (e.g., personified character, setting, etc.)

- What is important about the character's interaction with the earth or sky?
- Summary
- Theme of the story
- What is unique about this story's portrayal of the earth and/or sky?

Code your book with sticky notes, or write your response on a whiteboard or in your journal, before each section of the class chart is filled in. (RL.4.1, RL.4.2, RL.4.3, RL.4.5, RL.4.9)

3. WRITING ABOUT A FAVORITE STORY (OPINION WRITING)

Of the stories read in this unit, which was your favorite, and why? Choose a story about which to write a well-developed essay. Support your opinion by citing details from the favorite text. Edit your work for complete sentences, punctuation, and use of language and conventions (see Standards for more details) before turning it in to your teacher. Your teacher may ask you to type your opinion paper for publication on a class blog about the books read in this unit. (W.4.1, L.4.1, L.4.2, L.4.3, L.4.5)

4. CLASS DISCUSSION

Let's compare and contrast how the earth and sky are treated in Native American stories and other texts. Look back in the stories and poems we've read for specific lines or paragraphs in order to find specific details. (SL.4.1, RL.4.9, L.4.3)

5. CLASS DISCUSSION

First, read and discuss a story about rock carving, such as *And Still the Turtle Watched* by Sheila MacGill-Callahan. Then, read informational books, such as *The Mound Builders of Ancient North America* by E. Barrie Kavasch or *Mounds of Earth and Shell* by Bonnie Shemie, which tell why the Native Americans created structures and dwellings from the earth. Your teacher may ask you to write, on a sticky note, on a whiteboard, or in your journal, what you learned about the purposeful nature of Native American artifacts and structures. Finally, review the story and see if any additional information or insights are apparent that weren't noticed the first time. (RL.4.1, RL.4.3, RI.4.1, RI.4.3, RI.4.9, L.4.1a, SL.4.1, SL.4.2, L.4.3)

6. POETRY RESPONSE/FLUENCY

Read and discuss the meaning of the poem "Indian Names" by Lydia Howard Huntley Sigourney. What is the message of the poem? Locate the rivers from the poem on a map of the United States. Discuss additional names of places whose names may have Native American origins, especially local places, and keep an ongoing list in your journal. Divide the poem into stanzas, and, with a group of three other classmates, perform the poem as a quartet. Record the readings using a video camera to compare the similarities and differences in expression used by different groups. (RL.4.4, SL.4.1, SL.4.4c, L.4.3)

7. INFORMATIONAL TEXT GRAPHIC ORGANIZER

As a class, keep a chart of information learned about constellations using the categories below. With a partner, research a constellation on the Internet. Be sure to evaluate your sources for credibility, citing only the sources that gave you the most relevant and useful information.

Constellation Name

- Where does the name come from?
- What is the definition of a constellation?

- What is unique about this constellation?
- What does it look like? (Draw a picture.)

   In your journal, write what you learn, as well as where you found the information, in case you need to go back to find a reference. Present your findings to the class. As a class, complete the class chart of all the constellations. (SL.4.2, SL.4.3, SL.4.4, W.4.7, RI.4.1, RI.4.3, RI.4.7, RI.4.8, RI.4.9)

8. JOURNAL WRITING

Following partner presentations about constellations (in Activity 7), write a summary of what you learned, using appropriate facts and descriptive details. (W.4.2, W.4.4, W.4.7, L.4.1, L.4.2, L.4.3)

9. LITERARY RESPONSE

Choose one of the stories about the earth or sky, such as *Butterfly Eyes and Other Secrets of the Meadow* by Joyce Sidman and Beth Krommes or *A Pride of African Tales* by Donna L. Washington and James Ransome. Compare how the facts we know about the earth and sky are modified in order to make a good story. This is called taking "artistic license." Keep an ongoing T-chart in your journal with two columns—*Fact* and *Fiction*—to track the amount of artistic license taken in each book we read. Write a response to this question in your journal: "Why do you think the author changed some facts and kept others?" (RL.4.1, RL.4.9, W.4.4)

10. ART/NARRATIVE WRITING

After looking at and discussing as a class van Gogh's *The Starry Night* and El Greco's *View of Toledo*, students should select one of the two works and write a story that could take place at the time of day and in the location depicted in the painting. Ask students to look closely at the painting before beginning to write, and to refer back to it repeatedly. Begin by outlining your story using the "Somebody-Wanted-But-So" graphic organizer. Then, make a list of the main events for your story. Next, add details by incorporating some facts you learned from your research, as well as some imaginary information, because we have learned that taking artistic license is an effective technique that authors use to build a story. Write a draft of your story and work with a partner to choose words and phrases that have the effect you want and that fit the painting you selected. Once you and your partner believe your story is of the highest quality, record yourself reading it. Upload this as a podcast to the class web page, which will have van Gogh's and El Greco's paintings displayed nearby. (W.4.3, W.4.4, W.4.5, W.4.6, W.4.7, W.4.8, SL.4.5, L.4.1, L.4.2, L.4.3, L.4.5)

11. WORD STUDY

Let's examine words that describe the earth and sky. As an individual and as a class, keep an index card file of new words learned in this unit (i.e., *astronaut, astronomer, constellation, eclipse,* etc.). Keeping the words on index cards will allow you to use and sort the words by spelling feature, root words, prefixes, and suffixes. Find prefixes (*astro-*) and suffixes (*-ologist, -ology*) and discuss how the prefixes and suffixes add clues to the part of speech and meaning of the words. Consult reference materials to confirm pronunciations and clarify the meaning of the words and phrases. (*Note:* This will be an ongoing activity all year long.) In addition, you may be asked to create an individual semantic map of related words in order to help you explore understanding of the interconnectedness of words related to the earth and sky. (L.4.4a,b,c)

12. CLASS DISCUSSION AND INFORMATIVE/EXPLANATORY WRITING

As a class, summarize what was learned in this unit as it relates to the essential question ("How are the earth and sky portrayed in fiction and nonfiction?"). Following the class discussion, write your response in your journal. Work with a partner to edit and strengthen your writing. Shape your response into an informative/explanatory essay before sharing with your teacher. Your teacher may ask you to type your essay and respond to a poll about the unit on the classroom blog. (W.4.9a,b, W.4.4, W.4.5, L.4.1, L.4.2, L.4.3)

13. ART/CLASS DISCUSSION/INFORMATIVE/EXPLANATORY WRITING

Study Millet's and Constable's works closely. Note that they both include earth and sky and an individual figure. Students should compare and contrast the two works, answering questions such as: What different choices did each painter make to distinguish between the earth and sky, land and air—colors, textures, light? What role does the figure play in the work? Next, students should write a short essay outlining their responses. Have students present the works, along with their essay, to the class. (SL.4.1, SL.4.3, L.4.3)

14. ART/CLASS DISCUSSION

View Stieglitz's and Celmins's works closely. Ask students to guess which work is a photograph and which one a drawing. What is happening in each image of the sky? How has the artist depicted the sky? What types of artistic techniques has he or she employed? Is one depiction more mysterious than the other? (SL.4.1, SL.4.3)

15. MECHANICS/GRAMMAR WALL

As a class, continue adding to the Mechanics/Grammar bulletin board started in Unit One. Remember, once skills are taught in a mini-lesson and listed on the bulletin board, you are expected to edit your work for these elements before publication. (L.4.1, L.4.2, L.4.3)

16. GRAMMAR AND USAGE

Read *Eats, Shoots & Leaves* by Lynne Truss as a class and discuss how the placement of the comma changes the meaning of the sentences. Make a list of times when commas are used for effect (i.e., after an introductory phrase: After she went to the movie, she wanted to read the book.) Choose a piece of your own writing and circle punctuation used (reviewing periods, exclamation points, and question marks in addition to commas). Read your writing aloud to a partner and decide if the punctuation used gives the desired effect. Revise as necessary. (L.4.3b)

17. VOCABULARY/WORD WALL

As a class, continue adding to the Vocabulary Word Wall bulletin board where, throughout the year, you will add and sort words as you learn them in each unit of study. (L.4.4)

ADDITIONAL RESOURCES

- *Integrating Literacy Into the Study of the Earth's Surface* (ReadWriteThink) (W.4.7)
- *Earth Verse: Using Science in Poetry* (ReadWriteThink) (RL.4.5)
- *Science Writer Seymour Simon was Born in 1931* (ReadWriteThink) (W.4.7)
- *Constellation Myth Project* (MiddleSchoolScience.Com) (W4.3)
- *Native American Lore*
- *NASA: Spirit of Discovery, Stars and Constellations* (Southeast Missouri State University)
- *Star Bright, Starry Night* (artLibrary)

- *Our Earth as Art Gallery* (NASA, Goddard Space Flight Center)
- *Educator's Guide to Eats, Shoots & Leaves*
- "Somebody-Wanted-But-So" strategy (West Virginia Department of Education)

TERMINOLOGY

Artistic license	Legend	Narrative writing	Word choice
Details	Lore	Research	
Facts	Myth	Theme	

MAKING INTERDISCIPLINARY CONNECTIONS

This unit teaches:

Art: Vincent van Gogh, El Greco, Jean-Francois Millet, John Constable, Alfred Stieglitz, Vija Celmins

Science:

Space (a review of planets from grade 3)

Astronomy (e.g., the sun as a star and as a source of light and heat; how an eclipse happens; the Milky Way and Andromeda galaxies; constellations such as the Big Dipper; the moon and its phases, etc.)

History/Geography: Introduction to culture and life of Native Americans (e.g., mound builders)

This unit could be extended to teach:

Science:

The earth and its layers and formations (e.g., crust, mantle, core, volcanoes, hot springs and geysers, how mountains are formed, etc.)

The atmosphere (e.g., troposphere, stratosphere, mesosphere, thermosphere, exosphere; how the sun and the earth heat the atmosphere, etc.)

History/Geography: Introduction to culture and life of other native cultures, such as:

Mayas, (e.g., knowledge of astronomy and mathematics, located in Central America, etc.)

Aztecs (e.g., warrior culture, Tenochtitlan, located in Mexico, etc.)

Incas (e.g., empire along the coast of South America, Machu Picchu, Cuzco, etc.)

Grade Four, Unit Five Sample Lesson Plan

Can You Hear a Shout in Space? Questions and Answers About Space Exploration by Melvin Berger and Gilda Berger

In this series of four lessons, students read *Can You Hear a Shout in Space? Questions and Answers About Space Exploration* by Melvin Berger and Gilda Berger, and they:

Identify questions to explore (RI.4.1, RI.4.3)

Conduct exploration (RI.4.3, RI.4.7, RI.4.10, RF.4.4, W.4.8)

Document explorations (W.4.2, W.4.4, W.4.9b, W.4.10, L.4.1, L.4.2, L.4.6)

Share results (SL.4.1, SL.4.4, L.4.3)

Summary

Lesson I: Questions and Answers About Space Exploration	Lesson II: Researching Space Exploration
Explore the questions in *Can You Hear a Shout in Space? Questions and Answers About Space Exploration* by Melvin and Gilda Berger (RI.4.1, RI.4.3, RI.4.7, SL.4.1) Select a question to investigate (RI.4.3)	Explore NASA's website for more answers (RI.4.3, RI.4.7, RI.4.10, RF.4.4, W.4.8) Expand research (RI.4.7) Record results (in form of notes) (W.4.8)
Lesson III: Documenting Result of Exploration	**Lesson IV: Sharing Results**
Review notes (W.4.7, W.4.8) In paragraph form, document exploration results (W.4.2, W.4.4, W.4.9b, W.4.10, L.4.1, L.4.2, L.4.6) Revise paragraph (W.4.5) Rewrite paragraph (W.4.4, W.4.10, L.4.1, L.4.2, L.4.6)	Share answers to their explorations (SL.4.1, SL.4.4, L.4.3) Probe results (RI.4.7) Point to lingering questions (RI.4.7)

Lesson III: Documenting Result of Exploration

Objectives

Review notes (W.4.7, W.4.8)

(In paragraph form) document exploration results (W.4.2, W.4.4, W.4.9b, W.4.10, L.4.1, L.4.2, L.4.6)

Revise paragraph (W.4.5)

Rewrite paragraph (W.4.4, W.4.10, L.4.1, L.4.2, L.4.6)

Required Materials

☐ Notes taken in Lessons I and II

☐ Paper and pencils or pens

Procedures

1. **Lead-In:**
Review notes from Lessons I and II.

2. **Step by Step:**
   a. Students, in paragraph form, document results of their exploration (the answer to the question that they selected in Lesson I and the research they conducted in Lesson II). The paragraph must include:
      - The original question
      - A topic sentence that uses that question as a starting point
      - An answer to the question that is composed of at least four sentences
      - A concluding observation
   b. Students revise their paragraphs.

3. **Closure:**
Instruct students that for homework they will rewrite their paragraphs based on the in-class revisions. Also remind them that the original paragraph must be attached to the final draft.

Differentiation

Advanced

- If applicable to the research, students will go deeper into their question by creating a three-dimensional model showing an even richer understanding of the question. Students will present these displays to another class, sharing new learning.

- Students will find relevant websites and work with the teacher to create a WebQuest, pulling ideas for extended exploration from the questions and research.
- Students will use the final products of individual research to create a digital version of Jeopardy.

Struggling:

- Work closely with students to outline their paragraphs, revise and edit. Provide students with a graphic organizer for paragraph construction, if necessary.
- Choose websites to aid students in conducting research (and provide links to those websites through Internet-based bookmarking tools).
- Give students the option of using a word processing program at school (or home) to help with spell-check and grammar editing. (It may be helpful to use a shared spreadsheet with a partner.)

Homework/Assessment

Students rewrite paragraph.

Literary Heroes

This six-week unit ends the year by looking at heroes, real and imagined.

ESSENTIAL QUESTION

? Can heroism be conveyed in words?

OVERVIEW

Generate a definition of *hero* that will evolve over the course of this unit. Students choose a story from this unit to study using all the strategies and skills learned up to this point in the year. Through reading about overtly brave and courageous literary characters (e.g., King Arthur, Robin Hood) or real people who made an impact on the world (e.g., Shakespeare, Davy Crockett, Booker T. Washington), students continue to revise the definition of hero to accommodate what these varied people have in common. After reading about famous heroes, attention is turned to the unsung hero, and class discussions reveal the importance of those people who often remain unnoticed and behind the scenes. The class reviews characters from other novels read this year who, upon reflection, may be heroes. In a culminating project students design their own multimedia presentation of an unsung hero based on what they learned in this unit about heroism.

FOCUS STANDARDS

These Focus Standards have been selected for the unit from the Common Core State Standards.

RL.4.4: Determine the meaning of words and phrases as they are used in a text, including those that allude to significant characters found in mythology (e.g., Herculean).

RI.4.8: Explain how an author uses reasons and evidence to support particular points in a text.

W.4.1: Write opinion pieces on topics or texts, supporting a point of view with reasons and information.

SL.4.2: Paraphrase portions of a text read aloud or information presented in diverse media and formats, including visually, quantitatively, and orally.

L.4.6: Acquire and use accurately grade-appropriate general academic and domain-specific words and phrases, including those that signal precise actions, emotions, or states of being (e.g., *quizzed, whined, stammered*) and that are basic to a particular topic (e.g., *wildlife, conservation,* and *endangered* when discussing animal preservation).

SUGGESTED STUDENT OBJECTIVES

- Collaboratively define the word *hero*.
- Read and discuss a variety of fiction and nonfiction texts about literary and real heroes, from the Middle Ages and beyond.
- Explain how knowledge of classic stories such as *King Arthur* increases understanding of others, such as *Knights of the Kitchen Table*.
- Conduct short research projects on famous and not-so-famous heroes.
- Compare print and film versions of stories about heroes, such as *Robin Hood*.
- Write acrostic poems.
- Design and share a multimedia presentation about unsung heroes.

SUGGESTED WORKS

(E) indicates a CCSS exemplar text; (EA) indicates a text from a writer with other works identified as exemplars.

LITERARY TEXTS

Stories

Middle Ages

- *King Arthur* (Scholastic Junior Classics) (Jane B. Mason and Sarah Hines Stephens)
- *The Knights of the Kitchen Table #1* (Time Warp Trio) (Jon Scieszka and Lane Smith)
- *The Story of King Arthur & His Knights* (Classic Starts) (Howard Pyle and Dan Andreasen)
- *King Arthur* (Troll Illustrated Classics) (Howard Pyle, Don Hinkle, and Jerry Tiritilli)
- *The Kitchen Knight: A Tale of King Arthur* (Margaret Hodges and Trina Schart Hyman)
- *The Whipping Boy* (Sid Fleischman and Peter Sis)
- *The Adventures of Robin Hood* (Classic Starts) (Howard Pyle and Lucy Corvino)
- *Favorite Medieval Tales* (Mary Pope Osborne and Troy Howell)
- *Days of the Knights: A Tale of Castles and Battles* (DK Readers Proficient Readers, Level 4) (Christopher Maynard)
- *The Young Merlin Trilogy: Passager, Hobby, and Merlin* (Jane Yolen)
- *Sir Cumference and the First Round Table: A Math Adventure* (Cindy Neuschwander and Wayne Geehan)
- *Door in the Wall* (Marguerite De Angeli)
- *Christmas in Camelot* (Magic Tree House Book 29) (Mary Pope Osborne and Sal Murdocca)
- *Ella Enchanted* (Gail Carson Levine)
- *The Grey King* (The Dark is Rising Sequence) (Susan Cooper) (EA)
- *The Mystery of the Alamo Ghost* (Real Kids, Real Places) (Carole Marsh)

Other Time Periods

- *The Children's Book of Heroes* (William J. Bennett, Michael Hague, and Amy Hill)
- *Kaya's Hero: A Story of Giving* (American Girls Collection) (Janet Beeler Shaw, Bill Farnsworth, and Susan McAliley)
- *Adventures of the Greek Heroes* (Anne M. Wiseman, Mollie McLean, and Witold T. Mars)

- *Welcome to the Globe: The Story of Shakespeare's Theatre* (DK Readers Proficient Readers, Level 4) (Peter Chrisp)
- *The Library Card* (Jerry Spinelli)

Stories (Read Aloud)

- *Saint George and the Dragon* (Margaret Hodges and Trina Schart Hyman)
- *Merlin and the Dragons* (Jane Yolen and Li Ming)

Poems

- "Why Dragons?" (Jane Yolen)
- "Robin Hood and Little John" (Anonymous)
- "Robin Hood and Maid Marian" (Anonymous)

INFORMATIONAL TEXTS

Informational Books

- *England: The Land* (Erinn Banting) (E)
- *Illuminations* (Jonathan Hunt)
- *Knights And Castles* (Magic Tree House Research Guide) (Mary Pope, Will Osborne, and Sal Murdocca)
- *Knights: Warriors of the Middle Ages* (High Interest Books) (Aileen Weintraub)
- *Adventures in the Middle Ages* (Good Times Travel Agency) (Linda Bailey and Bill Slavin)
- *The Middle Ages: An Interactive History Adventure* (You Choose: Historical Eras) (Allison Lassieur)
- *Women and Girls in the Middle Ages* (Medieval World) (Kay Eastwood)

Biographies

- *Joan of Arc: The Lily Maid* (Margaret Hodges and Robert Rayevsky)
- *William Shakespeare & the Globe* (Aliki)
- *George Washington: Soldier, Hero, President* (DK Readers Reading Alone, Level 3) (Justine and Ron Fontes)
- *Davy Crockett: A Photo-Illustrated Biography* (Photo-Illustrated Biographies) (Kathy Feeney)
- *Booker T. Washington: A Photo-Illustrated Biography* (Photo-Illustrated Biographies) (Margo McLoone)
- *Henry Ford: A Photo-Illustrated Biography* (Photo-Illustrated Biographies) (Erika L. Shores)
- *Elizabeth Cady Stanton: A Photo-Illustrated Biography* (Photo-Illustrated Biographies) (Lucile Davis)
- *Chief Joseph of the Nez Perce: A Photo-Illustrated Biography* (Photo-Illustrated Biographies) (Bill McAuliffe)

ART, MUSIC, AND MEDIA

Art

- *The Unicorn Tapestries* (late fifteenth through early sixteenth centuries)
- Raphael, *St. George and the Dragon* (1504–1506)
- Donatello, *St. George* (1415–1417)

Film

- Michael Curtiz and William Keighley, dirs., *The Adventures of Robin Hood* (1938)
- Richard Thorpe, dir., *Knights of the Round Table* (1953)

SAMPLE ACTIVITIES AND ASSESSMENTS

1. INTRODUCTORY ACTIVITY

As a class, create a chart (using the Frayer Model) that outlines the definitions, characteristics, and examples of heroes as we know them. Continue to add to this chart as the literature and informational text read in this unit expand and alter the definition. (RL.4.4, RI.4.4, L.4.4a,c)

2. LITERARY RESPONSE

As a class, let's begin by examining our understanding of *hero* through one of its common definitions: "the primary character in a literary work." Record characteristics, examples, and nonexamples of the heroes that appear in the books. You will be asked to share your notes with a partner, and together share your ideas with the class. First, focus on the Red Cross Knight in *Saint George and the Dragon* by Margaret Hodges and Trina Schart Hyman. On another day, focus on Young Arthur in *Merlin and the Dragons* by Jane Yolen and Li Ming. After summarizing and discussing insights from these books with the class, write a response about how your understanding of the word *hero* changed or remained the same after hearing each story. (RL.4.2, RL.4.3, RL.4.9)

3. POETRY/LITERATURE RESPONSE

Read and discuss the poem "Why Dragons?" by Jane Yolen. How does knowing the story of St. George from reading the book *St. George and the Dragon* (see Activity 2) increase your understanding of, and appreciation for, this poem? What are the poetic techniques used that you recognize? Does this poem remind you of *Merlin and the Dragons* (since it's written by the same author and it's about the same time period)? Your teacher may ask you to write your own response on a whiteboard or on sticky notes before discussing as a class. After the class discussion, divide up the stanzas and recite the poem as a class. (RL.4.4, RL.4.5, RL.4.9, W.4.8)

4. LITERATURE RESPONSE

Choose an eventful scene or chapter from a Middle Ages story you are reading. Write a journal entry retelling the scene from another point of view (i.e., if it's in first person, rewrite it in third; if it's in third person, rewrite it in first). Trade your journal entry with a classmate who is reading the same book and ask him/her to tell you if your new version makes sense and why (or why not). Revise if needed. (W.4.4, RL.4.3, RL.4.6, RL.4.10)

5. RESEARCH REPORT

Work with a partner to generate some research questions about a historical event from the Middle Ages. Using the Internet, an encyclopedia, and informational texts, read as much as you can about the event. Present your findings in a short report with visuals, similar to the illuminated manuscript pages found in Jonathan Hunt's *Illuminations*, to the class. Your teacher may ask you to type your report, include visuals, and publish it on the class web page. (W.4.4, W.4.7, L.4.1, L.4.2, L.4.3, L.4.6)

6. OPINION WRITING

If heroism demands courage and taking risks, which legendary character, King Arthur or Robin Hood, is a better hero? Support your opinion with strong evidence from the text. (W.4.1. W.4.4, W.4.7, W.4.10, L.4.1, L.4.2, L.4.3, L.4.6)

7. LITERATURE RESPONSE

After reading the King Arthur myths, read the *Knights of the Kitchen Table* by Jon Scieszka and Lane Smith. Discuss how knowing the original story and historical information about the time period helps you appreciate the details in this humorous version. (SL.4.1, RL.4.9)

8. INFORMATIONAL TEXT GRAPHIC ORGANIZER

As a class, we will keep a chart of information, using the categories and research questions below, about the heroes we have learned about from a variety of times and places. Start with the nonfiction texts from this unit, but also review all historical figures studied this year. As the chart is filled in, use the information to talk about how this changes or reinforces our understanding of a *hero*.

- Person's name
- When did he/she live?
- Where did he/she live?
- Why is he/she considered a hero/heroine?
- Are there any fiction stories written about him/her? What are they?
- Other memorable/interesting facts

Write your own responses in your journal and share them with a partner before presenting your findings to the class. (RL.4.3, RL.4.4, RL.4.5, RI.4.1, RI.4.8, RI.4.9, RI.4.10, SL.4.1, SL.4.2, SL.4.4)

9. ACROSTIC POEM

Following a class discussion of heroes, write an acrostic poem about your favorite hero/heroine. Recall from grade 3 that an acrostic poem is one that uses each letter of a word to provide the first letter of each line. Use descriptive words to exemplify the hero's traits, and include words of history from the time period (e.g., *chivalrous* and *medieval*). Your teacher may ask you to type your poem, and insert a relevant picture of the person from the Internet, for publication in a class book. (RL.4.4, RI.4.4, W.4.4, W.4.7, L.4.1, L.4.2, L.4.3, L.4.6)

10. CLASS DISCUSSION

What is the role of point of view when describing heroes? Review an old favorite where the perspective of the story is turned around, such as *The True Story of the Three Little Pigs* by Jon Scieszka. Discuss how the "villain" portrays him/herself as a hero. Can this strategy—taking a different point of view in order to change the story—always work? Write your ideas in your journal, and share them with a partner before discussing as a class. How does point of view change our class definition of a hero or not? (SL.4.1, RL.4.5)

11. CLASS DISCUSSION

Compare film and print versions of a book such as *The Adventures Robin Hood* or *Knights of the Round Table*. (*Note:* You may need to ask your teacher which scenes would be appropriate to watch.) While viewing select scenes, discuss major differences between drama and prose, and structural elements (e.g., casts of characters, settings, descriptions, dialogue, and stage directions). (SL.4.1, RL.4.5)

12. JOURNAL RESPONSE

Does heroism require overt acts of courage and bravery? Who are some everyday people who are also heroes? Read the article titled "Foster Parents Are the Unsung Heroes of Kids" and then read descriptions of heroes from ABC Montana. After reading these articles, write a journal entry where you nominate someone you know who you feel is an unsung hero. Be sure to explain with strong reasons why you chose that person. (RI.4.8, W.4.4, W.4.9a,b)

13. MULTIMEDIA PRESENTATION

As a class, summarize what was learned in this unit as it relates to the essential question ("How does what we read teach us about heroism?"). Then, work with a classmate to revise and edit your unsung hero nomination (see Activity 12) to include as many new vocabulary words, phrases, and figurative language descriptions as make sense. Add audio recording and visual displays to enhance the impact of the nomination. Add your presentation to a class web page. As a culmination, host a ceremony where students share their presentations with each other about unsung heroes. (W.4.2, W.4.5, W.4.6, W.4.7, W.4.8, SL.4.5, SL.4.6, L.4.1, L.4.2, L.4.3, L.4.5, L.4.6)

14. MECHANICS/GRAMMAR WALL

As a class, continue adding to the Mechanics/Grammar bulletin board started in Unit One. Remember, once skills are taught in a mini-lesson and listed on the bulletin board, you are expected to edit your work for these elements before publication. (L.4.1, L.4.2, L.4.3)

15. VOCABULARY/WORD WALL

As a class, continue adding to the Vocabulary Word Wall bulletin board where, throughout the year, you will add and sort words as you learn them in each unit of study. (L.4.4)

16. ART/CLASS DISCUSSION

Explore the imagery in the *Unicorn Tapestries*. What do you see? Continuing with what you have learned about the medieval European world, who are the characters featured in the tapestries? What is the meaning of the medieval hunt? Why does the unicorn seem symbolic—is it treated specifically in the tapestries? What about other animal imagery? (SL.4.1, SL.4.3)

17. ART/CLASS DISCUSSION

Examine Raphael's painting of St. George. What imagery do you see? How has Raphael depicted St. George? How does he look? Now, look at the Donatello sculpture of St. George. What are the differences? How did each artist choose to render his character? Can you see any of the same elements in the St. George characterizations as you did in the *Unicorn Tapestries*? (SL.4.1, SL.4.3)

ADDITIONAL RESOURCES

- *Is Superman Really All That Super? Critically Exploring Superheroes* (ReadWriteThink) (RL.4.6)
- *Question and Answer Books—From Genre Study to Report Writing* (ReadWriteThink) (RL.4.5)
- *Heroes Around Us* (ReadWriteThink) (W.4.7)
- *Jane Yolen For Kids* (JaneYolen.Com)
- *Black History Month: Unsung Heroes Project* (National Association for the Advancement of Colored People, NAACP)
- *Contributions of Americans of Hispanic Heritage* (America USA)
- *"The Cullman Times* 2010 Unsung Heroes Named" *The Cullman Times*, March 28, 2010
- The Frayer Model (JustReadNow!)
- "Foster parents are the unsung heroes of kids," *The Wichita Eagle*, May 16, 2010
- *Unsung Heroes* (ABCMontanta)

TERMINOLOGY

Acrostic poem
Character development
Hero/heroine

Literary terms: novel, plot, setting
Perspective

Point of view
Unsung hero
Villain

MAKING INTERDISCIPLINARY CONNECTIONS

This unit teaches:

History:

Middle Ages (e.g., feudalism, life in a castle, chivalry, knights, castles, Joan of Arc, etc.)

Biographies (e.g., William Shakespeare, George Washington, Davy Crockett, Booker T. Washington, Henry Ford, Chief Joseph, etc.) and what makes people want to write about their lives

Art: medieval tapestry, Raphael, Donatello

This unit could be extended to teach:

Geography: geography of England and Western Europe (i.e., rivers, mountain ranges, etc.)

Mathematics: geometry (e.g., the circumference, diameter, and radius of circles; perimeter of quadrilaterals, etc.)

Grade Four, Unit Six Sample Lesson Plan

King Arthur by Howard Pyle

In this series of three lessons, students read *King Arthur* by Howard Pyle, and they:

- Explore the story of King Arthur according to Howard Pyle (RL.4.4, RL.4.10, RF.4.4)
- Conduct online exploration of King Arthur's life (RI.4.3, RI.4.8, W.4.7, W.4.8)
- Examine facts vs. fiction (RI.4.3, RI.4.8, RI.4.9)

Summary

Lesson I: King Arthur

- Explore the life of King Arthur, as told by Howard Pyle (RL.4.4, RL.4.10, RF.4.4)
- Examine King Arthur's role as a leader (RL.4.2, RL.4.3)
- Investigate King Arthur's legacy (RL.4.9)

Lesson II: Looking for Facts

- Recall details of Howard Pyle's book *King Arthur* (RL.4.1, RL.4.3, SL.4.1)
- Conduct research into the life of King Arthur (RI.4.3, RI.4.8)
- Explore a variety of sources (RI.4.3, W.4.7)
- Record findings (W.4.8)
- Note the emerging uncertainty about the facts surrounding King Arthur's life (RI.4.9, W.4.9b)

Lesson III: Facts and Fiction

- Present findings from Lesson II (SL.4.2, SL.4.4, L.4.6)
- Note differences concerning King Arthur's life that the sources reveal (RI.4.3, RI.4.8, RI.4.9)
- Consider Pyle's presentation of events (RL.4.3, RL.4.9)
- Point to the author's point of view (RL.4.6)
- Revisit King Arthur's role as a leader (RL.4.2, RL.4.3)

Lesson II: Looking for Facts

Objectives

Recall details of Howard Pyle's book, *King Arthur* (RL.4.1, RL.4.3, SL.4.1)

Conduct research into the life of King Arthur (RI.4.3, RI.4.8)

Explore a variety of sources (RI.4.3, W.4.7)

Record findings (W.4.8)

Note the emerging uncertainty about the facts surrounding King Arthur's life (RI.4.9, W.4.9b)

Required Materials

☐ *King Arthur* by Howard Pyle

☐ Computers with Internet access

Procedures

1. Lead-In:
Recall details of *King Arthur* by Howard Pyle.

2. Step by Step:
   a. Students, in several small groups (or individually), conduct online research about King Arthur. Steer the students toward multiple sites.
   b. Students record their findings.

3. Closure:
Class discussion reveals what emerges during research.

Differentiation

Advanced

- Using the results of the class research, students will create a multimedia presentation entitled "Facts and Fiction, The Making of a Legend." Tell students to alternate slides with factual information and slides with evolved fictional detail to reinforce the idea of how a legend evolves over time. Students take other legends or tall tales and do additional study on "Facts and Fiction."

- Students explore why legendary characters evolve and their role in culture.

Struggling

- Students will have five to ten minutes at the beginning of the class to review the Howard Pyle book and place sticky notes on pages with details they want to remember. Following the review time, they will turn and talk to a neighbor about the details they remember.
- Provide the students with a two-column graphic organizer showing the Howard Pyle detail on one side of the paper and the research finding on the opposite side.
- Choose websites to aid students in conducting research (and provide access to these websites through web-based bookmarking tools).

Homework/Assessment

In preparation for Lesson III, instruct the students to review their class notes. Then instruct them to be prepared to share with the rest of the class at least two conflicting facts about the life of King Arthur.

GRADE 5

Having built an elementary foundation in reading, writing, literature, history, and science, fifth-grade students are ready to start tackling complex literature and ideas. The fifth-grade units present a series of ideas related to the life of the mind: play, invention, clues, conflict, exploration, and coming of age. In the unit on playing with words, students explore the delight of literary language, exemplified in works such as Richard Wilbur's *The Disappearing Alphabet* and William Blake's "The Echoing Green." This leads into a unit on inventive thinking, where students learn about scientific, artistic, musical, and literary inventors. As the year progresses, students learn how literature can provide insight into culture and history. The units provide many connections with history, science, and the arts; students listen to Renaissance music, examine art from the Civil War, and consider how illustrations contribute to a text. While building vocabulary and learning multiple meanings of words, students begin to study etymology, thus gaining insight into the relationships among languages. Students develop their writing within many genres: reflective essays, reports, journals, stories, responses to literary and artistic works, and more. In their essays, they are able to articulate a central idea and illustrate it with examples, integrate information from several texts, and discuss literary themes. As they continue to learn grammatical concepts and refine their style, students at this level should demonstrate some command of Standard English grammar and usage. By the end of fifth grade, students are ready for deeper study of literature and the origins of words.

Standards Checklist for Grade Five

Standard	Unit 1	Unit 2	Unit 3	Unit 4	Unit 5	Unit 6	Standard	Unit 1	Unit 2	Unit 3	Unit 4	Unit 5	Unit 6
Reading—Literature							9b	A	A	A	A	A	A
1		A	FA	A	A		10						
2	FA	A		A	A	A	Speaking and Listening						
3		A		A	A	FA	1	FA	FA	A	A	A	A
4	A	A		A	A		1a	FA	A	A	A	A	A
5					FA		1b	FA	A	A	A	A	A
6			A	FA		A	1c		FA	A	A	A	A
7	A				FA	A	1d		FA	A	A	A	A
8 n/a							2					FA	A
9		FA	A	A		A	3			FA	A	A	
10						A	4		A		FA		A
Reading—Informational Text							5		A		A	A	FA
1	FA		FA				6					A	A
2	A	FA				A	Language						
3	A	A		FA		A	1	A	FA	FA	A	A	A
4	F	A					1a	A	FA	A	A	A	A
5					FA		1b	A	FA	A	A	A	A
6	A	A	A	A		FA	1c	A	A	FA	A	A	A
7			FA	A		A	1d	A	A	FA	A	A	A
8			A		FA		1e	A	A		A	A	A
9	A	FA		A			2	A	A		A	A	A
10						A	2a	A	A	A	A	A	A
Writing							2b	A	A	A	A	A	A
1		A	FA			A	2c	A	A		A	A	A
1a		A	A			A	2d	A	A		A	A	A
1b		A	A			A	2e	A	A		A	A	A
1c		A	A			A	3	A	A		A	A	FA
1d		A	A			A	3a	A	A		A	A	FA
2		FA	A	A		A	3b	A	A		A	A	FA
2a		A	A	A		A	4	A	A	FA	FA	A	A
2b		A	A	A		A	4a	A	A	A	A	A	A
2c		A	A	A		A	4b	A	A	A	FA	A	A
2d		A	A	A		A	4c	A	A	FA	A	A	A
2e		A	A	A		A	5	FA			A	FA	
3	A			FA	FA	A	5a	A			A	A	
3a	A			A	A	A	5b	A			A	A	
3b	A			A	A	A	5c	A			A	A	
3c	A			A	A	A	6						A
3d	A			A	A	A	Reading Foundations						
3e	A			A	A	A	1 n/a						
4	A	A	A	A	A	A	2 n/a						
5	A	A			FA		3	FA					
6	A		A			FA	3a	A					
7	FA	A	A	A	A	A	4		F	F	FA	FA	FA
8			A	A		FA	4a				FA		A
9	A	A	A	A	A	A	4b		FA	A	A	A	A
9a	A	A	A	A	A	A	4c			FA	A	A	A

F = Focus Standards; A = Activity/Assessment

Playing with Words

This four-week unit encourages students to experiment with language and to explore their personal writing style.

ESSENTIAL QUESTION

? Why (and how) do we play with language?

OVERVIEW

Reading both spoonerisms and classic poetry provides students a chance to explore and appreciate language. Students bring in a book about an important figure, such as an artist or an inventor, as a springboard for writing about their own interests and for researching famous scientists. Students explore word origins, compare literal and figurative language, and present a poem they have written. Students write an opinion essay in response to the essential question.

FOCUS STANDARDS

These Focus Standards have been selected for the unit from the Common Core State Standards.

RL.5.2: Determine a theme of a story, drama, or poem from details in the text, including how characters in a story or drama respond to challenges or how the speaker in a poem reflects upon a topic; summarize the text.

RI.5.1: Quote accurately from a text when explaining what the text says explicitly and when drawing inferences from the text.

RI.5.4: Determine the meaning of general academic and domain-specific words and phrases in a text relevant to a grade 5 topic or subject area.

RF.5.3: Know and apply grade-level phonics and word analysis skills in decoding words.

RF.5.3(a): Use combined knowledge of all letter-sound correspondences, syllabication patterns, and morphology (e.g., roots and affixes) to read accurately unfamiliar multisyllabic words in context and out of context.

W.5.7: Conduct short research projects that use several sources to build knowledge through investigation of different aspects of a topic.

SL.5.1: Engage effectively in a range of collaborative discussions (one-on-one, in groups, and teacher-led) on grade 5 topics and texts, building on others' ideas and expressing their own clearly.

SL.5.1(a): Come to discussions prepared, having read or studied required material; explicitly draw on that preparation and other information known about the topic to explore ideas under discussion.

SL.5.1(b): Follow agreed-upon rules for discussions and carry out assigned roles.

L.5.5: Demonstrate understanding of figurative language, word relationships, and nuances in word meanings.

SUGGESTED STUDENT OBJECTIVES

- Conduct research on people of interest (e.g., notable scientists), selecting and citing the most relevant and useful information gathered, and making a plan for presenting your findings.
- Devise ways to present research using available digital resources (i.e., multimedia presentations); present findings to the class or to a wider audience.
- Apply understanding of poetic devices (e.g., figurative language), word relationships, and nuances in word meanings in one's own writing of original poems.
- Develop an opinion about authors' use of figurative language and present it in an opinion essay.

SUGGESTED WORKS

(E) indicates a CCSS exemplar text; (EA) indicates a text from a writer with other works identified as exemplars.

LITERARY TEXTS

Stories

- *The Disappearing Alphabet* (Richard Wilbur and David Diaz)
- *The King Who Rained* (Fred Gwynne)
- *Baseball Saved Us* (Ken Mochizuki)
- *My Teacher Likes to Say* (Denise Brennan-Nelson)
- *In a Pickle and Other Funny Idioms* or *Mad as a Wet Hen! and Other Funny Idioms* (Marvin Terban)
- *What Are You Figuring Now? A Story about Benjamin Banneker* (Creative Minds Biography) (Jeri Ferris)
- *A Picture Book of George Washington Carver* (Picture Book Biography) (David Adler and Dan Brown)
- *What's the Big Idea, Ben Franklin?* (Jean Fritz)

Stories (Read Aloud)

- *The Phantom Tollbooth* (Norton Juster and Jules Feiffer)

Poems

- "Casey at the Bat" (Ernest Lawrence Thayer) (E)
- *Joyful Noise: Poems for Two Voices* (Paul Fleischman and Eric Beddows)
- "The Echoing Green" (William Blake) (E)

- "Little Red Riding Hood and the Wolf" (Roald Dahl) (E)
- "Eletelephony" (Laura Richards)
- "My Shadow" (Robert Louis Stevenson)
- *Runny Babbit: A Billy Sook* (Shel Silverstein)
- *Carver: A Life in Poems* (Marilyn Nelson)

Poems (Read Aloud)

- *The Tree is Older than You Are: A Bilingual Gathering of Poems & Stories from Mexico with Paintings by Mexican Artists* (Naomi Shihab Nye)

INFORMATIONAL TEXTS

Biographies

- *Tales of Famous Americans* (Peter and Connie Roop)
- *Who Was Thomas Alva Edison?* (Margaret Frith, John O'Brien, and Nancy Harrison)
- *In Their Own Words: Thomas Edison* (George Sullivan)
- *Who Was Albert Einstein?* (Jess M. Brallier and Robert Andrew Parker)
- *Alexander Graham Bell: An Inventive Life* (Snapshots: Images of People and Places in History) (Elizabeth MacLeod)
- *Amelia to Zora: Twenty-Six Women Who Changed the World* (Cynthia Chin-Lee, Megan Halsey, and Sean Addy)
- *The World at His Fingertips: A Story about Louis Braille* (Creative Minds Biographies) (Barbara O'Connor and Rochelle Draper)
- *John Muir: Young Naturalist* (Childhood of Famous Americans) (Montrew Dunham)
- *Rachel Carson: Pioneer of Ecology* (Women of Our Time) (Kathleen V. Kudlinski)
- *We Are the Ship: The Story of Negro League Baseball* (Kadir Nelson) (E)
- *Who Was Jackie Robinson?* (Gail Herman, Nancy Harrison, and John O'Brien)
- *Meet the Authors and Illustrators Volume 1: 60 Creators of Favorite Children's Books Talk About Their Work (Grades K–6)* (Deborah Kovacs and James Preller)
- *Who Was William Shakespeare?* (Celeste Mannis)
- *Who Was Dr. Seuss?* (Janet Pascal and Nancy Harrison)
- *Who Was Pablo Picasso?* (True Kelley)
- *Visual and Performing Artists* (Women in Profile) (Shaun Hunter)
- *Who Was Louis Armstrong?* (Yona Zeblis McDonough, John O'Brien, and Nancy Harrison)
- *Musicians* (Women in Profile) (Leslie Strudwick)

Reference

- *Scholastic Dictionary of Idioms* (Revised) (Marvin Terban)

ART, MUSIC, AND MEDIA

Art

- Joseph Cornell, *L'Egypte de Mlle Cleo de Merode, cours élémentaire d'histoire naturelle* (1940)
- Joseph Cornell, *Object (Roses des Vents)* (1942–1953)
- Joseph Cornell, *Cassiopeia 1* (1960)
- Joseph Cornell, *Untitled (Solar Set)* (1956–1958)

Music and Songs

- Benjamin Britten, *The Young Person's Guide to the Orchestra, Opus 34* (1946)
- Jack Norworth, "Take Me Out to the Ballgame" (1908)

Media

- Bud Abbott and Lou Costello, "Who's on First?" (c. 1936)

SAMPLE ACTIVITIES AND ASSESSMENTS

1. RESEARCH/BIO-POEM

Read all you can about an inventor, scientist, author, poet, illustrator, artist, sports figure, or musician who made a historic contribution to their field. To select the most relevant and useful information, make a chart in your journal that includes the following open-ended research questions:

- Name of your person
- Where he/she lived
- When he/she lived
- What did he/she do that made him/her famous?
- What are some additional facts you found interesting?

Design a plan for your informational search. After finishing this research, create a bio-poem based on the person you chose. Make sure you can explain why you chose the words you put into the bio-poem, and create a digital presentation of both. (RI.5.1, W.5.6, W.5.7, L.5.1a)

2. RESEARCH AND INFORMATIVE/EXPLANATORY WRITING

Since you and your classmates are reading and researching different scientists and inventors, keep track of information in categories similar to those in your journal (listed in Activity 1). After taking notes in your journal, select the most relevant and useful information gathered and make a plan for presenting your findings in a short report that is logically ordered and cites at least two sources of information. Edit your writing for correct use of conjunctions, prepositions, and interjections. Your teacher may ask you to publish your report and insert a picture of the person from the web. (RI.5.1, RI.5.2, RI.5.3, W.5.7, L.5.1a)

3. CLASS DISCUSSION

How are the scientists and inventors you've read about similar? How are they different? How and why do scientists and inventors "play"? (SL.5.1a,b, RI.5.9)

4. CLASS DISCUSSION

Compare and contrast the presentation of a topic in two different formats, such as baseball in "Casey at the Bat" (Ernest Lawrence Thayer) to *We Are the Ship: The Story of Negro League Baseball* (Kadir Nelson), drawing on specific details from the text. Your teacher may ask you to write your own response in your journal, and share it with a partner before or during the class discussion. (RL.5.2, SL.5.1a,b)

5. POETIC DEVICES

Not only do poets use a variety of forms, rhyme schemes, and meters, but they use specific devices to enliven their poems and reveal their themes. Find examples of similes, metaphors, alliteration, and onomatopoeia in poems from this unit, and mark them with coded sticky notes. Create a T-chart in your journal that lists the poetic devices and includes examples of each. Try to write your own poem that uses at least two of the devices found. If you write a poem with a partner, use a shared spreadsheet so you can work collaboratively on it. (RL.5.4, L.5.5, W.5.4)

6. NARRATIVE WRITING

Explore your own style of writing. Write your own humorous story or poem in which you incorporate figurative language or idioms learned. Share it with a classmate. Ask your classmate what he/she thinks would improve your writing. (L.5.5, W.5.4, W.5.5)

7. DRAMATIZATION/FLUENCY

Choose a poem, such as one from the anthology *Joyful Noise* (Paul Fleischman and Eric Beddows), to memorize and/recite with a classmate. After the performance, discuss specific passages and poetic devices that made the poem come alive. Record the readings using a video camera for future reference and to see how your fluency improves during the course of the year. (RF.5.3a)

8. CREATE A CLASS BOOK

Illustrate the literal and figurative meaning of an idiom from a text such as *The King Who Rained* (Fred Gwynne). We will compile these illustrations into a class book to share with younger students. Try to use phrases learned in your daily writing and speaking as well. Your teacher may ask you to create a slide of your idiom, including scanned illustrations or relevant photos from the Internet, before assembling them into a class book (either electronic or in print). (L.5.5b)

9. WORD STUDY

As an individual and as a class, keep an index card file of words and phrases learned from the stories and poems in this unit, especially homonyms (e.g., saw (noun)/saw (past participle of the verb "to see"; bat (the rodent)/bat (the baseball implement) and homophones, (i.e., sea/see; weather, whether). Keeping the words on index cards will help you when you sort words by prefix, suffix, root words, meaning, spelling feature, etc. (*Note:* This will be an ongoing activity all year long.) (L.5.4a, RI.5.6)

10. LISTENING/MUSICAL APPRECIATION

Listen to Benjamin Britten's *The Young Person's Guide to the Orchestra* as a class. Discuss how the ideas of "theme and variations" are expressed through music. As a class, choose a common topic about which to write, and then anyone who is interested may share their draft with the class. Discuss the similarities and differences in writing, just as "themes and variations" exist in music. (SL.5.1a,b)

11. OPINION ESSAY

Write an opinion essay response to the essential question ("Why [and how] do we play with language?"). Your teacher may give you the opportunity to "Give one, get one" before writing your response. Discuss at least three examples of figurative language or other word play (e.g., the inclusion in a poem of words with multiple meanings). Edit your writing for correct use of conjunctions, prepositions, and interjections before sharing with your teacher. Your teacher may ask you to type your essay and respond to a poll about the unit on the classroom blog. (W.5.5, W.5.7, W.5.9a,b, L.5.1a)

12. GRAMMAR AND USAGE

Your teacher will teach mini-lessons on the individual language standards. For example, he/she will explain what conjunctions are. Then, he/she will give you a set of three sentences to combine into one thought [i.e., (1) The girl walked to school. (2) The girl is named Jesse. (3) The girl wore a yellow skirt.] Using conjunctions, work with a partner to combine the three sentences. Select a piece of your own writing, circle shorter sentences, and try to use conjunctions to make longer, more interesting sentences. (L.5.1a)

13. MECHANICS/GRAMMAR WALL

As a class, create a Mechanics/Grammar bulletin board where, throughout the year, you will add to a checklist of editing topics as they are taught through targeted mini-lessons (e.g., proper use of punctuation, capitalization). Once skills are taught in a mini-lesson and listed on the bulletin board, you are expected to edit your work for the elements before publication. (L.5.1, L.5.2, L.5.3)

14. VOCABULARY/WORD WALL

As a class, create a Vocabulary Word Wall bulletin board where, throughout the year, you will add and sort words as you learn them in each unit of study. (L.5.4)

15. ART/CLASS DISCUSSION

Do visual artists "play" with materials the way other artists do? Examine the works of Joseph Cornell. This early twentieth-century American artist spent his life collecting and arranging objects into imaginative and whimsical works. What do you notice about his assemblages? What types of objects did he use? Are Cornell's boxes like visual poems? What questions are you left with once you look at each box? (SL.5.1)

16. ART/WRITING

The Joseph Cornell boxes are carefully arranged to let your eye wander and find hidden objects. Cornell has created an assemblage, or a three-dimensional artistic composition made out of found objects. If you could create an assemblage box in the manner of Cornell, what would you put inside? Would you hide objects in drawers and small spaces, or let your viewer see everything? Write a short narrative describing your process for creating an assemblage. (W.5.3, W.5.4)

ADDITIONAL RESOURCES

- *David Weisner's Book June 29, 1999, Showcases This Day* (ReadWriteThink) (RL.5.7)
- *Alliteration All Around* (ReadWriteThink) (RL.5.4)
- *Noah Webster Published His American Dictionary of the English Language in 1828* (ReadWriteThink) (L.5.4a,b,c)
- Spelling Patterns, "Go Fish" Card Game (ReadWriteThink) (L.5.4a,b,c)
- *Elizabeth Blackwell Became the First Woman to Earn a MD Degree in 1849* (ReadWriteThink) (RI.5.9)
- *Biographies for Children* (Pitara Kids Network)
- *All About Adolescent Literacy* (AdLit.Org)
- *Great People of the 20th Century* (Oracle ThinkQuest, By Students, For Students)
- "Give One Get One" (RRISD Math Team)

TERMINOLOGY

Biography

Dialogue

Homonym

Homophone

Idiom/cliché

Literal and figurative language

Poetic devices: rhyme scheme, meter, stanza, metaphors,

similes, alliteration, onomatopoeia

Spoonerism

Theme (and variation)

MAKING INTERDISCIPLINARY CONNECTIONS

This unit teaches:

Art: assemblage, Joseph Cornell

Science: Biographies (e.g., Albert Einstein, Alexander Graham Bell) and their (respective) related field of study (e.g., physics)

This unit could be extended to teach:

Science: Scientists and the type of science to which they contributed (e.g., ecology, biology, chemistry, astronomy, geology, meteorology, electricity, etc.)

History/Geography: Famous people throughout history (e.g., How have these people changed our world? What makes them famous?)

Physical Education: Baseball (i.e., rules and history)

Grade Five, Unit One Sample Lesson Plan

We Are the Ship: The Story of Negro League Baseball by Kadir Nelson

In this series of six lessons, students read *We Are the Ship: The Story of Negro League Baseball* by Kadir Nelson, and they:

> Explore the story of the Negro League along with Kadir Nelson (RI.5.2, RI.5.5)
>
> Conduct research that expands their appreciation of the league and its players (RI.5.9, W.5.7, SL.5.1)
>
> Publish their findings (W.5.2, W.5.4, W.5.5, W.5.7)

Summary

Lesson I/II: *We Are the Ship*

Identify and contextualize the term *Negro* (L.5.4)

Note the "nine-inning" format of the book (RI.5.5)

Examine the use of first-person narration (RL.5.6)

Explore Kadir Nelson's depiction of the Negro League (RI.5.2, RI.5.5)

Lesson III/IV: Investigating the Negro League

Expand the study of the Negro League (RI.5.7, RI.5.9)

Use online and library resources (RI.5.7, RI.5.9)

Extract necessary information (RI.5.7, RI.5.9)

Establish categories for investigation (RI.5.7, RI.5.9)

Record findings (W.5.8)

Identify areas for further research (SL.5.1)

Generate discussion of findings (SL.5.1)

Probe tensions (SL.5.1)

Note emerging themes (SL.5.1)

Lesson V/VI: Reporting the Story of the Negro League

Record the findings of the research (RI.5.9, W.5.7, SL.5.1)

Map out the presentation of the research (RI.5.9, W.5.7)

Coherently articulate findings (RI.5.9, SL.5.1)

Challenge conventions (W.5.6)

Produce a work for publication (W.5.2, W.5.4, W.5.5, W.5.7)

Publish research (W.5.7)

Lesson V/VI: Reporting the Story of the Negro League

Objectives

Record the findings of the research (RI.5.9, W.5.7, SL.5.1)

Map out the presentation of the research (RI.5.9, W.5.7)

Coherently articulate findings (RI.5.9, SL.5.1)

Challenge conventions (W.5.6)

Produce a work for publication (W.5.2, W.5.4, W.5.5, W.5.7)

Publish research (W.5.7)

(The class selects a format for publication: a newspaper; a magazine; a yearbook; a scrapbook; or a series of posters. Each of these works well for this type of collective effort.)

Required Materials

☐ Research material
☐ Computers
☐ Markers, glue, and paper

Procedures

1. Lead-In:
   Introduce the collective class project.
2. Step by Step:
   a. Students form groups based on the categories that were established in earlier lessons. They review the material they already have and begin to consider the type of presentation that is most suitable for their work (e.g., an article, a set of illustrations, letters, or photographs).
   b. Group work continues. Students write and edit articles, draw illustrations, and select photographs.
   c. Students put together the various components of the project. Student editors begin the process of assembling the material.
3. Closure:
   The students will share projects with each other, which gives them a chance to appreciate their collective efforts. Part of the class conversation should include reflection upon the experience and what they have learned about the Negro League.

Differentiation

Advanced

- If the students are good editors, have them peer edit the articles written by classmates.
- Students can choose a more challenging form of presentation (e.g., setting up a web page, electronic slides, or wiki where student presentations can be collected).
- Students should find additional modern-day resources to discuss how the current game of baseball is similar to or different from earlier years of baseball (i.e., *Baseball Saved Us* by Ken Mochizuki or *A Strong Right Arm* by Michelle Green).

Struggling

- Work with a small group in order to provide more intensive support. Students divide the categories for research tasks among the group members. Partners record their findings on index cards to facilitate sharing and sorting of information.
- Students may select a set of illustrations to record on a podcast to demonstrate understanding of the topic, discussing the illustrations prior to writing their article.
- Using a shared online document or a document camera, students collaboratively write their article. Print out the first draft for students to edit individually before editing as a group.

Homework/Assessment
N/A

Grade 5 ▶ *Unit 2*

Renaissance Thinking

This six-week unit focuses on the research process, as well as the creative and critical thinking used by writers, inventors, and famous people from the Renaissance and beyond.

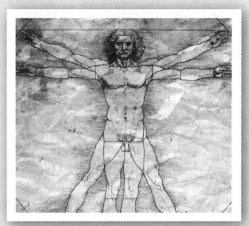

ESSENTIAL QUESTION

? How does creativity change the world?

OVERVIEW

Through the pairing of fiction and nonfiction books on related topics, this unit builds on students' understanding of the Renaissance as a period of new learning and discovery. This unit is particularly effective for teaching the research process, since the people involved or the historical context of particular inventions are most likely new to students. Students publish and present their research papers to the class. Students then find commonalities among inventors and innovators, share these insights in group discussions, and use this information as a springboard for their own innovative and creative writing. This unit sets in motion the reading, writing, researching, and word analysis processes that will be a hallmark of their fifth-grade year. This unit ends with an informative/explanatory essay in response to the essential question.

FOCUS STANDARDS

These Focus Standards have been selected for the unit from the Common Core State Standards.

RL.5.9: Compare and contrast stories in the same genre (e.g., mysteries and adventure stories) on their approaches to similar themes and topics.

RI.5.2: Determine two or more main ideas of a text and explain how they are supported by key details; summarize the text.

RI.5.9: Integrate information from several texts on the same topic in order to write or speak about the subject knowledgably.

RF.5.4: Read with sufficient accuracy and fluency to support comprehension.

RF.5.4(b): Read on-level prose and poetry orally with accuracy, appropriate rate, and expression on successive readings.

W.5.2: Write informative/explanatory texts to examine a topic and convey ideas and information clearly.

SL.5.1: Engage effectively in a range of collaborative discussions (one-on-one, group, and teacher-led) on grade 5 topics and texts, building on others' ideas and expressing their own ideas clearly.

SL.5.1(c): Pose and respond to specific questions by making comments that contribute to the discussion and elaborate on the remarks of others.

SL.5.1(d): Review the key ideas expressed and draw conclusions in light of information and knowledge gained from the discussions.

L.5.1: Demonstrate command of the conventions of Standard English grammar and usage when writing or speaking.

L.5.1(a): Explain the function of conjunctions, prepositions, and interjections in general and their function in particular sentences.

L.5.1(b): Form and use the perfect (e.g., *I had walked; I have walked; I will have walked*) verb tenses.

SUGGESTED STUDENT OBJECTIVES

- Read and compare information learned from fiction and nonfiction books about an inventor of choice (e.g., *Leonardo: Beautiful Dreamer* by Robert Byrd and *The Usborne Book of Inventors from DaVinci to Biro* by Struan Reid, Patricia Fara, and Ross Watton).
- Explain the characteristics of historical fiction.
- Compare and contrast historical fiction stories using those characteristics as a guide.
- Describe the value of primary source documents when studying a historical period, such as the Renaissance (e.g., Leonardo's notebook).
- Conduct research and develop/present a multimedia presentation that integrates information from more than one source (e.g., on an inventor of choice); anticipate and respond to questions from classmates.
- Explain the historical context surrounding an invention of choice, based on information gathered from multiple print or digital sources.
- Define related words and identify their parts of speech (e.g., *inventor, invention, venue, innovator, innovative, innovate, new*, etc.).

SUGGESTED WORKS

(E) indicates a CCSS exemplar text; (EA) indicates a text from a writer with other works identified as exemplars.

LITERARY TEXTS

Stories

- *Leonardo: Beautiful Dreamer* (Robert Byrd)
- *Leonardo da Vinci* (Diane Stanley)
- *Starry Messenger: Galileo Galilei* (Peter Sis)
- *The Invention of Hugo Cabret* (Brian Selznick) (*Note:* This book illustrates the creative process beautifully, but is not set in the Renaissance.)
- *Midnight Magic* (Avi)

- *Fine Print: A Story about Johann Gutenberg* (Creative Minds) (Joann Johansen Burch and Kent Alan Aldrich)
- *The Apprentice* (Pilar Molina Llorente and Juan Ramon Alonso)
- *The Children's Shakespeare* (Edith Nesbit and Rolf Klep)

Poems

- "Time" (Valerie Bloom)
- Riddles from Chapter Five, "Riddles in the Dark," *The Hobbit* (J.R.R. Tolkien)

INFORMATIONAL TEXTS

Informational Books

- *Toys! Amazing Stories Behind Some Great Inventions* (Don L. Wulffson and Laurie Keller) (E)
- *The New How Things Work* (David Macaulay and Neil Ardley)
- *So You Want to be an Inventor?* (Judith St. George and David Small)
- *The Usborne Book of Inventors from Da Vinci to Biro* (Struan Reid, Patricia Fara, and Ross Watton)
- *Women Inventors* (series) (Jean F. Blashfield)
- *Telescopes: The New Book of Knowledge* (Scholastic) (Colin A. Ronan) (E)
- *About Time: A First Look at Time and Clocks* (Bruce Koscielniak) (E)
- *Where Do You Get Your Ideas? Favorite Authors Reveal Their Writing Secrets* (Sandy Asher and Susan Hellard)
- *Amazing Leonardo da Vinci Inventions You Can Build Yourself* (Build It Yourself Series) (Maxine Anderson)
- *Leonardo da Vinci: A Nonfiction Companion to Monday with a Mad Genius* (Magic Tree House Research Guide) (Mary Pope Osborne, Natalie Pope Boyce, and Sal Murdocca)
- *Michelangelo* (Getting to Know the World's Greatest Artists) (Mike Venezia)
- *Outrageous Women of the Renaissance* (Vicki Leon)
- *Science in the Renaissance* (Brendan January)
- *Science in the Renaissance* (Renaissance World) (Lisa Mullins)
- *Renaissance Artists Who Inspired the World* (Explore the Ages) (Gregory Blanch and Roberta Stathis)
- *About Time: First Look at Time and Clocks* (Bruce Koscielniak)
- *The Renaissance* (History Opens Windows) (Jane Shuter)
- *You Wouldn't Want to Be Mary Queen of Scots: A Ruler Who Really Lost Her Head* (Fiona MacDonald and David Antram)
- *The Renaissance* (Understanding People in the Past) (Mary Quigley)

ART, MUSIC, AND MEDIA

Art

- Leonardo da Vinci, *Mona Lisa* (c. 1503–1506)
- Michelangelo, *Sistine Chapel Ceiling* (1508–1512)
- Michelangelo, *Dome of St. Peter's Basilica* (1506–1626)
- Raphael, *School of Athens* (1510–1511)

- Donatello, *St. George* (c. 1416)
- Pieter Bruegel, *Peasant Wedding* (1567)
- Leonardo da Vinci, *The Last Supper* (1495–1498)

Music and Songs

- Traditional, possibly Henry VIII of England, "Greensleeves" (1580)
- Canadian Brass, "English Renaissance Music"
- The King's Singers, *Madrigals*

SAMPLE ACTIVITIES AND ASSESSMENTS

1. LITERATURE RESPONSE

Works of historical fiction are set in the past, but have fictional characters or fictional elements as well. As a class, compare and contrast various historical fiction stories. In order to prepare for class discussions, create a T-chart in your journal where you take notes about people, places, or events that you believe are represented accurately; and about people, places, or events that you believe are fictional. Be sure to include in your notes the page number and book title for each example so you can refer back to the text. (RL.5.1, RL.5.9)

2. LITERATURE RESPONSE

In your journal, create a character map of the main character in the historical novel you are reading. Show how the character changes (or develops) over the course of the text. Compare your character with one chosen by a classmate. How are the characters similar? How are they different? (RL.5.2, RL.5.3)

3. INFORMATIONAL TEXT GRAPHIC ORGANIZER

As a class, keep a chart about the creative and inventive people read about; the chart will include the following information/research questions:

- Name of your person
- Where he/she lived
- When he/she lived
- What did he/she do that made him/her famous?
- What are some additional facts you found interesting?
- What adjectives would you use to describe this person? Why?

    Your teacher may ask you to write your own responses in your journal and share them with a partner before each section of the class chart is filled in. Be sure to include page numbers and the title of the book so you can refer back to the text if needed. Your teacher may also ask you to type your information into a shared spreadsheet so that you can collaboratively work on it as a class. (RI.5.4, RL.5.9)

4. CLASS DISCUSSION

How would you define creative/inventive thinkers? What are the common characteristics of the creative/inventive thinkers studied? (SL.5.1a, b, RI.5.9)

5. CLASS DISCUSSION

Read and compare what you learn about Leonardo da Vinci from fiction and nonfiction text (e.g., *Leonardo: Beautiful Dreamer* by Robert Byrd and *The Usborne Book of Inventors from DaVinci to Biro* by Struan Reid, Patricia Fara, and Ross Watton). How does knowing the historical information enhance your understanding of the fictional story? (RL.5.9, SL.5.1)

6. RESEARCH AND INFORMATIVE/EXPLANATORY WRITING (MULTIMEDIA PRESENTATION)

Using the Internet, biographies, and informational texts, read all you can about an inventor. As a class, create a timeline of the inventors studied in order to understand where each inventor "lived" chronologically in history. Write a short, informative/explanatory essay about an inventor of choice that answers the question "How is necessity the mother of invention?" Your response should be a well-developed essay with three sources of information cited. Edit your writing for form and use of the perfect tenses (see Standards for more details). Your teacher may give you the option of adding a multimedia component to your paper—either a slide presentation to highlight key points, a film, or a podcast. Publish both the paper and the digital presentation, and present them to the class. Anticipate and respond to questions from classmates. (RI.5.2, RI.5.3, RI.5.9, W.5.2, RF.5.4b, L.5.1a,b)

7. JOURNAL WRITING

Inventors are creative people who turn their ideas into reality. Leonardo da Vinci is one of many famous inventors who kept notebooks of ideas. Look at one of his original notebooks online. Start a section of your writing journal for ideas. What ideas for inventions do *you* have? Create lists and draw and label pictures. Share your ideas with a classmate to strengthen your ideas. (W.5.5, W.5.9b)

8. WORD STUDY

As an individual and as a class, keep an index card file of words studied (e.g., *Renaissance, inventiveness, inventor, innovation, creativity, creation,* etc.). Keeping the words on index cards will help you when you sort words by prefix, suffix, root words, meaning, spelling feature, and so on. How do the root words help you understand the meaning of the words? (*Note:* This will be an ongoing activity all year long.) You may also be asked to work in groups to create semantic maps of the words *creativity* and *innovation* in order to explore your understanding of these words. (RI.5.6, L.5.4a)

9. LISTENING/MUSICAL APPRECIATION

Listen to music from the Renaissance (see preceding Art, Music, and Media section). How does this music reflect the time period in which it was written? How is it similar to and different from music you listen to today? Discuss as a class. (SL.5.1a,b)

10. ART/ROLE PLAYING/WRITING

To help you appreciate, in some small part, the challenges that Michelangelo faced in painting the ceiling of the Sistine Chapel, tape paper under your desk and then draw a detailed picture for ten minutes without stopping. After ten minutes, switch from pencil to paint. With your classmates, discuss the experience, and how it helps you to appreciate the amount of work that went into creating the Sistine Chapel ceiling. Finally, write in your journal about what it must have been like for Michelangelo to tackle a project that took years to complete in difficult conditions. (SL.5.1a,b, W.5.1a,b,c,d,e,f)

11. CLASS DISCUSSION

Usually pictures enhance a story, but sometimes pictures are *part* of the story, such as in *The Invention of Hugo Cabret* by Brian Selznick. How do pictures tell a story? Justify your answer by citing specific pages from the text during class discussion. (SL.5.1, SL.5.5)

12. INFORMATIVE/EXPLANATORY ESSAY

Write an informative/explanatory essay in response to the essential question ("How has inventive thinking, as revealed in fiction and nonfiction, changed our world?"). Give at least three reasons/

examples. Your teacher may give you the opportunity to "Give one, get one" before writing your response. Edit your writing for form and use of the perfect tense (see Standards for more details) before sharing with your teacher. Your teacher may ask you to type your essay and respond to a poll about the unit on the classroom blog. (W.5.7, W5.9.a,b, SL.5.4, L.5.1a,b)

13. GRAMMAR AND USAGE

Your teacher will teach mini-lessons on the individual language standards. For example, he/she will teach the class about the form and use of the perfect tense, and then you will practice some cloze activities as a class: (i.e., I _____ walking my dog down the street before you came home. I _____ walking my dog down the street in an hour.) Next, your teacher will give you the start of a sentence (I had ... I have ... I will have ...) and you will have the opportunity to finish the sentence with a partner. Select a piece of your own writing, find examples of the perfect tense, and ensure that you have used the correct forms. (L.5.1c)

14. MECHANICS/GRAMMAR WALL

As a class, continue adding to the Mechanics/Grammar bulletin board started in Unit One. Remember— once skills are taught in a mini-lesson and listed on the bulletin board, you are expected to edit your work for these elements before publication. (L.5.1, L.5.2, L.5.3)

15. VOCABULARY/WORD WALL

As a class, continue adding to the Vocabulary Word Wall bulletin board where, throughout the year, you will add and sort words as you learn them in each unit of study. (L.5.4)

16. ART/CLASS DISCUSSION

Compare Raphael's *School of Athens* with da Vinci's *The Last Supper*. How does each artist create a narrative? Discuss the idea of composition—how does the artist organize the painting and the story it tells? Photocopy both images and have students draw on the pages, grouping the characters. Discover the underlying structure of each work and compare them. Identify the central figures in each story. Examine the way each artist chose to focus viewer's attention on those figures and then move the eye around the scene. What details did the artists include that help tell their stories? (SL.5.1, SL.5.5)

17. ART/CLASS DISCUSSION

Compare da Vinci's *Mona Lisa* and Donatello's *St. George*. How has the artist captured the subject's essence in this portrait? What is different between the two? Both portraits are believed to be of real people. How did each artist seem to take this into consideration in their portrayal? (SL.5.1)

ADDITIONAL RESOURCES

- *Write a Gem of a Poem* (ReadWriteThink) (RL.5.4, W.5.4)
- *Great American Inventors: Using Nonfiction to Learn About Technology Inventions* (ReadWriteThink) (RI.5.9)
- *Research Building Blocks: "Organize This!"* (ReadWriteThink) (RI.5.9)
- *Research Building Blocks: Skim, Scan, and Scroll* (ReadWriteThink) (RI.5.9)
- *Famous Inventors: A to Z* (About.Com)
- Leonardo da Vinci Notebooks (British Library)
- "Give One Get One" (RRISD Math Team)

TERMINOLOGY

Bibliography	Fiction	Paraphrase
Character development	Nonfiction	Primary source documents

MAKING INTERDISCIPLINARY CONNECTIONS

This unit teaches:

Science: Inventors through various time periods (e.g., Galileo and his contributions to astronomy; Thomas Edison and his contributions to telecommunications, electricity, and sound recording; Benjamin Banneker and his contributions to astronomy and mathematics); a study of "how things work" (e.g., similar to the information in the book by David Macaulay)

History/Geography: The Renaissance (e.g., a "rebirth" of ideas; patrons of the arts and learning; Leonardo da Vinci and Michelangelo); the Reformation (e.g., Gutenberg; Ptolemaic [earth-centered] vs. sun-centered models of the universe)

Art: Renaissance painting and sculpture, da Vinci, Raphael, Donatello

This unit could be extended to teach:

Science: The Scientific Method; force and motion (e.g., simple machines, etc.); astronomy (e.g., constellations, moon phases, etc.)

Art: Further study of Renaissance art and architecture (e.g. Botticelli, Michelangelo, Brunelleschi)

Grade Five, Unit Two Sample Lesson Plan

About Time: A First Look at Time and Clocks by Bruce Koscielniak

In this series of four lessons, students read *About Time: A First Look at Time and Clocks* by Bruce Koscielniak, and they:

> Explore the concept of time and the inventors of clocks (RI.5.1, RI.5.2, RI.5.5)
>
> Conduct research on inventors and their inventions (RI.5.1, RI.5.2, RI.5.5, RI.5.7, W.5.7, W.5.8)
>
> Present the collected data (RI.5.9, SL.5.2, SL.5.5)

Summary

Lesson I: *About Time: A First Look at Time and Clocks*

Expand understanding of time (RI.5.2, RI.5.3)

Explore early ways of telling time (RI.5.3)

Develop a detailed timeline for the invention of the clock (RI.5.3)

Reflect on the long process that leads inventors to their inventions (SL.5.1, SL.5.2, SL.5.4)

Lesson II: Inventors and Inventions

Examine the list of inventors and their inventions (SL.5.1)

Select an inventor (W.5.5, W.5.8)

Conduct research (RI.5.1, RI.5.2, RI.5.5, RI.5.7, W.5.7, W.5.8)

Review research material (SL.5.1, SL.5.2, SL.5.4, W.5.8)

Lesson III: Preparing to Present Data

Continue research (RI.5.1, RI.5.2, RI.5.5, RI.5.7, W.5.7)

Compose essays based on the data that was collected (W.5.2a,b,c,d,e; W.5.8, W.5.10)

Revise essays (W.5.5)

Draw illustrations of inventions (SL.5.5)

Lesson IV: Inventions Fair

Mount research results onto display boards (SL.5.2, SL.5.5)

Emphasize three sections: (SL.5.5)

Inventor

Invention

Significance in history

Survey peers' work (RI.5.5)

Lesson II: Inventors and Inventions

Objectives

Examine the list of inventors and their inventions (SL.5.1)

Select an inventor (W.5.5, W.5.8)

Conduct research (RI.5.1, RI.5.2, RI.5.5, RI.5.7, W.5.7, W.5.8)

Review research material (SL.5.1, SL.5.2, SL.5.4, W.5.8)

Required Materials

☐ Copies of Renaissance and Elizabethan Inventions and Inventors Timeline

☐ Computers with Internet access

☐ Printer

☐ Notebooks

☐ Pens and pencils

Procedures

1. Lead-In:

Students examine handouts of Renaissance and Elizabethan Inventions and Inventors Timeline

1450: Johannes Gutenberg invents the printing press with movable type in Germany

1510: Leonardo da Vinci designs a horizontal water wheel

1540: Toriano invents a mandolin-playing automaton

1543: John Dee creates a wooden beetle that can fly for an undergraduate production — one of the first robots

1565: Conrad Gesner of Switzerland invents the pencil

1583: Leonard and Thomas Digges invent the telescope

1589: William Lee invents the knitting machine

1590: Dutchmen Hans and Zacharias Janssen invent the compound microscope

1591: Sir John Harington invents the flush toilet in England

1593: Galileo Galilei invents a water thermometer

1609: Galileo Galilei introduces the first telescope to astronomy

Source of list (adapted): http://www.elizabethan-era.org.uk/elizabethan-inventions.htm.

2. Step by Step:

a. In groups of threes, students select an invention to research.

b. The focus of the research is on:

   • A biography of the inventor

   • A map locating the country where the inventor was born

- Data discussing his inventions
- A single important invention
- Illustrations or photographs of his inventions
- The impact of the invention on society

c. Students print informational texts that they select online.

d. Group members divide the research material among themselves. Individuals identify main ideas in the material and take notes.

3. Closure:

At the conclusion of the lesson, the groups reconvene. They share their notes and determine what further research is needed.

Differentiation

Advanced

- Students will create a commercial for an invention studied in the research. Using a musical composition or visual art masterpiece from the era in the commercial will yield extra points. Students will be allowed to create their commercial as an electronic slide presentation, record it using a video camera, or create it as a movie.

Struggling

- Students will work in heterogeneous groups, using a graphic organizer to aid in the research tasks and organization. Students may collaborate on a shared online spreadsheet, if desired.
- Intervene to be sure the student can be successful with his/her assigned part.
- Students may paste selected informational text into a document formatted for "text to speech" or partner with a student willing to read aloud the information.

Homework/Assessment

N/A

Clues to a Culture

This six-week unit focuses on aspects of Native American nations/cultures as revealed through pairings of literature and informational text.

ESSENTIAL QUESTION

? How does literature provide insight into a culture?

OVERVIEW

This unit begins with students collectively defining and discussing the word *culture*. Next, students compare nineteenth-century America from the Ojibway point of view in *The Birchbark House* to depictions in texts such as *Little House on the Prairie* and *If You Were a Pioneer on the Prairie*. In order to glean the similarities and differences across nations, students read trickster stories and informational text; they also listen to music and examine art from a variety of Native American cultures. Class discussions reinforce awareness of how someone's perspective can affect their view of events and people. This unit ends with an informative/explanatory essay in response to the essential question.

FOCUS STANDARDS

These Focus Standards have been selected for the unit from the Common Core State Standards.

RL.5.1: Quote accurately from a text when explaining what the text says explicitly and when drawing inferences from the text.

RI.5.1: Quote accurately from a text when explaining what the text says explicitly and when drawing inferences from the text.

RI.5.7: Draw on information from multiple print or digital sources, demonstrating the ability to locate an answer to a question quickly or to solve a problem efficiently.

RF.5.4: Read with sufficient accuracy and fluency to support comprehension.

RF.5.4(c): Use context to confirm or self-correct word recognition and understanding, rereading as necessary.

W.5.1: Write opinion pieces on topics or texts, supporting a point of view with reasons and information.

SL.5.3: Summarize the points a speaker makes and explain how each claim is supported by reasons and evidence.

L.5.1: Observe conventions of grammar and usage when writing or speaking.

L.5.1(c): Use verb tense to convey various times, sequences, states, and conditions.

L.5.1(d): Recognize and correct inappropriate shifts in verb tense.

L.5.4: Determine or clarify the meaning of unknown and multiple-meaning words and phrases based on grade 5 reading and content, choosing flexibly from a range of strategies.

L.5.4(c): Consult reference materials (e.g., dictionaries, glossaries, thesauruses), both print and digital, to find the pronunciation and determine or clarify the precise meaning of key words and phrases.

SUGGESTED STUDENT OBJECTIVES

- Compare fiction and nonfiction books about a specific topic (e.g., Native American nations during pioneer times in America), quoting accurately from the texts.
- Find similarities and differences in stories (e.g., trickster tales) from various cultures.
- Create a multimedia presentation based on information drawn from various types of sources (e.g., a presentation on a Native American nation of choice based on fiction, nonfiction, art or other media).
- Summarize and evaluate the content and structure of a classmate's presentation, evaluating how well they support their claims.
- Define related words and identify their parts of speech (e.g., *nation, national, nationality, nationwide, culture, cultural, cultivate,* etc.)

SUGGESTED WORKS

(E) indicates a CCSS exemplar text; (EA) indicates a text from a writer with other works identified as exemplars.

LITERARY TEXTS

Note: The list of Native American nations below is illustrative, not comprehensive; please choose a local nation to examine in a similar manner.

Stories
- *The Birchbark House* (Louise Erdrich) (E)
- *Little House on the Prairie* (Laura Ingalls Wilder and Garth Williams) (EA)
- *Knots on a Counting Rope* (John Archambault, Bill Martin Jr., and Ted Rand)
- *Dreamcatcher* (Audrey Osofsky and Ed Young)
- *Walk Two Moons* (Sharon Creech)
- *Guests* (Michael Dorris)
- *A Boy Called Slow* (Joseph Bruchac and Rocco Baviera)
- *Julie of the Wolves* (Jean Craighead George and John Schoenherr)
- *Island of the Blue Dolphins* (Scott O'Dell)
- *Sign of the Beaver* (Elizabeth George Speare)

Trickster Tales

- *Trickster Tales: Forty Folk Stories from Around the World* (World Storytelling) (Josepha Sherman)
- *How Rabbit Tricked Otter: And Other Cherokee Trickster Stories* (Gayle Ross and Murv Jacob)
- *A Ring of Tricksters: Animal Tales from North America, the West Indies, and Africa* (Virginia Hamilton and Barry Moser) (EA)
- *Raven: A Trickster Tale from the Pacific Northwest* (Gerald McDermott)
- *Coyote: A Trickster Tale from the American Southwest* (Gerald McDermott)

Poems

- "Dream Catchers" (Ojibway, Traditional)
- "You are Part of Me" (Cherokee, Lloyd Carl Owle)

INFORMATIONAL TEXTS

Informational Books

- *A History of US: The New Nation, 1789–1850* (Joy Hakim) (E)
- *A History of US: First Americans, Prehistory–1600* (Joy Hakim) (E)
- *If You Were a Pioneer on the Prairie* (If You … Series) (Anne Kamma and James Watling)
- *Black Frontiers: A History of African-American Heroes in the Old West* (Lillian Schlissel)
- *If You Lived with the Cherokees* (If You … Series) (Peter and Connie Roop and Kevin Smith)
- *If You Lived with the Sioux Indians* (If You … Series) (Ann McGovern and Jean Syverud Drew)
- *You Wouldn't Want to Be an American Pioneer! A Wilderness You'd Rather Not Tame* (You Wouldn't Want To … Series) (Jacqueline Morley, David Salariya, and David Antram)
- *The Nez Perce* (True Books) (Stefanie Takacs)

Informational Book (Read Aloud)

- *Sequoyah: The Cherokee Man Who Gave His People Writing* (James Rumford)

Speech

- "I will fight no more forever" (Chief Joseph the Younger, October 5, 1877)

ART, MUSIC, AND MEDIA

Art

Apache

- Edward S. Curtis, *Apache Still Life* (1907)
- Artist unknown, *San Juan, A Mescalero Apache Chief* (no date)
- Noah H. Rose, *View of two Native American Apache women outside their cloth-covered wickiups in a camp in Arizona* (1880)

Hopi

- Wooden Hopi Kachina doll (1925)
- *Hopi Girl with Jar* (no date)
- Edward Curtis, *East Side of Walpi* (1921)

Haida

- Haida mask (1879)
- Bill Hupe, *Dedication Potlach: The Honoring of Ancient Traditions* (2006)
- *Indian Village, Alaska* (artist unknown, 1897)

Music

- Thomas Vennum, *Ojibway Music from Minnesota: A Century of Song for Voice and Drum*

Media

- *Will Fight No More* (video of the speech of Chief Joseph)

SAMPLE ACTIVITIES AND ASSESSMENTS

1. CLASS DISCUSSION

What is meant by the word *culture*? For which elements does one look when learning about a culture? Write your ideas down on a sticky note and "Give one, get one." *(Note:* Answers may include language, social organization, customs/traditions, arts, religion, symbols, etc.) Create a class chart of elements to look for, and look to find examples in texts read during this unit. (SL.5.1)

2. LITERATURE RESPONSE

The Birchbark House by Louise Erdrich is described as a realistic and sympathetic portrayal of a Native American culture during the period of westward expansion. Compare pioneer life as presented from Omakayas's perspective in *The Birchbark House* with Laura's perspective in *Little House on the Prairie* by Laura Ingalls Wilder or *If You Were a Pioneer on the Prairie* by Anne Kamma and James Watling. Choose an event in the story and write about what surprised you the most about Omakayas's experience. (RL.5.1)

3. LITERATURE RESPONSE

The title of Sharon Creech's book *Walk Two Moons* comes from the Native American phrase, "Don't judge a man until you have walked two moons in his moccasins." What have you learned about the Native American nation studied? Turn and talk with a neighbor about this prompt before responding in your journal. (RL.5.1)

4. INFORMATIVE/EXPLANATORY WRITING (AND MULTIMEDIA PRESENTATION)

Read all you can about a Native American nation, drawing on information from multiple print or digital sources. Be sure that the digital and print sources are credible. Use indexes, tables of contents, digital searches, and key words as you work. Use the most relevant and useful information to write an informative/explanatory piece about your nation of choice. Your response should be a well-developed essay with three sources of information cited, including accurate quotations from the texts. Edit your writing for proper verb tenses and punctuation, especially commas (see Standards for more details). Your teacher may give you the option of adding a multimedia component to your paper—either creating an electronic slide presentation to highlight key points or sharing links to music and/or images of the Native American nation of choice. Publish both and present them to the class. Answer questions from classmates about your presentation. (RI.5.1, RI.5.7, RI.5.8, RL.5.1, W.5.2a,b,c,d; RF.5.4b,c, L.5.1a,b,c,d; L.5.2a,b)

5. LITERATURE RESPONSE

Sharon Creech uses sound imagery, often linked to personification, throughout her novel *Walk Two Moons*. Find an example of how these literary techniques were used to increase the feeling of being part of the story, mark it with a sticky note, and share it with a partner. (RF.5.4c)

6. OPINION WRITING

Consider the speech of Chief Joseph the Younger ("I will fight no more forever"). In your opinion, do you think he needed to be consoled or encouraged to go on? Write your position on a sticky note, and your teacher will divide the class based on your position. Share ideas with classmates who are of the same opinion. Then, begin by individually drafting an essay in your journal. Work with classmates to revise your essay, ensuring that it includes accurate quotations from the speech to support your opinion. Edit your writing for verb tense and punctuation, especially commas (see Standards for more details). Publish your essay on a classroom blog to encourage additional conversation. (SL.5.3, W.5.1a,b,c,d; W.5.6, L.5.1a,b,c,d; L.5.2a,b)

7. CLASS DISCUSSION

As a class, discuss how trickster stories can reveal insights into a culture different from your own. What did you learn about the nation from the trickster story you've just read? What does a story/poem reveal about a culture that reading solely from an informational text does not? Write your ideas down in your journal prior to class discussion. (RL.5.9, SL.5.3)

8. CLASS DISCUSSION

Why do tricksters ignore conventional cultural behavior? Why are these characters often personifications and not human? What impact does culture have on the tale? Talk with a classmate to share ideas and then write your favorite ideas down in your journal prior to class discussion. (RL.5.9)

9. WORD STUDY

As an individual and as a class, keep an index card file of words studied (e.g., *tribe, tribute, nation, nationality, nationwide, culture, cultural,* etc.). Keeping the words on index cards will help you when you sort words by prefix, suffix, root words, meaning, and so on. How do the prefixes and suffixes help you understand the meaning of the words while changing the part of speech? (*Note:* This will be an ongoing activity all year long.) (RI.5.6, L.5.4a,b,c)

10. MUSIC/ART APPRECIATION/OPINION WRITING

Discuss how art and music can provide insights into a culture. From which do you prefer to learn? Why? Your teacher may ask you to write your own response and reasons on sticky notes, on a whiteboard, or in your journal before discussing as a class. (SL.5.1)

11. INFORMATIVE/EXPLANATORY ESSAY

Write an informative/explanatory essay in response to the essential question ("How does literature provide clues to a culture?") Your teacher may give you the opportunity to "Give one, get one" before writing your response. Edit your writing for verb tense and punctuation, especially commas (see Standards for more details). Your teacher may ask you to type your essay and respond to a poll about the unit on the classroom blog. (W.5.4, W.5.7, W.9a,b, L.5.1a,b,c,d; L.5.2a,b)

12. ART/WRITING

View Rose's and Curtis's photographs, along with *Indian Village, Alaska*. What can we learn about these tribes through images of their housing? Why do you believe each tribe has a different form of home? For instance, why might the Apache build more temporary housing and the Hopi build into the land? What about these images can lead you to make educated guesses? Ask the students to write an essay describing what they have learned by viewing the photographs. (W.5.1, W.5.2, W.5.4, W.5.8)

13. ART/CLASS DISCUSSION

Compare the Haida mask with the Kachina doll. Are the colors, fabrics, and textures used similar? Why do you believe this is so? What is the purpose of each of these objects? Discuss the use of pattern in these two works. (SL.5.1)

ADDITIONAL RESOURCES

- *November is National American Indian Heritage Month* (ReadWriteThink) (RL.5.9)
- *Native Americans Today* (ReadWriteThink) (RI.5.7)
- *Culture Clues Expedition* (National Geographic) (RI.5.7)
- *Teaching Point of View with Two Bad Ants* (ReadWriteThink) (RL.5.6)
- *Life of a Navajo Weaver* (ArtsEdge, The Kennedy Center)
- *Native American Chants and Movement* (ArtsEdge, The Kennedy Center)
- *Countries and their Cultures* (EveryCulture.Com)
- Native American Indian Legends and Folklore (Native Languages of the Americas)
- "Give One Get One" (RRISD Math Team)

TERMINOLOGY

Culture	Perspective	Sound imagery
Personification	Point of view	Trickster tale

MAKING INTERDISCIPLINARY CONNECTIONS

This unit teaches:

History/Geography: Native American cultures (e.g., Great Basin and Plateau, Northern and Southern Plains, Pacific Northwest, etc.) and famous Native Americans (e.g., Chief Joseph the Younger); life in the American west (e.g., the transcontinental railroad, pioneers, wagon trains, etc.)

Art: photography, Native American decorative arts

This unit could be extended to teach:

History/Geography: Where different Native American tribes lived (e.g., Great Basin and Plateau, Northern and Southern Plains, Pacific Northwest, etc.), and how the shelters, clothing, and artwork varied based upon geography; conflicts between Native Americans and European settlers (e.g., American government policies, Bureau of Indian Affairs, Sand Creek Massacre, Little Big Horn, Wounded Knee, etc.); Native American nations or famous Native Americans (e.g., Tecumseh, Osceola, Sacagawea, Sequoyah, etc.); westward expansion before the Civil War (e.g., Lewis and Clark, Daniel Boone, Wilderness Trail, Erie Canal, Pony Express, etc.)

Grade Five, Unit Three Sample Lesson Plan

A History of US: The New Nation 1789–1850 by Joy Hakim

In this series of five lessons, the students read *A History of US: The New Nation 1789–1850* by Joy Hakim, and they:

Recall and list main events and important historical figures in The New Nation (RI.5.1, RI.5.3, RI.5.10, SL.5.1)

Expand their knowledge and understanding of late eighteenth- and early nineteenth-century America (RI.5.1, RI.5.2, RI.5.5, RI.5.6, RI.5.7, RI.5.10, W.5.7, W.5.8, RF.5.4)

Record their findings (RI.5.9, W.5.4, W.5.5, W.5.6, W.5.8)

Publish their findings (SL.5.2, SL.5.4, SL.5.5, L.5.3)

Summary

Lesson I: The New Nation	Lesson II/III: Researching The New Nation
(In groups) explore main events and important historical figures in The New Nation (RI.5.1, RI.5.3, RI.5.10, SL.5.1)	(In groups) conduct research of selected topic (RI.5.1, RI.5.2, RI.5.5, RI.5.6, RI.5.7, RI.5.10, W.5.7, W.5.8, RF.5.4)
(In groups) list the topics generated in the previous objective (RI.5.3, SL.5.1)	(In groups) record information (W.5.8)
Examine results of groups' research (SL.5.1, SL.5.2, SL.5.4, W.5.8)	(In groups) identify needs for further research (SL.5.1c)
Select research topics (W.5.5, W.5.8)	(In groups) conclude research (SL.5.1d)
Lesson IV: Document Findings	**Lesson V: The New Nation Revisited—Publishing Research**
Investigate options for presenting the data (poster boards, class news-paper, magazine, multimedia, etc.) (SL.5.5)	Display findings (SL.5.2, SL.5.4, SL.5.5, L.5.3)
Explore sections of presentation (essays, maps, photos etc.) (W.5.10)	Probe classmates' exploration of "The New Nation" (L.5.1, SL.5.1, SL.5.3)
Document results of research (RI.5.9, W.5.8)	Reflect upon the results (SL.5.1d)
Edit and revise all work (W.5.4, W.5.5, W.5.6)	

Lesson I: The New Nation

Objectives

(In groups) explore main events and important historical figures in The New Nation (RI.5.1, RI.5.3, RI.5.10, SL.5.1)

(In groups) list the topics generated in the previous objective (RI.5.3, SL.5.1)

Examine results of groups' research (SL.5.1, SL.5.2, SL.5.4, W.5.8)

Select research topics (W.5.5, W.5.8)

Required Materials

- ☐ Class set of *A History of US: The New Nation 1789–1850* by Joy Hakim
- ☐ Computers with Internet access
- ☐ Chart paper
- ☐ Markers

Procedures

1. Lead-In:
   Break the students into groups.
2. Step by Step:
   a. In the groups, students revisit *A History of US: The New Nation 1789–1850* by Joy Hakim, and generate a list of important historical figures and events in The New Nation.
   b. Still in groups, the students record their findings on chart paper. The lists are likely to include the presidents of the period, maps of Lewis and Clark explorations, the War of 1812, the growth of industry, the Abolitionists, and more.
   c. Lead a discussion of the students' findings.
3. Closure:
   Students select research topics.

Differentiation

Advanced

- After the list of people and events has been generated and discussed, students choose topics made more interesting by the multiple viewpoints of the contributions of a historical figure or a historical event.
- Throughout the research, students will discuss — at the upper end of Bloom's taxonomy (i.e., analyzing, evaluating) — the effects of the figure's or event's contribution to America.

Struggling

- Students will brainstorm a list of helpful informational text features to cue importance. (Chapter titles, subtitles, picture captions, bold print, table of contents, etc.)
- During the initial reading of this text, teachers and students may want to keep a running list of important people and events in ongoing preparation for this research project.

Homework/Assessment

N/A

America in Conflict

This nine-week unit focuses on the causes and consequences of the American Civil War, as revealed through literature and informational text.

OVERVIEW

Students read historical fiction and informational text about the Civil War in the United States and compare and contrast the ways in which each type of text describes key historical events. In order to gain a deeper understanding of the period beyond what is addressed in print, students listen to music and examine art from the Civil War period. The culminating activity is to compose a narrative that is set within a historical context, includes a fictional character with a conflict to grow from, and incorporates authentic facts, photos, or artwork.

ESSENTIAL QUESTION

? How are fictionalized characters and real people changed through conflict?

FOCUS STANDARDS

These Focus Standards have been selected for the unit from the Common Core State Standards.

RL.5.6: Describe how a narrator's or speaker's point of view influences how events are described.

RI.5.3: Explain the relationships or interactions between two or more individuals, events, ideas, or concepts in a historical, scientific, or technical text based on specific information in the text.

RI.5.5: Compare and contrast the overall structure (e.g., chronology, comparison, cause/effect, problem/solution) of events, ideas, concepts, or information in two or more texts.

RF.5.4: Read with sufficient accuracy and fluency to support comprehension.

RF.5.4(a): Read on-level text with purpose and understanding.

W.5.3: Write narratives to develop real or imagined experiences or events using effective technique, descriptive details, and clear event sequences.

SL.5.4: Report on a topic or text or present an opinion, sequencing ideas logically and using appropriate facts and relevant, descriptive details to support main ideas or themes; speak clearly at an understandable pace.

L.5.4: Determine or clarify the meaning of unknown and multiple-meaning words and phrases based on grade 5 reading and content, choosing flexibly from a range of strategies.

L.5.4(b): Use common, grade-appropriate Greek and Latin affixes and roots as clues to the meaning of a word (e.g., *photograph, photosynthesis*).

SUGGESTED STUDENT OBJECTIVES

- Compare and contrast the points of view in fictional and nonfictional texts about the same topic or time period.
- Compare and contrast the ways in which fictional and informational texts treat historical events (e.g., the Civil War and slavery in the United States).
- Analyze two accounts of the same event and describe important similarities and differences in the details they provide.
- Write a historical narrative, incorporating knowledge gained from fictional and informational text about a particular period in history (e.g., the Civil War).
- Define related words and identify their parts of speech (e.g., *civil, civilization, civilian*).

SUGGESTED WORKS

(E) indicates a CCSS exemplar text; (EA) indicates a text from a writer with other works identified as exemplars.

LITERARY TEXTS

Stories

- *Bull Run* (Paul Fleischman)
- *Maritcha: A Nineteenth-Century American Girl* (Tonya Bolden)
- *Ballad of the Civil War* (Mary Stoltz and Sergio Martinez)
- *Across Five Aprils* (Irene Hunt)
- *A Picture of Freedom: The Diary of Clotee, a Slave Girl, Belmont Plantation, Virginia, 1859* (Dear America Series) (Patricia C. McKissack)
- *Underground Man* (Milton Meltzer)
- *Steal Away . . . to Freedom* (Jennifer Armstrong)
- *Dear Austin: Letters from the Underground Railroad* (Elvira Woodruff and Nancy Carpenter)
- *A Light in the Storm: The Civil War Diary of Amelia Martin, Fenwick Island, Delaware, 1861* (Dear America Series) (Karen Hesse)
- *When Will This Cruel War be Over? The Civil War Diary of Emma Simpson, Gordonsville, Virginia, 1864* (Dear America Series) (Barry Denenberg)
- *After the Rain: Virginia's Civil War Diary, Book Two* (Mary Pope Osborne) (EA)
- *A Time To Dance: Virginia's Civil War Diary, Book Three* (Mary Pope Osborne) (EA)
- *The Journal Of James Edmond Pease: A Civil War Union Soldier, Virginia, 1863* (Dear America Series) (Jim Murphy) (EA)
- *Just a Few Words, Mr. Lincoln* (Jean Fritz)
- *Charley Skedaddle* (Patricia Beatty)

Picture Books (for the Introductory Activity)

- *Follow the Drinking Gourd* (Jeanette Winter)
- *Sweet Clara and the Freedom Quilt* (Deborah Hopkins)

Poems

- "The New Colossus" (Emma Lazarus) (E)
- "The Eagle" (Alfred Lord Tennyson)
- "I Hear America Singing" (Walt Whitman) (EA)
- "I, Too, Sing America" (Langston Hughes) (E)

INFORMATIONAL TEXTS

Informational Books

- *You Wouldn't Want to Be a Worker on the Statue of Liberty! A Monument You'd Rather Not Build* (You Wouldn't Want To . . . Series) (John Malam and David Antram)
- *A History of US: War, Terrible War, 1855–1865* (Joy Hakim) (E)
- "Underground Railroad": *The New Book of Knowledge* (Henrietta Buckmaster) (E)
- *You Wouldn't Want to Be a Civil War Soldier: A War You'd Rather Not Fight* (You Wouldn't Want To . . . Series) (Thomas Ratliff and David Antram)
- *If You Lived at the Time of the Civil War* (If You . . . Series) (Kay Moore and Anni Matsick)
- *If You Traveled on the Underground Railroad* (If You . . . Series) (Ellen Levine and Larry Johnson)
- *If You Lived When There was Slavery in America* (If You . . . Series) (Anne Kamma and Pamela Johnson)
- *The Abraham Lincoln You Never Knew* (James Lincoln Collier and Greg Copeland)
- *Outrageous Women of Civil War Times* (Mary Rodd Furbee)
- *Sojourner Truth: Ain't I a Woman?* (Frederick McKissack and Patricia C. McKissack)
- *The Abolitionist Movement* (Cornerstones of Freedom) (Elaine Landau)
- *Your Travel Guide to the Civil War* (Passport to History) (Nancy Day)
- *I Lift My Lamp: Emma Lazarus and the Statue of Liberty* (Nancy Smiler Levinson)

Speech

- *The Gettysburg Address* (Abraham Lincoln) (E) (*Note: The Gettysburg Address* is a CCSS exemplar text for grades 9 through 10.)

ART, MUSIC, AND MEDIA

Art

- Alexander Gardner, *President Abraham Lincoln in the tent of General George B. McClellan After the Battle of Antietam* (October 3, 1862)

Music and Songs

- Patrick S. Gilmore, "When Johnny Comes Marching Home" (1863)
- Julia Ward Howe, "The Battle Hymn of the Republic" (1861)
- Daniel Decatur Emmett, "Dixie" (1861)
- "Goober Peas"

Media

- Civil War photographs

SAMPLE ACTIVITIES AND ASSESSMENTS

1. SUGGESTED INTRODUCTORY ACTIVITY

Start this unit by reading aloud a favorite picture book about the Civil War, such as *Follow the Drinking Gourd* or *Sweet Clara and the Freedom Quilt*, not only to start building background knowledge of the Civil War period, but also to help your students understand what you will expect from them in journal entries and other assignments. (RL.5.1, SL.5.1, SL.5.3, W.5.4, W.5.8)

2. CLASS DISCUSSION

How do the symbols of America (e.g., the Statue of Liberty, the American flag, the bald eagle, etc.) provide strength during times of conflict? Discuss as a class, citing examples from the poems and stories you've read. (SL.5.1)

3. POETRY RESPONSE/NARRATIVE WRITING

Continue the Poetic Devices Chart (begun in Unit One) that includes examples of similes, metaphors, alliteration, and onomatopoeia in poems from this unit. Write your own poem about America that uses at least two of the techniques found. Your teacher may ask you to type your poem and insert a relevant picture or illustration for publication on the class web page. (RL.5.4, L.5.5, W.5.4)

4. ART/CLASS DISCUSSION

How is war depicted through art? View one of the most famous photos of the Civil War, *President Abraham Lincoln in the tent of General George B. McClellan After the Battle of Antietam*, and discuss what the image teaches viewers about the Civil War, even before learning facts and reading literature from that time period. (SL.5.1)

5. LITERATURE RESPONSE

While reading a story such as *Bull Run* by Paul Fleischman, keep an ongoing list of words to describe the main character(s). Mark the text with sticky notes and write the adjectives on the notes. After finishing the book, you will be asked to choose the best adjectives to describe the character's internal responses and external behaviors in response to conflicts experienced. (RL.5.1, RL.5.3, RL.5.6, RF.5.4a,b,c)

6. CLASS DISCUSSION

Read and compare what you learn about slavery in America from fiction and nonfiction text (e.g., *Dear Austin: Letters from the Underground Railroad* by Elvira Woodruff and Nancy Carpenter and *If You Lived When There was Slavery in America* by Anne Kamma and Pamela Johnson). How does knowing the historical information enhance your understanding of the fictional story? Talk with a classmate to share ideas prior to large-group discussion. (RL.5.9)

7. CIVIL WAR GRAPHIC ORGANIZER AND INFORMATIVE/EXPLANATORY WRITING

As a class, keep a chart of information about the Civil War period learned from a variety of fiction and nonfiction; the chart will track responses to the following questions:

- What is the conflict?

- Why does this conflict occur?
- Who is involved on each side of the conflict?
- How is the conflict resolved?
- How does this conflict affect our lives today?

Keep a list of your responses to these questions in your journal. Share thoughts with a partner who has read the same book as you, and collaboratively contribute to the class chart or a shared spreadsheet. After the class finishes the graphic organizer, individually write a summary explaining one of the conflicts studied. Your response should be a well-developed essay that includes at least three supporting details and a statement about how the event fits into the larger context of the Civil War. Check your writing for plagiarism. Edit your writing, especially for commas to set off the words *yes* and *no* and to indicate direct address (see Standards for more details). Your teacher may ask you to publish your essay on the class blog or the class web page. (RI.5.3, RI.5.5, RI.5.7, RI.5.9, RF.5.4a,b,c; W.5.2, W.5.4, L.5.1a,b,c,d; L.5.2a,b,c)

8. CLASS DISCUSSION

At the end of the unit, compare the lives of different characters, real and fictional, during the Civil War and discuss how they grew because of the conflict they experienced. (RI.5.3, RI.5.5, RI.5.7, RI.5.9, RF.5.4a,b,c)

9. RESEARCH ESSAY/MULTIMEDIA PRESENTATION

Write a research essay about an event from the Civil War, highlighting the causes and effects of the conflict. Part of your essay should explain the relationship or interaction between individuals or events. Alternatively, students may choose a person to write about, noting how that person contributed to the cause or to the resolution of this historical conflict. The well-developed research essay should be logically ordered with at least two to three sources of information cited. Edit your writing, especially for commas to set off the words *yes* and *no* and to indicate direct address (see Standards for more details). Your teacher may ask you to draw and scan illustrations or insert relevant photos from the Internet for publication on the class web page. (W.5.2, W.5.7, RI.5.3, SL.5.4, SL.5.5, L.5.1a,b,c,d; L.5.2a,b,c)

10. WORD STUDY

As an individual and as a class, keep an index card file of words studied (e.g., *secession, rebellion, abolition, confederate, rebel,* etc.). Keeping the words on index cards will help when you sort words by prefix, suffix, root words, meaning, and so on. How do word relationships (e.g., between *civil, civilization, and civilian*) help you understand the meaning of the words, while the prefixes and suffixes affect the part of speech and spelling? (*Note:* This will be an ongoing activity all year long.) (RI.5.6, L.5.4b,c)

11. (HISTORICAL) NARRATIVE WRITING

Write your own historical narrative that is set during the Civil War, includes a fictional character with a conflict to grow from, and incorporates authentic facts, photos, or artwork. Talk through your ideas with a partner before starting your first draft. You will have the opportunity to edit and revise your narrative with a partner, so that your final product is of the highest quality. The well-developed narrative should include ideas that flow logically, and at least five new vocabulary words or phrases that provide historical context. Edit your writing, especially for commas to set off the words *yes* and *no* and to indicate direct address (see Standards for more details). Publish your narrative on the class web page to encourage virtual conversation after the unit is over. (W.5.3, W.5.4, W.5.9a,b, SL.5.5, L.5.1a,b,c,d; L.5.2a,b,c)

12. MECHANICS/GRAMMAR WALL

As a class, continue adding to the Mechanics/Grammar bulletin board started in Unit One. Remember—once skills are taught in a mini-lesson and listed on the bulletin board, you are expected to edit your work for these elements before publication. (L.5.1, L.5.2, L.5.3)

13. VOCABULARY/WORD WALL

As a class, continue adding to the Vocabulary Word Wall bulletin board where, throughout the year, you will add and sort words as you learn them in each unit of study. (L.5.4)

ADDITIONAL RESOURCES

- *Engaging Students in a Collaborative Study of the Gettysburg Address* (ReadWriteThink) (SL.5.3)
- *Using Historical Fiction to Learn About the Civil War* (ReadWriteThink) (RL.5.2, W.5.7)
- *Critical Perspectives: Reading and Writing About Slavery* (ReadWriteThink) (RL.5.2, W.5.7)
- *Strategic Reading and Writing: Summarizing Antislavery Biographies* (ReadWriteThink) (RL.5.2, RI.5.1)
- *Examining Plot Conflict Through a Comparison/Contrast Essay* (ReadWriteThink) (RL.5.9)
- *Civil War Music* (ArtsEdge, The Kennedy Center)
- *Pictures of the Civil War* (The National Archives)
- *The U.S. Civil War 1861–1865 Timeline* (A History Place)

TERMINOLOGY

Ballad	Conflict	Symbolism
Cause and effect	Poetic terms: meter, rhyme	
Characterization	scheme, metaphor, simile	

MAKING INTERDISCIPLINARY CONNECTIONS

This unit teaches:

History/Geography: The Civil War (e.g., abolitionists, slave life, Abraham Lincoln, Gettysburg Address, yankees and rebels, Blue and Gray, First Battle of Bull Run/First Battle of Manassas, Sojourner Truth, Harriet Tubman, Underground Railroad, etc.)

This unit could be extended to teach:

History/Geography: Reconstruction (e.g., famous people, major events, etc.); Lincoln's assassination; slavery
Language Arts: "O Captain, My Captain" (Walt Whitman)

Grade Five, Unit Four Sample Lesson Plan

"The New Colossus" by Emma Lazarus
I Lift My Lamp: Emma Lazarus and the Statue of Liberty by Nancy Smiler Levinson

In this series of five lessons, students read "The New Colossus" by Emma Lazarus and *I Lift My Lamp: Emma Lazarus and the Statue of Liberty* by Nancy Smiler Levinson, and they:

Explore Emma Lazarus's place in history (RL.5.6, RI.5.1)

Explore Emma Lazarus's Jewish identity (RL.5.6, W.5.4, W.5.7)

Investigate the story of the Statue of Liberty (RL.5.6, RI.5.3, RI.5.9, SL.5.1)

Probe the relationship between Emma Lazarus and Ralph Waldo Emerson (RI.5.3, W.5.4, W.5.7, SL.5.1)

Examine the historical significance of "The New Colossus" (RL.5.2, SL.5.1, SL.5.2)

Summary

Lesson I: "Mighty Woman with a Torch" (Ch. 1 in *I Lift My Lamp*)	Lesson II: Young Emma Lazarus and "A Monumental Idea" (Ch.2–Ch. 6)
Critically read "The New Colossus" (RL.5.10, RF.5.4)	Investigate the early life of Emma Lazarus (RL.5.6, RI.5.1)
Investigate the allusion to the "brazen giant of Greek fame" (RL.5.4, L.5.4)	Explore the significance of America's idea of freedom (W.5.4, W.5.7)
Explore the notion of "the golden door" (RL.5.4, L.5.4)	Conduct online/library research into the origins of the Statue of Liberty (RI.5.1, RI.5.7, W.5.4, W.5.7)
Examine the theme of "The New Colossus" (RL.5.2)	Document findings of research (RI.5.9, W.5.4, W.5.7)
(While reading Ch. 1 in *I Lift My Lamp*) provide early information and lay a foundational, historical context to Emma Lazarus and the Statue of Liberty (RL.5.5, RL.5.6)	

Lesson III: Emma Lazarus and Ralph Waldo Emerson

Recall details of the relationship between Emma Lazarus and Ralph Waldo Emerson (in *I Lift My Lamp*) (RI.5.3)

Conduct online/library research on the relationship between Lazarus and Emerson (RI.5.3, W.5.4, W.5.7)

Explore details of the correspondence between Lazarus and Emerson (RI.5.3, W.5.4, W.5.7, SL.5.1)

Lesson IV: Emma's Jewish Identity and the Statue of Liberty (Ch.7—End)

Explore the significance of Lazarus's Jewish heritage (RL.5.6, W.5.4, W.5.7)

Identify reasons of Jewish immigration to America (RI.5.7, RI.5.9, W.5.4, W.5.7, SL.5.4)

Probe the origins of "The New Colossus" (RL.5.2, RL.5.5, L.5.4, W.5.4, W.5.7)

Contextualize Lazarus's role in establishing the Statue of Liberty as a beacon of freedom (RL.5.6, RI.5.3, RI.5.9, SL.5.1)

Lesson V: Lazarus, Emerson, the Statue of Liberty, and "The New Colossus"—Reflections

Recall how historical events, people, a monument, and a single poem all came together (RL.5.6, RI.5.3, RI.5.9)

Examine the lingering impact of "The New Colossus" (RL.5.2, SL.5.1, SL.5.2)

Lesson IV: Emma's Jewish Identity and the Statue of Liberty

Objectives

Explore the significance of Lazarus's Jewish heritage (RL.5.6, W.5.4, W.5.7)

Identify reasons for Jewish immigration to America (RI.5.7, RI.5.9, W.5.4, W.5.7, SL.5.4)

Probe the origins of "The New Colossus" (RL.5.2, RL.5.5, L.5.4, W.5.4, W.5.7)

Contextualize Lazarus's role in establishing the Statue of Liberty as a beacon of freedom (RL.5.6, RI.5.3, RI.5.9, SL.5.1)

Required Materials

- ☐ Class set of "The New Colossus" by Emma Lazarus
- ☐ *I Lift My Lamp: Emma Lazarus and the Statue of Liberty* by Nancy Smiler Levinson
- ☐ Computers with Internet access

Procedures

1. Lead-In:

Recall details of Chapters 9 and 10.

2. Step by Step:

(The progression of this part depends upon previous lesson's homework. The assumption here is that the students will have read the final chapters of the book for homework. Adjust the lesson if you do in-class reading of these chapters instead.

a. Discussion of Chapters 9 and 10:

- The persecution of European Jewry in the late nineteenth century
- Lazarus's response
- Jewish immigration to America
- Lazarus's involvement with Jewish refugees
- Lazarus's poetry and letters reveal her deep Jewish emotions

b. Revisit "Inspiration" and document the events that led to the composition of "The New Colossus."

3. Closure:

Read aloud (or have a student volunteer read aloud) "Her Words Forever Sing," the final chapter of *I Lift My Lamp: Emma Lazarus and the Statue of Liberty*.

Differentiation

Advanced

- Students will create a concept map based on the word *inspiration*, either on paper or using concept map software.
- Students will explore the word *inspiration* by posting facets of the word's meaning to a physical cube (e.g., they can choose to describe it, compare it to the word *creativity*, illustrate its relationship to a musician or visual artist, apply it to a poet's work, analyze its root word and origin, or argue for or against it).

Struggling

- Provide students with an outline to guide the reading of Chapters 9 and 10 for homework (or class work) or require them to use a particular number of sticky notes to mark important details in the text.
- Have the reading available for students to listen to on individual MP3 players.

Homework/Assessment

Students write a two-paragraph composition in which they discuss the historical significance of "The New Colossus." (The paper will be used for class discussion in the final lesson of the unit.)

Grade 5 ► *Unit 5*

Exploration, Real and Imagined

This five-week unit builds on the study of character development begun in Unit Four by having students articulate what we learn from real and fictional characters' experiences.

OVERVIEW

Students choose an exemplar text with a dreamlike context—such as *Alice in Wonderland* or *The Little Prince*—to read with their peers and to examine what we can learn from the characters' experiences and development. If students have the opportunity to view performances of the books they can also discuss how the performances are similar to and different from the book. Additionally, students read informational texts such as *My Librarian is a Camel: How Books are Brought to Children Around the World* or biographies of explorers in order to apply lessons learned from literature to informational text. Students also create an individual semantic map of the word *exploration* in order to help their understanding of the real and fictional characters studied in this unit. Finally, this unit ends with an informative/explanatory essay in response to the essential question.

ESSENTIAL QUESTION

? What do people, both real and imagined, learn from exploring their world?

FOCUS STANDARDS

These Focus Standards have been selected for the unit from the Common Core State Standards.

RL.5.5: Explain how a series of chapters, scenes, or stanzas fits together to provide the overall structure of a particular story, drama, or poem.

RL.5.7: Analyze how visual and multimedia elements contribute to the meaning, tone, or beauty of a text (e.g., a graphic novel, multimedia presentation of fiction, folktale, myth, [or] poem).

RI.5.8: Explain how an author uses reasons and evidence to support particular points in a text, identifying which reasons and evidence support which point(s).

RF.5.4: Read with sufficient accuracy and fluency to support comprehension.

W.5.3: Write narratives to develop real or imagined experiences or events using effective technique, descriptive details, and clear event sequences.

W.5.5: With guidance and support from adults and peers, develop and strengthen writing as needed by planning, revising, editing, rewriting, or trying a new approach.

SL.5.2: Summarize a written text read aloud or information presented in diverse media and formats, including visually, quantitatively, and orally.

L.5.5: Demonstrate understanding of figurative language, word relationships, and nuances in word meanings.

SUGGESTED STUDENT OBJECTIVES

- Compare similarities and differences between two exemplar texts (e.g., *Alice in Wonderland* and *The Little Prince*).
- Respond to poetry, prose, and informational text in writing and in class discussions.
- Explain how poetry is used within prose.
- Discuss how illustrations in *Alice in Wonderland* and/or *The Little Prince* play a role in telling the story.
- Recite poetry for classmates—original and parody versions.
- Continue defining related words and identify their parts of speech (e.g., *exploration, explorer, exploratory; character, characterization, characterize*).
- Interpret figurative language, including similes and metaphors.
- Research and report on an explorer.
- Write an exploration story.

SUGGESTED WORKS

(E) indicates a CCSS exemplar text; (EA) indicates a text from a writer with other works identified as exemplars.

LITERARY TEXTS

Stories
- *Alice's Adventures in Wonderland* (Lewis Carroll) (E)
- *The Little Prince* (Antoine de Saint-Exupéry) (E)
- *Down the Rabbit Hole:* An Echo Falls Mystery (Peter Abrahams)
- *The Nursery "Alice"* (Lewis Carroll and John Tenniel)
- *Alice in Wonderland* (Campfire Graphic Novel) (Lewis Carroll, adapted by Louis Helfand and Rajesh Nagulakonda)
- *The End of the Beginning: Being the Adventures of a Small Snail (and an Even Smaller Ant)* (Avi and Tricia Tusa)

Poems
- "Words Free as Confetti" by Pat Mora (E)
- "Against Idleness and Mischief" (Isaac Watts)
- "The Star" (Ann and Jane Taylor)

- "The Spider and the Fly" (Mary Howitt)
- "Queen of Hearts" (*Mother Goose*, anonymous)
- "How Doth the Little Crocodile" (from *Alice's Adventures in Wonderland*) (Lewis Carroll)
- "The Mouse's Tale" (from *Alice's Adventures in Wonderland*) (Lewis Carroll)
- "Twinkle, Twinkle, Little Bat" (from *Alice's Adventures in Wonderland*) (Lewis Carroll)
- "'Tis the Voice of the Lobster" ("Lobster Quadrille") (from *Alice's Adventures in Wonderland*) (Lewis Carroll)

Quotations

- "Grown-ups never understand anything by themselves, and it is exhausting for children to have to provide explanations over and over again." (Antoine de Saint-Exupéry, *The Little Prince*)
- "It is only with the heart that one can see rightly; what is essential is invisible to the eye." (Antoine de Saint-Exupéry, *The Little Prince*)

INFORMATIONAL TEXTS

Informational Books

- *My Librarian is a Camel: How Books are Brought to Children Around the World* (Margriet Ruurs) (E)
- *Camels* (Nature Watch) (Cherie Winner)
- *Desert Mammals* (True Books) (Elaine Landau)
- *Deserts* (True Books: Ecosystems) (Darlene R. Stille)
- *Who Is Neil Armstrong?* (Roberta Edwards, Nancy Harrison, and Stephen Marchesi)
- *Who Was Daniel Boone?* (Sydelle Kramer)
- *Who Was Ferdinand Magellan?* (S. A. Kramer, Nancy Harrison, and Elizabeth Wolf)
- *Who Was Marco Polo?* (Joan Holub, John O'Brien, and Nancy Harrison)
- *Kids During the Age of Exploration* (Kids Throughout History) (Cynthia MacGregor)
- *Women Explorers of North and South America* Series (Margo McLoon-Basta)
- *State-by-State Guide* (United States of America) (Millie Miller and Cyndi Nelson)

Biographies

- *René Magritte* (Getting to Know the World's Greatest Artists) (Mike Venezia)
- *Salvador Dalí* (Artists in Their Time) (Robert Anderson)

ART, MUSIC, AND MEDIA

Art

- Wilfredo Lam, *Untitled*, (1947)
- Roberto Matta, *Psychological Morphology* (1938)
- Giorgio de Chirico, *The Disquieting Muses* (1916)
- Salvador Dalí, *The Persistence of Memory* (1931)
- René Magritte, *The False Mirror* (1928)
- René Magritte, *Time Transfixed* (1938)
- Marcel Duchamp, *Bicycle Wheel* (1913)
- Jean (Hans) Arp, *Mountain, Navel, Anchors, Table* (1925)

Illustrations

- Sir John Tenniel, *Alice's Adventures in Wonderland*
- Antoine de Saint-Exupéry, *The Little Prince* (1943)

Music

- Danny Elfman, *Alice in Wonderland Soundtrack* (2010) (Walt Disney Records)
- Steve Schuch, *The Little Prince* (1997) (Night Heron Music)

Film

- Stanley Donen, dir., *The Little Prince* (1974)
- *Lewis Carroll's Alice in Wonderland* (Broadway Theater Archive) (1983)

SAMPLE ACTIVITIES AND ASSESSMENTS

Note: Students should have the opportunity to choose a book to read and to discuss in groups. Whole-class activities are listed after the specific activities by text title (following). If both *Alice's Adventures in Wonderland* and *The Little Prince* are above some students' reading levels, you can add a third group that reads *The End of the Beginning,* an easier book with similar characteristics.

1. INTRODUCTORY ACTIVITY

Your teacher will introduce ways we can learn from characters' experiences in books by reviewing characters in some old favorites—such as *The Little Red Hen* and *Lon Po Po* or *The Three Little Pigs* and *The True Story of the Three Little Pigs.* You will start with some easier and more familiar stories in order to practice how to examine characters with more challenging and new texts. Talk about the character's point of view as well as the sequence of events experienced—the interrelationship among these and other elements in the story. (RL.5.1, SL.5.1, SL.5.3)

ALICE'S ADVENTURES IN WONDERLAND

2. LITERATURE RESPONSE

What does Alice think she will find when she jumps down the rabbit hole? If you were Alice, would you have done this? Why or why not? Write your response in your journal, share ideas with a classmate, and revise your response if you get additional ideas you would like to use. (RL.5.2)

3. LITERATURE RESPONSE

Recall characters you have read about so far this year and compare them to characters from this text. For example, compare Alice's encounters in Wonderland with the Red Queen to another literary character that encounters a tyrant. What can you learn from Alice? Write your response in your journal, share ideas with a classmate, and revise your response if you get additional ideas you would like to use. (RL.5.3)

4. LITERATURE RESPONSE

To see *Alice* and its illustrations in a different light, your teacher will introduce you to (1) *The Nursery "Alice,"* a version of the story that Carroll prepared for very young children, (2) *Down the Rabbit Hole: An Echo Falls Mystery* (Peter Abrahams), and/or (3) the graphic novel version of *Alice in Wonderland* (Campfire Graphic Novels). Discuss similarities and differences between these versions. (RL.5.7)

5. LITERATURE RESPONSE

Summarize each chapter in your journal by answering the question, "What does Alice learn from her experiences in *Alice's Adventures in Wonderland*?" Cite specific examples and/or mark the text with a sticky note to facilitate group discussion. (RL.5.5)

6. ART/CLASS DISCUSSION

Examine the work of two surrealist artists: Salvador Dalí and René Magritte. Compare the dreamlike state of the artworks to the experiences Alice has in Wonderland. In what ways are Alice's adventures similar to dreams (or nightmares)? To surrealist art? (SL.5.1)

THE LITTLE PRINCE

7. LITERATURE RESPONSE

What does the little prince or the pilot learn about himself by exploring the world and thinking about his adventures? Write your response in your journal (citing evidence from the text), share ideas with a classmate who chose the same character, and revise your response if you get additional ideas you would like to use. (RL.5.3)

8. LITERATURE RESPONSE

Symbols and metaphors are present throughout *The Little Prince*. Do these make it easier or harder for you to understand the story? Why? (L.5.5a, RL.5.4)

9. LITERATURE RESPONSE

Summarize every three to four chapters of *The Little Prince* in your journal by answering the question, "What does the pilot learn from the little prince? What does the little prince learn from the pilot?" Cite examples from the text. (RL.5.5)

10. MUSIC APPRECIATION

Listen to the song "The Little Prince" by Steve Schuch. Read the lyrics. Discuss similarities and differences between the song and the book. (SL.5.1)

GENERAL

11. PARTNER DISCUSSION

At the end of your novel study, pair up with a partner who read a book that you did not. Share:

- What the character learned about himself/herself by exploring their unique world. (SL.5.2, SL.5.3, RF.5.4, RL.5.5)
- How the illustrations are part of the story, showing specific pages. (SL.5.2, RL.5.7)
- How the music/songs from this unit remind you of the story you read (if applicable). (SL.5.1)

12. DRAMATIZATION/FLUENCY

Choose a poem to perform interpretively from the suggested list or write your own. Memorization is not required, but optional for this performance. (Alternatively, pair with a partner where one of you learns the Lewis Carroll version, and the other learns the original version. Perform both versions for the class, and then discuss how knowing the original helps us to appreciate the parody even more.) Record the readings using a video camera in order to share with others on the class blog. (L.5.5a,b,c; SL.5.6)

13. MEDIA APPRECIATION

How is reading *Alice's Adventures in Wonderland* or *The Little Prince* similar to or different from watching a DVD version? Which do you prefer? Why? Write your initial thoughts in your journal before discussing as a class. (RL.5.7)

14. INFORMATIONAL TEXT RESPONSE

After reading *My Librarian is a Camel* (Margriet Ruurs), has your perspective about the school library and access to library books changed? What are some ways that the author influenced your thinking? Cite specific examples from the text during class discussion. In your journal, write a response to this question: "What did you learn from this text?" (RI.5.8)

15. RESEARCH REPORT

Not only do fictional characters learn from exploring their world, but real people do too. Research a famous explorer and his/her contributions to understanding of the world, and present your findings to the class. The research essay should be logically ordered with at least two to three sources of information cited. Edit your writing, especially correlative conjunctions, titles of works, and sentence variety (see Standards for more details). Your teacher may ask you to type your report, and insert relevant visuals from the web, for publication on the class web page. (W.5.7, L.5.1, L.5.2a,b,c,d; L.5.3a)

16. NARRATIVE WRITING

Write your own exploration story about a real or fictional character. Your story should have a moral or a lesson you want the reader to learn from your character. You will have the opportunity to edit and revise your narrative with a partner so that your final product is of the highest quality. The narrative should include ideas that flow logically and at least five new exploration vocabulary words. Edit your writing, especially correlative conjunctions, titles of works, and sentence variety (see Standards for more details). Your teacher may ask you to type your story, add visuals, and possibly even record it as a podcast or using a video camera, for publication on the class web page. (W.5.3, W.5.4, W.5.5, L.5.1, L.5.2a,b,c,d; L.5.3a)

17. WORD STUDY

As an individual and as a class, keep an index card file of words, literal and figurative, studied in this unit (e.g., *exploration, explorer, exploratory; character, characterization, characterize*). Keeping the words on index cards will help when you sort words by prefix, suffix, root words, meaning, and so on. How do word relationships help you understand the meaning of the words, while the prefixes and suffixes affect the part of speech and spelling? (*Note:* This will be an ongoing activity all year long.) In addition, you will create an individual semantic map of the word *exploration* in order to represent visually your understanding of the real and fictional types of exploration studied in this unit. (L.5.4a,b,c)

18. INFORMATIVE/EXPLANATORY ESSAY

Write an informative/explanatory essay in response to the essential question ("What do people, both real and imagined, learn from exploring their world?"). Your teacher may give you the opportunity to "Give one, get one" before writing your response. Include at least three examples of things learned. Edit your writing, especially for correlative conjunctions, titles of works, and sentence variety (see Standards for more details) before sharing with your teacher. Your teacher may ask you to type your essay and respond to a poll about the unit on the class blog. (W.5.9a,b, W.5.4, W.5.7, L.5.1, L.5.2a,b,c,d; L.5.3a)

19. ART/NARRATIVE WRITING

Have students select any one of the works. Students should inventory the visual elements in the work. Consider what the artists might be trying to communicate about the figure(s) or the setting through their juxtaposition of imagery and/or use of distortion. What role does color play in the work? Use the list to write a short story based on the work, referring back to it as the story is developed. Is the story similar to a dream? (W.5.3, W.5.4)

20. ART CONNECTION/CLASS DISCUSSION

The suggested artworks in this unit belong to two related schools of art—Dadaism and Surrealism. Duchamp's *Bicycle Wheel* is considered a Dadaist work. Dadaists created "anti-art" that attempted to go against long-established ideas of what art looked like. Duchamp made a series of works he called "readymades," which paired or simply presented commonplace objects in an art setting. Jean Arp was also a Dadaist. Read the title of Arp's work out loud as you examine it. What do you see? Now, look at Magritte's *Time Transfixed*. Magritte worked as a Surrealist, an approach to art making that developed out of Dadaism. Much of Magritte's work is dreamlike, featuring qualities found in Surrealism. Closely examine *Time Transfixed* and discuss as a class how Dadaism and Surrealism are similar and different. (SL.5.1, SL.5.5)

21. GRAMMAR AND USAGE

Your teacher will teach mini-lessons on the individual language standards. For example, he/she will explain correlative conjunctions. Then, he/she will give you a set of sentences and ask you to insert the correct conjunction (i.e., Connor has not gone to school today, _____ (nor/or) has he done his homework."). After the class understands this skill, you will select a piece of your own writing where you have used correlative conjunctions, or find part of your writing where adding these could enhance your writing. Edit to ensure that you used them correctly, and check your work with a partner. (L.5.1e)

22. MECHANICS/GRAMMAR WALL

As a class, continue adding to the Mechanics/Grammar bulletin board started in Unit One. Remember—once skills are taught in a mini-lesson and listed on the bulletin board, you are expected to edit your work for these elements before publication. (L.5.1, L.5.2, L.5.3)

23. VOCABULARY/WORD WALL

As a class, continue adding to the Vocabulary Word Wall bulletin board where, throughout the year, you will add and sort words as you learn them in each unit of study. (L.5.4)

ADDITIONAL RESOURCES

- *Character Trading Cards* (ReadWriteThink) (RL.5.5)
- *Using Picture Books to Teach Characterization In Writing Workshop* (ReadWriteThink) (RL.5.2)
- *Book Report Alternative: Examining Story Elements Using Story Map Comic Strips* (ReadWriteThink) (RL.5.5)
- *The Original Alice: Alice's Adventures Underground* (British Library)
- "Give One Get One" (RRISD Math Team)

TERMINOLOGY

Metaphor	Paradox	Style
Nonsense literature	Parody	Symbol

MAKING INTERDISCIPLINARY CONNECTIONS

This unit teaches:

History/Geography: Explorers (e.g., who they are, where/why they explored, etc.); geography of North and South America (e.g., fifty states, major oceans and rivers, etc.)

Science: Camels (e.g., where they live, what is their habitat, what makes them suited for desert life, etc.)

Art: surrealism, Salvador Dalí, René Magritte, Roberto Matta, illustration

This unit could be extended to teach:

History/Geography: Explorers (e.g., Prince Henry the Navigator, Bartolomeu Dias, Vasco da Gama, Cabral, Christopher Columbus, Ferdinand Magellan, Balboa, etc.); deserts of the world (e.g., Africa: Sahara, Kalahari; Asia: Gobi; North America: Mojave, Death Valley; South America: Atacama Desert, etc.)

Science: Oceanography (e.g., surface, subsurface land features, ocean floor, composition of sea water, currents, tides, marine life, etc.); desert habitats (e.g., what lives in a desert? what adaptations would be needed by people to live in a desert? etc.)

Grade Five, Unit Five Sample Lesson Plan

Alice's Adventures in Wonderland by Lewis Carroll
Alice in Wonderland: A Walt Disney Production

In this series of four lessons (that begin after students have read *Alice's Adventures in Wonderland* by Lewis Carroll), students watch the film *Alice in Wonderland*, and they:

> Note the differences between the novel and the movie (RL.5.1, RL.5.2, RL.5.7)
>
> Analyze the impact of the differences between the novel and the movie (RL.5.2)
>
> Articulate their observations in writing (W.5.1, W.5.4, W.5.9a, W.5.10, L.5.1, L.5.2, L.5.3)

Summary

Lesson I: *Alice in Wonderland*—The Movie	Lesson II: Alice's Adventures—The Novel and the Movie
Watch *Alice in Wonderland* (1951 Disney Production) (RL.5.7)	Reread assigned passage in *Alice's Adventures in Wonderland* (RL.5.1, RL.5.10, RF.5.4)
(Begin to) identify differences between the novel and the movie (SL.5.2, RL.5.7)	(In small groups) recall details of assigned scene in the movie (SL.5.1, SL.5.2, RL.5.5)
Lesson III: Alice's Adventures—The Novel and the Movie	**Lesson IV: Alice's Adventures—Assessing the Transition from the Novel to the Movie**
Analyze the movie's interpretation of the assigned scene (RL.5.5, RL.5.7, SL.5.2)	Recall ideas that were generated in Lessons II and III (W.5.8, SL.5.2)
Note the differences between the novel and the movie (RL.5.1, RL.5.2, RL.5.7)	Evaluate the impact that the differences between the novel and the movie have on the reader/viewer's understanding of Lewis Carroll's message (RL.5.2, W.5.1, W.5.4, W.5.9a, W.5.10, L.5.1, L.5.2, L.5.3)

Lesson IV: Alice's Adventures—Assessing the Transition from the Novel to the Movie

Objectives

Recall ideas that were generated in Lessons II and III (W.5.8, SL.5.2)

Evaluate the impact that the differences between the novel and the movie have on the reader/viewer's understanding of Lewis Carroll's message (RL.5.2, W.5.4, W.5.1, W.5.9a, W.5.10, L.5.1, L.5.2, L.5.3)

Required Materials

☐ Class set of *Alice's Adventures in Wonderland* by Lewis Carroll

☐ *Alice in Wonderland* (1951 Disney Production)

☐ Students' notes

Procedures

1. Lead-In:

Students review their notes (from Lessons I–III).

2. Step by Step:

a. Introduce the students to the in-class work. Students will create an outline in preparation for writing an essay. Their task is to evaluate the impact that the differences between *Alice Adventures in Wonderland*, the novel, and *Alice in Wonderland*, the movie, have on the reader/viewer's understanding of Lewis Carroll's message.

b. Using their notes, students begin to work on the outline of their essays. They should follow the essay outline template shown here.

Alice in Wonderland Essay Outline

Introduction

Lead sentence: Introduces the text and the movie

Contextualize: Introduces the specific passage on which the essay focuses

Thesis Statement: States the main point that the essay will make

Body Paragraph I

Topic Sentence: supports the thesis statement

Support detail 1

Support detail 2

Support detail 3

Body Paragraph II

Topic Sentence: supports the thesis statement

Support detail 1

Support detail 2

Support detail 3

Body Paragraph III

Topic Sentence: supports the thesis statement

Support detail 1

Support detail 2

Support detail 3

Conclusion

The conclusion will:

Refer to the thesis statement (not repeat it)

Articulate a lesson that the essay teaches

Point to a possible greater idea, a special insight that the essay suggests

   c. Students revise their outlines.

3. Closure:

   Remind the students that for homework, they will use their outlines to write essays. Both the outline and the essays will be collected.

Differentiation

Advanced

- After writing the essay, students will rewrite the movie scene to be more in line with the author's message in the book. Supply students with a model of how movie scripts are written. As an extension, students may present their movie scene to the class, recorded on a video camera or created using video editing software.
- Students will research other movies that correspond to books they have already read this year. They may want to lead a series of class or lunch discussions (i.e., "The Book Is Better Club") based on the message in the movie versus the message in the book.

Struggling

- Prepare pairs of movie scenes and passages for students to choose from for the focus of the essay. These can be collected for student review on portable media players.
- Students may work in small groups or with a partner to create outlines. Students can do this activity collaboratively on a shared spreadsheet.
- Give students the time they need to complete the essay, creating one paragraph each evening and reviewing/revising it with a partner and/or teacher the following day.

Homework/Assessment

Write essay.

Coming of Age

This final six-week unit focuses on the genre of the novel, and uses "coming of age" as a unifying theme.

ESSENTIAL QUESTION

? How can literature help us understand what it means to "grow up"?

OVERVIEW

In this unit, students choose one of many exemplar novels to study, using all the strategies and skills learned throughout the year. Coming of age is the recurring theme in the texts for this unit. Students compare and contrast characters' experiences in novels to develop their own definition for "coming-of-age novels." Students research the historical context behind a novel, such as the Great Depression as the historical context for *Bud, Not Buddy,* by Christopher Paul Curtis. Striving to answer the essential question, students create multimedia presentations about coming of age.

FOCUS STANDARDS

These Focus Standards have been selected for the unit from the Common Core State Standards.

RL.5.3: Compare and contrast two or more characters, settings, or events in a story or drama, drawing on specific details in the text (e.g., how characters interact).

RI.5.6: Analyze multiple accounts of the same event or topic, noting important similarities and differences in the point of view they represent.

RF.5.4: Read with sufficient accuracy and fluency to support comprehension.

W.5.6: With some guidance and support from adults, use technology, including the Internet, to produce and publish writing as well as to interact and collaborate with others; demonstrate sufficient command of keyboarding skills to type a minimum of two pages in a single sitting.

W.5.8: Recall relevant information from experiences or gather relevant information from print and digital sources; summarize or paraphrase information in notes and finished work, and provide a list of sources.

SL.5.5: Include multimedia components (e.g., graphics, sound) and visual displays in presentations when appropriate to enhance the development of main ideas or themes.

L.5.3: Use knowledge of language and its conventions when writing, speaking, reading, or listening.

L.5.3(a): Expand, combine, and reduce sentences for meaning, reader/listener interest, and style.

L.5.3(b): Compare and contrast the varieties of English (e.g., dialects, registers) used in stories, dramas, or poems.

SUGGESTED STUDENT OBJECTIVES

- Define the term *coming-of-age novel.*
- Compare the treatment of coming of age in a variety of novels.
- Compare and contrast novels and their film versions.
- Compare and contrast how characters in a story respond to challenges and what they learn from their experiences.
- Compare and contrast the experiences of real people during different historical time periods.
- Generate interview questions; interview people who can serve as sources of information on a research topic; relate their answers to research questions.
- Research the steps that would be involved in turning a hobby or interest into a career; communicate findings.

SUGGESTED WORKS

(E) indicates a CCSS exemplar text; (EA) indicates a text from a writer with other works identified as exemplars.

LITERARY TEXTS

Stories

- *Where the Mountain Meets the Moon* (Grace Lin) (E)
- *M. C. Higgins, the Great* (Virginia Hamilton) (E)
- *The Secret Garden* (Frances Hodgson Burnett) (E)
- *Tuck Everlasting* (Natalie Babbitt) (E)
- *Then Again, Maybe I Won't* (Judy Blume)
- *Flying with the Eagle, Racing the Great Bear: Stories from Native North America* (Joseph Bruchac)
- *Cat with a Yellow Star: Coming of Age in Terezin* (Susan Goldman Rubin and Ela Weissberger)
- *The Wall: Growing Up Behind the Iron Curtain* (Peter Sis)
- *Blue Willow* (Doris Gates)
- *Bud, Not Buddy* (Christopher Paul Curtis) (E)
- *Out of the Dust* (Karen Hesse)
- *A Long Way From Chicago* (Richard Peck)
- *A Year Down Yonder* (Richard Peck)
- *The Journal of C. J. Jackson: A Dust Bowl Migrant, Oklahoma to California, 1935* (Dear America Series) (William Durbin)
- *Rose's Journal: The Story of a Girl in the Great Depression* (Marissa Moss)
- *Walk Two Moons* (Sharon Creech)

- *Survival In the Storm: The Dust Bowl Diary of Grace Edwards, Dalhart, Texas, 1935* (Dear America Series) (Katelan Janke)
- *Christmas After All: The Great Depression Diary of Minnie Swift, Indianapolis, Indiana, 1932* (Dear America Series) (Kathryn Lasky)

Poems
- "Freedom" (William Stafford)
- "I'm Nobody! Who are you?" (Emily Dickinson) (EA)
- "Dreams" (Nikki Giovanni) (EA)

INFORMATIONAL TEXTS
Informational Books
- *The Kid's Guide to Money: Earning It, Saving It, Spending It, Growing It, Sharing It* (Steve Otfinoski) (E)
- *Gorilla Doctors: Saving Endangered Great Apes* (Scientists in the Field) (Pamela S. Turner)
- *Quest for the Tree Kangaroo: An Expedition to the Cloud Forest of New Guinea* (Scientists in the Field) (Sy Montgomery and Nic Bishop) (E)
- *Setting Career Goals* (Stuart Schwartz and Craig Conley)
- *Getting Ready for a Career As . . .* (Series)
- *The Great Depression* (Cornerstones of Freedom) (Elaine Landau)
- *Kids During the Great Depression* (Kids Throughout History) (Lisa A. Wroble)

Informational Books (Read Aloud)
- *Children of the Great Depression* (Russell Freedman) (EA)
- *Children of the Dust Bowl: The True Story of the School at Weedpatch Camp* (Jerry Stanley)
- *Dust to Eat: Drought and Depression in the 1930s* (Michael L. Cooper)

ART, MUSIC, AND MEDIA
Art
- Edward Hopper, *House by the Railroad* (1925)
- Dorothea Lange, *Migrant Mother* (1936)
- Hugo Gellert, *The Working Day, no. 37* (c. 1933)
- Conrad A. Albrizio, *The New Deal* (1934)
- Blanche Grambs, *No Work* (1935)
- Bernard Joseph Steffen, *Dust Plowing* (c. 1939)

Music
- Marsha Norman and Lucy Simon, *The Secret Garden* (musical) (1991)
- Artie Shaw and His New Music, "Whistle While You Work" (no date)
- Jack Yellen and Milton Ager, "Happy Days Are Here Again" (1929)
- E. Y. "Yip" Harburg and Jay Gorney, "Brother, Can You Spare a Dime?" (1931)
- Duke Ellington and Irving Mills, "It Don't Mean a Thing (If It Ain't Got That Swing)" (1931)
- Jerome Kern and George Gard "Buddy" DeSylva, "Look for the Silver Lining" (1920)

Film

- Doug Atchison, dir., *Akeelah and the Bee* (2006)
- Robert Stevenson, dir., *Old Yeller* (1957)
- Victor Fleming, dir., *The Wizard of Oz* (1939)

SAMPLE ACTIVITIES AND ASSESSMENTS

Note: Students choose a coming-of-age novel to read. Discussion groups are based on the novel chosen by each student.

1. CLASS DISCUSSION

What is meant by the term *coming-of-age novel*? (*Note:* Prompting may be needed and answers could include: a story where a main character grows up by gaining knowledge or life experience; a story where I see a character transition from childhood to adulthood; a story where characters take on adult responsibility or learn a lesson, etc.) Create a class chart of characters read about and the ways they grow up in stories. After reading our novels, try to generate a definition of your own that will enable you to write your coming-of-age story. (SL.5.1)

2. LITERATURE RESPONSE

Keep a journal about your coming-of-age novel that specifies:

- The main character
- The obstacles faced
- The characteristics that enable him/her to overcome obstacles
- The character's internal responses and external responses to these obstacles
- The events that lead up to the climax and, ultimately, the character's growth
- Notes about varieties of English (dialects, registers) or other literary techniques used in the novel (L.5.3)

After reading your novel, create a coming-of-age comic strip that outlines the key events and supporting details that the main character went through to grow up. You may want to use comic strip software to publish your ideas. (RL.5.2, W.5.8)

3. GRAPHIC ORGANIZER

As a class, keep a chart with the following categories of the novels we've read, on paper or in a shared spreadsheet. As the chart is filled in, and at the end of the unit, use this information to make comparisons and generalizations about characters (and people) who undergo changes in their development:

- Setting
- Main character who undergoes a change, and adjectives that describe him/her
- Obstacles faced by the main character
- Climax (where the main character resolves the conflict)
- Resolution (how the story ends; what the character learns)
  (RL.5.2, RL.5.3)

4. CLASS DISCUSSION

Be prepared to compare and contrast two or more characters, settings, or events across novels, drawing on specific information from each novel. What did you learn about yourself from these characters? Your teacher may ask you to write a personal response to this last question on a sticky note or in your journal before the class discussion begins. (SL.5.1, RL.5.3, RL.5.6, RL.5.9, RL.5.10, RF.5.4)

5. OPINION WRITING

Of the novels read in fifth grade, which was your favorite, and why? Write a convincing paper on why next year's fifth graders should be encouraged to read this novel. Write a well-developed essay that includes an engaging opening statement of your opinion, at least three supporting details, and a conclusion. Edit your work for all grammar studied this year, including language conventions (see Standards for more details). Your teacher may ask you to type your essay and draw or scan a favorite illustration for publication on the class web page. (W.5.1, SL.5.1, L.5.1, L.5.2, L.5.3a,b, L.5.6)

6. COMPARING MOVIES AND LITERATURE

As an alternative means of examining the elements involved in coming-of-age stories, select a movie version of one of the stories to watch and discuss the elements from the graphic organizer (see Activity 3). Did the novel or movie address a question or issue with which you (or a friend) have struggled? (RL.5.7)

7. POETRY RESPONSE

Read and discuss the connection between the two people in Emily Dickinson's poem "I'm Nobody! Who are you?" Relate the experience of the characters in the poem to the characters in your coming-of-age novel. Which characters can you see having a similar conversation? Justify your answer, citing specific details from the text. With whom has the main character in your book connected? Is the character an outsider? Your teacher may ask you to write a personal response to this last question on a sticky note or in your journal and share responses with a classmate before the class discussion begins. (SL.5.1, SL.5.2, L.5.6)

8. PARTNER CONVERSATION

Pair with a partner who read a different coming-of-age novel than you did. Collaboratively generate interview questions, keeping track of them in a shared spreadsheet, and then participate in mock interviews where you pretend to be the main character in the book you read (such as Mary Lennox from *The Secret Garden*, Sal from *Walk Two Moons,* or Mayo Cornelius from *M. C. Higgins, the Great*). Write about what you learned from your interview, and then have your partner check it for accuracy. (Alternatively, write interview questions for the author of your book and conduct research online to see if you can find answers to your questions for the author.) (L.5.3a,b, RL.5.3, SL.5.6)

9. RESEARCH PROJECT/PRESENTATION

Part of coming of age means moving into adulthood and getting a job. Read informational text about people who followed their interests and turned them into careers, such as Lisa Dabek in *Quest for the Tree Kangaroo*. What challenges did they encounter as part of their work? Conduct research about what steps you need to take to be ready for the profession(s) in which you are interested. Then write an essay about your research. Your research essay should be logically ordered and cite at least three sources of information. Edit your work for all grammar studied this year, including language conventions (see Standards for more details). Include visual displays in your presentation to the class as appropriate. Your teacher may ask you to type your essay, and possibly add relevant visuals for publication on the class web page. (RI.5.6, RI.5.10, RL.5.6, W.5.7, SL.5.1, L.5.1, L.5.2, L.5.3a,b, L.5.6)

10. RESEARCH ESSAY

Read the biography of Peter Sis on his website and listen to the interview with Sis about his memoir, *The Wall: Growing Up Behind the Iron Curtain*. Read informational text about communism in order to better understand how the communist form of government under which Sis lived suppressed his personal and artistic freedom. Conduct research about what was involved in seeking asylum in the United States, and how that experienced changed Sis in his mid-thirties. Your research essay should be logically ordered and cite at least three sources of information. Edit your work for all grammar studied this year, including language conventions (see Standards for more details). Include visual displays in your presentation as appropriate. Share your findings with the class. (RI.5.6, RI.5.10, RL.5.6, W.5.7, SL.5.1, L.5.1, L.5.2, L.5.3a,b, L.5.6)

11. RESEARCHING HISTORICAL CONTEXT

Coming-of-age novels are "timeless" because they take place in a variety of contexts and settings. For example, *Bud, Not Buddy* by Christopher Paul Curtis takes place during the Great Depression. You have learned this year that knowing the historical context increases your understanding and appreciation for historical fiction. Research an event from the Great Depression, focusing on how that event affected people of the time. What lessons did people or society learn from the Great Depression? If possible, start by interviewing someone who lived during the Great Depression. (Your teacher may bring in a guest speaker with a personal connection to the Great Depression time period.) Present your findings to the class so you can generate a better understanding of that historical period. Your research essay should be logically ordered and cite at least three sources of information. Edit your work for all grammar studied this year, including language conventions (see Standards for more details). (W.5.2, W.5.7, RI.5.3, SL.5.4, L.5.1a,b,c; L.5.2a,b, L.5.3a,b, L.5.6)

12. INFORMATIVE/EXPLANATORY ESSAY

Look back to what you learned during the America in Conflict unit (Unit Four), and compare it to what you learned about life during the Great Depression. Write an informative/explanatory essay about how life changed for African Americans between the start of the Civil War to the end of the Great Depression. How did it stay the same? Your response should be a well-developed essay that includes at least three supporting details. Edit your work for all grammar studied this year, including language conventions (see Standards for more details). (RI.5.2, W.5.2, W.5.4, W.5.8, L.5.1, L.5.2, L.5.3a,b, L.5.6)

13. MUSIC/WRITING

Listen to music from the Great Depression. Discuss how music can provide insight into historical events. What do you learn about these events by listening to music? How do the arts provide comfort and solace in times of conflict? Your teacher may ask you to write your own response on sticky notes, on a whiteboard, or in your journal before discussing as a class. (SL.5.1)

14. NARRATIVE/MULTIMEDIA PRESENTATION

A culminating project is for you to create your own coming-of-age multimedia presentation. You can create a movie or a keynote presentation, write a poem or a song, start a blog, and so forth. Create a character with an obstacle to overcome. How does he/she overcome it? The presentation should begin with an introduction that answers the essential question ("How can literature help us understand what it means to 'grow up'?"). Use at least ten new words or phrases that we've learned and studied throughout the year. Edit your work for all grammar studied this year, including language conventions (see Standards for more details) before publishing in an online format. (W.5.3, W.5.6, W.5.8, W.5.9a,b, RI.5.10, SL.5.5, SL.5.6, L.5.1, L.5.2, L.5.3, L.5.3a,b, L.5.6)

15. MECHANICS/GRAMMAR WALL

As a class, continue adding to the Mechanics/Grammar bulletin board started in Unit One. Remember—once skills are taught in a mini-lesson and listed on the bulletin board, you are expected to edit your work for these elements before publication. (L.5.1, L.5.2, L.5.3)

16. VOCABULARY

In small groups, select a passage from a book read in this unit, such as *Bud, Not Buddy,* that has a unique dialect. Discuss whether the use of slang-like language helped to add to the tone and authenticity of the book. Discuss 1930s slang words from the book *Bud, Not Buddy* and try to think of contemporary words that could replace the 1930s version. Remember—slang is acceptable to use in story dialogue, but shouldn't be used in formal writing. You will have the opportunity to rewrite a section of *Bud, Not Buddy* in contemporary language and compare the new presentation to the original version. (L.5.3b)

17. VOCABULARY/WORD WALL

As a class, continue adding to the Vocabulary Word Wall bulletin board where, throughout the year, you will add and sort words as you learn them in each unit of study. (L.5.4)

18. ART/CLASS DISCUSSION

View Edward Hopper's *House by the Railroad*. Does the house appear occupied or abandoned? Does the railroad track appear to cut off access to the house, at least visually? What feelings do you get when you view this image? Note that Hopper claimed to try not to depict emotion in his paintings, only facts. Do you think Hopper was trying to depict the status of society at this time—or just a house? Would you describe this painting as happy, sad, or neither? (SL.5.1. SL.5.4)

19. ART/CLASS DISCUSSION

Compare the Dorothea Lange photograph with the drawing by Blanche Grambs. Can you still feel emotion looking at the drawing, even though you are not seeing the character's face? What about in Lange's photograph? What makes this image so powerful? (SL.5.1. SL.5.4)

ADDITIONAL RESOURCES

- *Once They're Hooked, Reel Them In: Writing Good Endings* (ReadWriteThink) (W.5.3, W.5.4)
- *Creating Family Timelines: Graphing Family Members and Significant Events* (ReadWriteThink) (RI.5.7)
- *Literature as a Jumping Off Point for Nonfiction Inquiry* (ReadWriteThink) (RL.5.9)
- *Actor Sidney Poitier was Born in 1924* (ReadWriteThink) (W.5.1)
- *Web-Based Thematic Unit: Bud, Not Buddy* (Eduscapes)
- *The Impact of the Great Depression on Family and Home* (Novelguide.com)
- *A New Deal for the Arts* (The National Archives)
- Interview with Peter Sis about *The Wall: Growing Up Behind the Iron Curtain* (Book Expo America)
- Peter Sis's website

TERMINOLOGY

Climax

Dialogue

Foreshadowing

Idioms such as "act your age," "at the tender age of . . . ," "ripe old age"

Imagery

Resolution

Style

MAKING INTERDISCIPLINARY CONNECTIONS

This unit teaches:

Art: Edward Hopper, Dorothea Lange

Economics: Money (e.g., employment, private enterprise, banks, budgets, taxes, investments, etc.)

History/Geography: The Great Depression (e.g., stock market crash, unemployment, "Hoovervilles," "Dust Bowl," etc.)

This unit could be extended to teach:

Science: (as an extension of *The Secret Garden*): Plant structures and processes (e.g., vascular and nonvascular plants, photosynthesis, plant cell structures, classification, etc.)

Mathematics: Money (e.g., solving multiplication problems with money, savings and checking accounts, etc.)

Grade Five, Unit Six Sample Lesson Plan

The Secret Garden by Frances Hodgson Burnett

In this series of ten lessons, students read *The Secret Garden* by Frances Hodgson Burnett, and they:

- Annotate the novel for listed lessons' objectives (RL.5.1, RL.5.10, RF.4.4, W.5.8, W.5.9)
- Identify the literary elements of the novel (RL.5.3, RL.5.5, RL.5.6, SL.5.5)
- Follow the protagonist's evolution (RL.5.2, RL.5.3)
- Investigate the plot of the novel (RL.5.3)
- Probe the significance of the indoor and the outdoor settings (RL.5.3)
- Identify key conflicts (RL.5.2)
- Note the role of the minor characters (RL.5.3, L.5.3b)

Summary

Lesson I: Meet Mary Lennox (Ch. I–Ch. III)

- (Begin to) discover the purpose of annotations (RL.5.1, RL.5.10, RF.4.4, W.5.8, W.5.9)
- Note details of Mary's life before her departure for England (RL.5.1, RL.5.2)
- Examine early presentation of Mary (RL.5.1, RL.5.2)
- Explore Mary's arrival at Misselthwaite Manor (L.5.3b, RL.5.5)
- Probe the emerging conflict (RL.5.2, SL.5.1)

Lesson II: Mary's New Life Begins (Ch. IV–Ch. VI)

- Explore Martha's perception of Mary (RL.5.1, RL.5.3)
- Record early details of Dickon (RL.5.1, RL.5.3)
- Note Mary's early attraction to the "mysterious garden" (RL.5.1, RL.5.5)
- Follow Mary's explorations (RL.5.5)
- Trace the mystery that unfolds (RL.5.1, RL.5.5)

Lesson III: Discoveries (Ch. VII–Ch. IX)

- Explore Martha's impact on Mary (RL.5.1, RL.5.3)
- Examine the relationship between Mary and the Robin (RL.5.1, RL.5.3)
- Note Mary's early actions as she enters the garden (RL.5.1, RL.5.3)

Lesson IV: Dickon (Ch. X–Ch. XII)

- Explore Mary's and Dickon's first meeting (RL.5.1, RL.5.3)
- Examine the purpose of Dickon's mention of the "missel thrush" (RL.5.1, RL.5.3, L.5.4a)
- Detail Mary's meeting with Mr. Craven (RL.5.1, RL.5.3)
- Revisit Mary's evolving character (RL.5.3)

Lesson V: Colin (Ch. XIII–Ch. XV)

Explore the first meeting between Mary and Colin (RL.5.1, RL.5.3)

Note Mary's growing influence over Colin (RL.5.1, RL.5.3)

Juxtapose Colin's and Dickon's personalities (RL.5.1, RL.5.3)

Examine Mary's relationship with the two boys (RL.5.1, RL.5.3)

Lesson VI: Mary's Growth (Ch. XVI–Ch. XVII)

Note Mary's growing independence (RL.5.1, RL.5.2)

Explore the narrator's claim that Colin's fight with Mary (Ch. XVI) was "rather good for him" (RL.5.3)

(Continue to) juxtapose Colin's and Dickon's personalities (RL.5.3)

Note Mary's reaction to Mr. Craven's gift (RL.5.3)

Lesson VII: "I shall live forever and ever and ever!" (Ch. XVIII–Ch. XX)

Note Colin's gradual transformation (RL.5.1, RL.5.3)

Explore Mary's role in Colin's transformation (RL.5.1, RL.5.3)

Examine the nature of Dickon's growing influence on both Mary's and Colin's transformations (RL.5.1, RL.5.3)

Lesson VIII: Magic (Ch. XXI–Ch. XXIII)

Probe Colin's growing inner strength transformation (RL.5.1, RL.5.3)

Explore the relationship between magic and actions (RL.5.4)

Examine Colin's interpretation of magic (RL.5.4)

Lesson IX: (Ch. XXIV–End)

Examine Dickon's mother's role in reaching the novel's climax (RL.5.2, RL.5.3, RL.5.5)

Explore the relationship among Mary, Martha, Dickon, and Colin (RL.5.3)

Probe the thematic strands in the novel (RL.5.2)

Lesson X: Annotations Revisited

Revisit the objectives of the lessons

Explore the annotations (RL.5.1, RL.5.10, RF.4.4, W.5.8, W.5.9)

Revisit the themes of the novel (RL.5.2)

Trace a single theme (in the form of an argumentative essay) (RL.5.2, W.5.1, W.5.4, W.5.9, W.5.10, SL.5.4, L.5.1, L.5.2, L.5.6)

Lesson I: Meet Mary Lennox (Ch. I–Ch. III)

Objectives

(Begin to) discover the purpose of annotations (RL.5.1, RL.5.10, RF.4.4, W.5.8, W.5.9)

Note details of Mary's life before her departure for England (RL.5.1, RL.5.2)

Examine early presentation of Mary (RL.5.1, RL.5.2)

Explore Mary's arrival at Misselthwaite Manor (L.5.3b, RL.5.5)

Probe the emerging conflict (RL.5.2, SL.5.1)

Required Materials

☐ Class set of *The Secret Garden* by Frances Hodgson Burnett

☐ Sticky notes

Procedures

1. Lead-In:

Introduce the lesson's objectives and instruct the students to reread the first three chapters (the assumption here is that students will have read those chapters for homework). Instruct the students to annotate the chapters for the lesson's objectives. (Students use the sticky notes to make the annotations.)

2. Step by Step:

   a. Students annotate Chapters I, II, and III for the lesson's objectives. You may choose to provide the students with samples. Here are a few annotations for a description of Mary's early life:

   "She had not wanted a little girl at all, and when Mary was born she handed her over to the care of an Ayah [*Mary is not loved*], who was made to understand that if she wished to please the Mem Sahib she must keep the child out of sight as much as possible. So when she was a sickly, fretful [*Her mother considers her "ugly"*], ugly little baby she was kept out of the way, and when she became a sickly, fretful, toddling thing she was kept out of the way also. She never remembered seeing familiarly anything but the dark faces of her Ayah and the other native servants, and as they always obeyed her and gave her own way in everything, because the Mem Sahib would be angry if she was disturbed by her crying, by the time she was six years old she was as tyrannical and selfish [*This is why she becomes so selfish.*] a little pig as ever lived."

   b. Lead a class discussion in which the students use their annotations to help explain their understanding of Mary's early life. Remind the students to continue annotating during the discussion.

3. Closure:

Explain the homework.

Differentiation

Advanced

- Working ahead of the class, students create digitized dramatic readings of chapters, recorded on portable media players or using video cameras. (These readings can be used to aid less advanced readers.)

- Choose a favorite chapter and create a script for a scene of a play. Follow a framework for script writing. As time allows, choose characters and direct the short play in rehearsals and performance. Record using a video camera.

- Students may need an audio text (CD, play-away, text-to-speech, portable media player) available to them to ease the volume of reading in this unit.
- Students will limit annotations to only one or two of the class objectives.
- Provide a graphic organizer to sort the annotations according to the lesson's objectives.

Homework/Assessment

Read Chapter IV through Chapter VI and annotate (follow the class activity) for the objectives of Lesson II:

- Explore Martha's perception of Mary
- Record early details of Dickon
- Note Mary's early attraction to the ''mysterious garden''
- Follow Mary's explorations
- Trace the mystery that unfolds

ABOUT COMMON CORE

Common Core is a nonprofit 501(c)3 organization formed in 2007 to advocate for a content-rich liberal arts education for all students in America's K–12 schools. We believe that a student who graduates from high school without an understanding of culture, the arts, history, literature, civics, and language has been left behind. To improve education in America, we promote programs, policies, and initiatives at the local, state, and federal levels that provide students with challenging, rigorous instruction in the full range of liberal arts and sciences. We also undertake research and projects, such as the Common Core Curriculum Mapping Project, which aim to provide educators with tools that will help students to become strong readers and learners. Go to www.commoncore.org for more information. Despite the coincidence of name, Common Core and the Common Core State Standards are not affiliated.

Common Core has been led by Lynne Munson, as president and executive director, since its founding. From 2001 to 2005, Munson was deputy chairman of the National Endowment for the Humanities. In that post, Munson conceived of and designed Picturing America. The most successful public humanities project in NEH history, Picturing America put more than 75,000 sets of fine art images and teaching guides into libraries, K–12 classrooms, and Head Start centers. From 1993 to 2001, Munson was a research fellow at the American Enterprise Institute, where she wrote *Exhibitionism: Art in an Era of Intolerance*. Munson has written on contemporary cultural and educational issues for numerous national publications, including the *New York Times, The Wall Street Journal, USA Today, Educational Leadership,* and *American Educator*. She has appeared on CNN, FoxNews, CNBC, C-SPAN, and NPR.

Joy Hakim, author, *A History of the US* and *The Story of Science*

Bill Honig, president, Consortium on Reading Excellence (CORE); former California superintendent of public instruction

Carol Jago, director, California Reading and Literature Project at UCLA; former president, National Council of Teachers of English (NCTE)

Juan Rangel, chief executive officer, United Neighborhood Organization (UNO)

ACKNOWLEDGMENTS

Common Core and I, personally, have many people to thank for their support of and contribution to this mapping project. The Bill & Melinda Gates Foundation's support of these Maps was central to their creation. Jamie McKee and Melissa Chabran deserve our deepest thanks. Dane Linn from the National Governors Association encouraged this project all along. David Coleman and Sue Pimentel of the Common Core State Standards ELA writing team have become wonderful colleagues in the course of this work. Our expert advisors—David Driscoll, Toni Cortese, and Russ Whitehurst—provided crucial guidance. And Checker Finn, Pat Riccards, and Andy Rotherham each offered well-timed counsel that was always on target. Wiley's Kate Bradford is an engaged and enthusiastic editor.

We are tremendously thankful to the American Federation of Teachers members, Milken educators, National Alliance of Black School Educators representatives, and the many other teachers and administrators who reviewed our Maps with care, thoroughness, and honesty. I am grateful for the wise guidance and unwavering encouragement of Common Core's trustees. Extra thanks to trustees Pat Forgione, Jason Griffiths, and Carol Jago, who each played a key role in this work. I'm grateful to research assistant Stephanie Porowski, her predecessor James Elias, as well as interns Meagan Estep and Denise Wilkins, each of whose investigatory skills is surpassed only by their ability to keep track of the nearly 200 documents that comprise these Maps. Thanks to Ed Alton for converting our Maps into a navigable—and now interactive—digital feast. And to Shannon Last, Laura Bornfreund, and Kathleen Porter-Magee for perfecting our every last word. Diana Senechal, Melissa Mejias, and Leslie Skelton each made important contributions to our high school Maps. Many thanks to Jack Horak, Ed Spinella, Christine Miller, Donald Holland, and also to Stephen Griffith, for keeping our increasingly complex affairs in order.

We've made many new friends as a result of this work as calls and e-mails have poured in from nearly every state. Very special thanks to Buddy Auman and Teresa Chance of the Northwest Arkansas Educational Cooperative, who have helped us to see our Maps in action. Julie Duffield from WestEd introduced us to twenty-first-century outreach. Donna Perrigo, Karen Delbridge, Linda Diamond, Joe Pizzo, Julie Joslin, and Laura Bednar have helped to spread word of our Maps in Arizona, Wyoming, California, New Jersey, North Carolina, and Arkansas. Many others from those states—and from New York, Florida, Ohio, Pennsylvania, and Utah, in particular—deserve our gratitude.

Lastly, the teachers who wrote the Maps deserve the utmost thanks. Each of our lead writers brought deep dedication, along with years of experience, to the project: Sheila Byrd Carmichael, our project coordinator and lead writer of the high school Maps, is an expert on education standards and former leader of the American Diploma Project; Ruthie Stern, who, in addition to her work on the high school Maps, led the writing of the seventy-six sample lesson plans, is a longtime New York City Public Schools teacher and a professor at Columbia Teachers College; Lorraine Griffith, lead writer for the elementary grades, is a fifth-grade teacher in Asheville, North Carolina, coauthor of numerous books on reading, and a Common Core trustee; Cyndi Wells, lead writer for the middle grades, is a teacher and fine arts facilitator in Charlottesville, Virginia, and our project's jack-of-all-trades; and Louisa Moats, author of our pacing guide for reading foundations, is a writer of the CCSS in reading and a true leader in her field. These women stuck with this project as it grew, wonderfully, beyond what any of us originally had imagined. They did all of this despite the challenges of the school schedules, motherhood, book deadlines, family vacations, and much else. It was an honor for me to have the opportunity to work alongside these teachers as they drew on their wealth of knowledge and experience to forge what we hope are tools that their peers nationwide will enjoy.

Lynne Munson
President and Executive Director, Common Core
Washington, D.C.
September 2011

INDEX OF SUGGESTED WORKS

This index lists the creators and titles of works included in the Maps. To search for other information (for example, ideas, places, events) please go to the online version of the Maps at http://commoncore.org/maps/ and use the search function.